Culture, Media, Language

Culture, Media, Language

Working Papers in Cultural Studies, 1972–79

in association with

the Centre for Contemporary Cultural Studies
University of Birmingham

First published 1980 by the Academic Division of
Unwin Hyman (Publishers) Ltd

Reprinted 1992, 1996
by Routledge
11 New Fetter Lane, London EC4P 4EE
29 West 35th Street, New York, NY 10001

Typeset in IBM Press Roman by Donald Typesetting, Bristol
Printed and bound in Great Britain at the University Press, Cambridge

British Library Cataloguing in Publication Data
Culture, media, language.
1. Culture-Addresses, essays, lectures
1. Hall, Stuart *b.* 1932
301.2'08 HM101

ISBN 0-415-07906-3

Contents

Preface

The Centre for Cultural Studies is a post-graduate research centre at the University of Birmingham; its staff and students research and publish in the field of Cultural Studies.[1]* It was established in 1964 under the Directorship of Richard Hoggart, then Professor of Modern English Literature. The aim was to inaugurate research in the area of contemporary culture and society: cultural forms, practices and institutions, their relation to society and social change. The principal inspiration behind its formation was the work which Richard Hoggart had undertaken in *The Uses of Literacy* – a pioneering study, published in the mid 1950s, offering an analysis of how recent developments were transforming and reshaping the cultures of the 'traditional' working class.[2] The Centre was intended to provide a base for the serious analysis of these questions, within the framework of higher education, and in a centre principally devoted to post-graduate research. In 1968 Richard Hoggart left to become an Assistant Director-General at Unesco, and, between 1968 and 1979, Stuart Hall was its Director.

The Centre has greatly expanded since those early days. It now consists of three staff members, two research fellows working on specific funded projects, and over forty post-graduate research students. It has left the original home provided for it within the English Department, and has gained a reputation of its own in the field on the basis of an independent programme of intellectual work, research and publishing.[3] More or less coterminous with its growth – though by no means as the exclusive effect of its work – programmes of study under the general rubric of 'Cultural Studies' have been widely initiated in other sectors of education.[4] This has led to the establishment of Cultural Studies degree courses and research programmes and to an expansion of the Cultural Studies element in a variety of courses and disciplines.

The *raison d'être* of this volume of essays, which is drawn from the Centre's work up to 1979, is not simply that it reflects the Centre's work over these years, but that it is addressed to, and may help in, the on-going work of clarification of this emergent field of study. Cultural Studies is not, however, a 'discipline', but an area where different disciplines intersect in the study of the cultural aspects of society. The particular complex of disciplines involved, and the types of approach adopted, naturally differ from place to place. This volume, based as it is on the Birmingham Centre's work, reflects only one particular tendency. While aimed in general at supporting and underpinning these initiatives, there is no intention that

*Superior figures refer to the Notes and references on pages 277–304.

this volume should stamp the field indelibly with the Centre's particular concerns. We hope that the 'openness' of our approach is reflected in the selections which follow, and that readers and users of the volume will bear this *caveat* in mind as they read.

The selection of articles in this volume has been drawn from the first nine issues of the Centre's journal, *Working Papers in Cultural Studies* (*WPCS*), from the Centre's list of Stencilled Papers and from some more recent work.[5] The early issues of the journal are now all out of print. The journal itself has been absorbed into the CCCS/Hutchinson series of books and now appears as the annual 'Special Number', along with other volumes.[6] In the interim some of those earlier articles and issues, however, have become 'collector's items'. In any event, the founding of the journal was an important moment in the Centre's development, and its early numbers reflect many key themes and topics in the formative phase of Cultural Studies. So we responded positively to Hutchinson's proposal that a selection should be made available, drawing principally on those earlier sources of work, though including one or two pieces in each section more representative of our recent work. A number of things should therefore be said, by way of guidance to the reader, about how the book is organized. First, it does *not* reflect the full range of Centre work. For example, work on the position and oppression of women is the core of the second Special Number already published in our new series, *Women Take Issue.* This theme is therefore not given a section on its own here, though the impact of feminism is reflected in several of the more recent contributions published in this volume (see below). Work in the 'subcultures' area did appear in *WPCS* 7/8, subsequently reprinted as *Resistance Through Rituals.* But this book appeared some three or four years ago. Moreover, there have been important developments in the work in this area, which deserve recognition. The 'ethnographic' emphasis which marked it from the outset has been retained, but its focus has shifted, first, to more 'mainstream' aspects of youth formation (Roger Grimshaw's study of the Scout Movement, extracted here, is an example), and then to the more central institutions and relations (for example, recent work on the transition from school to work of working-class boys and girls; on young manual workers; and women's domestic and paid work). These have thoroughly transformed the earlier, more 'subcultural', concerns.[7] These developments did seem to require some reference here (see the section on Ethnography). The growing base in Centre work of studies in such areas as education and educational institutions, the family, race and ethnicity, aspects of the state, together with the general redirection of Centre work towards more broadly 'historical' concerns - the analysis of particular periods, the welfare state, work on cultural history and on the problems of history and theory - are not substantially represented in these pages. Some of these topics are, however, scheduled as the main themes of Centre volumes now in preparation or shortly due to appear: for example, the collection of historical essays on *Working Class Culture* already published, and the volumes on *Unpopular Education, History and Theory* and *Citizenship and the Welfare State*, already planned or completed and due to be published in the Hutchinson series.[8]

These absences have three consequences which readers might bear in mind. First, this collection does not accurately reflect the *present spread* of Centre work. Second, it prioritizes a set of concerns which characterized the Centre's most recent work – mainly from 1972, when the journal was founded, up to about 1978. Third, it gives to Cultural Studies an emphasis on the analysis of texts and cultural forms, rather than on practices and institutions, which obscures more recent developments and which may therefore appear to tie the Centre too closely to its originating topics of interest. While in no way representing a rejection of these earlier concerns, it is important that this selection should not be taken as fixing Cultural Studies in an anachronistic mould. The shifts which have produced new kinds of work must be understood as just as essential to the definition of Cultural Studies as those represented here. The different phases of Centre work are more extensively marked and discussed in the Introduction and section introductions below.

The present volume is divided into four main sections. They deal with ethnographic work, the media, language and English studies. Each has an introductory overview piece, charting the changing interests and directions in these areas. This is followed by a selection of extracts mainly drawn from journal articles, theses or published papers, reflecting projects and seminar work over the period 1972–8. There has been no attempt to update these pieces retrospectively or to bring them into line with present thinking. In this respect, the 'Working Papers' of our title is an accurate guide to actual Centre practice and to how the results of that practice are represented in the volume. The exception is English Studies, which, leaving aside the 'mapping the field' extract (from an early journal, *WPCS* 4), has been largely rewritten especially for this volume and draws mainly on present work. For a time, literary studies as such were not widely pursued in the Centre. It is only more recently that we have again been able to find a serious basis for this work – one which, while drawing on the analysis of texts, breaks with the literary-critical tradition of a too text-bound practice, as well as with the text–context framework of the so-called 'sociology of literature', and relocates both in the analysis of literary formations and in literature as an institutional practice.[9] There was therefore, in this case, no continuing body of Centre work to draw on. As has already been said, the 'historical' dimension of Centre work is certainly not accurately reflected in these selections. But the move to a more concrete, historical mode of work – one of the most important aspects of recent Centre thinking – is briefly indexed by Richard Johnson's review article, looking back at the Anderson/Thompson debate about the 'peculiarity' of Britain's historical development, which helped to inaugurate this historical phase in the Centre.[10] This article therefore forms a second, 'introductory' piece to the volume.

In each section we have retained the different problematics which underpinned our work in these areas at different stages. There has been no attempt to update them in the search for a definitive or 'correct' position. We wanted to stress the necessarily open, provisional nature of work in a novel and emergent area like Cultural Studies. We also wished to underscore the diversity of approaches, the sense of developing from position to position, which has characterized our approach throughout. We have tried, at each stage, to be as rigorous as we could be, within our limits, but we have not presumed to offer a final truth in any of these fields. Orthodoxy here is, in our view, the enemy of a truly 'open' science. A larger issue is signalled here. Intellectual and academic advances in areas cognate to our own have sometimes been marked in recent years by an acute sectarianism, sustained by what has often seemed a false search for scientific correctness. Though we have learned a great deal from, and been instructed by, these advances, we have tried to develop them within a different intellectual practice.

We have, accordingly, consciously adopted the strategy of allowing our stops and starts, our moments of progress, marking time and retreats, our shifts of direction and 'new beginnings' to show through as they actually occurred at the time. Readers must not, therefore, expect to find here a consistent theoretical position, unfolding from the beginning to its appointed conclusion: nor even a unified set of findings. This is definitively not *the* reader in Cultural Studies in general - which is a larger, more ambitious task, remaining to be undertaken. We hope, of course, when such a text (or texts) come to be prepared, that the work of clarification to which the papers in this volume bear witness will be found helpful and instructive. On a less ambitious plane, we hope those now working in Cultural Studies will find here something instructive, both substantively in the areas covered and, more generally, in terms of the necessary perils and costs which attend an intellectual project and intervention of this order. When such a definitive work comes to be written, we feel certain that it will draw fruitfully on wider experiences than we can recapitulate here and will require the mobilization of intellectual strengths and resources well beyond the capacity of the Birmingham Centre. We know it will reflect pertinent differences and variations rather than that spurious unity with which Cultural Studies has sometimes been charged.

The volume as a whole was edited, on behalf of the Centre, by an Editorial Group consisting of Steve Baron, Michael Denning, Stuart Hall, Dorothy Hobson, Andy Lowe and Paul Willis. The Ethnography section was edited by Dorothy Hobson and Paul Willis; the Media section by Stuart Hall; the Language section by Andy Lowe; and the English Studies section by Michael Denning. Steve Baron and Andy Lowe were responsible for the editorial work on Richard Johnson's article. An outline for the Introduction was provided by Stuart Hall and Andrew Lowe and extensively discussed by the Editorial Group. The main text was drafted by Stuart Hall. The drafts were discussed by the Editorial Group and the Centre as a whole and substantially revised in the light of suggestions proposed. We are especially grateful to Richard Johnson and Michael Green for their detailed comments. Where appropriate, particular articles and extracts are attributed to individual authors, as are the related section introductions. Chris Weedon, Andrew Tolson and Frank Mort were responsible for the extensive new materials contained in the Language section (with additional drafting by Andrew Lowe). With the exception of the opening extract - authored by an earlier Literature Group at the Centre, which was responsible for putting together *WPCS* 4 - the section on English Studies has been prepared, discussed and written collectively by the present English Studies Group,

1978-9 (including Janet Batsleer, Rob Burkitt, Hazel Corby, Tony Davies, Michael Denning, Michael Green, Rebecca O'Rourke, Michael O'Shaughnessey, Roger Shannon, Stephen Shortus and Michael Skovmand).

Part One

Introduction

1 Cultural Studies and the Centre: some problematics and problems*

Stuart Hall

The first issue of *Working Papers in Cultural Studies* appeared in 1972.[1] The title 'Working Papers' was deliberately intended to set the terms of our approach in a number of respects. This was *not* the scholarly journal of the field – which, indeed, hardly as yet existed.[2] We laid no proprietary claim on it. We recognized that, if Cultural Studies 'took off', it would deploy a greater variety of approaches than we could reproduce within the Birmingham Centre (at that time, less than half its present size). We also recognized that a particular 'mix' of disciplines woven together at Birmingham to form the intellectual base of Cultural Studies would not necessarily be reproduced exactly elsewhere.[3] We could imagine Cultural Studies degrees or research based, just as effectively, on visual (rather than literary) texts, on social anthropology (rather than sociology) and with a much stronger input of historical studies than we drew on in the early days. Such courses have indeed been initiated since then – with conspicuous success.[4] The Centre had, perforce, to work with the intellectual raw materials it had to hand. It chose to specialize in those areas which the small staff felt capable of supervising.[5] It approached the problems of interdisciplinary research from those more established disciplines already present in the complement of staff and students working in Birmingham at that time.[6] But we tried not to make the mistake of confusing these starting positions – over which we had relatively little control – with a *theoretically informed* definition of Cultural Studies as such. Hence, the journal specifically refused, at the outset, to be a vehicle for defining the range and scope of Cultural Studies in a definitive or absolute way. We rejected, in short, a descriptive definition or prescription of the field.[7] It followed that, though the journal did not offer itself as a conclusive definition of Cultural Studies, it *did* confront, from its first issue, the consequences of this refusal: namely, the need for a sustained work of theoretical clarification.

On the other hand, the journal was conceived as an intellectual *intervention.* It aimed to define and to occupy a space. It was deliberately designed as a 'house journal' – a journal or tendency, so to speak. Nearly all of its contributors were Centre members.[8] Its aim was to put Cultural Studies on the intellectual map. It

*This introductory survey was based on outlines proposed by Stuart Hall and Andrew Lowe. It was extensively discussed by the Editorial Group. The main text was drafted by Stuart Hall and revised in the light of comments offered by the Editorial Group and other members of the Centre.

declared an interest in advancing critical research in this field. The phrase, 'Working Papers', however, underlined the tentative character of this enterprise, as we saw it.

In real terms, its publication and production was made possible by a small educational bequest made over to the Centre by Sir Allen Lane and Penguin Books in the early days - and without strings - to give the Centre some small independent financial support.[9] Otherwise the journal had no official sponsorship or financial support: it was self-financed and self-produced. In conception and execution it was a collective venture, the product of staff and students working together. With the Stencilled Paper series, which was initiated at about the same time, it gave the Centre, and Cultural Studies, a necessary public presence.[10] The first issue was designed and overseen by Trevor Millum, one of our first successful Ph.D students, in a period of post-thesis euphoria.[11]

The development of the Centre, and of Cultural Studies, can be resumed in a number of different ways. We look at three aspects in this introduction: first, the changes in theoretical perspective and in the main problematics which have staked out the Centre's development through the 1970s; second, the question of the different areas of concrete research in which the Centre has been centrally engaged; third, the modes of organization, the intellectual practices of analysis and research, through which that work has been practically realized.

Foundations of cultural studies

The search for origins is tempting but illusory. In intellectual matters absolute beginnings are exceedingly rare. We find, instead, continuities and breaks. New interventions reflect events outside a discipline but have effects within it. They most often work to reorganize a set of problems or field of inquiry. They reconstitute existing knowledge under the sign of new questions. They dispose existing elements into new configurations, establish new points of departure. Cultural Studies, in its institutional manifestation, was the result of such a break in the 1960s. But the field in which this intervention was made had been initially charted in the 1950s. This earlier founding moment is best specified in terms of the originating texts, the original 'curriculum', of the field - Hoggart's *The Uses of Literacy*, Raymond Williams's *Culture and Society* and *The Long Revolution*, E. P. Thompson's critique of the latter work and the 'example' of related questions, worked in a more historical mode, in *The Making of the English Working Class.*[12]

These were not textbooks for the inauguration of a new discipline: though they were the results of disciplined intellectual work of a high order. They were responses of different kinds to a decisive historical conjecture. They brought disciplined thought to bear on the understanding of their own times. They were far from neutral or scholarly: they were cultural interventions in their own right. They addressed the long-term shifts taking place in British society and culture within the framework of a long, retrospective, historical glance. What these writers in their various ways confronted, precisely, was post-war British society, recently emerged from the upheavals of total war, entering a period of change and development whose parameters were set by the terms of the post-war 'settlement'. The depression and the war appeared to have established certain critical breaks with earlier developments. The 'settlement' – defined by the revival of capitalist production, the founding of the welfare state and the 'Cold War' – appeared to bring economic, political and cultural forces into new kinds of relation, into a new equilibrium. But what sort of qualitative break with the past did this constitute? Had there been a decisive rupture with the determining historical forces which had shaped Britain's 'peculiar' route through the earlier phases of industrial capitalist development, or merely their recomposition into new continuities? Was Britain still a capitalist civilization or a 'post-capitalist' one? Did welfare capitalism represent a fundamental or merely a superficial reordering of society? The earlier phases of industrial capitalist development had produced a complex but distinctive type of social formation: what type of social formation was now in the making? Such transformations in the past had entailed profound cultural shifts and upheavals: as E. P. Thompson remarked, when surveying the deep changes in the social apprehension of Time which sustained an earlier moment of 'transition', 'there is no such thing as economic growth which is not, at the same time, growth and change of a culture . . . .'[13] What did such cultural changes amount to now? What would be the consequences for traditional class relationships, for class formation, and their cultures – hitherto, the very basis of the cultural order itself? Were there new, emergent cultural forces and tendencies? Above all, how were these historical processes to be qualitatively understood and assessed?

These issues were being widely debated at the time. They formed, for example, a constitutive part of the agenda of the early 'New Left', with which many of the contributors identified above had been associated. They set the terms of the post-war 'cultural debate' which, with many changes of emphasis, continues today. They also defined the space in which Cultural Studies emerged, defined its objectives and its agenda. From its inception, then, Cultural Studies was an 'engaged' set of disciplines, addressing awkward but relevant issues about contemporary society and culture, often without benefit of that scholarly detachment or distance which the passage of time alone sometimes confers on other fields of study. The 'contemporary' – which otherwise defined our terms of reference too narrowly – was, by definition, hot to handle. This tension (between what might loosely be called 'political' and intellectual concerns) has shaped Cultural Studies ever since. Each of the books referred to above inhabited this tension in a different way. Each addressed the problems defined by a decisive conjuncture – even when the mode of analysis was 'historical'. Each sought fresh direction from within a tradition of intellectual inquiry, which it then both developed and transformed. Each insisted that the answers should match, in complexity and seriousness, the complexity of the issues it addressed. Each supposed that those answers, when and if found, would have consequences beyond the confines of an intellectual debate. This tension necessarily situated Cultural Studies awkwardly with respect to the existing division and branches of knowledge and the scholarly norms legitimated within the higher learning. Marked in this way by its origins, Cultural Studies could in no sense be viewed as the establishment of yet another academic sub-discipline. This prevented its easy absorption and naturalization into the social division of knowledge. It also made the enterprise problematic from the outset in the eyes of the powers that be - with near fatal consequences, on occasions, for the whole venture.

One important question was the relation of Cultural Studies to the existing disciplines in which its problems were being rethought. Could this work be pursued in a disciplined, analytic way, yet break from some of the founding propositions of the intellectual fields in which it was situated? Each of the texts mentioned above referred itself and its readers to existing traditions of thought. The *Uses of Literacy,* which attempted to chart the process of change within the traditional cultures of the urban working class, employed methods similar to those developed by Leavis and the *Scrutiny* critics, attempting to rework their procedures and methods so as to apply them to the study of living class cultures.[14] This aim was altogether different from the purposes behind the initial inspiration of 'Leavisite' criticism - and was accordingly repudiated by its 'master'. The continuities nevertheless remained. For behind the emphasis on 'practical criticism' ('These words in this order') Leavisite criticism had always, in its own way, been profoundly sensitive to questions of cultural context, the sub-text of its 'texts':[15] even if its definition of culture was peculiarly conservative, fundamentally anti-democratic, and depended on the historically dubious search, through an infinite regress, for some stable point of reference in a hypostatized 'organic culture' of the past.[16] Leavis himself had always stressed the intricate relationship between the internal organization of experience, through language, in the preferred texts of the 'Great Tradition' and the general 'state of the language', which he took as a paradigm of the culture.[17] In his 'Sketch for an English School' Leavis also revealed a deep, if idiosyncratic, historical sense.[18] The *Uses of Literacy* refused many of Leavis's embedded cultural judgements. But it did attempt to deploy literary criticism to 'read' the emblems, idioms, social arrangements, the lived cultures and 'languages' of working class life, as particular kinds of 'text', as a privileged sort of cultural evidence. In this sense, it continued 'a tradition' while seeking, in practice, to transform it.

Culture and Society undertook a work of contemporary description only in its conclusion. What it did was to resume and trace a tradition of English thought and writing, a line of critical thinking about English culture and society, back to certain social thinkers, writers and intellectuals of the nineteenth and early twentieth centuries. These writings - now often safely enshrined in academic curricula - Williams revealed as engaged, critical interventions in their own time in a set of key debates about the relations between culture and industry, democracy and class.[19] What united these various writers into *a* 'culture-and-society' tradition, in Williams's view, was not their particular, often very different, actual positions and judgements, but the mode of sustained reflection they gave to qualitative questions about the impact on culture of the historic transformations of the past. Arnold's *Culture and Anarchy* and Leavis's *Mass Civilization and Minority Culture* were both shown as deeply engaged, embattled pieces of cultural criticism, hiding their partisanship a little behind the invocation to a fixed set of standards nominated as Culture with a capital 'C'. It is true that, in emphasizing this highly literary tradition in critical bourgeois thought, Williams may have underplayed more radical alternative traditions and evidence from more popular, radical and artisan cultures not easily fitted into the literary framework. This was one criticism which Thompson levelled at *The Long Revolution* in a seminal critique, of which he gave a magisterial counter-demonstration in *The Making of the English Working Class.* Nevertheless, the condensations which *Culture and Society* effected - giving the thought of 'the past' an immediate reference and connotation in present debates, detaching them from their traditional moorings in the Eng. Lit. syllabus - was formidable.

Yet in reconstituting this tradition Williams also, in a sense, brought it to a decisive close. *The Long Revolution*, which followed almost immediately, was a seminal event in English post-war intellectual life. It marked the opening of a strikingly different kind of reflection on past and present. It linked with the 'culture-and-society' debate in its literary–moral points of reference. But in its theoretical mode and ambition it clearly also broke with that tradition.[20] It attempted to graft on to an idiom and mode of discourse irredeemably particular, empirical and moral in emphasis, its own highly individual kind of 'theorizing'. It shifted the whole ground of debate from a literary–moral to an anthropological definition of culture. But it defined the latter now as the 'whole process' by means of which meanings and definitions are socially constructed and historically transformed, with literature and art as only one, specially privileged, kind of social communication. It also engaged, if in a highly displaced fashion, the Marxist tradition, and its way of describing the relation between culture and other social practices, as the only viable (but, in its existing English form, unsatisfactory) alternative to more native traditions.[21] The difficult, somewhat abstract quality of some of the writing in *The Long Revolution* can largely be ascribed to its status as a 'text of the break'. Bearing in mind the cultural and intellectual climate of the 'Cold War' in which it was conceived and written one can only register, without further comment here, the intellectual boldness of the whole venture.[22]

It was quickly followed by Thompson's critique and *The Making.* The latter, in its radically democratic emphasis, and its heroic labour of recovery of popular political cultures hitherto largely lost to serious historical work, is the most seminal work of social history of the post-war period. It was informed throughout by a sense of how impossible it would be, after it, to give an account of that formative historical 'transition', the 1790s to the 1830s, without a sustained account of the 'cultural dimension'. It was rigorously and, in the best sense, 'empirically' grounded in historical particularity, though its brief opening pages on 'class relationships' constituted a brief but resonant statement, 'theoretical' in effect, if not in manner or intent. Thompson stressed the dimensions of historical agency through which a distinctive class formation made itself - the active tense in the title was fully intentional. His definition of culture was rooted in the collective experiences which formed the class in its larger historical sense. The book situated culture in the dialectic between 'social being' and 'social consciousness'. In doing so, it broke with a kind of economic determinism, and with an institutional perspective, which had marked and limited certain older versions of 'labour history', which it effectively displaced. It also obliquely - by demonstration, as it were - challenged the narrow, elitist conception of 'culture' enshrined in the Leavisite tradition, as well as the rather evolutionary approach which sometimes marked Williams's *Long Revolution.* It affirmed, directly, the relevance of historical work to the task of analysing the present. Thompson insisted on the historical specificity of culture, on its plural, not singular, definition - 'cultures', not 'Culture': above all, on the necessary struggle, tension and conflict between cultures and their links to class cultures, class formations and class struggles - the struggles between 'ways of life' rather than the evolution of '*a* way of life'. These were seminal qualifications.

All these works, then, implied a radical break with previous conceptualizations. They inflected the term 'culture' away from its traditional moorings, getting behind the inert sense of 'period' which sustained the text/context distinction, moving the argument into the wider field of social practices and historical processes. It was difficult, at first, to give these breaks a precise location in any single disciplinary field. They appeared to be distinctive precisely in the ways in which they broke across and cut between the disciplinary empires. They were, for the moment, defined as 'sociological' in a loose sense - without, of course, being 'proper' sociology.

The break with sociology

Some elements within sociology 'proper' were, indeed, preoccupied at this time with similar themes. One thinks, for example, of the work of the Institute of Community Studies and of the wider preoccupation with the idea of 'community' which could be considered as a sort of analogue, within sociology, of the emergent concern with cultures elsewhere.[23] But by and large British sociology was not predisposed to ask questions of this order. This was the period - the 1950s - of its massive dependence on American theories and models. But American sociology, in either its Parsonian theorization or its structural-functionalist methodology, was theoretically incapable of dealing with these issues.[24] It was systematically functionalist and integrative in perspective. It had abolished the category of contradiction: instead, it spoke of 'dysfunctions' and of 'tension management'. It claimed the mantle of a science. But its premises and predispositions were highly ideological. In fact, it responded to the question posed earlier - what sort of society was this now? - by giving a highly specific historical answer: all post-capitalist, post-industrial societies were tending to the model of the American dream - as one representative work put it, to the 'first new nation'. It celebrated the triumph of 'pluralist society', constantly counterposed to 'totalitarian society', a highly ideological couplet which was advanced as a concluded scientific fact. It did not deal with 'culture', except within the terms of a highly pessimistic variant of the 'mass society/mass culture' hypothesis. Instead, it referred to 'the value system' in the singular - into which, as Shils eloquently put it, on the basis of pluralism, the 'brutal culture' of the masses was destined to be gradually and successfully incorporated.[25] It militantly refused the concept of ideology.[26] What was said earlier needs now to be somewhat qualified. It did, after all, provide a sort of reply to the questions being posed: it *transposed* them into its own, highly distinctive theoretical framework. At the same time, it preferred a methodology - *the* method of the social sciences - modelled on a highly outdated version of the natural sciences, militantly empiricist and quantitative.

Perry Anderson has - in our view, correctly - argued that such a sociology could produce no concept of 'totality' and, without that, no concept of 'culture' either.[27] Anderson argues that this 'absent centre' was filled in Britain, but in a displaced form, by other disciplines, in which the concept of 'totality' assumed a partial existence. He mentions anthropology and literary criticism; we might now add the 'new' social history. One way of thinking of Cultural Studies is as the intellectual space where the convergences between these displaced traditions occurred. 'Driven out of any obvious habits, the notion of totality found refuge in the least expected of studies . . . .'

This is no mere speculation. It refers directly to the politics of academic life in which Cultural Studies, from the moment of its inception, was immersed. Hoggart's inaugural lecture, 'Schools of English and Contemporary Society', which announced the programme of the Birmingham Centre, was an originating document.[28] Its principal way of conceiving the field ought to have given little offence to academic *amour propre.* It indexed Cultural Studies as primarily concerned with 'neglected' materials drawn from popular culture and the mass media, which, it suggested, provided important evidence of the new stresses and directions of contemporary culture. This gave the Centre's initial impetus a distinctly 'literary' flavour' - with the *Uses of Literacy* as an exemplary feat. It recommended the adaptation of literary-critical methods in reading these texts for their qualitative cultural evidence: a modest proposal - in retrospect, perhaps, too modest. But its relative 'conservatism' may have reflected that historic compromise required to get these illicit questions posed at all, within a traditional academic framework. Nevertheless, it triggered off a blistering attack specifically from sociology, which, while not concerned with such issues, reserved a proprietary claim over the territory. For example, the opening of the Centre was greeted by a letter from two social scientists who issued a sort of warning: if Cultural Studies overstepped its proper limits and took on the study of contemporary society (not just its texts), without 'proper' scientific (that is quasi-scientistic) controls, it would provoke reprisals for illegitimately crossing the territorial boundary.

It may be hard for us - confronted as we are now by the immense disarray of 'mainstream' sociology - to recall a time when British sociology was so confident of its claims and proprieties. But this was no idle threat. It was compounded by an equally conservative reaction from those 'humanists' who might have been expected to know better (after all, they too were under notice to quit from an emergent technicist positivism). They regarded 'culture' as already inscribed in the texts they studied and in the values of liberal scholarship. Anything more modern was, by definition, a sign of cultural decline and debasement. Spending time analysing modern cultural forms was a positive collusion with the 'modern disease'. They shared, in fact, with Leavis, the assumption that culture and democracy were unalterably opposed. 'Organic culture' lay irredeemably in the past. Everything else was 'mass culture'. Despite these areas of agreement with what Leavis called the 'diagnosis', they refused his moral seriousness and strenuous programme as too embattled for their tastes. It seemed vulgar, then, to point out that this whole definition of culture had been framed in very specific and peculiar historical conditions: that it entailed its own peculiar reading of history; that it enshrined its questionable ideological judgements as 'truths'; that it was militantly elitist in practice. Cultural studies then was either hopelessly unscientific or a product of the very disease it sought to diagnose - either way, a treason of the intellectuals. The relative caution and uncertainty which accompanied the inauguration of the Centre was due in no small measure to this inhospitable climate. For years 'Cultural Studies' found itself required to survive by running the gauntlet, skilfully, between these two entrenched - but, in their different ways, philistine and anti-intellectual - positions.

This was not without its real effects. When the Centre gained its first funded project[29] - a study of social change through an examination of the popular press, 1930-64 - it was proposed that since we were not equipped to undertake 'proper sociological' investigation, we should analyse the 'texts' by methods of cultural reading, and then the social scientists might be recruited to 'test' our (soft) hypotheses by the appropriate (hard) scientific methods. A not dissimilar argument was advanced when we first applied to the Social Science Research Council (SSRC) for the funds which eventually led to the project undertaken by Paul Willis (and subsequently reported in *Learning to Labour*). Fortunately, so far as the Rowntree project was concerned, this broken-backed strategy found no takers, and we simply had to do the whole job ourselves. Actually, the common meeting-ground in the project itself between these two irreconcilable alternatives was provided not so much by sociological methods as by a return to the ground of concrete historical analysis. This was the first time, in a real sense, that historical questions came firmly into play within the Centre's practice. In our view, the book which resulted from breaking this methodological sound barrier, and which dissolved the false literary *versus* sociological antithesis - *Paper Voices* - was a much better one than could have been produced in the way originally proposed: and it was the combination of literary and historical work which sustained it.[30] This was certainly one early point where the Centre began to desert its 'handmaiden' role and chart a more independent, ambitious, properly integrated territorial space of its own.

The 'sociological encounter' could be described in many different ways. It led to a quite new range of work in the Centre, taking into previous definitions of that work new emphases on 'lived cultures' - the study of youth cultures, for example; the concern with subcultures and the study of deviance; attention to the institutions of schooling and the relations of the workplace. What was also at issue was the need to confront theoretically, and in a manner appropriate to ourselves, the dominant discipline which cast its proprietary shadow across our path. This could not be done by simply grafting sociology on to Cultural Studies from the outside – though this was often what, at the time, 'interdisciplinary' was taken to mean. With the extension in the meaning of 'culture' from texts and representations to lived practices, belief systems and institutions, some part of the subject matter of sociology also fell within our scope. Yet the dominant ways of conceptualizing these relationships within structural-functionalism prevented our posing these questions correctly.

However, it was also clear that there were more mansions in the sociological kingdom than its guardians suggested. Thus began the Centre's appropriation of sociology from within. We staked out a line for ourselves through the 'classic' texts and problems. Here, alternative traditions within sociology itself began to make their appearance. Structural-functionalism turned out to be not science itself but a particular kind of theoretical construct and synthesis, put together in a very specific historical moment: the moment of American world-cultural hegemony. But there were other traditions which *did* attempt to deal with social action and institutions as 'objectivated structures of meaning'. They examined types of historical societies ('capitalist' ones, for example) from the perspective of their ideological formations (for example, the 'Protestant Ethic').[31] They proposed two types of sociological explanation for cultural phenomena: the societal and historical forces which produced them, and those phenomena analysed in terms of their 'relevance for meaning'.[32] In their very different ways these approaches connected with the theory of communication outlined in *The Long Revolution* and the project of 'reading' working-class life in terms of its 'lived meanings' which *The Uses of Literacy* had attempted.

It is clear, in retrospect, where this line of thinking pointed. It tended to give Cultural Studies a distinctively 'Weberian' gloss. This is clear enough in Weber's own work. But similar lines can also be traced elsewhere in the German idealist tradition and in the famous 'debate over method' from which German sociology first emerged.[33] They can be identified with the *verstehen* or 'interpretative' hermeneutic stress which characterizes early historical sociology and the *Geistwissenschaft* approach in general (Dilthey and Simmel are representative figures here).[34] At the same moment as we began to excavate this neglected tradition in classical sociology, a parallel movement of recovery began within sociology itself. Sociologists began to speak of the 'two sociologies' – counterposing Weber to Durkheim.[35] Gradually these themes began to be reappropriated within 'mainstream' sociology itself. They are to be found in the phenomenological reprise associated with Berger and Luckmann's 'social construction of reality' approach and based on the rediscovery of the work of Alfred Schutz;[36] later, in ethnomethodology, with its interest in the 'common-sense' foundations of social action, its focus on language and conversational analysis as a sort of paradigm for social action itself.[37]

More significant for us was the rehabilitation of 'social interactionism'. This had a distinguished, if subordinate, history within American mainstream sociology –

especially in the work of Mead and the 'Chicago School'.[38] But it had recently been revived in the writings of Howard Becker and the subcultural theorists.[39] They chose to work at a more ethnographic level. They were sensitive to the differences in 'lived' values and meanings which differentiated subcultures from the dominant culture. They stressed the importance of the ways in which social actors define for themselves the conditions in which they live – their 'definitions of situation'. And they deployed a qualitative methodology. This emphasis on qualitative work has exercised a formative influence within Cultural Studies and can be traced in the early work on youth cultures, in Paul Willis's study of the cultures of school and work and, in more recent research on women, on women's work and experience.[40] It posed the question of the status of the experiential moment in any project of research in 'lived' cultures as an irreducible element of any explanation.[41] The tension between these experiential accounts and a larger account of structural and historical determinations has been a pivotal site of Centre theorizing and debate since then.[42] Moreover, the ethnographic tradition linked Cultural Studies with at least two other kinds of related work: with the descriptive emphases of some kinds of social anthropology (for example, the anthropological study of the interpretative schema or 'folk ideologies' which social groups employ to give their conditions of existence meaning);[43] and with the 'history from below' which characterizes the new social history – for example, the 'oral history' movement, the work of Centerprise and *History Workshop*, a great deal of feminist historical writing (the work of Sheila Rowbotham, for instance) and that whole body of work inspired by Thompson's *The Making.*[44]

There was, however, another aspect not so readily assimilated by this route. The 'lived accounts' which social actors gave of their experience themselves had to be situated. They had their own determinate conditions. Consciousness is always infused with ideological elements, and any analysis of social frameworks of understanding must take account of the elements of 'misrecognition' which are involved. They also had material and historical conditions which decentred them from any full 'authenticity': men/women make history, but under conditions which are not of their own making . . . . This more 'structural' approach had been precisely the purchase offered by structural-functionalism. The problem was that the latter secured its 'structural' view by evading the dialectic between agency and conditions: it thought 'structures' as uncontradictory, integrative, functionalist in an evolutionary and adaptive sense. Weber had rescued the 'meaning' dimension – but at the cost of a heuristic reduction of social action to individual motivation: his 'methodological individualism'. Schutz and the phenomenologists tried to give Weber's 'meaning construction' a more societal dimension – but at the cost of absorbing everything, including the material foundations of culture, into thought and language: the study of historical societies, from this perspective, became a sort of 'sociology of knowledge'.[45]

Much of this emphasis derived from its Kantian or neo-Kantian basis in German idealist thought. But reference to Weber, Simmel and the 'Heidelberg Circle' reminds us of another seminal thinker formed in the same intellectual space: George

Lukács. Lukács's name indexes an alternative working through of many of the same problems, but on a 'Hegelian' rather than a Kantian foundation and in the context not of an 'empirical social science' but of 'Western Marxism'.[46] This term refers to that complex Marxism, consciously counterposed to the vulgar reductionism of the Marxism of the Second and Third Internationals, which was much preoccupied with questions of culture, ideology and 'the superstructures', whose filiation Anderson has recently retraced.[47] (It was the absence of this brand of Marxism from the English intellectual scene in the 1930s which made Williams remark, in *Culture and Society*, that against the mechanical reductionism of what passed for 'Marxism' in England at that time, Leavis and *Scrutiny* not only 'won' the argument but deserved to win.) It was therefore of the utmost importance that at precisely this moment many of these long-forgotten or unknown 'Western Marxist' texts began to appear in translation, largely through the mediation of New Left Books and Merlin Press. English Cultural Studies thus had to hand, for the first time, an alternative source of theorizing within Marxism about its characteristic problems: in Lukács's literary historical work, Goldmann's *Hidden God*, the first translations of Walter Benjamin, the early texts of the 'Frankfurt School' (known previously only because American 'mass-society theorists' were taken to have successfully refuted Adorno's pessimistic critique), Sartre's *Question of Method.*[48]

These texts marked a decisive second 'break' in Cultural Studies: the break into a complex Marxism. They restored to the debate about culture a set of theorizations around the classical problem of ideologies. They returned to the agenda the key question of the determinate character of culture and ideologies – their material, social and historical conditions of existence. They therefore opened up a necessary reworking of the classical Marxist question of 'base' and 'superstructures' – the decisive issue for a non-idealist or materialist theory of culture. This reworking of Cultural Studies on the ground of the 'base/superstructures' metaphor was a highly significant moment, which had a formative impact on the Centre's work – for example, in media studies, in historical work, in the debates concerning the methods of ideological analysis, in the kind of theoretical argument sustained at that time in our General Theory seminar (the place where these issues were constantly thrashed out).

It was here that the charge of 'theoreticism' was first advanced. And there is no doubt that the Centre was, for a time, over-preoccupied with these difficult theoretical issues. It has to be said, however, that we had no alternative but to undertake a labour of theoretical definition and clarification at the same time as we attempted to do concrete work in the field. The two could not be separated. The term 'culture' could not be simply taken on loan from other traditions of thought and surreptitiously applied, by infinite extension, to an unfolding series of new objects. It could not just be 'tested' empirically. There were different definitions of the term 'culture'. Each implied a different programme of work. Each was only one term in a matrix of related concepts and propositions. To establish the field required a break with older problematics and the constitution of new ones. More recently, Althusser's discussion of how new knowledges are developed by an 'epistemological rupture' with previous ideological problematics has greatly exaggerated the absolutism of such breaks and has helped to induce a practice in which texts are not only read 'symptomatically', for their underlying problematics, but actually *reduced* to them.[49] But his general argument stands. Terms and concepts cannot be treated or changed in isolation; they must be judged in terms of their position in a set of concepts – 'the problematic' – and in relation to the 'constitutive unity of effective thoughts that make up the domain of an existing ideological field'.[50] This is not cited in defence of every twist and turn of the theoretical screw, but it explains the *necessarily* theoretical nature of our enterprise as opposed to the obviousness of empirical common sense.

The break into a complex Marxism was made possible, though not easier, by the creative disintegration from within of sociology itself in its mainstream form. After a period of methodological certainty, sociology too entered its theoretical agony. The theory of the self-regulative properties of advanced capitalist societies was shown to be penetrated by highly ideological notions. More important, the 'tension-managing' capacities of liberal-pluralist societies – for which, at the time, America provided the paradigm case – began to look increasingly precarious under the impact of the political events and upheavals of American society in the late 1960s. Advances were made here not simply by taking thought but through the perceptible impact of real historical events on a particular structure of knowledge. When Martin Nicolaus, the translator of Marx's *Grundrisse,*[51] asked his distinguished American sociological colleagues, 'What is this science which only holds good when its subjects stand still?' he marked not the turning of another methodological corner but the break-up of a certain structure of thought under the force of historical events it could not explain. From this rupture there emerged new kinds of questions about the 'politics of culture' (all that was resumed in the cultural revolution of 1968 and after) which gave the work of the Centre a new dynamic and a new relevance to the emergent contradictions in contemporary advanced societies. The Centre did not, of course, bring about this reversal single-handed: though we were prescient in sensing, quite early, that the whole armour-plated craft of structural-functionalism was less seaworthy than it had appeared. But we did not fire the releant torpedo. Simply, it became possible to pose – as it were, against sociology – certain 'sociological' questions (for example, the question of ideology) to a 'science' which had only given us the reassuring vista of the 'end of ideology'. If the ensuing disarray caused consternation in the sociological camp, it also released intellectual energies, set people free to undertake new kinds of work.[52] Certainly, so far as Cultural Studies was concerned, it gave us a much-needed theoretical breathing-space. Its effect has been, in the long run, profoundly liberating, intellectually.

New dimensions of culture and the impact of the 'structuralisms'

From this point onwards, Cultural Studies is no longer a dependent intellectual colony. It has a direction, an object of study, a set of themes and issues, a distinctive problematic of its own.

First, there was the move away from older definitions of culture to new formulations. Culture no longer meant a set of texts and artefacts. Even less did it mean the 'selective tradition' in which those texts and artefacts had been arranged, studied and appreciated.[53] Particularly it did not mean the values and ideals, which were supposed to be expressed *through* those texts – especially when these were projected out of definite societies in historical time – and deployed as an 'ideal order' (what Williams called a 'court of appeal'), against which the (widely assumed) inevitable process of cultural decline could be measured. These constituted very much the going 'Humanities' definition of culture. It seemed to us to ascribe a general and universal function to values in the abstract which could only be understood in terms of their specific social and historical contexts: in short, an ideological definition, as important for what it obscured as for what it revealed. This definition had to be, to use an ugly neologism, 'problematized'.

The abstraction of texts from the social practices which produced them and the institutional sites where they were elaborated was a fetishization – even if it had pertinent societal effects.[54] This obscured how a particular ordering of culture came to be produced and sustained: the circumstances and conditions of cultural reproduction which the operations of the 'selective tradition' rendered natural, 'taken for granted'. But the process of ordering (arrangement, regulation) is always the result of concrete sets of practices and relations. In constituting a particular cultural order as 'dominant', it implied (though this was rarely examined) the active subordination of alternatives – their marginalization and incorporation into a dominant structure: hence, also, the resistances, antagonisms and struggles which result from regulation.[55] Strikingly, these concepts were altogether absent: they had been 'naturalized' out of existence. Making culture problematic meant therefore raising these absences to visibility. What were the processes by means of which a dominant cultural order came to be 'preferred'?[56] Who preferred *this* order rather than that? What were the effects of a particular ordering of the cultures of a social formation on the other hierarchized social arrangements? How did the preferred cultural order help to sustain 'definite forms of life' in particular social formations? How and why did societies come to be culturally 'structured in dominance'? Broadly speaking, two steps were involved here: First, the move (to give it a too condensed specification) to an 'anthropological' definition of culture – as cultural *practices*; second, the move to a more historical definition of cultural practices: questioning the anthropological meaning and interrogating its universality by means of the concepts of social formation, cultural power, domination and regulation, resistance and struggle. These moves did not exclude the analysis of texts, but it treated them as archives, decentring their assumed privileged status – one kind of evidence, among others.

Second, the question of the relation between cultural practices and other practices in definite social formations. Here we posed the issue of the relation of the 'cultural' to what we may call – again, for shorthand purposes – the economic, political and ideological instances.[57] This was part of the project to develop a materialist definition of culture.[58] It referenced, immediately, the problems of 'base'/'superstructure' and the question of determination. But the classical terms of that metaphor were now clearly inadequate.[59] The work of revision had indeed already commenced.

Thompson had called attention to the

> dialectical interaction between culture and something that is not culture. We must suppose the raw material of life experience to be at one pole, and all the infinitely complex human disciplines and systems, articulate and inarticulate, formalized in institutions or dispersed in the least formal ways, which 'handle', transmit or distort this raw material to be at the other. It is the active process – which is at the same time the process through which men make their history – that I am insisting upon.[60]

In the effort to give culture its own specificity, place and determinate effect, *The Long Revolution* had also proposed a radical revision to the 'base/superstructure' metaphor. It said, in effect, all the practices - economic, political, ideological, cultural - interact with effect on each other. This rescued culture from its residual status as the mere expression of other forces: but at the expense of a radical relativism, skirting the problem of determination. Other related traditions (Williams at this stage noted the convergences between his own work and that of Goldmann and Lukács)[61] retained the old 'base'/'superstructure' distinction but expanded the complexity and 'reciprocal effect' of the latter (in which culture–ideology was firmly located) on the former. This retained the determinacy - but in an elongated, 'last instance only' fashion. Did it go far enough? Sartre attempted to go behind this formulation by isolating the aspect of *signification* as the specifically cultural element:

> Because we are men and because we live in the world of men, of work and of conflicts, all the objects which surround us are signs. By themselves they scarcely mask the real project of those who have made them thus for us and who address us through them. Thus significations come from man and his project but they are inscribed everywhere in things and in the order of things . . . .[62]

These reworkings all tended to bring together again things which had been dispersed into the binary poles of the 'base'/'superstructure' metaphor, on the ground of a common, general *praxis*: human activity, 'the process through which men made history', with none of that false abstraction which their assignment to different levels of effective determinacy seemed to imply.[63] This was close to the position taken by Marx in *The German Ideology*, with its 'consciousness/being' dialectic, and its affirmation that all abstractions could be resolved into the general historical process itself - 'which is nothing but the activity of men'. This had a radically historicized philosophical anthropology as its basis. It entailed a very specific way of conceptualizing the totality: a 'whole', in which each social practice mediated every other practice, or, to adopt Williams's distinctive gloss, conceiving *praxis* as the essential forms of human energy. It also entailed thinking of society as an 'expressive totality'.

The major phase of theoretical development which followed must therefore be broadly identified with all those influences which interrupted this search for unities and underlying 'totalities'. These were linked with a different conception of a social totality – as a necessarily 'complex structure', which does not express a unity but is 'structured in dominance'. Here, as Marx argued in the 1857 *Introduction*, unity is the 'result of many determinations', the product of a particular articulation of distinctions and differences rather than of similarity and correspondence.[64] Determinacy had to be thought not as emanating from one level of the social totality – for example, 'the base' – in a unilinear fashion but as an 'over-determination'.[65] The problematic of Cultural Studies thus became closely identified with the problem of the 'relative autonomy' of cultural practices. This was a radical break. It goes far beyond the impact of the 'structuralisms' – though they were instrumental in a major way in bringing this question to the fore. But, actually, the strongest thrust in 'structuralism' as a mode of thought is towards a radical diversity – the heterogeneity of discourses, the autonomization of instances, the effective dispersal of *any* unity or ensemble, even that of a 'relatively autonomous' one.[66] So the problematic of 'relative autonomy' is more accurately characterized as the site where 'structuralism' and Marxism confront each other at their theoretical limits.[67] It was precisely at this juncture that Engels began his long, difficult and seminal 'correction' of the economistic and mechanical applications of Marxism which had become orthodox in his time. It is now commonly agreed that what Engels did was to identify the core problem of a non-reductionist Marxism, and to provide the elements only of a possible 'solution': the solutions he offered remain (as, surprisingly, both Althusser and Thompson have recently acknowledged)[68] unsatisfactory. 'Relative autonomy' is/was therefore not an accomplished position, theoretically secure against all comers. If anything, its inadequacies only reinforced a general recognition of the major *lacunae* in classical Marxist theory in relation to the whole problem of the 'superstructures'. It signalled work to be done, knowledge to be produced – an open Marxism – rather than the application of ready-made schema.

If structuralism forced on us this question in a peculiarly urgent form, it was certainly not alone in this respect. And its 'solutions' were also, themselves, open to serious question. Its formalism and rationalism, its privileging of the highest levels of abstraction as the exclusive mode of operation of 'Theory' with a capital 'T', its obsession with epistemological issues, themselves constituted formidable barriers to the solution of problems which structuralism itself posed. In noting the impact of structuralism, therefore, we are signalling a formative intervention which coloured and influenced everything that followed. But we are *not* charting a fixed orthodoxy to which we subscribed uncritically. Indeed, here we have not a single influence but a succession, a series. Critiques and rejections of structuralism are as significant in this part of the story as influences absorbed and positions affirmed. We attempt to assess this formative phase and to indicate something of its complexity, in a shorthand way, by taking four representative instances, which reinforce the point.

The first can be identified with the initial impact of the early work of Lévi-Strauss and Barthes. Both deployed the models of structural linguistics as a paradigm (some would say, infinitely expandable) for the scientific study of culture.

Indeed, then and since language has been used as a paradigm figure through which all social practices could potentially be analysed, in effect holding out the promise – which long eluded the 'human sciences' – of a mode of analysis at one and the same time rigorous, scientific and non-reductionist, non-positivist. Language, which is the medium for the production of meaning, is both an ordered or 'structured' system and a means of 'expression'. It could be rigorously and systematically studied – but not within the framework of a set of simple determinacies. Rather, it had to be analysed as a structure of variant possibilities, the arrangement of elements in a signifying chain, as a practice not 'expressing' the world (that is, reflecting it in words) but articulating it, articulated upon it. Lévi-Strauss employed this model to decipher the languages (myths, culinary practices and so on) of so-called 'primitive' societies.[69] Barthes offered a more informal 'semiotics', studying the systems of signs and representations in an array of languages, codes and everyday practices in contemporary societies.[70] Both brought the term 'culture' down from its abstract heights to the level of the 'anthropological', the everyday.

If the weakness of the positions outlined earlier was their tendency to *dissolve* the cultural back into society and history, structuralism's main emphasis was on the specificity, the irreducibility, of the cultural. Culture no longer simply reflected other practices in the realm of ideas. It was itself a practice – a *signifying* practice – and had its own determinate product: meaning. To think of the specificity of the cultural was to come to terms with what defined it, in structuralism's view, as a practice: its internal forms and relations, its internal structuration. It was – following Saussure, Jakobsen and the other structural linguists – the way elements were selected, combined and articulated in language which 'signified'. The stress therefore shifted from the substantive contents of different cultures to their forms of arrangement – from the *what* to the *how* of cultural systems.[71]

This was a radical departure. In Sartre, the link between signification and praxis had been founded theoretically on the intentional and expressive project of men (fetishized, masked by their objectivated, alienated appearance in 'the order of things': see above). Modern structuralism proposed instead to think of men as spoken by, as well as speaking, their culture: spoken through its codes and systems. The latter aspect (the linguistic system, the social part of language, the *langue*) rather than individual utterances (*paroles*) was what could be studied systematically. In this, as in much else, Lévi-Strauss recapitulated, within structuralism, many of the conditions of a 'science of society' first proposed in Durkheim's *Rules of Sociological Method* (for instance, the suicide rate, not individual suicides, was for Durkheim the properly constituted 'social fact').[72] In the same way Lévi-Strauss established the 'rule' as central in the construction of all ordered human systems. He imposed 'difference' and 'distinction' where previously there had been correspondences and unities (compare Goldmann's protocol for a sociology of literature in *The Hidden God*).

Structuralism thus constituted a fundamental *decentring* of cultural processes from their authorial centre in 'man's project'. Culture was as much constituted by its conditions of existence as it constituted them. It established constraint and regulation alongside expression and agency in the analysis of structured practices. Structuralism thus marked a radical break with the dominant forms of theoretical humanism. It bracketed the terms 'consciousness' and 'intention'. Culture was better understood as the inventories, the folk taxonomies, through which social life is 'classified out' in different societies. It was not so much the product of 'consciousness' as the unconscious forms and categories through which historically definite forms of consciousness were produced.[73] This brought the term 'culture' closer to an expanded definition of ideology - though now without the connotations of 'false consciousness' which the term had previously carried.

Lévi-Strauss helped to rehabilitate the work of Durkheim and to demonstrate his varied lineage: where Parsons had worked towards the structural-functionalist synthesis via the Durkheim of *Suicide*, Lévi-Strauss directed attention to Durkheim and Mauss's *Primitive Classification*, which he identified as an integral part of structuralism's 'uncompleted programme.[74] In polemical fashion, Lévi-Strauss privileged the synchronic level of analysis over the diachronic - an anti-historical inversion with which, from the outset, we were far from happy. For, while it powerfully moved the level of analysis back to that of 'system' and 'structure', this was at the cost (never fully reckoned with by its devotees) of reconstituting some of the fundamental positions of structural-functionalism (for example, society as a 'system of systems') which earlier positions had correctly contested. With these costs Cultural Studies had at once to reckon. In a wider sense, Lévi-Strauss tilted the intellectual pendulum sharply from German to French influences and models, and from a neo-Hegelianism to a distinctive variant of neo-Kantianism.[75] Yet the impact of structuralism, one must repeat, does not consist of positions unqualifiedly subscribed to. We must acknowledge a major theoretical intervention. Whatever else it could not do, structuralism displaced 'man in general' from the full intentional centre of the cultural project. It thus ended a certain theoretical innocence, whatever the critiques of structuralist theories which had then to be made. It made culture, in its expressive sense, conditional - because conditioned. It obliged us really to re-think the 'cultural' as a set of practices: to think of the material conditions of signification and its necessary determinateness.

This may seem strange since Lévi-Strauss, by concentrating so absolutely on the *internal* relations of 'the cultural', effectively side-stepped the issue of determinacy. He resolved the problem cognitively by reference to a set of universal elements and rules common to *all* cultural practices, which he ascribed to the structure of the human mind as such - *l'esprit humain.*[76] In this sense - as Ricoeur observed and Lévi-Strauss acknowledged - he remained a 'Kantian without the transcendental imperative' (that is, God). He was also, if only in a deep sense, a 'Durkheimean', founding culture at the level of reciprocal exchange rather than on production.[77] His work also exemplified a sustained formalism - the price of his proper attention to forms. Nevertheless, a conception of determinate practice lay somewhere near the centre of his work. It could not be constrained for long inside its Kantian and Durkheimean brackets, the limits of his structuralism.

This is clearly demonstrated by what rapidly succeeded it - the work of the

Marxist structuralists, here personified in the example of Althusser. Marxist structuralism looked initially like a take-over bid; but it is important to see the internal logic which drove structuralism from its Durkheimean to its Marxian inflexion. If language is a social practice, it can be adequately reduced neither to the mere sum of the individual speakers nor to the individual utterances spoken in it. It must be defined in terms of the 'systems of relations' which make these individual interventions possible and which structure, determine and limit them. There is, despite all their radical differences, a common starting-point here between Durkheim and Marx – in Marx's insistence that we must start with relations, and Durkheim's insistence that the object of social science is 'the social *sui generis*'. On the irreducibility of a 'structure' to the conscious intentions of its individual elements *both* agree – at least as to this necessary level of abstraction. There the salient compatibilities end. For where Durkheim isolated 'the social' (as Lévi-Strauss, following him, abstracted 'the cultural'), Marx insisted on the relations *between* material relations – thinking of 'societies' as ensembles. And where Lévi-Strauss centred his analysis on the 'rule', the codes and formal oppositions, Marx worked from relations and contradictions. Nevertheless, the manner in which Althusser attempted to rethink structuralism on Marxist foundations owed much more to Lévi-Strauss (and through him, inevitably, to Durkheim) than he or his followers have been willing to acknowledge.

Althusser's impact is harder to detail satisfactorily. Here one can only select certain key themes. The first is the break (powerfully established in the early *For Marx* essays) with expressive and totalizing ways of thinking about the relationships between different practices in a social formation. It is well known that there are more ways than one in which this rethinking appears in his work. There is the notion of societies as necessarily complex, unevenly determining and determinate practices, caught in his concepts of 'relative autonomy' and 'over-determination'. There is the full-blown 'structural causality' of *Reading Capital*, where each practice is only the condensed effect of the structure as a whole. The differences between these positions cannot be commented on further here. Crudely, the important innovation was the attempt to think the 'unity' of a social formation in terms of an articulation. This posed the issues of the 'relative autonomy' of the cultural-ideological level and a new concept of social totality: totalities as complex structures.

Second, but closely related, was Althusser's attempt to reformulate the problem of determination in a non-reductionist way (or ways). Third, there were the varied, sometimes internally inconsistent, ways in which he defined *ideology*. This work on ideology was of special relevance to Cultural Studies. It revived two earlier stresses and added two new ones. It reasserted the conception of ideologies as practices rather than as systems of ideas. It defined ideologies as providing the frameworks of understanding through which men interpret, make sense of, experience and 'live' the material conditions in which they find themselves.[78] This second emphasis was very close to the 'culture' of Lévi-Strauss; but it employed a more Marxist connotation, stressing the degrees of mis-recognition involved in these framings and classifications of social existence.[79] Thus, for Althusser, ideologies were those images, representations, categories through which men 'live', in an imaginary way, their real relation to their conditions of existence. To these, Althusser added two further, more controversial, propositions. Ideologies were materially located and were therefore best examined, in their practico-social effect, in the institutional sites and apparatuses (the ISAs) which elaborated them.[80] But also ideologies worked by constituting or interpellating 'subjects'. The 'I', the seat of consciousness and the foundation of ideological discourses, was not the integral Cartesian centre of thought but a contradictory discursive category constituted by ideological discourse itself. Here Althusser, whose borrowings from Freud were already strategic (for example, the concept of 'over-determination'), now ambiguously made another, more tactical, 'loan' from the psychoanalytic work of Lacan.[81]

The problems with the Althusserean formulations on these key theoretical issues (and on the related epistemological questions concerning the relation between science and ideology, knowledge and the 'real') are well rehearsed and cannot be resumed here. We must include in any such account a substantive critique made from within the Centre itself.[82] Basically, the concepts of 'relative autonomy' and 'over-determination' proved fruitful and have been developed – even though they are by no means theoretically secure (what is relative? how autonomous is 'autonomy'?). 'Structuralist causality' has been amply shown to be just another, larger, self-sufficient and self-generating 'expressive totality': all its effects are given in the structure which is itself the sum of all the practices – even if this is a totality of a Spinozean rather than a Hegelian variety. Ultimately, it proved both form[...] and functionalist in character, giving a basis for Thompson's subsequent caric[...] of Althusser's 'structure' as a sort of self-generating machine. Althusser's lat[...] work – critical of both the formalism and the theoreticism of his earlier ef[...] returns us to more acceptable positions, but these are descriptively rathe[...] theoretically established.[83]

In its integral form, then, 'Althussereanism' remained an internally [...] position. In its fully orthodox form it never really existed for the C[...] people swallowed *Reading Capital* whole – though elsewhere it did [...] acquire doctrinal status. But again the impact was not a matter o[...] Althusser interrupted certain previous lines of thinking in a dec[...] have gone on to further developments nevertheless continue t[...] his shadow, after his 'break'. Many who have definitively cri[...] standing on his shoulders.

One last aspect of his influence must be noted. This c[...] Althusser himself, and those influenced by him, reshape[...] the relationship between ideologies/culture and class f[...] lived practices of social groups in definite societies p[...] on the major social formations of industrial capital[...] In many ways the earlier Marxist tradition – Lukā[...] plifications here – conducted the analysis of spe[...] conceiving them as the products or expression[...]

sistent
ew
ime,
ubscription.
. Those who
nd think in
m are still
e ways in which
ral issue of
Cultures as the
evitably, a focus
class formations.
mann are good exem-
formations largely by
ural-ideological level, of

framings and classifications of social existence.[79] Thus, for Althusser, ideologies were those images, representations, categories through which men 'live', in an imaginary way, their real relation to their conditions of existence. To these, Althusser added two further, more controversial, propositions. Ideologies were materially located and were therefore best examined, in their practico-social effect, in the institutional sites and apparatuses (the ISAs) which elaborated them.[80] But also ideologies worked by constituting or interpellating 'subjects'. The 'I', the seat of consciousness and the foundation of ideological discourses, was not the integral Cartesian centre of thought but a contradictory discursive category constituted by ideological discourse itself. Here Althusser, whose borrowings from Freud were already strategic (for example, the concept of 'over-determination'), now ambiguously made another, more tactical, 'loan' from the psychoanalytic work of Lacan.[81]

The problems with the Althusserean formulations on these key theoretical issues (and on the related epistemological questions concerning the relation between science and ideology, knowledge and the 'real') are well rehearsed and cannot be resumed here. We must include in any such account a substantive critique made from within the Centre itself.[82] Basically, the concepts of 'relative autonomy' and 'over-determination' proved fruitful and have been developed - even though they are by no means theoretically secure (what is relative? how autonomous is 'autonomy'?). 'Structuralist causality' has been amply shown to be just another, larger, self-sufficient and self-generating 'expressive totality': all its effects are given in the structure which is itself the sum of all the practices - even if this is a totality of a Spinozean rather than a Hegelian variety. Ultimately, it proved both formalist and functionalist in character, giving a basis for Thompson's subsequent caricature of Althusser's 'structure' as a sort of self-generating machine. Althusser's later work - critical of both the formalism and the theoreticism of his earlier efforts - returns us to more acceptable positions, but these are descriptively rather than theoretically established.[83]

In its integral form, then, 'Althussereanism' remained an internally inconsistent position. In its fully orthodox form it never really existed for the Centre. Few people swallowed *Reading Capital* whole - though elsewhere it did, for a time, acquire doctrinal status. But again the impact was not a matter of mere subscription. Althusser interrupted certain previous lines of thinking in a decisive way. Those who have gone on to further developments nevertheless continue to work and think in his shadow, after his 'break'. Many who have definitively criticized him are still standing on his shoulders.

One last aspect of his influence must be noted. This concerns the ways in which Althusser himself, and those influenced by him, reshaped the central issue of the relationship between ideologies/culture and class formations. Cultures as the lived practices of social groups in definite societies produced, inevitably, a focus on the major social formations of industrial capitalist societies: class formations. In many ways the earlier Marxist tradition - Lukãcs and Goldmann are good exemplifications here - conducted the analysis of specific cultural formations largely by conceiving them as the products or expressions, at the cultural-ideological level, of the 'world outlooks' or *visions du monde* of particular classes. Class structures, class domination and class contradictions also constituted, at the level of cultures and ideologies, parallel formations - class ideologies. Althusser not only challenged any attempt to reduce the specificity of the 'ideological instance' to the simple effect of the economic base (hence, 'over-determination' and uneven relations and relative autonomy): he also challenged the expressive notion of a simple correspondence between class formations (mainly determined by economic relations) and cultural formations. He did not deny mutual and reciprocal effects between them within the structured complexity of social formations, but he refused any simple transparencies and correspondences. Two related steps were involved here. First, the argument that classes were not simple 'economic' structures but formations constituted by *all* the different practices - economic, political and ideological - and their effects on each other. ('Contradiction' and 'over-determination' were, indeed, Althusser's attempt to 'think' this proposition, which he derived from Engels's letters, against a reductionist Marxist economism, on what he conceived as a more theoretically adequate basis.) Secondly, classes were not integral formations and did not, as Poulantzas put it, carry their ideologies already prescribed and prearranged like number plates on their backs.[84] The manner in which Althusser tried to reformulate this relationship has been the subject of extended critiques. But as a general protocol for the field of study, the force with which it posed the cultures/classes question cannot be overestimated. He asked, to put it simply, how the relationship of cultures/ideologies to classes could be conceived, if one were to avoid reducing the former to the latter.

In sum, one might say that structuralism posed, rather than answered satisfactorily, certain absolutely critical questions for Cultural Studies. This summary proposition could, of course, be divided into many more subdivisions than we have space for here. It offered the challenge of further work on the problem of a materialist, non-reductionist theory of culture.

We have noted the importance of Althusser's 'Ideological state apparatuses' essay.[85] This influential paper was important because its definition of ideologies embraced many of the wider ways in which we had come to define culture - also, because of its stress on 'practices' rather than merely on 'ideas'. It was influential, too, because it retained a classical Marxist emphasis on the 'function' which ideology performed in reproducing the conditions and relations necessary to the mode of production of class societies. This third emphasis was important because it initiated ways of thinking about the relationship of ideologies to class-structured social formations (that is, through reproduction), without reducing the former to classes.[86] It related the production of ideologies to 'dominant ideologies' and to all those apparatuses which produce and reproduce the ideological structures of society, located in the state and in the institutions of civil society (churches, trade unions, the family, the social, cultural apparatuses and so on).[87] But it tended to conceptualize these relations as 'functional supports' for a given system of dominant social arrangements. Thus it consistently down-played the notion of cultural contradiction and struggle. For all practical purposes, the domain of ideology was, for Althusser, the domain of the '*dominant* ideologies'.[88] Althusser attempted to redress the functionalist balance of this essay in a footnote on ideology as 'struggle' - but, so far as the theoretical structure of his argument was concerned, this eleventh-hour revision was merely 'gestural'.[89] This was a critique of his work which the Centre began to develop from its first encounter.[90] And the importance of this critique may be indicated by naming another influential figure - Antonio Gramsci - who provided, for us, very much the 'limit case' of Marxist structuralism and whose work has therefore been widely influential, in a different way, for the Centre.

Like the structuralists, Gramsci steadfastly resists any attempt neatly to align cultural and ideological questions with class and economic ones. His work stands as a prolonged repudiation of any form of reductionism - especially that of 'economism': 'It is the problem of the relations between structure and superstructure which must be accurately posed and resolved if the forces which are active in the history of a particular period are to be correctly analysed and the relation between them determined.'[91] This connection and specificity is elaborated in Gramsci through his extended work on the nature of the state and civil society in developed capitalist societies; in his discussion of 'the specificity of the political'; in his work on 'national-popular' cultures and the role and formation of intellectuals; in his analysis of 'common sense' as the ground on which different organized ideologies intervene; in his emphasis on the practico-social role which ideologies have in organizing and mobilizing masses of people; and in the complex notion which he has of what constitutes a 'class' formation and the complex role of class alliances within a historical bloc.

Gramsci brings these ideas together within the framework of the concept of 'hegemony', which has played a seminal role in Cultural Studies.[92] This is an enlarged and complex idea. In essence, it refers to all those processes whereby a fundamental social group (Gramsci speaks of alliances of class strata, not of a unitary and unproblematic 'ruling class'), which has achieved direction over the 'decisive economic nucleus', is able to expand this into a moment of social, political and cultural leadership and authority throughout civil society and the state, attempting to unify and reconstruct the social formation around an organic tendency through a series of 'national tasks'. Gramsci speaks of this elaboration of a tendency into a civilization as the 'passage from the structure to the complex superstructure' - a formative and connective moment, requiring new kinds and levels of intervention

in which previously germinated ideologies become 'party', come into confrontation and conflict, until one of them or at least a combination of them tends to prevail, to gain the upper hand, to propagate itself throughout society - bringing about not only a unison of economic and political aims, but also intellectual and moral unity, posing all the questions around which the struggle rages, not on a corporate but on a 'universal' plane, and thus creating the hegemony of a fundamental group over a series of subordinate groups.[93]

Here one finds Gramsci thinking of complex social formations and the relations between their different aspects in a connective but non-reductionist way. 'Hegemony' retains its base in the way the productive life of societies is organized.[94] But it raises as critical the formative and educative tasks which are required if this is to become the basis of a profound revision of the whole social formation – the structures of civil and political life, culture and ideologies. The important point is that such 'moments' assume a different character, have different degrees of success and provoke qualitative challenges of different kinds at different times, depending on the definite forms of society, the balance of contending forces and the historical conjuncture. In this respect Gramsci massively corrects the ahistorical, highly abstract, formal and theoreticist level at which structuralist theories tend to operate. His thinking is always historically specific and 'conjunctural'.[95] It is conjunctural in two senses. It is always made specific to a particular historical phase in specific national societies; but, further, the concept of hegemony is elaborated specifically in relation to those advanced capitalist societies in which the institutions of state and civil society have reached a stage of great complexity, in which the mobilization and consent of the popular masses is required to secure the ascendancy of a particular tendency and in which 'reform' requires an extended and complex process of struggle, mastery, compromise and transformation to reshape society to new goals and purposes. Gramsci's thinking is thus peculiarly relevant to societies like ours, in which political and cultural power has been stabilized through the parliamentary and representative political system, with a complex state structure and a massive development of the cultural institutions of civil society.

For Gramsci, 'hegemony' is never a permanent state of affairs and never uncontested. He distances himself from both the 'ruling class/ruling ideas' propositions of *The German Ideology* and the functionalist conception of 'dominant ideology' in Althusser's essay. 'Hegemony' is always the (temporary) mastery of a particular theatre of struggle. It marks a shift in the dispositions of contending forces in a field of struggle and the articulation of that field into a tendency. Such tendencies do not immediately 'profit' a ruling class or a fraction of capital, but they create the conditions whereby society and the state may be conformed in a larger sense to certain formative national-historical tasks. Thus particular outcomes always depend on the balance in the relations of force in any theatre of struggle and reform. This rids Gramsci's thinking of any trace of a necessitarian logic and any temptation to 'read off' political and ideological outcomes from some hypostatized economic base. Its effect is to show how cultural questions can be linked, in a non-reductionist manner, to other levels: it enables us to think of societies as complex formations, necessarily contradictory, always historically specific.

Gramsci, of course, remains within the basic terms of a materialist theory. But there have been other influences which, in certain areas of our work, have taken the line of thinking beyond these terms of reference. One may think here of the difficult but important work stemming from the critique of earlier semiotic models of language, and of parallel developments based on an appropriation of psychoanalytic theories. These tendencies may be conveniently represented by Foucault,[96] in whose work one finds an even more radical attempt to break with any model of a hierarchy of determining factors through the concept of 'discursive practices'. Foucault's name must be taken here as 'personifying' a whole set of theoretical developments based on the critique of the early models of language promulgated in the first phase of semiotic theory and structural linguistics. In his notion of 'discourse' Foucault goes some way to breaking down the dichotomy, which most other positions appear to retain in some form, between the signifying ('discursive') and the 'extra-discursive' aspects of any practice.[97] This work privileges, but in a new way, the study of textual archives and the sites through which the 'discursive' practices of a society are constructed. His analysis of the practices of sexuality or of punishment examines the rules and regularities through which, at different moments, the objects of these practices are formulated and elaborated. Foucault, following the lead of Lévi-Strauss, though in a very different way, directs attention to the *internal* relations and regularities of any field of knowledge. He remains agnostic about their general determining conditions and about their 'truth'. He examines them largely from a 'topographical' or genealogical vantage point – studying their arrangement, their disposition, their interventions on each other, their articulation and transformation. This, once again, skirts the difficult question of determination, but it has provided the basis for extensive, concrete studies of different fields of knowledge and practice.[98] He has helped further to break down that dichotomy between social practices and the ways they are represented in ideologies, in discourse and in particular regimes of knowledge. He has opened up again the problem of 'representation' itself, on which so many theories of ideology and symbolic representation have been based.

We have deliberately not attempted here to resume the entire theoretical spectrum of the Centre's recent work in this period. We have referenced some major turning-points through a selection of representative instances. This abbreviated account should not be taken as marking a steady and unified 'long march' through the theoretical continents. Different theorists and positions outlined above have been more or less influential in different areas of the Centre's work. While maintaining a consistent level of debate and discussion about and between them, a certain theoretical 'pluralism' has been both necessary and inevitable. Thus, to give an example: the Centre's work on language (see below) explored very fully the post-Saussure critique of semiotic models and has worked fairly consistently on terrain staked out by Derrida, Foucault, Kristeva, the 'Tel Quel' group and Lacanian psychoanalysis (the contribution to this volume amply demonstrates this in detail). By contrast the media group has been critical of the 'autonomy' it saw implied in those positions and the universalism entailed by the revisions of psychoanalysis advanced by Lacan (see below). Despite these real differences in theoretical perspective, the two groups have learned much from each other. Another example: analysis in the Work Group has always retained an earlier stress on the importance of observational methods and the accounts actors give of their experience: nevertheless, this work has moved progressively towards its own distinctive ways of conceptualizing the structural conditions of the labour process (for example, Part 2 of Paul Willis's

Learning to Labour). Much of this research now relates to women's work, reflecting a more developed feminist perspective (see below), but within this work *both* kinds of emphases are present. (This is discussed in *Women Take Issue*.) In feminist research more generally the emphasis on experience and consciousness (in, for example, Sheila Rowbotham's work) sharply contrasts with 'Althusserean' and Lévi-Straussean emphases (for example, Juliet Mitchell's *Psychoanalysis and Feminism* or the Lacanian positions of the journal, *M/F*). Yet another example: the Centre's History Group, which pursued the rationalist position on history and theory as far as it could be taken, then went on to provide one of the most developed and formative critiques of this position. Theoretical openness has by no means been easy to sustain within the Centre, but the Centre has consciously attempted to undercut any attempts to establish an 'orthodoxy' (in the sense of a set of prescribed positions to which everyone had to adhere).

The impact of the feminisms

We have traced the complex and uneven impact of 'the structuralisms'. The most profound challenge to any attempt to establish a Cultural Studies 'orthodoxy' has, however, undoubtedly arisen from the emergence of feminism within the Centre's work. In challenging the male-oriented models and assumptions and the heavily masculine subject-matter and topics which for long constituted the assumed terrain of Cultural Studies (in a profoundly unconscious and unreflexive way), feminism has had an obvious impact on Cultural Studies. It has forced a major rethink in every substantive area of work. But its impact can in no sense be limited to these substantive reworkings. It is impossible, from a vantage point inside feminism, to retain a reductionist theory of culture. In posing all those areas and sites in any social formation which need to be rethought from the perspective of the position and the oppression of women and the centrality of patriarchal relations, feminism has provoked a break with any residual attempt to give the term 'material conditions' an exclusively economistic or 'productivist' meaning. In raising the question of how to think of both the causes and the effects of the contradictions of gender, it has displaced forever any exclusive reference to class contradictions as the stable point of reference for cultural analysis. All that is involved in thinking about the specificity of 'gender' – distinct from, even though it can be shown to be articulated with, 'class' – has moved Cultural Studies away from its tendency to a complex class reductionism.[99] We have seen that the question of 'determination' has been one of the principal theoretical motors of work in this area. But the attention to the structuring principle of gender and to questions of sexual difference and patriarchal relations has rendered it impossible to fall back behind the intrinsic heterogeneity and necessary complexity of different kinds of contradiction, attributable in neither a 'first' or 'last' sense to the 'economic' in its simple designation.

Feminism has thus been responsible not only for setting 'reproduction', alongside 'production', as a key site for the elaboration of cultural structures, but also for profoundly rethinking the concept of 'production' itself. Both Gramsci and Althusser cited the school and the family as key instances in the construction of 'hegemony'. But neither school nor family can be seriously considered outside the sexual division of labour, the construction of gender roles, identities and relations and the principle of sexual difference. The institutions of state and civil society are both 'capitalist' and 'patriarchal' in character, in their very mode of operation: but capitalism and patriarchy have distinct histories, different conditions of existence, different cross-cutting effects and consequences, which make impossible any neat alignment or correspondences between them. A theory of culture which cannot account for patriarchal structures of dominance and oppression is, in the wake of feminism, a non-starter. But patriarchal relations are not amenable to simple extensions, marginal qualifications or emendations to other theories which - but for this question - retain their general validity. The problematics of these theories have had to be profoundly recast, their premises brought into radical question, because of the absence, in their very theoretical structure, of the question of sexual difference.

Feminism has therefore radically altered the terrain of Cultural Studies. It has, of course, brought whole new concrete areas of inquiry, new sites of investigation into being within the Cultural Studies agenda, as well as reshaping existing ones. But its larger impact has been theoretical and organizational - all that has been required to think the whole field anew from the site of a different contradiction and all that this has meant, in its consequences, both for what is studied in the Centre and for how it is studied: the organization of a new intellectual practice. The attempt really to take these questions into account - not simply to nod, generally, in their direction - has been a painful exercise at times (as those who have read the account by women in the Centre in *Women Take Issue* will readily understand):[100] not so much a crisis of intent - which was subscribed to at an early stage, though not without resistance - but rather of bringing about a deep change in practice and in the modes of intellectual work in the Centre. The resistances have been all the stronger because of the depth and extent of what had been repressed, the hard-won certainties which, rightly and necessarily, were challenged and undermined. In one area after another of the Centre's work feminism has sent certainties and orthodoxies back to the drawing-board. It has redrawn the map of Cultural Studies, as it is slowly redesigning every area of critical intellectual life. The transformations it has provoked are profound and unstoppable.

Concrete studies

The charting of problematics will, we hope, have given the reader some sense of what has been involved in the attempt to give Cultural Studies a better definition and a more secure theoretical basis. It may, however, have left the impression that difficult positions are hardly won before they are dissolved in a further methodological and theoretical reprise. In fact, this has not been the case. There has never been a rigidly imposed unitary theoretical position in the Centre: though there always has been a general project - the elaboration of a non-reductionist theory of cultures and social formations - and a defined 'universe of discourse' within whose framework different positions and emphases are exposed to mutual critique.

Different lines of concrete work and research have, as we suggested earlier, employed different paradigms, taken different stresses. Paul Willis's work, while increasingly taking into account the determining impact of wider sets of relations, remains rooted in a critical ethnography and in the 'recovery' of the experience and understandings of the groups of actors so constrained. It insists on the irreducibility of this moment to any larger terms of a 'structural' explanation. The early work on subcultures exemplified a strong base in this tendency, but in subsequent work it has been modified and recast by the deployment of Gramsci's concept of 'hegemony' and by more sustained work on historically specific forms of resistance. By contrast, media work - because of the centrality of textual analysis - has continued to be more profoundly influenced than other areas by linguistic and semiotic traditions. Recent research on the state, education and the family has been influenced by the 'new social history', by structuralist and feminist theories. The work on language has been deeply marked by the new concerns with 'discursive practices' and their regulative properties. 'Cultural history' has addressed itself to post-war historiographical traditions and to the relationship, posed in these alternative traditions, between history and theory. Thus when one turns from theoretical questions *per se* to concrete research in the Centre, we find recurring emphases: but also a greater plurality of approaches than the monolithic impression which may have been suggested by this necessarily compressed account.

Priorities in the areas of concrete research have also changed over time. 'Accreted' sometimes seems a more appropriate term, since problems never simply disappear, nor are they displaced by the opening up of new areas but are transformed and developed within a different problematic. Centre work is full of these recoveries and reprises. In the early days Centre research was mainly concentrated in three areas: the media, literary analysis and popular culture. Work on the media has continued throughout. But the shifts of perspective and problematic are significant (they are charted in more detail below). Literary studies, as we noted earlier, have had a somewhat chequered career: but this is a history which the Centre shares with literary studies everywhere. Again, the internal transformation of this field is very amply discussed in the relevant section. Popular culture was always a problematic area: largely descriptive in definition (often no more than a mere listing of residual customs and forms) and inscribed within the inadequate terms of the 'cultural debate' (with its 'popular/high' culture oscillations). The analysis of popular texts has, however, recently revived within both the Media Studies and English Studies areas. And this development is complemented by a quite novel concern with 'the popular' in a radically new sense: national-popular cultural traditions, popular ideologies, the popular as the ground of common sense in which more developed and organized 'philosophies' intervene, the popular as the stake in the struggle for hegemony and consent (populist/popular democratic elements in political discourses and their articulation with different class practices, for example).[101] A combination of some of these interests, within the framework of a more developed theory of the state and with an attempt at the analysis of a specific historical conjuncture, resulted in a collective Centre enterprise, eventually published in *Policing the Crisis*.[102]

This did mark the beginning of a whole new phase of concrete research more directly concerned with political formations, state and civil institutions, institutional policies and practices. It also marked the beginning of a new concern with questions of historical periodization and the attention to specific historical conjunctures in their own right. Indeed, there has been a thorough-going 'historicization' of the Centre's previously rather theoreticist practice, which seems to us an unqualified gain. This is now beginning to deliver its own provisional results, in work to come on state formations in the 1880s–1920s and the 1930s; 1945, the Welfare State and the terms of the post-war settlement; literary formations and women's writing in the 1930s and 1950s; the post-war legislation on sexuality, and the restructuring of women's work; and the labour process and the post-war history of race relations. The most general consequence is the pressing of this whole range of work – whether contemporary or 'historical' – towards historical specificity and a sense of the present conjuncture (these only appear to be antithetical and opposed emphases if the term 'historical' is taken, simple-mindedly, to refer to the past, but we have attempted, rigorously, to break with this disabling, descriptively inert definition).

We have already mentioned the impact of feminism. This too has had its consequences for the areas and directions of concrete research. For some time work in this area was organized within the Women's Studies group. But after an initial phase this has been abandoned in favour of making questions of gender and patriarchal relations central to the concerns of all our research groups and no longer the responsibility of women alone to sustain. Thus one can find these concerns now best developed in (for example) the analysis of the impact of schooling on girls and of paid/unpaid domestic work on women; in the analysis of feminine representations in literary and media discourses; in the study of feminist political representation; in the examination of state policies and strategies directly addressed to women, strongly marked in their patriarchal forms; in the connections between school and family. More generally, the articulation between gender and class relations is now a consistent theme in all the Centre's present work.

The different areas of concrete research have also retained distinct *methodological* emphases: in some, the emphases on ethnographic field work and interviewing; in some, the centrality of texts and discourse and the practices of representation; in some, the difficult methodological moves entailed in moving from formal ideologies to their 'lived' historical implementation – their implementation, in particular, in institutional practices and policies; in some, the appropriation of historical methods of research on archives, documentary and other sources. Like the substantive themes reviewed earlier, these are no longer neatly distributed between the different research groups, but are combined and recombined in ways appropriate to the concrete objects of research, across the groupings. There is a continual dialogue and debate across these substantive areas and an attempt to appropriate methods to problems. There is a delicate question of balance here – a tension between probing more deeply the substantive and methodological areas of specialization and developing a more integrated style of work. There has, inevitably, been a certain 'regionalism' in a Centre which spans so wide a spectrum of concrete areas. Each 'region' continues to have an intellectual responsibility – to know and to confront, critically, the strategies, methods and findings as these have been defined in the dominant practice in that area. Each, however, also has a responsibility to make such progress as it is able to make within its own 'region' openly available to other groupings and thus to develop Cultural Studies as a whole and to advance it as a field of study. The combination of these 'regional' and general emphases is one of the central and strategic organizational intellectual tasks for the Centre, to which much energy and many resources have been directed over the years and for which Centre members are asked to take a collective responsibility.

Developing a practice of intellectual work

We have dealt, so far, with the theoretical problems which have staked out the Centre's development and with concrete research. But this account would be incomplete without some attempt directly to address the actual question of organizing a practice. It is only 'in practice' that aims, goals and intentions can be actually and effectively (or ineffectively) realized. Though this aspect comes last, it has been, in many ways, our first priority throughout – and something genuinely distinctive about the Centre. Here we have striven for what has sometimes seemed to us and to our critics to be the 'near-impossible': to be, at once, rigorous *and* open; to be *both* theoretical and concrete. A certain critical self-reflexivity has been one necessary consequence of working in a field of inquiry which has no clear precedents, no fixed reference points, no scholarly orthodoxy. We have had to make problematic for ourselves what others could take for granted. We have had to investigate the premises and assumptions behind a range of available theories and methods – and have thus, one might say, fallen into the habit of constantly questioning our own starting-points. If this has appeared, at times, a form of theoretical self-indulgence, we would simply point to the elegant studies and the sophisticated theorizing in our own areas of work which have elaborated their protocols, done their field work, questioned their respondents, read their documents, produced their accounts and results – and all on the unexamined premise that the world, for all practical purposes, is 'masculine'. Faced by this blinding obviousness, who now would have the courage to insist that we ought simply to have just done more 'good empirical research'?

The issue of 'theoreticism' is not an irrelevant one, certainly.[103] We are aware of the many turning-points where we have fallen into an imitative dependency, or where we have allowed theoretical debates to obscure the absolutely necessary test of concrete work and exemplification. In the last five years the Centre has struggled both to make its own critique of 'theoreticist' positions (including its own) and to reshape its work to give it a substantially greater concrete and historical basis. Though we would not claim success in every department, we feel far more confident than we did five years ago about getting the theoretical and concrete aspects of our work into a better and more productive balance. This struggle - for the best kind of theoretically informed concrete practice - continues: it is one of our highest, most self-conscious priorities. We have attempted to monitor and to transform our organization of intellectual work in the light of it. We believe our future work will show the positive effects of struggling with ourselves in this way for a 'best practice'. It is the only way we know of developing a real intellectual practice which does not merely reproduce The Obvious. This has given the Centre a built-in and unchallenged subscription to the 'necessary complexity' of the field. It has also required us to think hard about the actual conditions for the production of knowledge, and to think about our own strategies in ways which - to use Gramscean terms - are necessarily 'organizational and connective'. Gramsci argued:

> It has to be established that every research has its own specific method and constructs its own specific science, and that the method has been developed and elaborated together with the developments and elaborations of this specific research and science, and forms with them a single whole. To think that one can advance the progress of a work of scientific research by applying to it a standard method chosen because it has given good results in another field to which it was naturally suited is a strange delusion which has little to do with science. There do however exist certain general criteria which could be held to constitute the critical consciousness of every man [and woman] of science, whatever his [or her] specialization. Thus one can say someone is not a scientist if he displays a lack of sureness in his particular criteria, if he does not have a full understanding of the concepts he is using, if he has scant information and understanding of the previous state of the problems he is dealing with, if he is not very cautious in his assertions, if he does not proceed in a necessary but an arbitrary and disconnected fashion, if he cannot take account of the gaps that exist in knowledge acquired, but covers over and contents himself with purely verbal solutions and connections, instead of stating that one is dealing with provisional positions which may have to be gone over again and developed, etc.[104]

The emphasis in that passage on the actual forms of an intellectual practice are crucial. They remind us that intellectual work does not consist only of what has been studied, of the theories and methods employed or even of the provisional results obtained. It also has to do with the *practice itself* - with how it is performed. The Centre has, alongside the kind of task already outlined, also attempted in this period to generate a new kind of intellectual practice and to give it an organizational form. Especially, it has experimented with ways of involving all its members, staff and students, in the shaping of that practice and in the decisions and responsibilities for setting that practice to work in a specific organizational setting. But this, in turn, always requires taking account of the existing practices, dominant elsewhere, which it has been necessary to challenge, displace or transform.

Here, one can think of the lonely, isolated, individualized and competitive-possessive form in which much research in the humanities and social sciences is conceived and conducted. This is indeed how most of us - including the youngest recruits to the Centre - have learned to learn to try to produce knowledge. It has seemed to us largely an obsolete and archaic kind of 'knowledge production' (knowledge in the handicraft or artisan mode), thoroughly out of keeping with modern conditions of intellectual work and the real division of intellectual labour. This we have tried, in different ways, to displace. But to set a practice aside is different - and easier - than actually replacing it with an alternative real practice: the will to go in another direction is not the same thing as sustaining a changed or transformed practice, in intellectual matters as in all others.[105] In general, what has been involved here has been the attempt to make intellectual work more collective in the actual forms of its practising: to constitute research and groups of projects and studies around working collectives rather than serial groups of competing intellectuals, carrying their very own thesis topics like batons in their knapsacks. This has involved trying to make real the general commitment that each, in his or her own way and sphere of interest, is, at the same time, responsible for developing the field of knowledge as a whole; it has involved, too, the more difficult exercise of genuinely sharing knowledge, of exposing ideas at a critical, primary stage of their formulation, and the even more arduous task of trying to research and to write as a collective group.

A particular form of organization of the Centre's intellectual practices has been one of the consequences. For some time there were no distinct research groupings. Individual students were linked with the field through their individual research topics: the enterprise was framed, first, by a 'general theory' seminar and, later, by a regular series of 'work-in-progress' sessions. At a certain point the 'general theory' seminar became too large and unwieldly for our purposes. The size of the seminar became inhibiting for new members, and it depended too much on prior knowledge, privileged access to the discourse and a false search for abstraction at a rarified level. A major innovation was introduced at this point, which largely set the framework of Centre practice up to the present. Work was divided between different research groups, each organized around a particular theme or field. These groupings first arose as a drawing together, in each area, of individual thesis topics. They were designed to constitute a common framework of reading, discussion and research in which individual and group concerns could be more properly integrated. But this 'collectivization' made possible a more sustained engagement with existing fields and regions of research and their characteristic problematics. This necessary specialization, in 'regional' studies, was combined with an annual review, in which each research group presented to the Centre as a whole some aspect of its work during the year. On the occasion of these annual presentations - a regular feature now of the Centre's year - the cross-cutting themes in common between groups could be identified, the differences of the appropriation of common approaches to each distinct field of inquiry marked and debated. This division into specialized and general work led to an immense leap in intellectual productivity. It made it possible, for example, to develop particular issues of our journal, and more recently of our book series, around particular themes, based on, even if not exclusive to, the specialized work of the different research groups. From these groups developed projects on which individual group members worked, which then retrospectively rephrased their particular research and thesis topics, giving them a more integral relation to the collective interests of their grouping, as well as a degree of collective support. The inauguration of our taught MA was the first attempt to give an abbreviated introduction to, and account of, Cultural Studies as a field, in a relatively integrated way: but MA students are also attached to research groups for their specialist studies, thereby attempting to integrate the MA level of work with the organic process of building up Cultural Studies as a whole in the Centre, whatever the mode or level of attachment of each individual student. In this sense, despite the greater degrees of specialization entailed, concrete attempts have been made in the ways we organize ourselves and our work to ensure that, through our individual and collective practices, a more general practice - developing Cultural Studies as a field - is also thereby sustained.

The difficulties and constraints on such experiments in practice are numerous. Still, research students get what financial support they do, are admitted to study and must deliver the goods to be judged on a wholly individual basis. Hierarchies of knowledge, differences in age, experience and intellectual formation, genuine differences in theoretical orientation or emphasis have been determinate conditions working against its realization.[106] The intellectual division of labour, in which the sexual division is so profoundly inscribed, does not disappear at the whisk of a collective wand. Nevertheless, we would claim, against other models, to have made some advances. The weaknesses of the experiment, but also its gains, are plain for all to see, especially where we are most free to put these ideas into practice: in published work in the journal, working papers, books and articles. The strengths must speak for themselves. The weaknesses must not be glossed over. There is a kind of intensity of concentration, a sureness of grasp, a style of individual cognitive organization which collective projects find it difficult to reproduce. Collective writing rarely has the force and concision of a comparable individual piece of work: it tends to be more loosely organized and to lack a certain intellectual density. We claim, however, at least to know something of, and to have explored some of the problems consequent on, trying to develop new forms of collective intellectual practice. We know something of what this means as a practical condition of intellectual work. In this sense, we feel we have begun to anticipate some of the difficulties not of the past but of the future. No attempt should or could be made here to underestimate the tensions and contradictions produced by this mode of work. They are objective - in our situation - as well as subjective, and they are not to be resolved without costs. But they are at least 'of our time': they belong to the present; they are not archaic, or merely inhabited and inherited out of academic habit.

Of course, the project has offered no guarantees of success. We too operate within the existing division of intellectual labour, which has a merciless logic and has imposed itself on the Centre as much as elsewhere. In the face of that logic the so-called 'unity' of theory and practice appears a somewhat empty slogan.[107] It is really exceedingly difficult both to do serious intellectual work in an advanced, interdisciplinary area and to write and produce in an immediately accessible way. This is not an excuse for the retreat into private languages. The Centre has been criticized more than once for the difficulty and obscurity of its language - and the criticism is a valid one (even if it is produced with what sometimes appears to be a sort of triumphal glee). It arises from a too unreflexive practice. But it is also inscribed in the terrain and the institutions where we work. It arises, in part, from trying to do good and serious work in a field as yet hardly mapped out. It arises, in part, from the necessity to bend language and inflect its meanings and concepts to purposes which cannot be simply culled from the storehouse of common-sense knowledge. It arises, most acutely, from the fragmentation of knowledge, its ruthless division into watertight compartments; from the *doxa* and orthodoxy of those divisions and the ways in which they are politically defended, policed and regulated; and from the wider division of intellectual labour which they reproduce.

In these circumstances we have attempted to *work towards* a greater unity, without expecting to conjure it out of thin air or the 'will to knowledge'. Our aim, in this respect, could be defined as the struggle to form a more 'organic' kind of intellectual. Gramsci spoke of the distinction between those 'traditional' intellectuals who set themselves the task of developing and sophisticating the existing paradigms of knowledge and those who, in their critical role, aim to become more 'organic' to new and emergent tendencies in society, who seek to become more integral with those forces, linked to them, capable of reflecting what Gramsci called the 'intellectual function' in its wider, non-specialist and non-elitist sense. He also designated two tasks for those aiming to become 'organic' intellectuals: to challenge modern ideologies 'in their most refined form', and to enter into the task of popular education. Two tasks, not one, both difficult to realize, especially at the same moment. 'Given all this,' he remarked, 'the question of language in general and of languages in the technical sense must be put in the forefront of our inquiry.'

The Centre has been faced with this hard truth since its inception. We have tried, within the available limits and resources, to work both sides of this difficult road - to address ourselves to central and relevant problems and issues, even if their original formulation required a specialist language not instantly available; and also, where and when we could, to undertake the by no means easy task of translating ourselves into more widely available vocabularies. Those who have attempted this combination will know that the latter is no more technical task. It has to do not with summoning up a 'common experience', which in fact does not exist, but with attempting actively to construct, to forge, a unity of knowledge and practice. This is what Gramsci would have called an essentially 'organizational' task and function: the organizational and connective function of the 'organic' intellectual. Caught between the harsh alternatives just outlined, the Centre has struggled *not* to affirm (against the clear evidence) that it already is, but constantly to *become more organic*. That requires not the pretence that no social division of knowledge exists, but a more organized and effective kind of intervention in that division. There is no social organization without the intellectual function, in its widest sense, Gramsci argued: no organic intellectual formation 'without the theoretical aspect of the theory-practice nexus being distinguished concretely by the existence of a group of people – "specialized" in conceptual and philosophical elaboration of ideas'. But also there is none without 'an analogous movement on the part of the mass', who 'raise themselves to higher levels of culture and . . . extend their circle of influence towards the stratum of specialized intellectuals, producing . . . groups of more or less importance'. To produce work which is progressively more 'organic' in this reciprocal sense has been, throughout, the Centre's task and goal. But as Gramsci also noted, 'the process of creating intellectuals is long, difficult, full of contradictions, advances, retreats, dispersals and regroupings, in which the loyalty of the masses is often sorely tried'.[108]

2 Barrington Moore, Perry Anderson and English social development*

Richard Johnson

It is useful to start by sketching what might be the specifically *historical* concerns of a Centre of Contemporary Cultural Studies. One central task is to reconstruct, in concepts and in imaginative understanding, the succession of cultural formations within the capitalist epoch. We might concede to our title word 'contemporary' that our interests should not normally stretch much beyond the 1880s. It is certainly in that decade that many 'modern' developments begin. And we will also tend to continue to focus on Britain, perhaps within a widening comparative span. As a main object of study we might take the systems of culturally mediated social relations between classes and their internal cultural resources and repertoires. This must include cultural differences *within* classes, for, whether within a dominant or a subordinate class, these often supply the means of control. It must include too a continued attention to the subject's experience and to the records of this in literature or autobiographical fragment. Attention to the subjective moment is not a mere romanticism. It is only through the conscious, social and more or less creative activity of individual men, women and children that the systems of class-cultural relations are reproduced. It is they who within given conditions reinforce in their lives the cultural patterns or make their breaks with them. The histories of intention and consciousness (and also of emotional economy and the only-partially-conscious) are necessary components in any explanatory history at all.

It is especially important to chart cultural *movement.* We might think of this as a process of transition from one more or less stable set of relations to another. The record shows a history of such transitions: from periods of manifest challenge to periods of relative 'order', from dissent to consent, from manifest contradiction to apparent resolution. These phases, movements of a mid-term duration, are a principal, immediate and urgent object of study. They are the subject of a history of hegemony. But they rest, in the last resort, on shifts of a more subterranean nature and of a longer duration that roll right through the epoch as a whole. We have to understand this underlying movement too.

The second aim is to examine further what Edward Thompson has called the

*This article first appeared in *Culture and Domination, WPCS* 9 (1976). It is a twice-revised version of two papers given to the Theory Seminar at the Centre in November 1974. Earlier versions were also given to the Social History Seminar at Birmingham. Acknowledgements to everybody in a mind-stretching first year at the Centre.

'peculiarities of the English'. What is distinctive about British social development in comparison with other countries that have taken the capitalist route? Like the knowledge of conjunctures, this is necessary knowledge, '*really* useful knowledge', as nineteenth-century radicals would have called it. It is needed to inform a political practice that is not chauvinistically blind to 'foreign' lessons and sympathies, nor yet incapable of seeing, through a concern with 'absences', the most evident features of an immediate world. Of particular importance in this understanding of place are the most persistent long-term features, the most 'structural' and abiding peculiarities, the contours that need to be observed.

Finally, we need to engage with the ways of studying history that are already in the field and with which we have, of necessity, been brought up. *This* is important because the kind of history we should practise here remains quite unformed. It can only develop through a series of critiques of existing modes. We have not, in this Centre, defined our 'cultural history', and we are not even sure if that is the right phrase. All we have are some rules of practice and slogans ('Struggle against idealism and other common reductions!' 'Keep it complex/concrete!' 'Preserve the authenticity of subjective experience!') and some powerful but incomplete or incompletely understood models (Marx as historian; historians of the Marxist revival in France and Britain; the *Annales* school as the historical variant of the French structuralist family; Gramsci for his suggestive and profoundly historical 'notes'). This is not much more than a beginning.

A project like the one outlined above sounds grandiose, especially in England, where historical ambitions are meagre. It has to be collective and long-term. This paper is meant to clear a tiny bit of ground for one part of the enterprise – sketching the peculiarities of the English – by considering those who have been there before.

In November 1844 Engels finished his *Condition of the Working Class in England.* Written from 'personal observation and authentic sources', it marked an important point in the development of Marxism, serving to repair the young Hegelians' ignorance of 'the real condition of life of the proletariat', helping to ground their communism not, as hitherto, in the critique of philosophy and political economy, but in the experience of the first working class.[1] Engels now planned a bigger project: 'As soon as I am through with that [he wrote to Marx] I shall tackle the history of the social development of the English, which will cost me much less effort, because I have the material for it all ready and arranged in my head, and because the whole business is perfectly clear to me.'[2] This plan was never carried out and if one traces Marx and Engels's encounter with the English it seems that the initial clarity was clouded. After 1848 the English experiences seemed more and more paradoxical: the oldest capitalist country with the most 'developed' working class seemed immune to revolution and 'the general social evolutions of European society'.[3] So they returned again and again to the English problem, seeking the levers of change.[4] In 1892 Engels, who lived to see new unionism (which excited him) and the Socialist revival (which often irritated him enormously), recorded a final English verdict. Its mixture of fine leading insights and a certain puzzlement is typical. Significantly, it was couched as an analysis of ideology and of a political culture.

> By its eternal compromises gradual, peaceful political development such as exists in England brings about a contradictory state of affairs. Because of the superior advantages it affords, this state can within certain limits be tolerated in practice, but its logical incongruities are a sore trial to the reasoning mind. Hence the need felt by all 'state-sustaining' parties for theoretical camouflage, even justification, which, naturally, are feasible only by means of sophisms, distortions and, finally, underhand tricks. Thus a literature is being reared in the sphere of politics which repeats all the wretched hypocrisy and mendacity of theological apologetics and transplants the theological intellectual vices to secular soil.[5]

Puzzled or not, then, Engels's original project – 'the social development of the English' – is *our* project – and the original markers, especially Marx's journalistic pieces, remain invaluable.

It ought to be a matter of some shame that after all this while English social history, even in its Marxist variants, has not done what Engels promised. The best work has been bounded by period, while the study of peculiarities requires the long view. Historians like Hilton, Hill, Hobsbawm and Edward Thompson have contributed massively within their own ranges, yet none of them has put his own and the others' work together in the kind of synthesis we need. Edward Thompson was drawn into a wider speculative sweep only by Anderson's 'provocation'. So it is that we have to turn outside 'history' for more recent starting-points: to a long political essay by an editor of *New Left Review* and to the formidable comparative social history of a 'loner' among American sociologists. In what follows I will discuss Barrington Moore's *Social Origins of Dictatorship and Democracy* first, then Perry Anderson's 'Origins of the present crisis'. But I will also draw on Marx's and Engels's original formulations, on Perry Anderson's most recent book and on the debate provoked by the Anderson/Nairn theses.[6]

Moore's book hinges on three related concerns. The most general of these is 'modernization'. As several reviewers noted, Moore has a tendency to use terms like this ubiquitously, without ever defining them. This derives in part from his method, for he is concerned to build his concepts empirically, from the comparison of instances. He is impatient with 'tiresome word games as a substitute for the effort to see what really happened'.[7] This is a fine corrective to all those abstract formulations of the principal features of 'traditional' and 'modern' societies in which there often lurk Western, 'democratic' or capitalist models of excellence. But the trouble with Moore's cavalier treatment of concepts is that he tends to employ them without an adequate critical exposition. We shall see some of the consequences of this later.

It is clear, however, that Moore's 'modernization' means more than industrialization, or 'the transformation from agrarian societies to modern industrial ones'. It also involves the emergence of the nation state, 'democratic' or 'totalitarian'. It necessarily brings fundamental changes in the position and the relations of traditional social classes. Moore's inclusion of China shows he has more in mind than industry. For here is a society still hugely agrarian entering the modern world presumably by virtue of the transformation of its rural structure and the creation of a new form of state.

If modern societies are, in some ways, similar, modernizing routes have differed greatly. It is the differences that interest Moore most. He is concerned to identify the particular constellations of modernizing forces in each of the (large) societies, European and Asian, that he chooses to study.[8] From particular histories he constructs three styles, or routes. France, England and America share one common route: 'bourgeois revolution', capitalism, democratic political regimes. Japan, Germany (sketchily portrayed) and Italy (very shadowy indeed) form a second type. Here 'modernization' occurs through a 'revolution from above', with no decisive break from the past generated by popular forces. Instead, 'modernization' is enforced by long periods of conservative rule, allied to capitalist business and culminating in Fascism. Russia and China, of course, represent the non-capitalist adaptation, in which the main motor of a communist transformation are late peasant rebellions.

The three routes are *alternatives* only in a limited sense. Moore is concerned to show why each country took the route it did and not some other. He signals points along the way where different paths seemed possible. He notes the reactionary potential of Britain in the 1790s and the failed peasant rebellions of French and German history. Yet once these moments pass, the outcome seems heavily determined. The routes are also *phases.* They are grouped in time, and missed opportunities are not recoverable. The route via bourgeois democracy is essentially a first-phase modernization, a modernization of the pioneers, unrepeatable elsewhere. If modernization is delayed, it may occur through conservative rule in the late nineteenth century. Or it may occur through Communism – a peculiarly late, telescoped form: perhaps the most likely twentieth-century route?

Since Moore is only concerned with the key moments in modernization, his individual histories have different temporal spans. One consequence of this is that we learn little of the contemporary peculiarities of England, France, Germany, the USA and Japan. A more serious criticism, addressed to the avowed purpose, is that Moore's method – a set of domestic histories over different periods of time – allows no space for reciprocal reactions between states. How far, for example, did the perpetual European rivalries affect domestic histories? How does the larger imperial conflict bear on Moore's themes? He argues that late modernizers may in some sense learn from earlier cases, but this is a very weak, idealist version of Marx's 'world-historical' dimension.

Moore's third concern is with the role of agrarian social classes in modernization. His central thesis is that lord and peasant have played a major part in determining routes into the modern world. Forms of agriculture and landed social relations have been 'decisive factors in determining the political outcome'.[9] Throughout the book, often with great ingenuity, this thesis is pushed as far as it will go. It is represented as a major revision of Marxist orthodoxy which holds, according to

Moore, that it is the new insurgent classes that have shaped the modern world.[10] The most forceful formulation of this is in connection with the radicalism of peasants and small producers which is discussed in that odd, residual chapter, 'Reactionary and revolutionary imagery', which stands in for a more organic treatment of culture and ideology. Moore notes that 'Marxist thinkers' have often dismissed peasant radicalism, and that anti-Marxists have often scoffed at this. He insists that peasants and artisans have been the 'chief social basis of radicalism'. He concludes that 'the wellsprings of human freedom lie not only where Marx saw them, in the aspirations of classes about to take power, but perhaps even more in the dying wail of a class over whom the wave of progress is about to roll'.[11]

This passage illustrates Moore's characteristic stance: his scholarly, Marcusean pessimism, his dissociation from both 'Marxist thinkers' and their obviously ideological critics, his half-break with American political science.[12] It illustrates, too, the problem with the book: the necessary one-sidedness of the thesis. For, of course, in the transition to industrial capitalism emergent and residual social classes coexist. History will not be wholly determined by either. So the danger with Moore's thesis is that his preferred emphasis (on lord and peasant) will seriously truncate his social histories, systematically demoting working class and bourgeoisie. We will return to this problem later, but it is clear that Moore is aware of the problem and has devised a solution, at least for the bourgeoisie. This solution is the notion of the modernizing alliance.

We may now look, in broad outline, at Moore's three routes. One way of simplifying his very complex argument is to see him as using four sets of determinations. These are:

1 the forms of agriculture
2 the inherited forms of the state
3 the nature of modernizing coalitions
4 the absence or presence of revolutionary violence.

By far the most important determinations are the agrarian modes of production and their attendant social relations. There are two crucial dimensions: the strength or weakness of the tendency towards commercialization and the form in which it occurs. A strong and early commercial impulse has distinguished the capitalist from the communist routes. This is so, Moore argues, because communist revolution has depended less on an industrial proletariat than on exploited peasant communities which have retained their internal cohesion, yet face the strains of late modernization. And the peasantry's communal institutions survive best when the solvent of commercial agriculture is weak or absent – hence the Russian and Chinese patterns. But the *form* of commercialization is as important as the degree of penetration. Form distinguishes democratic and reactionary routes within the capitalist family. The most favourable form for capitalist democracy involves the elimination of peasantry by agrarian capitalist enterprise (England); the least favourable is some 'labour-repressive' mode by which peasant production is retained, the work-force held on the land and the surplus extracted by highly coercive political means (for example, Eastern Europe). 'Labour-repressive' modes have several effects inimical to democracy. They preserve a peasantry which, this time with little political potential of its own, may form a reservoir of popular anti-capitalism of a twentieth-century Fascist type. They require a repressive state apparatus and an authoritarian and militaristic political culture incompatible with bourgeois freedoms. They permit a non-capitalist landed class to persist with a hold on state power and a dominance in the landed/bourgeois alliance. They make this class dependent on state power, bolstering a backward agrarian base. Presiding over a booming capitalist agriculture with no 'peasant problem', nineteenth-century English 'aristocracy' could afford a Whiggish strategy; German *junkers* could not. One wonders whether the distinction between 'labour-repressive' and other agrarian modes can really be sustained, but these parts of the book are, to the non-expert in peasantry, among the most interesting and convincing.

Moore's second determination is the state, which is viewed not so much as an independent factor, more as the product of social friction. Moore notes that all his societies (except America) developed centralized governments in the sixteenth or seventeenth centuries.[13] In democratic adaptations, however, central government was tamed by alliances independent of royal absolutism or bureaucracy. Ideally, as once more in the English paradigm, this should happen only *after* monarchy has tamed the feudal lord and unified the nation. Unless both processes occur a totalitarian outcome is likely. Moore pursues here a familiar pluralist argument – democracy derives from a 'balance' of social forces. But his version is characteristically subtle: balance must change in appropriate directions over time (to monarchy and away again); the anti-absolutist forces must be properly constituted (with capitalist elements predominant) and past struggles may be exceedingly violent (the Puritan and French Revolutions).

The third distinguishing feature of the three routes is the strength of what Moore usually calls, rather coyly, 'town dwellers'. He identifies the class fractions of the bourgeoisie as the main carriers of democracy and of liberal political notions. So modernizing alliances dominated by the bourgeoisie favour democratic solutions; reaction rests on the predominance of a non-capitalist landed class. Moore registers 'strong agreement with the Marxist thesis that a vigorous and independent class of town dwellers has been an indispensable element in the growth of parliamentary democracy. No bourgeois, no democracy'.[14] Thus, at the risk of punching a hole in his thesis, he accommodates the dominant class of modern times within his histories. The bourgeoisie becomes, indeed, 'the principal actor'. If one adds (as Moore also acknowledges) that the impulse to commercialize agriculture, the first move in the chain of causation, also owes much to bourgeois trade, transport and urban markets, the way is open to a major simplification of his case. A simpler equation now reads: early capitalism equals democracy. But if this blunts, rather, Moore's revisionism, it does not undermine the value of his thesis in constructing a more complete model.

Finally, in a running scrap with Conservative apologetics, Moore insists that revolutionary violence is creative. Popular violence checks royal absolutism in England and France; the American Civil War – 'a bloody gash across the whole record'[15] – guarantees, by destroying the plantation system, a democratic form of American capitalism. Violence is especially important in France, finely poised in the eighteenth century at the entry-point to different routes. The *ancien régime* showed features which elsewhere proved antithetical to democracy: a weak industrial bourgeoisie; a middle and upper class parasitic upon the court; a very strong form of royal absolutism; a large peasant class only partially emancipated from feudal entanglements in systems of agriculture lying between English agrarian capitalism and the estates of Eastern Europe. Hence the necessity (for democracy) of a violent revolution, 'bourgeois' in that it removed inhibitions to capitalism and democracy, but pushed on in its destructive work by the radicalism of peasants and *sans culottes*. Hence, too, once bourgeois and wealthier peasant reaction had checked the revolutionary impulse, the extreme vulnerability of French democratic institutions.[16]

It seems valid to test Moore's thesis by examining one route in more detail, so long as the inquiry turns on 'grand facts' and not on petty corrections. Viewed like this, broadly, Moore's English route is the nearest thing to a success story in a pessimistic book. The success is twofold: for capitalism and for 'freedom'. England is the paradigmatic case of capitalist democracy. Let us look at each aspect of 'success' in turn.

Moore shows that by the early nineteenth century all the major historical inhibitions to capitalism and the rule of capitalist classes had been swept away. Feudalism and feudal nobility were long dead, checked by monarchy, eroded by commercialization, replaced by 'peasant' or small producer or, later, by the classic English forms of agrarian capitalism – landlord, tenant, labourer. By the eighteenth century the English gentry were a thoroughly capitalist class. In the next one hundred years or so they completed the transformation of countryside by destroying, through the legal violence of enclosure, what was left of peasant agriculture. They thus removed from the historical agenda the problems of peasant rebellion or peasant inertia. Finally, the characteristic English alliance of landed/mercantile capital developed in opposition to the Crown, weakening it and, with it, the whole apparatus of the state. By 1800 neither monarchy (nor Church) could check economic progress and Parliament was in the hands of the class that was economically dominant.

There is plenty to criticize in the detail here. A few points of intermediate generality relevant to Moore's method must suffice. His discussion of the early role of monarchy and the weakness of English absolutism is much inferior to Perry Anderson's recent version, typically in the neglect of international determinations.[17] His interpretation of the Puritan Revolution – a revolution *for* capitalism and parliamentary rule – is heavily based on Tawney's researches, yet still convinces. It is arguable that he overstates the significance of the Revolution (as a violent passage) to strengthen his overall thesis. He certainly is incurious about religious issues, and this matches his tendency to neglect *the cultural and ideological forms* of political struggles. Later, concerned to show that peace was built on violence in the shape of enclosure, he post-dates the persistence of social groups that can be usefully described as peasantry. The people who undoubtedly *were* proletarianized by enclosure were less 'peasants', more independent small agrarian producers (peasants without a lord; little yeomen?) or semi-proletarians, living mainly on wages but with some marginal access to land. The difficulty of finding a language for these and similarly placed industrial groups is testimony to the continued crudity of our concepts (between 'peasant' and 'working class') and to the actual complexity of formations (between feudalism and industrial capitalism).

A more serious criticism is Moore's loose and uncertain use of the key concept - capitalism. Despite his close attention to agrarian formations throughout the book, the distinction between a merely commercial and actually capitalist agriculture remains unclear. In the English chapter at least Moore's implicit definitions of capitalism appear Weberian or Tawneyesque rather than Marxist. It is perhaps a case in which the quite studied avoidance of a Marxist language actually leads to a loss of clarity and explanatory force. Thus capitalism appears in Moore's account less a distinctive mode of production than a rather random scatter of elements of organization or attitude. He writes about the 'capitalist principle', a 'commercial and even a capitalist outlook', an attitude to land as 'modern capitalist private property', a belief in 'self-interest and economic freedom as the natural basis of human society', the adoption of revolutionary agrarian techniques and so on.[18] He misses the historical centre of the system. Though he illustrates the social logic of capitalism in revolutionizing relations on the land from the sixteenth century onwards, he does not fully express the fact that *capitalist requires proletarian* and that *capitalism creates the political problem of the proletarian presence and the means of class control.* Although there were groups of proletarian and semi-proletarian workers long before the nineteenth century (and also sets of characteristic class relations) the one-sided definition of capitalism is most seriously defective when applied to the nineteenth century.[19] We shall return to this in discussing 'freedom'.

Moore's basic point, however, is surely correct: all the problems characteristic of the transition to industrial capitalism in France and Germany were, in England, solved very early and very completely. The early, powerful, successful and pervasive bourgeois thrust in land, commerce, industry, politics (and even ideology) is the key to English social development.

It is worth stressing that Moore's view is very close to what might be called the 'classic' Marxist version. It is the main line which informs Edward Thompson's critique of Perry Anderson. He stresses the deeply bourgeois character of the English gentry, even to their town-dwelling; the centuries-old capitalist presence and 'the great arch of bourgeois culture'.[20] Perhaps the most striking formulations are Poulantzas's, for he is, in some respects, inclined to Anderson's positions. Although he uses the term 'feudal' in describing some aspects of English society since the seventeenth century, he stresses the success of the bourgeois revolution in England, the thoroughness of the whole transition to capitalism: 'The British revolution was particularly successful in that it allows the open domination of the CMP [capitalist mode of production] over the other modes of production in the social formation. This open domination brings it about that the matrix of this mode of production decisively permeates this formation.' He compares this with the French situation, where the domination of the capitalist mode of production was less complete. The consequences were the persistence of peasant agriculture and small-scale industry, the need politically to accommodate peasantry and *petit bourgeoisie* and hence the marked instability of bourgeois rule.[21]

The argument here is very similar indeed to Moore's, if much more schematic. Behind both (openly in Poulantzas, more covertly in Moore) stand Marx's original formulations. For it is easy to trace these arguments to his journalistic work on mid nineteenth century England and his analyses in *Class Struggles in France* and the *Eighteenth Brumaire.* He pointed the difference most succinctly: 'while the old bourgeoisie fights the French Revolution, the new one conquers the world market'.[22]

Moore's treatment of 'freedom' is much less convincing. 'Why,' he asks, 'did the process of industrialization in England culminate in the establishment of a relatively free society?'[23] His answer is phrased both in terms of the legacy from a violent past and in terms of specifically nineteenth-century developments. The legacy included strong parliamentary institutions adapted to the peaceful solution of social conflict, a relatively weak repressive state apparatus, an adaptive, landed upper class that did not need to resist the 'advance of industry' and, of course, no 'peasant problem'. Yet nineteenth-century progress in liberalism was by no means inevitable. From 1790 to about 1822 English society passed through a 'reactionary phase'. This did not amount to Halevy's 'reign of terror' but marked a break with liberalism.[24] Why was the phase so short-lived? In part the legacy, including cutting off the head of a tyrannous king, did not supply the materials. But since repression can be improvised (and was), this explanation is inadequate. The key, according to Moore, was that landed upper-class and industrial bourgeoisie had no permanent, structural need for repression. The former did not need to hold down a rebellious peasantry, for it had already eliminated it; industrial capital required little help from the state to create the preconditions for industrialization and to discipline a workforce. It completed these tasks itself. So instead the landed upper class continued to hold formal political power and the ruling-class fractions entered into a complex relationship, part rivalry for 'mass support', part aristocratic concession, part social and cultural osmosis. Since English agriculture remained buoyant up to the 1870s, aristocracy was enabled to make a long strategic retreat into the *alter ego* of industry and trade. At no point, after the 1790s, did it attempt a last-ditch stand or turn its bourgeois alliance into a reactionary path. The German type of coalition was avoided. On the whole, the aristocratic contribution in England to a tolerant politics and an amateur culture was exemplary.[25]

It is as well to note the positive aspects of this account before turning to criticism. Moore's portrayal of internal ruling-class relations is subtle. It is, as we shall see, more accurate than Anderson's. And again, nuances apart, it is similar to the 'classic' Marxist version. Like Edward Thompson and Poulantzas, Moore holds to something like Marx's formulation of the landed-industrial relationship. According to Marx, the aristocratic cliques that held formal political position held it on condition that they exercised power in the interests of industrial capital. The chief, the most willing vehicle was Whiggery – hence Marx's vivid satire on Lord John Russell. At face value this is a character assassination of the quintessential Whig politician; at a deeper level it is a personification of aristocratic powerlessness in an industrial world.[26] Marx sought to show precisely how the camouflage of surrogate rule *by* aristocracy *for* industrial bourgeoisie worked in terms of the mechanisms of political party, the Whiggish alliance and 'pressure from without'.[27] Similarly, Edward Thompson has argued that after 1832 had eroded the 'secondary complex of predatory interests' that was the nearest thing to 'aristocracy' in England there were two main developments: the steady pursuit of bourgeois policies by landed politicians and the steady erosion of landed power, even in its county bastions. A more aggressive policy by industrial bourgeoisie was simply unnecessary.[28] Moore's account lacks the powerful sophistication of the notion of 'old corruption', is more indulgent to Whig 'statesmen' and allows them a little more autonomous influence, but his basic formulation is not dissimilar. Aristocratic politicians worked the levers of power but learned the limitations of their own. It is misleading, he notes, to mark only the strength of their formal position in the political apparatus.[29]

But in other respects Moore's account is seriously flawed. His nineteenth-century section is much less successful than the earlier passages. In part this relates to the whole thesis about traditional social classes. At the point when industrial bourgeoisie *and* working class become major actors, determinations from a landed past are made to carry too great a burden of explanation. As I shall suggest later, the active presence of a working class-in-the-making is actually needed to explain fully the patterns which Moore portrays. Its virtual absence here and the absence of precursors earlier in the story might partly be explained by his failure fully to absorb the argument of *The Making of the English Working Class,*[30] but it is also related to his attenuated notion of capitalism and the neglect of the problem of class control. One consequence is that he accepts much too readily the rather assured portrayal, out of ruling-class sources, of ruling-class dilemmas conveyed in the quite Whiggish English historians whose work he uses, notably Kitson Clark, Woodward, Mather, Namier and F. M. L. Thompson. This portrayal is deeply embedded in the historical and political cultures and is not easily penetrated – especially, perhaps, by an American Anglophile. So having stressed past violence, having broken with Whiggish assumptions to that extent, he accepts, with only a hint of parody, the usual combinations of 'moderate and intelligent statesmen', 'legislation to improve the condition of the poor', the Whig devotion to the 'ideal of liberty' and even, if he does not indeed *intend* a parody, the 'age of peaceful transformation when parliamentary democracy established *itself* (*sic*!) and broadened down from precedent to precedent'. These formulations are not helped by the failure to analyse 'parliamentary democracy', both as a concept in liberal political science and as a concrete form of the state. One realizes with a sense of shock that Moore's question about England

(and, indeed, one part of his whole problematic) is phrased within a Whiggish tradition. His question is about England's relative 'freedom'. A more penetrating question, which nonetheless accepts his as a premise, might run as follows: 'Since in England both the coercive and bureaucratic apparatuses of state power were (for good historical reasons) rather weak, how was a particularly strong popular challenge contained?'

The problem is not posed because the class to which it refers is given, in the theory and in the historiography, no active role. The absence starts with the historical precursors of the working class. Moore implies a passivity in the English populace both before and during the Industrial Revolution. The vigorous resistances of Edward Thompson's artisans, weavers, labourers and *petit bourgeois* radicals are largely overlooked, much more so than across the Channel, where their incursions seem more spectacular. Moore's 'peasants' are purely victims. And this is a very important omission indeed. For it means that he greatly underestimates the difficulty of managing a popular resistance and transforming the inherited culture of proletarianized groups. This in turn bears upon early nineteenth-century uses of the state and thence on the English potential for a reactionary or a bureaucratic adaptation. Moore underestimates this possibility and he therefore finds it too easy to explain why it did not occur. So the early working class is easily disciplined 'with a minimum of help from the state'. Chartism makes a rather routine appearance, presenting an alien threat of violence, but is treated with lenience. One wonders what happened in all this to 'rural police', new Poor Law, Education Department, spy system and army of the north.

Against the familiar stereotypes one should insist that the new working-class presence was *determining*. It not only made itself but contributed to the making of nineteenth-century society and, not least, to 'bourgeois' (or aristocratic) freedoms. It is arguable that it was not so much middle-class agitation or the amateur culture of aristocracy that made England 'relatively free' but a plebeian agitation and culture, or, more accurately still, the friction of all three. If space allowed, this could be demonstrated in several critical areas: in the actual achievement of parliamentary *democracy* (as opposed to a wholly propertied parliamentary system); in the liberty of the press and of public meeting, both freedoms being won or maintained by *popular exercise*; and, not least, in the stemming of a very real impulse to a bureaucratic state, signalled in the popular defeat of the full Chadwickian programme of Poor Law reform.[31] Certainly, in the early nineteenth century, working-class movements seem to have been the main bearers of the notions of natural and civic rights.

This does not, of course, solve the problem, unfairly fathered on Moore, of how the popular challenge was contained. We shall return to it, in a quite different guise, later. In the meantime it is worth noting that a part of the answer is contained, as so often in this extremely rich book, in another part of the story. For in a later chapter Moore presents us with a critique of both conservative historiography and the idealist conception of culture. It is a pity these dimensions did not inform his English history – particularly in this passage:

The assumption of inertia, that cultural and social continuity do not require explanation, obliterates the fact that both have to be recreated anew in each generation, often with great pain and suffering. To maintain and transmit a value system human beings are punched, bullied, sent to jail, thrown in concentration camps, cajoled, bribed, made into heroes, encouraged to read newspapers, stood up against a wall and shot and sometimes even taught sociology. To speak of cultural inertia is to overlook the concrete interests and privileges that are served by indoctrination, education and the entire complicated process of transmitting culture from one generation to the next.[32]

It is quite true that in nineteenth-century England there was more bribing, cajoling, making of heroes, supplying newspapers and teaching in schools than the more brutally repressive alternatives. Political economy was taught, not sociology. Also ideology and a cultural control had deeper roots and a more organic origin than Moore's mere accumulation of apparatuses might suggest. Yet, to say it again, it is just this dimension that ought to have informed Moore's English story – and did not.

As we have seen, the key note of the 'classic' Marxist version of English social development is success – success of a peculiarly early and complete capitalist transformation and the masked political success of the English bourgeoisie under nineteenth-century conditions. The Nairn and Anderson version centres, by contrast, on failures, failures of the modern social classes. The first and most determining feature is a characteristic and abiding relationship between the classes within the ruling bloc: a failed or flawed bourgeoisie and a hegemonic 'aristocracy'.[33] There are five main stages in this argument. First, Anderson agrees that the Puritan Revolution was a succcessful revolution *for* capitalism (the view is similar to Moore's) but argues that the commercial bourgeoisie remained a subaltern class and that the Revolution left no bourgeois ideological legacy. In a sense it failed because impure and too early. Second, the Industrial Revolution created both an English proletariat and the industrial fraction of the bourgeoisie. Both had heroic moments. The industrial bourgeoisie forced the reform of Parliament and the repeal of the Corn Laws but its courage (in some mysterious way) waned, and it delegated its power to 'aristocracy'. Thus far one can speak of two classes – 'aristocracy' and bourgeoisie; after about 1850, in a third stage, they fuse, become a 'detotalized totality'. Yet still within this hegemonic bloc, through its hold on formal politics and through its socializing institutions, 'aristocracy' remains the dominant fraction. Fourth, just when it is losing its base in the agricultural depression, it receives a further lease of life through imperialism. This set the culture of the dominant class in a 'normatively agrarian mould', which it has not lost since. Finally, Britain escaped most of the creative domestic effects of two world wars. Even now (1964) the 'aristocratic' segment of the dominant class remains ascendant, and it is *its* culture which is monolithicly hegemonic.

The second British failure was the failure of Labour or Labourism. Nairn's starting-point was a paradox: the British Labour Party was 'one of the greatest political forces of the capitalist world', with the almost undivided loyalty of the working class in 'an overwhelmingly proletarian nation'. Why, then, had it repeatedly failed, even in 1945, to grasp 'the revolutionary opportunity'?[34]

Nairn and Anderson answer this question on two levels: a general thesis about the historical development of the English working class and a more detailed discussion of the internal dimensions of Labourism and the more persistent and structural problems of the British Left. The general theory, since it is an integral part of their view of English social development as a whole, is the part which concerns us here, but it should be stressed that there are elements of great independent value in their whole discussion of the Labour Party.

For the New Left Reviewers, the British working class, that exasperating entity, has had one abiding characteristic. After the defeat of Chartism it became, and has ever since remained, obstinately 'corporate'. They give a particular meaning to this word, nearer to Gramsci's usage than to that of Raymond Williams.[35] A corporate culture is self-identifying, inward-looking, purely indigenous, the opposite to hegemonic. 'A corporate class is one which *pursues its own ends within a social totality whose global determination lies outside it'.*[36] It is acknowledged, following Williams and Hoggart, that English working-class culture has been peculiarly dense and specific in its hinterlands. Often penetrated by bourgeois ideas, it has never been entirely assimilated. But nor has it acquired a world view complete or oppositional enough to combat hegemony over the whole range of society. Its characteristic state has remained that of social *apartheid*. Thrust into isolated subordination in the early nineteenth century, it has remained there ever since.

This subordination is mainly a reflex of the failure of the bourgeoisie. As Anderson puts it: 'It is a general historical rule that a rising social class acquires a significant part of its ideological equipment from the armoury of the ruling class itself.'[37] So, since English bourgeoisie had 'no impulse of liberation, no revolutionary values, no universal language', 'a supine bourgeoisie provided a subordinate proletariat'.[38] The only real bourgeois legacy was Fabianism, the pedigree of which is accurately traced to Utilitarianism, the nearest but partial attempt at a hegemonic bourgeois ideology. In the absence of Marxism in England, or an intellectual socialism worth the name, the working class was infected by the Fabian taint or groped empirically towards pragmatic solutions. The typical form of this blind activity has always been trade unionism, to whose search for limited gains the Labour Party became an adjunct.

The third failure was the failure of English intellectuals in the critical domain of the human sciences. Again, to do justice to part of the project that does not fall within the scope of this essay, it is important to stress the value of Anderson's discussion of the English intellectual world, at least the 'social scientific' part of it. 'Components of the national culture', Anderson's major essay in this field, belongs to a later historical moment than 'Origins' – to the student movement of the late 1960s rather than the Wilson election of 1964. Like all of Anderson's early historical work, it is enormously stimulating and suggestive. His map of English 'social science' is indispensable. Yet, though there are some changes of emphasis or some clarifications in the light of Edward Thompson's formidable criticisms, the treatment of intellectuals is still contained within the theme of bourgeois failure.[39]

Since bourgeoisie never 'achieved a political or social revolution in England', it never generated a 'revolutionary ideology'. Its thinkers were confined within a bourgeois corporatism: they never thought society as a whole - hence, their parochialism, empiricism, failure to penetrate the English fog of traditionalism and the long-continued absence of either a serious Marxist tradition or a complete political theory or a classical theoretical sociology of any kind. The most creative intellectual work has occupied the peripheries (literary criticism, anthropology) or been contained and isolated (psychoanalysis). It has also frequently been the province of émigrés. So where a revolutionary or synthetic tradition ought to have been, there is an 'absent centre'. English intellectual life is, indeed, a *history of absences*: no Durkheim, Pareto or Weber; no Lukács or Gramsci; no Sartre, Goldmann or Althusser. Much of the weakness of the British Left is traced to this source.

The final failure - and the outcome of all this - is the nature of British society in the mid 1960s: 'sclerosed', 'archaic', fossilized. One of the Nairn/Anderson questions is why the oldest capitalist society appeared fixed in an almost pre-industrial, pre-capitalist mould. The language of their analysis stresses this: 'the mythology of rank order', 'the pseudo-feudal coloration of British society', 'a comprehensive, coagulating conservatism', 'the patrician political style' and even, in a reference to the inter-war period, 'the pseudo-feudal class structure'.[40]

The distinctive feature of the Nairn/Anderson essays was the writing of history from a stand-point in the present. In practice all history does this (usually pretending not to), but these were emphatically political-historical essays. They broke with a history that is either merely contemplative (for its own sake) or merely professional (based on standards of mutual evaluation among people called 'historians'). It is important both to mark the seriousness of this intellectual-political intervention and to encounter it on its own ground - the ground of 'really useful knowledge'.

It is easy to see how the theme of failure was suggested by the immediate context of post-Macmillan Britain and the Wilson election campaign of 1964, with its modernizing, technocratic rhetoric. As Edward Thompson convincingly argues, it was strengthened by an implicit model of revolutionary and intellectual excellence based on the no-less-specific experiences of 'Other Countries', notably France.[41] In the absence of an explicitly comparative dimension, the project seemed to be informed by a rather self-indulgent Anglophobia.

It is obvious, in retrospect, that this was not the most useful way to approach the history. The theory of failure, indeed, coexists throughout the Anderson/Nairn early project with a contradictory half-recognition of the ideological and political *resources* of the dominant classes in England, a powerful defence in depth. Viewed differently, each of the Anderson/Nairn failures can also be read as *assets*, as symptoms of *strength*, as a large but finite repertoire of *solutions.* So by far the best part of Anderson's analysis of the 'present crisis' is the passage which deals with the barriers between a Labour electoral victory and qualitative social change. He points to the polycentricity of power in late British capitalism, the relative unimportance of military and bureaucracy, and to what he calls the 'extreme importance of cultural institutions'.[42] These points should have provided Anderson's problematic. They would have led not to questions about failure but to an analysis of strengths and how to penetrate them. Another way of putting this is to say that a backward-looking history is dependent on the adequacy with which the present is grasped.

A second criticism concerns the kind of history Anderson was writing, quite apart from its schematic character and its over-determination by too narrowly conceived a political moment. The most convincing typification is Anderson's own – that he was writing a kind of totalizing history but of an idealist kind, a history of superstructures in the manner of Lukācs.[43] It is indeed true that while Anderson's avowed project was 'the distinctive trajectory of British society since the emergence of capitalism' or 'the global evolution of the class structure' no less,[44] he focused on ideology, political society and the state and ignored both the forms of civil society and the mode and social relations of production. It is important to note the consequences of this very un-Marx-like method.

First, an idealist history, applied to the British instance, reinforces, quite arbitrarily, the *a priori* search for bourgeois failures. For, as we have seen, it is a feature of the British route that the bourgeois thrust in the domains of production and material life have been masked at the levels of ideology and state, especially, perhaps, at the level of political society and party. An idealist history cannot penetrate this formation, for it cannot compare the real relations and their representation in ideology. Consequently, Anderson and Nairn's main explanatory notion (aristocratic hegemony) *turns out to be nothing more than the principal theme of English Liberal ideology*. For from Ricardo and the utilitarians to J. A. Hobson and late popular liberalism, not to mention a large part of the Social Democratic tradition, the root of evils has been seen *precisely* as 'feudal', 'aristocratic' or 'military' residues in an industrial-democratic world.[45] The *New Left Review* analysis conforms to this very English tradition of radical liberalism: it does not surpass it, still less unmask it. The failure is compounded by a very one-sided reconstruction of the English Ideology itself, in which agrarian-conservative elements are magnified and the liberal-industrial counter-points virtually ignored.[46] Edward Thompson's criticism here is absolutely right, and the trouble is that the ideology of liberalism is actually present in the Anderson/Nairn story, but invisibly.

Second, this very unmaterialist version exaggerates the political moment in a history of determinations. Anderson's formative episodes, each of which fixes something permanently in the social structure, are political moments, not, for instance, trends in social and economic life. Against this it could be argued (classically, for a Marxist) that the most determining moments are the periods of transition from one mode of production to another, or from one sub-epoch to another, within the capitalist mode. To give two obvious examples without the elaboration they need: one 'grand fact' of British development is the very early entry, first by half a century or more, into industrial capitalism; another is the rather late, muted, defensive adoption of the forms of monopoly capital. Both features have tremendous power for the 'peculiarities of the English'. The Nairn/Anderson theme of bourgeois failure, for instance, might best be applied not to the whole span of history since the seventeenth century but, obviously enough, to the British transition to monopoly capitalism and the persistent twentieth-century failure to 'modernize'. This, anyway, would be a good starting-point and the one adopted by Hobsbawm in much of his work. A closer look might also show, however, that this 'failure' is also of considerable ideological utility and usually appears in exaggerated, one-dimensional versions.

Third, idealism produced an attenuated and formalistic history of class. Edward Thompson's criticisms on this score seem extraordinarily well aimed. In effect, Anderson's treatment of class fails doubly: it lacks the experiential, phenomenological dimensions of Thompson's own Marxism, but also any kind of historical sociology. *This* (Anderson/Nairn) working class has no economic function or social being. It is fooled in the head by ideas but not exploited and governed in the factory. Class experience does not change along any of these dimensions. Nor do classes have an internal structure of sets of internal social relations - other than those of party or trade union. As James Hinton observes, it is very unhistorical to suppose that at some time (the 1850s) a class can acquire fixed attributes (corporateness) which will persist independently of social and economic developments which change the class itself in internal configurations and external relations.[47] Edward Thompson's class-in-the-making was a very different set of people from Hinton's class of World War I, threatened or benefited by dilution. The same points could be made, of course, about the bourgeoisie and its fractions. All the classes are moved about in an ahistorical, mechanical manner. conveying with them abiding characteristics of mentality or world view.

A third set of criticisms, still of a historical-theoretical kind, concern Anderson's misuse of Gramsci's notions of hegemony and corporateness. Gramsci's formulations are frequently ambiguous but superbly historical and dialectical.[48] Anderson's are clear but also flat, static, lacking tensions. For Gramsci hegemony is a state of politico-cultural relations between classes *through which* a class or class alliance dominates by consent. If it can be seen as *belonging* to a class alliance, it belongs by virtue of the fact that it is their *work.* For Anderson, by contrast, hegemony is a property of the class which dominates. Its content is the content of the culture of the dominant class, whereas Gramsci's notion embraces all kinds of negotiations and concessions by which the dominant class alliance speaks to the conditions of subaltern or even subordinate classes and actively wins their consent. Gramsci's analytical repertoire is also immeasurably richer than Anderson's: Anderson's schema allows two basic situations - one in which a class dominates hegemonically and the subordinate classes are corporate and another in which subordinate classes prepare for power by developing a counter-hegemonic potential. This two-stage model is a very blunt instrument indeed for analysing whole tracts of historical experience (for example, the whole of British history from 1875 to 1951!). This accounts for some of the flatness of Nairn's working-class history, an analysis of unending corporateness. Gramsci, by contrast, saw in history many more situations: crises in hegemony; states of partial or incomplete or shifting hegemony; situations of 'Caesarism', in which the class that is dominant in the mode of production has to rule through another agent; situations in which there is little winning of consent at all, order being maintained mainly (but never purely) through the coercion of the economic process itself and the repressive apparatuses of the state.

The final point about hegemony is that the Anderson/Nairn view is very in-dialectical. Stuck in its corporate mode, the working class seems incapable of any kind of challenge. Secure in its hegemony, the dominant class is spared the trouble of continually refurbishing its armoury, accommodating new elements, *constructing* hegemony from a selection of the materials offered by real relations. A sense of the necessary friction, the necessary incompatibility of bourgeois and proletarian conditions of existence, seems altogether lost. The system is surprisingly self-policing - or if any real change is to be secured, it must come from outside, from Marxist intellectuals.

Against this view - which is not altogether a parody - one would want to insist on a pattern of challenge and response, action and *re*action, problem and 'solution', threat and containment (but containment always on a higher level): a pattern, in short, of struggle. At least this permits a curiosity about periods of working-class challenge, even if these *ended up* being contained within the corporate adaptation. For it is a matter of historical record that every now and again Nairn and Anderson's supine, untheoretical giant (who is usually preoccupied by less dramatic but necessary forms of subversion) has flexed muscles, hunched back and shaken the whole edifice. Then, of course, the politicians and the ideologues have got busily to work again, tying him down, eroding his gains, conceding the inevitable but patching the bigger breaches - hence a new 'order', incorporating a few real gains, exhausting one part of a repertoire of 'solutions' but representing an advance minute in proportion to the original effort.

To think in these terms is useful in two ways. It helps to make sense of an obvious feature of the story: the periodicity of crisis and relative stabilization. This is a recurrent, if irregular, pattern. One crude periodization might go like this:

Stabilization	*Crisis*
	1790–1845
1845–75	
	1875–95
1895–1911	
	1911–22
1922–37	
	1937–48
1948–70	
	1970 . . .

Each crisis or dissolution, of course, has its own determination and configuration; a cyclical pattern is not intended.

To think in these terms also allows us to give a proportionate historical role to the living force of 70 to 80 per cent of historical populations. For at the base of every moment of challenge are the experiences of a working class, or groups of working people, trying to live their everyday lives under capitalism. What these lives are like, and how the mass of the people understand them, and how control enters into that understanding are therefore key themes for our history.

The principal and determining fault in the *substance* of the Nairn/Anderson account is their recreation of the relationship of industrial and landed groups within the dominant class since the Industrial Revolution. It is possible to marshal an even stronger case than that proposed by Edward Thompson against the view of continued 'aristocratic' hegemony. What follows is an attempt to recreate more accurately the peculiar sources of strength of the English bourgeoisie, concentrating on the pre-monopolist period and relations between the landed and industrial fractions.

The agrarian-capitalist legacy was undoubtedly very important. Throughout most of the nineteenth century one finds coexisting within the same state two rather different kinds of social formation. These cohered around agrarian and industrial capital, the former in relative decline but in a flourishing state until the last decades of the century, the latter economically predominating. At first these two kinds of capital were perfectly complementary, since both capitalist agriculture and capitalist industry needed to create 'free labour' by transforming a rural social structure. In the long term they were, as Marx argued, likely to converge in the shape of 'agricultural industry', in which land would become a commodity like any other. In the meantime there were, it is true, some real antagonisms, but these were largely resolved (and resolved early) in favour of industrial capital.

Yet the estate, however capitalistically farmed, remained a different kind of unit of production from the business. There are numerous passages in Marx's writings where he examines this difference. One of the most revealing formulations is also an early one: 'Landed property in its distinction from capital is private property - capital - still afflicted with local and political prejudices.'[49] This catches perfectly the position of estate and landowners. For the estate had a value much more than economic value, more than could be cashed on the market. It carried a stock of status, the 'deference' (or anyway the voting power) of tenantry, and an enormous stock of cultural capital and of leisure. These assets derived from the internal character of landed capital. Through his intermediary, the tenant farmer, the owner of ground rent won both money and time, cash and leisure, for all the gentry's political functions: conspicuous consumption, ideological show (Edward Thompson's 'theatre'), amateur justice, all kinds of patronage and, of course, politics at the centre. Around the estate system were also preserved all kinds of social values that were alien to industrial capital but not antithetical to it - much of the whole conservative/Anglican repertoire, rooted not in 'feudalism' but in the genuinely hegemonic system of class-cultural relations which we might call 'gentry paternalism'.[50] The conservative repertoire continued to be reproduced not merely on the estates themselves but within a whole set of social institutions created in the days when landed wealth was king. The most important of these was the Anglican Church, always rurally centred, never wholly adapting to city, yet having a near-monopoly of formal education at most levels and undergoing quite a marked organizational and theological revival in the first half of the nineteenth century. Similarly linked to this system were the professional cousinhoods of law and the army. The nineteenth-century professions as a whole, especially those conferring a higher status, developed as a kind of hyphen between land and industry, with a social ideal that hybridized a bourgeois with a landed culture but which cannot be seen as 'aristocratic' in any simple way.[51]

Now, these assets did not stand over and against industrial capital except in some popular adaptations (for example, Cobbett's or Oastler's radicalism) or some literary formulations (Raymond Williams's 'culture and society' tradition). The former was a real component in popular resistance; the latter usually stopped short at a 'moral' anti-capitalism or merely provided a gloss of romantic rejection. Mostly the landed-conservative repertoire *was pressed into the service of capital as a whole.* So it came about that the first working class whose theories, forms of organization and strategies had, in any case, to be improvised from the start, faced always a double armoury: the economic power of manufacturer *and* farmer/landlord; the ideologies of deference *and* of self-help; High Tory Anglicanism *and* militant Dissent or popular anti-Catholicism; Chadwick's and Peel's newly professionalized police *and* gentry justice; popular political economy *and* 'moral and religious education'; utilitarian political philosophy *and* an anti-democratic conservatism or Whiggery; bourgeois special constabulary *and* an aristocratically led plebeian army.

This repertoire clearly had considerable stopping power. But, more important, it could deflect. It deeply influenced the nature of English radicalism, making it possible to construct the 'camouflaged' forms of politics on which Marx so often commented.[52] For while English 'aristocracy' persisted (and 1850 is much too soon for the point of fusion),[53] it could continue to appear to dominate English politics and to be the main butt of popular resentment. The division of large landed capitals and (relatively) small industrial capitals was sufficiently real to permit the construction of a whole national politics on this basis. So it was that the commonest form of English radicalism was an anti-aristocratic populism, not, or only imperfectly or temporarily, any kind of socialism. Apart from the Chartist/Owenite interlude of 1838–45 and, perhaps, the late nineteenth-century 'socialisms', this was true from Tom Paine to the early Chamberlain and the late Lloyd-George. The most powerful mystification of all was the mid nineteenth-century Liberal party.[54] Offering, concretely, very little to working people, it consisted of a leadership which was Whig, landowning and (if anyone was) 'aristocratic', plus the organizing, propagandizing power of Dissent and the big bourgeoisie, plus a rank and file of shopkeepers and artisans, all held together by an ideology that was basically anti-aristocratic. The counterpoint to this was a populist, demagogic conservatism, ringing the changes on themes of Nation and Empire and (perceptibly from the 1860s, markedly from the 1880s) attracting the support of property of all kinds.[55]

Exactly this political dialectic has been less marked since the decline of the big landed capitalist or his transmutation into another kind of *rentier*. Yet liberalism, in classic forms or in the mutant shapes of 'social reform', has been astonishingly persistent and pervasive in English political life. It has, indeed, formed that 'absent centre' for which Anderson searched, together, as Edward Thompson stresses, with elements in English bourgeois religion. One can go further. Liberalism in England has been carried in 'socialism', in the Labour Party and in the mainstream traditions of left intellectualism. So pervasive is this legacy from the Victorian dichotomy of industry and land that it is evidently almost invisible. It has as good a claim to have been the characteristic content of the English ideology than any kind of 'pseudo-feudalism'. The means to a real unmasking, however, is to *recognize the coexistence of the two.*

Postscript

This account is unrevised since 1974, and bits of it now cause unease. It will be important, sometime, to return to the major theme. Meanwhile, contemporary practice offers several models for a postscript. The first suggests that the author's jejune comments be read 'historically', perhaps as a record of 'experience'. (Does it show how one lumpen intellectual started to get drunk on Theory and was lured to the lair of the Monster Althusser?) Alternatively, 'the text' could be subjected to a really rigorous auto-critique on matters of theory, epistemology and 'pertinence' – on which grounds it would certainly fail. Both these kinds of self-digestion require peculiar stomachs (strong but also extremely agile) and lots of time and space. So this postscript is limited to re-emphasizing some points (which still seem *right*) in the light of later developments.

The Nairn/Anderson themes have also been restated. The first chapter of Tom Nairn's *The Break-Up of Britain*[56] takes account of some criticisms but consigns others to a footnote, where they 'answer themselves'.[57] In several ways the new account is less vulnerable than the old. It takes off from a new conjuncture: the crisis of the state in a dis-United Kingdom faced by the rise of the new nationalisms. It focuses on the development of the British 'state form', on inter-state relations and on the political cultures of England, Northern Ireland, Scotland and Wales. The shift of focus from the 1960s essays is not, then, so great: the puzzle remains the peculiarities of hegemony in Britain. The key questions are: Why has the old British state system lasted so long? And why has the threat of secession apparently eclipsed that of the class struggle in the 1970s? The answers lie in 'the historical character of the British state itself'.[58]

There are several important adjustments to the earlier argument. There is a more plausible portrayal of the ruling alliance in twentieth-century Britain. The inherent absurdity of unending 'aristocratic' hegemony is replaced by the convergence of finance capital ('the permanent victory of the City over the British economy') and 'the English intellectual class', a hugely influential grouping whose world view is a conservative liberalism. These social forces have preserved the peculiar character of the state, formed first under the dominance of agrarian capital and persistently 'intermediate', 'transitional' or 'pre-modern'. A 'patrician essence' - in state, in society and in the argument - is thus preserved.

A second major modification concerns international determinants on state forms. Nairn's general explanation associates nationalism with 'uneven development'. Nationalisms arise mainly (or initially?) in peripheral or hegemonized societies encountering coercion or competition from more advanced sectors. British development, being especially early, lacked any such moment of reactive popular nationalism. The later reliance on free-trade imperialism further inhibited a modernizing drive, feeding instead a passive nationalism of an inter-class kind, mainly mobilized in war-time. The peculiarities of the British state can best be understood, then, in terms of a 'world political economy'. Its dominant classes have been especially successful as rulers and conciliators, but the cost of the whole historical pattern has been the failure to modernize.

The third main change in the argument has been hinted at already: a concern with nationalisms of different kinds as a feature of political ideologies. Nationalism is seen as a major - perhaps *the* major - form of popular politics. In this way the *New Left Review* rediscovers the popular in the form of the nationalist. We'll look at the implications of this in a moment.

Yet many of the tendencies of the older account remain. The British route remains fundamentally flawed, giving rise to a society that is comprehensively blocked. In an argument now organized, explicitly, around the theme of 'modernization', this route is necessarily deviant. Britain has lacked 'that "modernizing" socio-political upheaval that ought to have refashioned both society and state in logical conformity with the demands of the new age'.[59] Internal forms of social struggle, especially of a popular kind, are still more or less absent as major determinants of outcomes. Popular forces are contained or incorporated without major consequences for the British 'state form'. This is partly because of insistence on the patrician essence, partly because the account is more concerned with how the state appears and how it is talked about than with what state agencies actually do, and partly because the whole theorization of struggle remains static and unrelational. Struggles happen but produce fixed and permanent outcomes. Hegemony is still thought of in terms of the world views of classes in simple relations of domination and subordination. Transformations must, in this model, be externally induced; they cannot be internally generated. The older account stressed the need for the importation of Marxist theory; the newer account reposes hope in the nationalisms of the British periphery. The old pessimism about the British working class is reinforced by the genuine insights of the new account, which stress the contradictions of unevenness at the expense of those of class.

Subsequent events make the account look idiosyncratic. Theoretically, it represents a pre-structuralist moment - despite the frequent use of the word 'structure'. If the debt is to Gramsci, it is to a Gramsci read through Lukācs, Sartre or Goldmann, not through the 'complex unity' of post-Althusserian structuralisms. It is strange that the influence of a structuralist work is quite minimal on writers usually held responsible for admitting these tendencies to Britain. Nicos

Poulantzas's sharp criticisms of 'Origins' seem quite repressed and are certainly not responded to. While the main tendency of theoretical work in the later 1970s has been to stress complexity, autonomies and even 'dispersions', these accounts still use notions of relatively simple social wholes, linked to 'history' by long evolutionary sequences. Social formations (patrician Britain) continue to have essences by which they can be understood. Classes continue to have homogeneous world views arranged around a few principles. Key features of political ideology represent, unproblematically, developments of another kind: the archaic appearances of the British state are held to represent its essence, whatever transformations are occurring in particular state apparatuses. It is odd that the main promoters of 'theory' remain so wedded to the ideas they were using in the mid 1960s.

Politically, too, the account remains problematic. As we've seen, popular forces, absent or supine in the earlier account, now appear as popular nationalisms. The earlier project argued a principled case for concentration on a narrowly intellectual culture. The uncomplicated populism of the old New Left was rejected; the task, pursued with some success, was to create a radical culture strongly influenced by continental Marxisms. This was always a paradoxical position for socialists to occupy, and the contradictions have deepened since. The new tendencies lacked indigenous popular roots and encouraged self-indulgent and esoteric styles of theorization and expression. At the same time the popularity of existing forms of Left politics was further eroded, popular spaces being occupied by forces not easily analysable in *NLR*-ish terms, especially a popular, anti-statist Toryism which, once in office, set about 'modernization' in a highly coercive form. The new analysis does not offer much in response – unless the future really does lie with the 'new' (now waning?) nationalisms or with some other form of radical popular nationalism. But this hope (which seems to me to smack of desperation) produces further paradoxes. Given the deep ambiguities of nationalisms of all kinds (which Nairn interestingly describes) and the likely association of nationalism and racism in the British context, the Nairn argument looks more like a loophole from pessimism than real grounds for hope. And anyway why must the desire for a better, non-capitalist world always appear in disguise? Is socialism such a peculiar and unpopular thing that it can only work indirectly, by proxy?

There is the problem, too, of the broader political tendency of the analysis. I still think that the original criticism here was correct: the analysis points to 'radical liberal' conclusions (to 'modernization' rather than to a socialist transformation of capitalist social relations). The tendency of the argument may be at odds with the politics of the authors. It is a matter of where the central contradictions are seen to lie. In the Nairn/Anderson accounts they lie between the needs of modern capitalism (never very precisely defined) and powerful determinations from the past. The contradictions are between old and new, or between archaic superstructural elements and the needs of development of the economy. Such contradictions are certainly important and not limited to the British case (see, for instance, Gramsci on Italy in 'Americanism and Fordism'). But given overwhelming stress, this form of analysis may altogether disguise the internal contradictions of bourgeois societies and the still contradictory character of the 'modernization' solution. It locates resistance to change (which is assumed, one-sidedly, to be good) in archaic residues and survivals, not in contradictions and necessary popular struggles central to capitalist relations themselves. At worst, allied to a New Left elitism, it points to the need for an *alternative* intelligentsia, which may secure 'the second bourgeois revolution' or technocratic revolution from above. This would be to reproduce the politics of radical liberalism as well as its analyses. At best, acceptance of the analysis tends to reduce socialist ambitions; like all good 'social democrats', we become mere 'modernizers'.

Against this it is important to assert the need for a politics that is both popular and socialist. This implies the need for analysis which takes popular movements and a 'lived' popular culture as central sets of concerns. These popular conceptions are the ground of socialist political practice; it is essential to understand how they are formed. This is not a return to the simple populism of the 1950s and 1960s; it is necessary to analyse the position of different constituents of the popular - the working class, women, blacks, those relatively removed from capitalist relations - and not to fuse all in 'the people'. But for these tasks the substantive accounts we have been discussing and the theories informing them do seem positively disabling.

Part Two

Ethnography

3 Introduction to ethnography at the Centre

Roger Grimshaw, Dorothy Hobson, Paul Willis

The extracts in this section have been chosen to show something of the use and development of this broad ethnographic range of work at the Centre. Also; we have borne in mind the general demand for particular articles which are no longer available in our original publications. Our extracts *are not* organized according to substantive terrain or specific theoretical focus, and this whole section should not be taken as a guide to the current state of ethnographic work at the Centre nor to the form of its theoretical/methodological integration in current projects. What we have attempted in the limited space available to us, is to indicate the *presence* within Cultural Studies of a method – through shifting theoretical and substantive focuses – which continues to offer, it seems to us, an important mode of the production of concrete studies of the cultural level.

Historically, ethnographic work has arisen from an awareness of the benefits of personal participation in, and communication with, an integral group involved with a characteristic way of life or cultural form. Developed intensively to tackle the problems of studying 'alien' cultures, ethnographic studies have come to be used more and more as a tool of mainstream sociological investigation. A reawakened interest in *verstehen*,[1] subjective meanings and sociological phenomenology after the breakdown of the dominance of structural-functionalism has accompanied a growing interest in methods capable of delivering qualitative knowledge of social relations, with all the rich distinctions and tones of living societies. Theoreticians such as Schutz and Cicourel[2] have become the reference points for this change of interest from quantitative statistical methods to qualitative modes of inquiry able to use documents, artefacts and records of various kinds, as well as the direct observation and interviews usually associated with ethnography. Within anthropology the study of ethnographic materials has become a launching-pad for the theoretical method of structuralism whose doyen is Lévi-Strauss.

Symbolic interactionism has enabled some measure to be taken of the nature and consequences of transactions between separate groups, such as public agencies and their clients.[3] The emphasis of symbolic interactionism, represented by theorists like Blumer, has been to record empirically social action and interpretation which are oriented to immediate others. Hence there developed an interest in labelling and its consequences for thought and behaviour. Such empirical concerns could be integrated into conflict theories of society, demonstrating aspects of the relations between larger social groups through study of encounters between, for example, deviants and controllers.

In terms of our own much shorter history, one of the central foci of our work has been to analyse and gauge the complex relations between representations/ ideological forms and the density or 'creativity' of 'lived' cultural forms. If the 'structuralist revolution' has warned against an inflation of the latter on any naive humanist trust, its 'theoreticist' descendants warn against the all-engulfing power of the former. It seems to us that the 'post-Althusserian' and even 'Gramscian' formulations conducted *within* theory still run the risk of inclining towards a purely formalist account of cultural forms. What we want to mark is the distinctiveness of a 'qualitative' methodological approach within the range of those available in Cultural Studies. This is the capacity of the ethnographic project, in Paul Willis's terms, to 'surprise' us and, if not generate alternative accounts of reality, at least question, compromise, negate or force revision in our existing accounts. There is a certain principle of the connectedness of cultural forms, as exposed (at best) through ethnographic study, which exerts a pressure against merely dredging methodologically unreflexive data for examples of a previously constituted theory. Of course, we recognize here the dangers of empiricism and the difficulties of developing a theoretically informed concrete account. The ethnographic interest at the Centre has undoubtedly been affected and brought to a degree of self-consciousness by recent theoretical developments discussed in Part One. Also, the method's historic roots in Weberianism, phenomenology, anthropology and, more recently, symbolic interactionism, give it an in-built tendency towards either idealism in its theoretical categories or an atheoreticalness which seems to suggest that theory can arise somehow naturally from the data. It is this very weakness, of course, which is a strength against theoretical reductionism. The problem, partially explored in Paul Willis's article extracted here, is to maintain the potential within this tradition to immunize accounts against theoretical violence while transcending some of its other limits in the overall materialist account of cultural forms.

We do not accept that the use of 'qualitative' methods automatically confines the resulting account to a theoretical Weberianism or to a merely descriptive, albeit 'rich', account. Even the early ethnographic work of the Centre, and certainly Phil Cohen's seminal article, part of which is extracted here, was theorized and addressed to analytic and theoretical questions much beyond an interest in 'experience' for its own sake or for its own guarantee. And later ethnographic work, some of which is extracted here, is in an explicit and developing relation with theoretical and critical concerns developing in the Centre generally: Paul Willis's work with questions of cultural reproduction, education and the labour process;[4] Angela McRobbie's with gender socialization, patriarchy and youth culture;[5] Dorothy Hobson's with the structures of female domestic experience and media discourses;[6] Roger Grimshaw's with structures of masculinity, ideology and the family.[7] In all of these areas, we would argue, the particular relation of theory and ethnography has allowed a real complexity and an explanatory power which can be seen in themselves as theoretical developments. It is to be hoped that in future the emphasis of ethnography on substantive explanation, with all the necessary complexity, precision and structure required in such work, will be supplemented by theory and general concepts which have an adequate firmness and relevance for the tasks which ethnography demands of them.

Still there exist certain conventions about how ethnographic work came about and developed in the Centre and elsewhere, and it is worth briefly charting how our interests have developed in relation to what are taken as the basic models. 'Early' forms of ethnography in the recent British context are taken to be associated with work on subcultures, deviancy labelling and amplification theory and the overall agenda of the National Deviancy Conference. In fact, this 'sceptical' revolution occurred mainly in theory, usually without (excepting Becker's pioneering work) serious or detailed ethnographic work. And, of course, Phil Cohen's seminal study of working-class culture and youth culture in the East End was most noticed for its theoretical contribution of 'magical displacement' which set the basic terms for much subsequent work, including *Resistance Through Rituals*. In fact, it was this later work which saw the arrival – though still patchily – of fuller ethnographic work in the articles by D. Hebdidge, P. Willis, P. Corrigan and others.[8]

We do not particularly want to question here the provenance of the ethnographic method so much as to chart its subsequent development in Cultural Studies and the work of the Centre. Most important, the method has been generalized now for use in the study of central and mainstream cultural forms and for the study and explication of these forms in relation to their material contexts – web of external determinations – and the contribution they make to the social reproduction of society generally and of its patriarchal and productive relations. The aim is not merely to classify ideas or forms but to show the non-reductive and non-mechanical relationship of these forms to basic material relationships. Paul Willis's recent work maintains an interest in the complexity and multifacetedness of cultural forms but relates them to fundamental aspects of school organization and the logic of the labour process to which working-class kids are destined. Current Centre work is developing this interest in the area of the transition from school to work of working-class girls and different occupational and gender cultures of the workplace.

The increasing presence of feminist concerns in the ethnographic project is, of course, no accident and a further indication of the potential for the method to be emancipated from its Weberian or phenomenological roots. The feminist interest in 'qualitative' methods springs from no idealist concern with self-generating (or merely classified) 'horizontal' cultural forms, but from a directly theoretical interest and a concern with determinations. For where the available Marxist theories could not account for the specificity of female experience – its oppressed form often first recorded in an ethnographic moment – it was necessary to return to experience and the subjective plane both to record and to substantiate this reality as a firm critique of available theory and to find materials towards the preliminary construction of alternative and more adequate theories. The privileging of 'the personal' was first developed in the Women's Liberation Movement through small-group consciousness-raising, where women learned to talk about personal experiences and to recognize that their experiences were shared by other women. Part of the ethnographic project for feminists has been to give a voice to the personal experience of the women and girls who are studied in the research.

The Marxist tradition had always emphasized the prior necessity of the analysis of fundamental economic structures in order to understand other features of social life. Unfortunately, the ambition of deducing other cultural features from basic economic structures, as Marx projected in *Capital*, has proved intractable beyond the preliminary stage of tracing correspondences and echoes between such spheres of activity. It is only comparatively recently, with the emergence of theorists of alienation and relative autonomy, the representatives of 'Western Marxism', that the possibility of adequate cultural analysis within a Marxist tradition has arisen. In our view, the complex bridging operation between economic, patriarchal and other social domains must run side by side with, use and be used by, a reassessment of the theoretical principles, method and concrete contributions of ethnography. Ethnography does not simply 'illustrate' an open concrete Marxism but helps to develop and internally test it.

The articles

The first extract (pages 78–87) comes from Phil Cohen's early influential article, 'Subcultural conflict and working-class community', which marked the beginning of a long arc of Centre interest in subcultures and the use of the ethnographic method. The article is based on his experience of a localized working-class area and proposes an original view of how the disintegration of a community is related to the forms of its youth cultures.

Paul Willis's article (pages 88–95) arises out of the early discussions of the Work Group on the status of the 'human objects' of the ethnographic method. It is interesting as a preliminary attempt to critique the implicit positivism in mainstream 'qualitative' methods and to outline a project for the more critical use of the method. He argues that a commitment to self-reflexivity engages the investigator's subjectivity, challenges previous assumptions and sets out fresh lines of inquiry, precisely when positivism withdraws into a cataloguing of factual and unanalysed descriptions. In some ways it marks the limits of a radical humanist version of the method, affirming it and taking it to a logical conclusion, but it also attempts to show how this might be combined with certain analytic Marxist categories – a project attempted, however unevenly, in his later *Learning to Labour*.

Roger Grimshaw's study of a Scoup camp (pages 96–104) illustrates some of the themes of his Ph.D thesis, *The Social Meaning of Scouting*. An ethnographic investigation of a Scout group forms the basis for an analysis of this particular culture, its processes and transactions, and the forms in which its codes practically address public and personal meanings. Substantively, the study charts the metaphorical association between a type of masculinity and a form of social and political conservatism.

Dorothy Hobson's account of the consumption of broadcasting by women (pages 105–14) forms part of her recent MA thesis, which is concerned with the classification of feminine experience acquired through an ethnographic technique.

A social theory of women's dependence and oppression supplies a notion of women's experience in terms of a sensitive comparison with men's social world. This form of study provides concrete materials towards understanding the links between reproduction, the patriarchal family and the reproduction of capitalism. Specifically, this extract offers a preliminary analysis of the role of radio and television in the lives of the women, as a means both of combating their isolation and coping with their lives.

4 Subcultural conflict and working-class community*

Phil Cohen

The fifties saw the development of new towns and large estates on the outskirts of east London (Dagenham, Greenleigh and so on), and a large number of families from the worst slums of the East End were rehoused in this way. The East End, one of the highest-density areas in London, underwent a gradual depopulation. But as it did so, certain areas underwent a repopulation as they were rapidly colonized by a large influx of West Indians and Pakistanis. One of the reasons why these communities were attracted (in the weak sense of the word) to such areas is often called 'planning blight'. This concept has been used to describe what happens in the take-off phase of comprehensive redevelopment in the inner residential zones of large urban centres. The typical pattern is that as redevelopment begins, land values inevitably rise and rental values fall; the most dynamic elements in local industry, which are usually the largest employers of labour, tend to move out, alongside the migrating families, and are often offered economic incentives to do so; much of the existing dilapidated property in the area is bought up cheaply by property speculators and Rachman-type landlords, who are only interested in the maximum exploitation of their assets - the largest profits in the shortest time. As a result the property is often not maintained and becomes even further dilapidated. Immigrant families with low incomes, excluded from council housing, naturally gravitate to these areas to penetrate the local economy. This in turn accelerates the migration of the indigenous community to the new towns and estates. The only apparent exception to planning blight in fact proves the rule. For those few areas which are linked to invisible assets - such as houses of 'character' (late Georgian or early Victorian) or amenities such as parks - are actually bought up and improved, renovated for the new middle class, students, young professionals who require easy access to the commercial and cultural centre of the city. The end result for the local community is the same: whether the neighbourhood is upgraded or downgraded, long-resident working-class families move out.

As the worst effects of this first phase, both on those who moved and on those who stayed behind, became apparent, the planning authorities decided to reverse their policy. Everything was now concentrated on building new estates on slum sites within the East End. But far from counteracting the social disorganization of the area, this merely accelerated the process. In analysing the impact of redevelopment on the community, these two phases can be treated as one. No one is denying

*This extract is taken from the longer article which appeared in *WPCS* 2 (1972).

that redevelopment brought an improvement in material conditions for those fortunate enough to be rehoused (there are still thousands on the housing list). But while this removed the tangible evidence of poverty, it did nothing to improve the real economic situation of many families, and those with low incomes may, despite rent-rebate schemes, be worse off.

The first effect of the high-density, high-rise schemes was to destroy the function of the street, the local pub, the corner shop as articulations of communal space. Instead there was only the privatized space of family units, stacked one on top of each other, in total isolation, juxtaposed with the totally public space which surrounded them and which lacked any of the informal social controls generated by the neighbourhood. The streets which serviced the new estates became thoroughfares, their users 'pedestrians' and, by analogy, so many bits of human traffic – and this irrespective of whether or not they were separated from motorized traffic. It is indicative of how far the planners failed to understand the human ecology of the working-class neighbourhood that they could actually talk about building 'vertical streets'! The people who had to live in them weren't fooled. As one put it: they might have running hot water and central heating but to him they were still prisons in the sky. Inevitably, the physical isolation, the lack of human scale and the sheer impersonality of the new environment was felt most keenly by people living in the new tower blocks which have gradually come to dominate the East End landscape.

The second effect of redevelopment was to destroy what we have called 'matrilocal residence'. Not only was the new housing designed on the model of the nuclear family, with little provision for large low-income families (usually designated 'problem families'!) and none at all for groups of young single people, but the actual pattern of distribution of the new housing tended to disperse the kinship network; families of marriage were separated from their families of origin, especially during the first phase of the redevelopment. The isolated family unit could no longer call on the resources of wider kinship networks or of the neighbourhood, and the family itself became the sole focus of solidarity. This meant that any problems were bottled up within the immediate interpersonal context which produced them; and at the same time family relationships were invested with a new intensity to compensate for the diversity of relationships previously generated through neighbours and wider kin. The trouble was that although the traditional kinship system which corresponded to it had broken down, the traditional patterns of socialization (of communication and control) continued to reproduce themselves in the interior of the family. The working-class family was thus not only isolated from the outside but also undermined from within. There is no better example of what we are talking about than the plight of the so-called 'housebound mother'. The street or turning was no longer available as a safe playspace, under neighbourly supervision. Mum or Auntie was no longer just around the corner to look after the kids for the odd morning. Instead, the task of keeping an eye on the kids fell exclusively to the young wife, and the only safe playspace was the 'safety of the home'. Feeling herself cooped up with the kids and cut off from the outside world, it wasn't surprising if she occasionally took out her frustration on those nearest and dearest! Only market research and advertising executives imagine that the housebound mother sublimates everything in her G-plan furniture, her washing machine or her non-stick frying pans. Underlying all this, however, there was a more basic process of change going on in the community, a change in the whole economic infrastructure of the East End.

In the late fifties the British economy began to recover from the effect of the war and to apply the advanced technology developed during this period to the more backward sectors of the economy. Craft industries and small-scale production in general were the first to suffer; automated techniques replaced the traditional handskills and their simple division of labour. Similarly, the economies of scale provided for by the concentration of capital resources meant that the small-scale family business was no longer a viable unit. Despite a long rearguard action, many of the traditional industries – tailoring, furniture making, many of the service and distributive trades linked to the docks – rapidly declined or were bought out. Symbolic of this was the disappearance of the corner shop; where these were not demolished by redevelopment they were replaced by larger supermarkets, often owned by large combines. Even where corner shops were offered places in the redevelopment area, often they could not afford the high rents. There was a gradual polarization in the structure of the labour force: on the one side, the highly specialized, skilled and well paid jobs associated with the new technology and the high-growth sectors that employed them; on the other, the routine, dead-end, low-paid and unskilled jobs associated with the labour-intensive sectors, especially the service industries. As might be expected, it was the young people, just out of school, who got the worst of the deal. Lacking openings in their fathers' trades, and lacking the qualifications for the new industries, they were relegated to jobs as van boys, office boys, packers, warehousemen and so on, and to long spells out of work. More and more people, young and old, had to travel out of the community to their jobs, and some eventually moved out to live elsewhere, where suitable work was to be found. The local economy as a whole contracted, became less diverse. The only section of the community which was unaffected by this was dockland, which retained its position in the labour market and, with it, its traditions of militancy. It did not, though, remain unaffected by the breakdown of the pattern of integration in the East End as a whole *vis-a-vis* its sub-community structure. Perhaps this goes some way to explaining the paradoxical fact that within the space of twelve months the dockers could march in support of Enoch Powell and take direct action for community control in the Isle of Dogs!

If someone should ask why the plan to 'modernize' the pattern of East End life should have been such a disaster, perhaps the only honest answer is that given the macro-social forces acting on it, given the political, ideological and economic framework within which it operated, the result was inevitable. For example, many local people wonder why the new environment should be the way it is. The reasons are complex. They are political in so far as the system does not allow for any effective participation by a local working-class community in the decision-making process at any stage or level of planning. The clients of the planners are simply the local authority or the commercial developer who employs them. They are ideological in so far as the plans are unconsciously modelled on the structure of the middle-class environment, which is based on the concept of *property* and private *ownership*, on individual differences of status, wealth and so on, whereas the structure of the working-class environment is based on the concept of community or collective identity, common lack of ownership, wealth, etc. Similarly, needs were assessed on the norms of the middle-class nuclear family rather than on those of the extended working-class family. But underpinning both these sets of reasons lie the basic economic factors involved in comprehensive redevelopment. Quite simply, faced with the task of financing a large housing programme, local authorities are forced to borrow large amounts of capital and also to design schemes which would attract capital investment to the area. This means that they have to borrow at the going interest rates, which in this country are very high, and that to subsidize housing certain of the best sites have to be earmarked for commercial developers.

All this means that planners have to reduce the cost of production to a minimum through the use of capital-intensive techniques - prefabricated and standardized components which allow for semi-automated processes in construction. The attraction of high-rise developments ('tower blocks', outside the trade) is that they not only meet these requirements but they also allow for certain economies of scale, such as the input costs of essential services, which can be grouped around a central core. As for 'non-essential' services, that is, ones that don't pay, such as playspace, community centres, youth clubs and recreational facilities, these often have to be sacrificed to the needs of commercial developers - who, of course, have quite different priorities.

The situation facing East Enders at present is not new. When the first tenements went up in the nineteenth century they provoked the same objections from local people, and for the same very good reasons, as their modern counterparts, the tower blocks. What *is* new is that in the nineteenth century the voice of the community was vigorous and articulate on these issues, whereas today, just when it needs it most, the community is faced with a crisis of indigenous leadership.

The reasons for this are already implicit in the analysis above. The labour aristocracy, the traditional source of leadership, has virtually disappeared, along with the artisan mode of production. At the same time there has been a split in consciousness between the spheres of production and consumption. More and more East Enders are forced to work outside the area; young people especially are less likely to follow family traditions in this respect. As a result, the issues of the workplace are no longer experienced as directly linked to community issues. Of course, there has always been a 'brain drain' of the most articulate, due to social mobility. But not only has this been intensified as a result of the introduction of comprehensive schools, but the recruitment of fresh talent from the stratum below - from the ranks of the respectable working class, that is - has also dried up. For this stratum, traditionally the social cement of the community, is also in a state of crisis.

The economic changes which we have already described also affected its position and, as it were, *destabilized* it. The 'respectables' found themselves caught and pulled apart by two opposed pressures of social mobility – downwards, and upwards into the ranks of the new suburban working-class elite. And, more than any other section of the working class, they were caught in the middle of the two dominant but contradictory ideologies of the day: the ideology of spectacular consumption, promoted by the mass media, and the traditional ideology of production, the so-called work ethic, which centred on the idea that a man's dignity, his manhood even, was measured by the quantity or quality of his effort in production. If this stratum began to split apart, it was because its existing position had become untenable. Its bargaining power in the labour market was threatened by the introduction of new automated techniques, which eliminated many middle-range, semi-skilled jobs. Its economic position excluded its members from entering the artificial paradise of the new consumer society; at the same time changes in the production process itself have made the traditional work ethic, pride in the job, impossible to uphold. They had the worst of all possible worlds.

Once again, this predicament was registered most deeply in and on the young. But here an additional complicating factor intervenes. We have already described the peculiar strains imposed on the 'nucleated' working-class family. And their most critical impact was in the area of parent/child relationships. What had previously been a source of support and security for both now became something of a battleground, a major focus of all the anxieties created by the disintegration of community structures around them. One result of this was to produce an increase in early marriage. For one way of escaping from the claustrophobic tensions of family life was to start a family of your own! And given the total lack of accommodation for young, single people in the new developments, as well as the conversion of cheap rented accommodation into middle-class, owner-occupied housing, the only practicable way to leave home was to get married. The second outcome of generational conflict (which may appear to go against the trend of early marriage, but in fact reinforced it) was the emergence of specific youth subcultures in opposition to the parent culture. And one effect of this was to weaken the links of historical and cultural continuity, mediated through the family, which had been such a strong force for solidarity in the working-class community. It is, perhaps, not surprising that the parent culture of the respectable working class, already in crisis, was the most 'productive' *vis-à-vis* subcultures; the internal conflicts of the parent culture came to be worked out in terms of generational conflict. What I think is that one of the functions of generational conflict is to decant the kinds of tensions which appear face-to-face in the family and to replace them by a generational-specific symbolic system, so that the tension is taken out of the interpersonal context, placed in a collective context and mediated through various stereotypes which have the function of defusing the anxiety that interpersonal tension generates.

It seems to me that the latent function of subculture is this: to express and resolve, albeit 'magically', the contradictions which remain hidden or unresolved in the parent culture. The succession of subcultures which this parent culture generated can thus all be considered so many variations on a central theme – the contradiction, at an ideological level, between traditional working-class puritanism and the new hedonism of consumption; at an economic level, between a future as part of the socially mobile elite or as part of the new lumpen proletariat. Mods, parkas, skinheads, crombies all represent, in their different ways, an attempt to retrieve some of the socially cohesive elements destroyed in their parent culture, and to combine these with elements selected from other class fractions, symbolizing one or other of the options confronting it.

It is easy enough to see this working in practice if we remember, first, that subcultures are symbolic structures and must not be confused with the actual kids who are their bearers and supports. Secondly, a given life-style is actually made up of a number of symbolic subsystems, and it is the way in which these are articulated in the total life-style that constitutes its distinctiveness. There are basically four subsystems, which can be divided into two basic types of forms. There are the relatively 'plastic' forms – dress and music – which are not directly produced by the subculture but which are selected and invested with subcultural value in so far as they express its underlying thematic. Then there are the more 'infrastructural' forms – argot and ritual – which are more resistant to innovation but, of course, reflect changes in the more plastic forms. I'm suggesting here that mods, parkas, skinheads, crombies are a succession of subcultures which all correspond to the same parent culture and which attempt to work out, through a system of transformations, the basic problematic or contradiction which is inserted in the subculture by the parent culture. So one can distinguish three levels in the analysis of subcultures; one is historical analysis, which isolates the specific problematic of a particular class fraction – in this case, the respectable working class; the second is a structural or semiotic analysis of the subsystems, the way in which they are articulated and the actual transformations which those subsystems undergo from one structural moment to another; and the third is the phenomenological analysis of the way the subculture is actually 'lived out' by those who are the bearers and supports of the subculture. No real analysis of subculture is complete without all those levels being in place.

To go back to the diachronic string we are discussing, the original mod life-style could be interpreted as an attempt to realize, *but in an imaginary relation*, the conditions of existence of the socially mobile white-collar worker. While the argot and ritual forms of mods stressed many of the traditional values of their parent culture, their dress and music reflected the hedonistic image of the affluent consumer. The life-style crystallized in opposition to that of the rockers (the famous riots in the early sixties testified to this), and it seems to be a law of subcultural evolution that its dynamic comes not only from the relations to its own parent culture, but also from the relation to subcultures belonging to *other class fractions*, in this case the manual working class.

The next members of our string – the parkas or scooter boys – were in some senses a transitional form between the mods and the skinheads. The alien elements introduced into music and dress by the mods were progressively de-stressed and the indigenous components of argot and ritual reasserted as the matrix of subcultural identity. The skinheads themselves carried the process to completion. Their life-style, in fact, represents a systematic inversion of the mods - whereas the mods explored the upwardly mobile option, the skinheads explored the lumpen. Music and dress again became the central focus of the life-style; the introduction of reggae (the protest music of the West Indian poor) and the 'uniform' (of which more in a moment) signified a reaction against the contamination of the parent culture by middle-class values and a reassertion of the integral values of working-class culture through its most recessive traits - its puritanism and chauvinism. This double movement gave rise to a phenomenon sometimes called 'machismo' - the unconscious dynamics of the work ethic translated into the out-of-work situation; the most dramatic example of this was the epidemic of 'queer-bashing' around the country in 1969-70. The skinhead uniform itself could be interpreted as a kind of caricature of the model worker - the self-image of the working class as distorted through middle-class perceptions, a metastatement about the whole process of social mobility. Finally, the skinhead life-style crystallized in opposition both to the greasers (successors to the rockers) and the hippies - both subcultures representing a species of hedonism which the skinheads rejected.

Following the skinheads there emerged another transitional form, variously known as crombies, casuals, suedes and so on (the proliferation of names being a mark of transitional phases). They represent a movement back towards the original mod position, although this time it is a question of incorporating certain elements drawn from a middle-class subculture - the hippies - which the skinheads had previously ignored. But even though the crombies have adopted some of the external mannerisms of the hippy life-style (dress, soft drug use), they still conserve many of the distinctive features of earlier versions of the subculture.

If the whole process, as we have described it, seems to be circular, forming a closed system, then this is because subculture, by definition, cannot break out of the contradiction derived from the parent culture; it merely transcribes its terms at a microsocial level and inscribes them in an imaginary set of relations.

But there is another reason. Apart from its particular, thematic contradiction, all subcultures share a general contradiction which is inherent in their very conditions of existence. Subculture invests the weak points in the chain of socialization between the family/school nexus and integration into the work process which marks the resumption of the patterns of the parent culture for the next generation. But subculture is also a compromise solution to two contradictory needs: the need to create and express *autonomy and difference* from parents and, by extension, their culture, and the need to maintain the security of existing ego defences and the *parental identifications* which support them. For the initiates the subculture provides a means of 'rebirth' without having to undergo the pain of symbolic death. The autonomy it offers is thus both real (but partial) and illusory as a total 'way of liberation'. And far from constituting an improvised *rite de passage* into adult society, as some anthropologists have claimed, it is a collective and highly ritualized defence against just such a transition. And because defensive functions predominate, ego boundaries become cemented into subcultural boundaries. In a real sense, subcultural conflict (greasers *versus* skinheads, mods *versus* rockers) serves as a displacement of generational conflict, both at a cultural level and at an interpersonal level within the family. One consequence of this is to foreclose artificially the natural trajectory of adolescent revolt. For the kids who are caught up in the internal contradictions of a subculture, what begins as a break in the continuum of social control can easily become a permanent hiatus in their lives. Although there is a certain amount of subcultural mobility (kids evolving from mods to parkas or even switching subcultural affiliations, greasers 'becoming' skinheads), there are no career prospects! There are two possible solutions: one leads out of subculture into early marriage, and, as we've said, for working-class kids this is the normal solution; alternatively, subcultural affiliation can provide a way into membership of one of the deviant groups which exist in the margins of subculture and often adopt its protective coloration, but which nevertheless are not structurally dependent on it (such groups as pushers, petty criminals, junkies, even homosexuals).

This leads us into another contradiction inherent in subculture. Although as a symbolic structure it *does* provide a diffuse sense of affinity in terms of a common life-style, it does not in itself prescribe any crystallized group structure. It is through the function of *territoriality* that subculture becomes anchored in the collective reality of the kids who are its bearers, and who in this way become not just its passive support but its conscious agents. Territoriality is simply the process through which environmental boundaries (and foci) are used to signify group boundaries (and foci) and become invested with a subcultural value. This is the function of football teams for the skinheads, for example. Territoriality is thus not only a way in which kids 'live' subculture as a collective behaviour, but also the way in which the subcultural group becomes rooted in the situation of its community. In the context of the East End, it is a way of retrieving the solidarities of the traditional neighbourhood destroyed by redevelopment. The existence of communal space is reasserted as the common pledge of group unity - you belong to the Mile End mob in so far as Mile End belongs to you. Territoriality appears as a magical way of expressing ownership; for Mile End is not owned by the people but by the property developers. Territorial division therefore appears within the subculture and, in the East End, mirrors many of the traditional divisions of sub-communities: Bethnal Green, Hoxton, Mile End, Whitechapel, Balls Pond Road and so on. Thus, in addition to conflict between subcultures, there also exists conflict within them, on a territorial basis. Both these forms of conflict can be seen as displacing or weakening the dynamics of generational conflict, which is in turn a displaced form of the traditional parameters of class conflict.

A distinction must be made between subcultures and delinquency. Many criminologists talk of delinquent subcultures. In fact, they talk about anything that is not middle-class culture as subculture. From my point of view, I do not think the middle class produces subcultures, for subcultures are produced by a dominated culture, not by a dominant culture. I am trying to work out the way that subcultures have altered the pattern of working-class delinquency. But now I want to look at the delinquent aspect.

For during this whole period there was a spectacular rise in the delinquency rates in the area, even compared with similar areas in other parts of the country. The highest increase was in offences involving attacks on property - vandalism, hooliganism of various kinds, the taking and driving away of cars. At the simplest level this can be interpreted as some kind of protest against the general dehumanization of the environment, an effect of the loss of the informal social controls generated by the old neighbourhoods. The delinquency rate also, of course, reflected the level of police activity in the area and the progressively worsening relations between young people and the forces of law and order. Today, in fact, the traditional enmity has become something more like a scenario of urban guerrilla warfare!

There are many ways of looking at delinquency. One way is to see it as the expression of a system of transactions between young people and various agencies of social control, in the subcultural context of territoriality. One advantage of this definition is that it allows us to make a conceptual distinction between delinquency and deviancy, and to reserve this last term for groups (for example, prostitutes, professional criminals, revolutionaries) which crystallize around a specific counter-ideology, and even career structure, which cuts across age grades and often community or class boundaries. While there is an obvious relation between the two, delinquency often serving as a means of recruitment into deviant groups, the distinction is still worth making.

Delinquency can be seen as a form of communication about a situation of contradiction in which the 'delinquent' is trapped but whose complexity is excommunicated from his perceptions by virtue of the restricted linguistic code which working-class culture makes available to him. Such a code, despite its richness and concreteness of expression, does not allow the speaker to make verbally explicit the rules of relationship and implicit value systems which regulate interpersonal situations, since this operation involves the use of complex syntactical structures and a certain degree of conceptual abstraction not available through this code. This is especially critical when the situations are institutional ones, in which the rules of relationship are often contradictory, denied or disguised but nevertheless binding on the speaker. For the working-class kid this applies to his family, where the positional rules of extended kinship reverberate against the personalized rules of its new nuclear structure; in the school, where middle-class teachers operate a whole series of linguistic and cultural controls which are 'dissonant' with those of his family and peers, but whose mastery is implicitly defined as the index of intelligence and achievement; at work, where the mechanism of exploitation (extraction of surplus value, capital accumulation) are screened off from perception by the apparently free exchange of so much labour time for so much money wage. In the absence of a working-class ideology which is both accessible and capable of providing a concrete interpretation of such contradictions, what can a poor boy do? Delinquency is one way he can communicate, can represent by analogy and through non-verbal channels the dynamics of some of the social configurations he is locked into. And if the content of this communication remains largely 'unconscious', then that is because, as Freud would say, it is 'over-determined'. For what is being communicated is not one but *two different* systems of rules: one belonging to the sphere of object relations and the laws of symbolic production (more specifically, the parameters of Oedipal conflict), the second belonging to property relations, the laws of material production (more specifically, the parameters of class conflict).

Without going into this too deeply, I would suggest that where there is an extended family system the Oedipal conflict is displaced from the triadic situation to sibling relations, which then develops into the gang outside the family. When this begins to break down the reverse process sets in. In the study of the structural relations for the emergence of subcultures the implications of this are twofold: first, changes in the parameters of class conflict are brought about by advanced technology where there is some class consensus between certain parent cultures, and that level of conflict appears to be invisible or acted on in various dissociated ways; second, the parameters of Oedipal conflict are becoming replaced in the family context but are refracted through the peer-group situation. It is a kind of double inversion that needs to be looked at not only in terms of a Marxist theory, which would analyse it simply by reference to class conflict and the development of antagonistic class fractions simply syphoning down vertically into another generational situation, but also in psychoanalytic terms, through the dynamics of Oedipal conflict in adolescence. We need to look at the historical ways in which class conflict and the dynamics of Oedipal conflict have undergone transformation and have interlocked, reverberating against each other.

5 Notes on method*

Paul Willis

If the 'naturalist' revolt was directed against positivism's inability to understand and record human subjectivity, mainstream sociology has nevertheless found it possible to assign participant observation (PO) and case study work a legitimate place in the social sciences.[1]

I shall be arguing that positivism's unwilling acceptance of 'qualitative' methodology sees more clearly than its own admissions that the emphasis on *methodological* variety may leave the heartland of the positivist terrain untouched. In its recognition of a *technical* inability to record all that is relevant - and its yielding of this zone to another technique - positivism may actually preserve its deepest loyalty: to its object of inquiry truly as an 'object'.[2] The duality and mutual exclusivity of the over-neatly opposed categories, 'qualitative' methods and 'quantitative' methods, suggest already that the 'object' is viewed in the same unitary and distanced way even if the *mode* is changed - now you measure it, now you feel it.

Still, there is much that is valuable in the 'naturalist' revolt. It has certainly dissociated itself from simplistic causal thinking, and it has developed a set of rules and research procedures which do offer an alternative concrete starting-point to the positivist methods. This article aims to identify the really central principles of the 'qualitative' method and to suggest what is worth preserving and what is worth firmly rejecting in a preliminary attempt to outline a method genuinely adapted to the study of human meanings.

The tradition which has most clearly used the 'qualitative' methods under discussion here was outlined in the last issues of *WPCS*.[3] The 'Chicago School' of the 1920s and 1930s originated this tradition.[4] W. F. Whyte's work in the 1940s marks a continuance of the tradition into a second phase.[5] The major expansion came in the 1950s and 1960s, with the work of Becker, Geer, Strauss, Polsky and others.[6] The tradition crossed to Britain most clearly when the work of this 'third wave' was taken up by D. Downes,[7] S. Cohen and particularly those associated with the 'sceptical revolution' institutionalized by the National Deviancy Conference.[8] There has been a sporadic but noticeable interest in, and use of, PO in Britain which is not specifically in this Chicago-derived tradition.[9] The method itself has been systematized and presented as a 'respectable' methodology in two recent readers.[10]

*This is an edited version of an article which first appeared in *Culture and Domination*, *WPCS* 9 (1976).

It may well be that my critique traduces certain texts in the ethnographic tradition. Certainly, there are examples in which a final account transcends the limitations of its own stated methods. In what follows I have mainly relied on codifications of method, such as those above, which are increasingly accepted as authoritative guides for those wishing to use 'qualitative' methods.

The manifest posture

The most obvious thrust of 'qualitative' methodology has been *against* traditional sociological theory and methods modelled on what are taken to be the procedures and tests of the natural sciences. To simplify, the fear seems to be that a theory can only, ultimately, demonstrate its own assumptions. What lies outside these assumptions cannot be represented or even acknowledged. So to maintain the richness and authenticity of social phenomena it is necessary, certainly in the early stages of research, to receive data in a raw, experimental and relatively untheorized manner – 'Allowing substantive concepts and hypotheses to emerge first on their own'.[11] It is recognized, of course, that there will have to come a time of closure.[12] It is hoped, however, that the selectivity and theorization of the final work will reflect the patterning of the real world rather than the patterns of received theory.[13] These 'anti'-theoretical concerns generate a profound methodological stress on contacting the subject as directly as possible. It is as if the ideal researcher's experience can achieve a one-to-one relationship with that of the researched.

This conviction, and the general distrust of theory, are most clearly expressed through and by the techniques and methods it is proposed to use.[14] The researcher is to work in the environment of his/her subjects rather than in the laboratory and is to enter the field as free as possible from prior theory. S/he is to participate in the round of activities of his/her subjects but to avoid 'disturbing' the field. S/he should not question his/her subjects directly but be as open as possible to the realm of the 'taken-for-granted'. S/he must take great care to plan his/her entrance into the field, prepare a feasible role and assiduously court those who might sponsor his/her membership in selected social groups.

It is the openness and directness of this methodological approach which promises the production of a final account which, like an icon, will bear some of the marks, and recreate something of the richness, of the original.

The hidden practice

If the techniques of 'qualitative' methodology mark a decisive break from 'quantitative' ones, the way in which they are *usually applied* makes a secret compact with positivism to preserve the subject finally as an object. Indeed, what the all-embracing concern for techniques and for the reliability of the data really shows us is a belief that the object of the research exists in an external world, with knowable external characteristics which must not be disturbed.

The central insistence, for instance, on the *passivity* of the *participant observer* depends on a belief that the subject of the research is really an object. The concern is to minimize 'distortion of the field', with the underlying fear that the *object* may be *contaminated* with the subjectivity of the researcher.[15] Too easily it becomes an assumption of different orders of reality between the researched and the researcher.

The insistent, almost neurotic, technical concern with the differentiation of PO from reportage and Art is also a reflection of the subterranean conviction that PO belongs with the 'sciences' and must, in the end, respect objectivity.[16] There is a clear sociological fear of naked subjectivity.[17] The novel can wallow in subjectivity - this is how it creates 'colour' and 'atmosphere' - but how do we know that the author did not make it all up? Indeed, in one obvious way he or she did make it all up! So the search must be for a unified object which might be expected to present itself as *the same* to many minds. The first principle of PO, the postponement of theory, compounds the dangers of this covert positivism. It strengthens the notion that the object can present itself directly to the observer.

On the role of theory

In fact, there is no truly untheoretical way in which to 'see' an 'object'. The 'object' is only perceived and understood through an internal organization of data, mediated by conceptual constructs and ways of seeing the world. The final account of an object says as much about the observer as it does about the object itself. Accounts can be read 'backwards' to uncover and explicate the consciousness, culture and theoretical organization of the observer.

However, we must recognize the ambition of the PO principle in relation to theory. It has directed its followers towards a profoundly important methodological possibility - that of *being 'surprised'*, of reaching knowledge not prefigured in one's starting paradigm. The urgent task is to chart the feasibility, scope and proper meaning of such a capacity.

If we are to recognize the actual scope for the production of 'new' knowledge, we must avoid delusions. We must not be too ambitious. It is vital that we admit the most basic foundations of our research approach and accept that no 'discovery' will overthrow this most basic orientation. The theoretical organization of the starting-out position should be outlined and acknowledged in any piece of research. This inevitable organization concerns attitudes towards the social world in which the research takes place, a particular view of the social relationships within it and of its fundamental determinations and a notion of the analytic procedures which will be used to produce the final account. It would also explain why certain topics have been chosen for research in the first place.

This theoretical 'confession', however, need not specify the *whole* of social reality in a given region; it has merely specified the kind of world in which its action is seen as taking place. Although it involves the general form of, it does not include, *specific* explanation - especially concerning the *manner,* the 'how' or the degree of external determination of a given social region - nor does it anticipate the particular meaning of the future flow of data.

It is indeed crucial that a qualitative methodology be confronted with the maximum flow of relevant data. Here resides the power of the evidence to 'surprise', to contradict, specific developing theories. And here is the only possible source for the 'authenticity', the 'qualitative feel', which is one of the method's major justifications. It is in this area – short of any challenge to one's world view – that there is the greatest possibility of 'surprise'.

This is not to allow back an unbridled, intuitive 'naturalism' on impoverished terms. Even with respect to what remains unspecified by the larger 'confession', we must recognize the necessarily theoretical form of what we 'discover'. Even the most 'naturalistic' of accounts involves deconstruction of native logic and builds upon reconstruction of compressed, select, significant moments in the original field experienced. There is an art concealing art which precisely obscures the theoretical work that has taken place.

Having recognized the inevitability of a theoretical component, it can be used more self-consciously to probe those areas about which knowledge is incomplete.

We will find in any cultural form and related form of consciousness a submerged text of contradictions, inconsistencies and divergencies. If we are tuned in to an illusory attempt to present a single-valency account without interpretative or reductive work, we shall more usually miss (or, at best, simply reproduce) this sub-text. It is necessary to add to the received notion of the 'quality' of the data an ability to watch for inconsistencies, contradictions and misunderstandings and to make theoretical interpretations of them. We must maintain the richness and atmosphere of the original while attempting to illuminate its inner connections. Certainly, the necessary and inevitable level of interpretative theorizing within the method can be used to explicate chosen topics without running greater dangers than are run conventionally in an *unrecognized* way.

On reflexivity: the politics of fieldwork

If we wish to represent the subjective meanings, feelings and cultures of others, it is not possible to extend to them less than we know of ourselves. What is so often taken as the 'object' and the researcher lie parallel in their humanity. The 'object' of our inquiry is in fact, of course, a subject and has to be understood and presented in the same mode as the researcher's own subjectivity – this is the true meaning of 'validity' in the 'qualitative' zone. The recognition of this truism is not, however, to declare against all forms of 'objectivity'. We are still in need of a method which respects evidence, seeks corroboration and minimizes distortion, *but which is without rationalist natural-science-like pretence.*

Though we can only know it through our own concepts, there is nevertheless a *real* subject for our inquiry, which is not entirely spirited away by our admission of its relativized position. If our purpose is a fuller understanding and knowledge of this subject, then we must have some concern for the reliability of the data we use. Furthermore, if our focus is not on isolated, subjective meanings but on their associated symbolic systems and cultural forms, then we are concerned also with real material elements. It is perfectly justifiable to use rigorous techniques to gain the fullest knowledge of these things. This is, therefore, to go partly down the road of traditional 'objectivity': many of the techniques used will be the same. The parting of the ways comes at the end of this process. The conventional process takes its 'objective' data-gathering as far as possible and then consigns the rest (what it cannot know, measure or understand) to Art or 'the problem of subjectivity'. Having constituted its object truly as an 'object', and having gained all possible knowledge about this 'object', the process must stop; it has come up to the 'inevitable limitations of a quantitative methodology'. But it is precisely at this point that a reflexive, 'qualitative' methodology comes into its own. Never having constituted the subject of its study as an 'object', it is not surprised that there is a limit to factual knowledge. What finally remains is *the relationship between subjective/cultural systems.*

The rigorous stage of the analysis, the elimination of distortion, the cross-checking of evidence and so on have served to focus points of divergence and convergence between systems. Reducing the confusion of the research situation, providing a more precise orientation for analysis, allows a closer reading of separate realities. By reading moments of contact and divergence it becomes possible to delineate other worlds, demonstrating their inner symbolic qualities. And when the conventional techniques retire, when they cannot follow the subjects of subjects themselves – this is the moment of *reflexivity*. Why are these things happening? Why has the subject behaved in this way? Why do certain areas remain obscure to the researcher? What differences in orientation lie behind the failure to communicate?

It is here, in this interlocking of human meanings, of cultural codes and of forms, that there is the possibility of 'being surprised'. And in terms of the generation of 'new' knowledge, we know what it is precisely *not* because we have shared it – the usual notion of empathy – but because we have *not* shared it. It is here that the classical canons are overturned. It is time to ask and explore, to discover the differences between subjective positions, between cultural forms. It is time to initiate actions or to break expectations in order to probe different angles in different lights. Of course, this is a time of maximum disturbance to researchers, whose own meanings are being thoroughly contested. It is precisely at this point that the researcher must assume an unrestrained and hazardous *self-reflexivity*. And it is the turning away from a full commitment, at this point, which finally limits the methods of traditional sociology.

It is in these moments also that there can be a distinctive relationship with a specifically Marxist form of analysis. The terrain uncovered and explored during this reflexive stage is likely to concern contradictions and tensions, both within the field of study – contrasting moments of subjective experience, tensions between what is said and done, differences between what collective forms or materials seem to say or promise and what *actually* happens or is experienced – and between the researcher's expectations, codes and cultural forms of understanding and those which he or she is uncovering. It is likely to be a difficult field of contradictions, picked up at this point precisely because it is the notion of *contradiction* which the traditional 'naturalistic' technique is unable to register or registers only as a weakness or breakdown in its method, or as the 'limit case' to the researcher's effectivity in the field – beyond which lies only 'going native' or withdrawal. With only a notion of 'what follows' taken from the surface reality of the 'object' and picked up transparently in the universal codes of 'science', contradictory messages, conflicts or breakdowns between codes and broken communication can only be understood as 'failures', to be transcended ultimately by better technique.

However, if these moments of crisis can be seen as a creative uncertainty, entered through a structured social relationship, indicating and arising from important contradictions, then further theoretical and methodological options become available. For the theoretical understanding developed through what I am characterizing as a more active and reflexive method can be in the form of a reformulation and more precise articulation of what I called earlier the larger theoretical 'confession' and, in particular, a more concrete extension of the way in which larger determinations and categories are seen to relate to the particular relationships and patterns of determination within the regional area under study. And often this must be through recognizing a necessary unevenness and complexity in the way that external forces or ideologies pattern a given area. This is a non-mechanistic, non-reductive view of the relationship between levels, which may wish to leave some scope for reciprocal effectivity between located cultural forms, subjective experience and larger structures or may insist on indirect or mediating processes, but which is still concerned with determination. This greater theoretical elaboration, extension and specification – especially within a theory which recognizes the play of contradiction – will then allow the better grasp and explanation of the now more complex and layered subject of study and the nature of the relationship which has uncovered it so far. It should also suggest *particular* questions and difficulties which renewed and more unconventional methods can seek to clarify. There is thus the possibility of a circular development between a progressively more specified 'theoretical confession' and the specific contradictions and tensions of fieldwork on to, in the return sweep, reconstituted forms of theory and back to the specifics of the fieldwork relation. This is the project of producing, finally, a fuller explanatory presentation of the concrete.

I am not necessarily arguing that the final account should show the several stages of this often tortuous process, or that these stages are necessarily always self-conscious: I would argue that it is something of this sort, often unconscious or even denied, which has taken place in the research work of those 'naturalistic' accounts which do have explanatory power. Nor am I denying that, as in the more classical notion of the Marxist method, this circular movement cannot occur after fieldwork is finished or upon secondary data, through the principles of search and selectivity on existing or received materials. What I am arguing, in the context of 'qualitative' methods, is that significant data are collected not through the purity or scientificism of its method, but through the status of the method as a social relationship, and specifically through the moments of crisis in that relationship and its to-be-discovered pattern of what is/what is not shared: the contradictions within and between these things. And, furthermore, that where the fieldwork is really extensive or where the researcher, in whatever form, can theorize, so to speak, on his/her feet, for all the difficulties and disorientations, reflexivity can allow the progressive constitution of the concrete in relation to theory, not merely as an analytic protocol but as a dynamic, dialectical method. This can give a concentration and an obstinate capacity to penetrate through successive layers of 'blank' data in the pursuit of particular themes not available to other methods. Not only the quality of the data, nor even its (however qualified) capacity to 'surprise', but this potential, at least, for a cyclic control and focus of method in the rich veins of 'lived' contradiction is what can most distinguish the 'qualitative' approach.

On technicism

The notion of a reflexive methodology, then, takes us beyond a simple concern with techniques of data-gathering. It is often stated as a truism that forms of data collection and analytic procedures are profoundly interconnected. I am arguing that it is precisely a *theoretical* interest which induces the researcher to develop certain kinds of technique, to make comparative forays, to invent or invert methodological canons, to select certain 'problems' for analytical explication. Though techniques are important, and though we should be concerned with their 'validity', they can never stand in the place of a theoretical awareness and interest arising out of *the recognition of one's role in a social relationship and its variable patterning.* Without this theoretical quickening, the techniques merely record uncritically only the apparent outward face of an external 'reality'.

We should resist, therefore, the hegemonizing tendency of technique. It seeks to take command whenever there is uncertainty. It disguises the creative potential of uncertainty. In particular, we should deconstruct the portmanteau, heavily mystified notion of PO, whose mere invocation and taxonomical description seem to guarantee the quality of an account. We should break down and detail its parts, along with a number of other techniques, to give us a flexible range of particular techniques to be drawn upon according to our theoretical needs. Within its spectrum the following techniques can be specified:

participation
observation
participation as observer
observation as participant
just 'being around'
group discussion
recorded group discussion
unfocused interview
recorded unfocused interview.

It is clearly misleading to think of these techniques as constituting one blanket methodology. Techniques lower down this list, for example, are more likely to be applied to a phenomenon from the past (cf. the development of 'oral history'). A particular strength can be gained by a more self-conscious combination of methods, where different modes of data collection, used at different times, give important cross-checks, as well as indicating the particular layered configuration of important contradictions. All of these techniques are relevant to the principles of 'qualitative' methodology, and each should be rigorously thought through in its particular research context.

Conclusion

Traditional sociology, then, provides a useful starting-point. But we must submit its methods to a rigorous screening to make explicit the denied theoretical account and to remove the hidden tendency towards positivism. We must liberate the whole notion of 'methodology' and argue, finally, for a recognition of the reflexive relationship of researchers to their subjects.

6 Green Farm Scout Camp*

Roger Grimshaw

Having just entered the troop, I had my first lesson in the niceties of Scouting's social relations on the first night of the camp – Friday. It was only a week since I had met the leaders, and our acquaintance was still quite recent. This explains the following incident, in which I was 'put right' by Bruce. Here I learned the spatial rules which underpin leader control.

Just before we all went to bed Bruce, Tim and I were sitting in Bruce's tent chatting when, somewhat lost for conversation, I noticed that the groundsheet was folded back from the door of the tent. So I remarked that it was a good thing that the groundsheet did not reach the entrance to the tent, since this would save people from trampling on the groundsheet when they entered. Bruce immediately responded in a firm tone. There was a rule in Scouting, he said, that boys never entered the Scouters' tents. I gave ground by saying something to the effect that I understood what he meant. It was, of course, quite understandable that Bruce should see a non-uniformed stranger as a person liable to make errors and that he should be alert to the possibility of correcting him, should the need arise. What Bruce was reminding me of sums up a whole (largely unspoken) set of rules about the relations between leaders and lads. While the leader has the power to find out what is happening in a tent occupied by lads, the same power is denied to the lads in relation to the leaders. Nor is it possible for a leader to invite lads into his tent except for special reasons.

While these rules are embodied mainly in practice and reveal themselves only in responses to their breach, they are nonetheless powerful indicators of the field of social relations operating at camp. Where there is a need actively to enrol some of the boys as agents of leadership for a particular purpose this can be signified, in rare instances, by an invitation to enter tents within the leader's terrain.[1] The Patrol Leaders (PLs) are, of course, the most likely people to be given this privilege. Pat was observed to invite them into his tent to give them information, to outline special tasks or indicate the future course of camp activities. They would also be told, in this context, about the running totals achieved in the patrol competition. In so far as the leader's tent belongs to the leadership's sphere of action, the choice of this situation to remind the PLs of their responsibilities is an apt one. We can see that the rule, as enunciated by Bruce, was not to be interpreted entirely literally;

*This is an extract from Roger Grimshaw's unpublished Ph.D thesis, 'The Social Meaning of Scouting: Ethnographic and Contextual Analysis Relating to a Midlands Industrial City'.

few common-sense rules are to be viewed in that way. There were tacit assumptions behind his remark which came out in the course of the camp, the purpose of the remark being to inform an outsider of the basic parameters of camp relations.

Boys would come up for information or advice in a casual way while we were engaged on some task of our own, such as cooking or cleaning. In a culture which stresses the participation of leaders and boys in common activities, however, it is the function of boundary maintenance to 'hold the line' against incursions which might undermine the ultimate responsibility and control of the leaders. The participation of leaders in the life of the boys was for the most part utilitarian (finding out about something, sorting out a problem) and always directly connected with the programme of the camp and its activities. So a social boundary remained between the two groups. This is the reason why the leaders remain leaders, and it is up to them to see that they do not deviate from the line of patterned interaction except in certain negotiated circumstances. Pat, Bruce and Tim seemed to constitute a leadership group because they constructed their own separation from the boys by the maintenance of physical and social boundaries.

The status and role of the PLs was partially evident at the camp, in terms of certain special responsibilities accorded to them. But these responsibilities were here marked by their subordination to the central planning and regulating function of the adult leadership. For instance, the three PLs were given the task of arranging clues on a 'treasure hunt' by concealing messages at various points around the grounds of the farm. The part played by the PLs in actually initiating formal activities was clearly a very small one. Older boys were typically likely to shape the pattern of long-running games once the leaders had started them; for example, one morning a marathon game of football went on after the leaders had lost interest. On an excursion I noticed that it was Wyn, an extrovert PL, who seemed to hold a pre-eminent position; he independently started a stalking game on the grass by the pond, in which all the younger ones joined. Wyn, I later found, was one of the most popular of the PLs with both lads and leaders. Even before the camp I noticed Pat take Wyn aside to tell him to look after one of the boys in his patrol. Pat's action signified their mutual understanding of the 'paternal' responsibilities of leadership. The need for such a role stemmed from the inexperience of the younger lads, quite a number of whom had not camped before.

The members of the camp took part, as usual, in a continuous patrol competition over the weekend. This competition was based on the leaders' evaluation of the patrol's performance in all relevant activities of the camp; in the first place, the competition revolved around the turn-out of kit and the cleanliness of the patrol's site and equipment at morning inspection. Full inspection is the most drastic concession of space made to the leadership by the boys. Not only is the patrol tent open to their eyes but all personal kit is laid out in open view, while the lads stand in a row before it. The whole of this inspection was organized on a patrol basis, so that the performance of individuals, whether good, bad or indifferent was significant only in so far as it affected the differential positions of the patrols in the competition. There was, in general, less emphasis on smart uniform, clean shoes and so on in the military manner than on the labour-oriented signs of good camping – properly brailed tents, clean utensils, a litter-free site. However, on the occasion of full kit inspection the leaders singled out for praise those lads who had conscientiously arranged their kit in a precise, meaningful order – for example, hat at the top, clothes in the middle, shoes at the bottom of the groundsheet. In my own view, the standard was, as usual, very punctilious, with very few differences between patrols that the evaluation could highlight. It indicated that the inexperience and youth of the boys did not detract from their assimilation of the standards of cleanliness and so on of the milieu. The results of the inspections were the main visible subject of evaluation by the leaders. But this did not rule out evaluation of other things, notably the 'effort' put in by individuals when participating in certain activities. It was customary for Pat to award marks to the patrol who got all its members to the flagpole before any other when the troop was called together. Thus evaluation and competition were harnessed by Pat to the norms both of labour and of social discipline operative in the special context of Scouting.

The Scouter who here most visibly embodied disciplinary and organizational authority was Pat. In short, he decided what should be done next; he was the one who addressed the boys as a body; he took the main responsibility for the camp's arrangements. The predominance of this aspect of the Scouter's role in the case of Pat can be contrasted with the different emphases of Bruce's approach. This difference corresponds to the difference between traditionalist and fraternalist styles respectively.

Bruce emphasized, in effect, the creative and productive side of his role. It was, for instance, seen as his responsibility to adjust the calor gas stoves when they became temperamental. One afternoon he casually built a temporary chair by lashing together a few left-over spars and poles. On the other hand, he kept more in the background when the troop was gathered together for some purpose and minimized his public visibility in this way. Bruce displayed his ability to exert practical mastery when we had need of firewood on one occasion. The best kind of firewood is dead wood found on the tree rather than on the ground, since the wood needs to be dry. As we were cooking on calor gas stoves for the most part, there was only one occasion when firewood had to be obtained, and the technique for doing so was revealed to me by Bruce. First, one makes a 'monkey-knot' at the end of a length of rope; one then has a rounded knot of rope which, when it is thrown up towards the tree branches, will catch in the interstices of the branches. By levering on the knot it is possible to break off dead branches, having assessed likely candidates by their absence of leaves. This technique belongs to the lore of backwoodsmen who master a hostile environment by the application of ingenuity and a few simple tools and pieces of equipment. Bruce was the custodian of this kind of skill in the troop, and he took the largest part in the gathering of wood in this ingenious manner. Soon he was climbing other trees with an axe and raining branches down on the wooded glade below. The manner of his involvement in these practical skills recalled the self-reliance of Baden-Powell's *Scouting for Boys*, with its hints on becoming a backwoods artisan. He turned his knowledge to account by making a 'commando' rope walk, tying parallel ropes, one above the other, between two trees – later even crossing them over. An informal toy was thus created for the lads, one with objective connotations of athletic physical mastery. For Bruce it seemed that the role of backwoodsman and pioneer had a simple meaning, tied to self-expression and practical mastery rather than to any overwhelming desire to organize. Technical mastery was typically associated with the fraternalist style.

Pat represented a different aspect of the Scouter's role – the capacity to manage and direct, to organize the activities of the campers in a co-ordinated way. Pat was willing to take on the responsibility that this task involved and carried it through with few signs of an inability to cope. He had, however, none of the calculated reserve which leads to accusations of stuffiness, formality and so on. This command was reinforced by Pat's bearing and appearance; a tall, strong young man, he gave a powerful impression of the physical competence and vigour which indeed characterized all of the leaders. As the tallest, Pat possessed the 'natural' appearance of supreme leader in the situation. He had sometimes a way of standing four-square to his audience with chin uplifted, feet planted apart and hands behind the back, which seemed to be an attempt to endow his authority with the stamp of physical superiority. This was the most 'artificial' aspect of his public persona, though it coincided with his stress on decisive authority. Pat's bearing had a self-awareness on occasions that was absent from the bearing of the other leaders and, indeed, of the lads. Perhaps he learned that repertoire of physical attitudes in his experience as a football referee, that classical exponent of gestural dramaturgy! It turned out, in fact, that the entire male membership of his family (father and three brothers) were trained football referees. On the last night of the camp Pat organized a football competition on a knock-out basis, in which the leaders took part. Pat created for the occasion, and punctiliously enforced, a special rule: swearing meant that you could be sent off, as at least one boy was. One could see that Pat was used to the position of referee, and that he had taken the opportunity of the game to introduce, for the occasion, a certain puritanism, without having shown a large amount of zeal in that direction previously. One of the objective effects of the no-swearing rule was to link performance at a play-oriented activity with observance of traditional 'decent' norms.

One of my first observations of Pat's style of leadership came when I was faced with a discipline problem of my own. I was with a group of boys, attempting to show them how to construct a paper balloon. There was a noise; I looked up from my work and saw a biggish boy called Tip hit another boy fairly firmly. I called Pat, saying, 'There's been a bit of a fracas!' and then told Tip to explain to Pat what he'd done. He mumbled something contritely amid a general silence. Pat told him and the victim of the blow to come outside. A minute later the lads returned. Much later on in the day Pat remarked to me that he felt Tip was a bit inclined to be violent. He displays his skill in concrete leadership by grasping that, in the absence of any general problem with the group of boys as a whole, it is best to 'take out' the problem pair and deal with their grievances concretely, rather than start an abstract harangue in front of an already cowed audience. Pat's style is thus concrete and particular, adjusting to the situation's requirements without losing disciplinary grip.

The different styles of leadership exemplified here correspond to two necessary aspects of the Scout leader's role. On the one hand, Pat's orientations refer to the function of active social control; on the other hand, the activities of Bruce represent the technical requirements of Scout camping activities and the practical skills necessary to their expressive realization.

The balloon construction exemplified the meaning of creative activities for the boys. Leonard had put up the idea as a general one for the half-dozen troops camping on the site. The purpose behind it was to create an opportunity for all the troops to witness a little *divertissement* in the evening, as the balloons were launched. Pat decided to give me the job of explaining to a group of lads how it was to be made and to supervise them as they did it. I suppose the 'arty-crafty' implications of the project made it appear suitable for me; there was no risk of anything untoward occurring, and it happened that I had been the first to peruse the plans. The main problem, I immediately apprehended, was that there was going to be little opportunity for revisions or corrections as we worked, so the project needed to be supervised. But I hoped to let the lads take on definite parts of the project and thus participate in its making. Ensconced as we were in the old farm stables, I noticed what one or two other troops were doing and followed the example set for me. In practice it meant that a Scouter made the balloon with the assistance of boys seconded from each of the patrols. Only one or two boys could be working on it at one time, so there was a problem of occupying the rest, who drifted in and out talking to one another. Eventually, despite the initial interest of some of the lads, I was left with only two – Tip, who has been mentioned before, and Lance; these two were Assistant Patrol Leaders (APLs) and therefore the oldest of the original bunch. Tip spent some time discontentedly rapping on the keys of an abandoned piano in a random manner, while Lance brightly asked me some intelligent questions about what I was doing with the troop. In truth, the whole activity must have been rather boring for them, partly because of the limited resources available compared with the number of lads. This reaction led to the eventual withdrawal of most of them from the 'place of work'. That their attitude was understood by Pat was, I think, clear; he made no attempt to harangue them for their lack of perseverance and himself assisted in the latter part of the work. I think we can assume the existence of shared understandings of what is and what is not rewarding in the spectrum of Scout activities. What set out to be a creative activity thus bore little relation to the concerns of the boys, not because it was distasteful but because it lacked an immediate appeal to the imagination.

After dinner we went back to the project to fasten the 'engine' of the balloon, a rag soaked in methylated spirit and attached to a cross piece. The whole balloon had to be examined for tears and loose edges so that patches could be applied. Meanwhile, we began to inflate our balloon by placing under the air hole a lighted gas stove. It was at this point that the project came to life for me (and evidently for others) as the various troops made their final preparations before the launching.

Instead of a passive pattern of paper shapes, the object had now become rounded and voluminous, about 1.5 metres high and tricked out in the troop's distinctive colours. The whole activity thus became implicitly redefined in terms of the cultural connotations of flight. Here, then, we were moving into the mythical world, novel, spectacular, which was suggested by the results of a creative activity in the distinctly improvisatory Scouting tradition. The members of the troops concerned gathered in the main field at Green Farm as dusk approached, and the leaders of the boys took it upon themselves to inflate their balloons, swelling them out with the hot air of gas stoves and finally launching them into the air, the smoke from the ignited rag at the bottom dwindling up into the balloons as they rose, one after the other, into the still air. At this stage there was a great deal of enthusiasm among the boys - precisely, it seemed to me, through the recognition of the *mythos* of flight represented by these collective objects. It was thus in the moment of consumption that the activity gained a meaning it had not possessed previously; it was then that the imagination was seized, rather than in the routines of production. In most cases the balloons floated for a couple of hundred metres over fields and fences pursued by hordes of shouting boys, were retrieved and, thanks to the exceptionally favourable weather conditions, relaunched as twilight turned into darkness. (I should add that this experience seemed to fire a certain enthusiasm for the project later on; for instance, at summer camp the older lads who had been at Green Farm made a balloon that, owing to weather conditions, unfortunately keeled over and caught fire.)

The conditions for a successful creative activity were thus founded in the moment of consumption, which thereafter prompted future production. The project was successful, but only in that it had a spectacular *dénouement*; its beginnings were distinctly unpromising and were quickly defined as a chore. We can learn from the reception of this activity something about the methods of Scouting and their relevance to its subjects. First, labour in Scouting operates necessarily by means of improvised 'pioneer' materials - bits of paper and wood in our case. Second, it posits creativity in a form of labour and enjoyment in an immediate consumption of the product of labour, but in practice the 'moment of production', even in such a simple pattern of creative activity, remains somewhat separate and apart from the 'moment of consumption' unless the producers possess an idea of the product adequate to their requirements. In other words, the project was not acceptable to the boys until positive results appeared and a satisfactory outcome could be envisaged. Third, voluntarily or otherwise, Scouters played a bigger substantive role in facilitating, even performing, creative activity than one might have assumed. Fourth, the connotations of this particular product of labour (which generally defines it as creative, as enjoyment) concerned a phenomenon with no substantive connection with the romance of the backwoods and the *veldt*, the territory of Baden-Powell, but a good deal of similarity. The balloon represented the 'frontier' technology of the early pioneers of aviation, in fact, the counterparts of the cowboy and the frontier scout, who figure in the Baden-Powell romance. In general, the task of the Scout leaders is to match the form of the activity with the imaginative life of their members; in this case the boys were more attracted by the consumption of the product, while the leaders were ready to fill the role of producers, in accord with the structure of avuncularity.[2] The latter regularly comes into play when novel or exceptional conditions arise for boys in the performance of work. However, the project represents a cultural enterprise in which both are imaginatively engaged – the celebration of a simple, practical mastery. This takes the form of a handicraft object, whose patterning evokes a typical, youthful, masculine interest in aviation. The simple immediacy of the method of production and consumption is thus typically joined to a specific imaginative effect, which derives from the repertoire of possibilities set up by the founding romance. Hence the concrete and particular forms of task usually can be coherently linked to the structure of the romance. In our terms, the simple immediacy of the method is here associated with pioneer skills, while the imaginative effect draws on pioneer and reconnaissance themes. It is the idea of the product or end-in-view that draws spontaneous interest in Scout labour tasks.

It has been indicated that the particular concern of the symbolic activity here did not coincide with the conventional backwoods form of Scouting. But there was one activity at the camp that did call on the techniques and evoke the imaginative connotations of the backwoods. This was the occasion when the whole troop cooked a meal 'backwoods-style' (without utensils, that is). It was the convention of backwoods cooking that made it necessary to leave the calor gas stoves and to build a big fire in order to accommodate all the individual cooks – for the technique lends itself to individual self-reliance. This feature again provides a close mediating link between labour and product, because it is the individual who cooks by himself, and what he cooks, in principle, he eats. Everyone was therefore drawn into the activity. Little equipment is allowed in the technique, so as to point up the 'backwoods' aura. The standard technique is reminiscent of the barbecue: green sticks (used as skewers for grilling) and aluminium foil (used as a cover for baking food) were the only items of equipment. The position of responsibility that the leaders defined as their own was illustrated by the fact that it was they who built up the fire and oversaw it, not the PLs or the lads. Instruction in the technique of cooking, however, passed 'invisibly', by example and imitation, without a phase of a general talk by the leaders to the collectivity. This activity was the clearest index, during the camp, of a traditional Scouting approach and style. As the wood fire had been replaced in the troop's repertoire by the gas stove, backwoods cooking distinctively evoked the atmosphere of the founding text, *Scouting for Boys*.

Hence the camp saw instances of two different forms of creative activity – the balloon construction and the backwoods cooking. While the balloon recalled the primitive days of flight, the cooking symbolized the primitive romance of the backwoods. The cooking has a highly traditional character, which yokes it, in a literal bond, to that form of Scouting which developed in the hands of its founder. Thus Pat's traditionalist style often favoured this suitable programme item. The oversight of (and participation in) these craft tasks by leaders was observed on other occasions, especially when the tasks were unfamiliar or required considerable strength, as some projects do. This sharing of tasks recalls the structure of avuncularity referred to earlier.

Observation and interaction during the weekend produced some interesting data which may contribute to a more in-depth account of informal or subterranean values in Scouting.

Sunday afternoon had a certain desultory quality, once the troop had returned from their activities outside the camp. The weather was very hot, baking the grass to a stiff dryness. Shirts had been discarded in the attempt to mitigate the effects of the heat. As I was casually standing about, with the Scouters by my side, I noticed a group of lads approach, one or two of them carrying billycans. They walked towards us, laughing and joking. Suddenly I noticed that Freddie, an APL, was coming towards me, a bucket of water in his hand. I suddenly felt myself isolated. With a smile he showed me the water in the bucket, and I smiled and looked unperturbed, thinking I was safe. Suddenly he made a move and, unable to step out of the way quickly enough, I was drenched with water. Simultaneously, the other lads attacked. I immediately raced after Freddie's rapidly retreating back. I knew that I had to make a positive, physical response to his provocation; what I had underestimated was the speed of his flight. I finally had to give up the chase after about thirty seconds, when a Scouter from a different troop suddenly warned us away from the region of his car. I had thought to retain my adult status, my symbolic invulnerability, and failed, while the echo of this sense of status made me ashamed to be treated by the Scouter as if I was a boy. Freddie had given me a challenge, thrown down the gauntlet, and engaged me in a conflict of physical mastery; I had accepted the invitation to enter his own terrain and, for the moment, had lost. Thereafter we developed something of a relationship out of this incident because he teased me about it.

The water fight at this moment became a general conflict, with groups of laughing lads running around, water canisters in their hands. But immediately the fight developed into a struggle between the adults and the boys. Each side tried to get hold of the supplies of water and store up 'ammunition'; then there would be running skirmishes, with attempts to isolate and then drench those who flagged behind. While the leaders enjoyed the better supplies, the lads were more numerous, so that the fight became a defensive battle for the most part, as far as we leaders were concerned. The lads enjoyed themselves immensely, in so far as the special status of the leaders, their privileged role in the troop, was undermined for the period of the game, and the role relationship became the site of a competitive struggle on the distinctive terrain of the boys.

Later in the day, after supper, a good-humoured rough-and-tumble developed on the field, with leaders on one side and boys on the other. This time, however, it was started by the Scouters, notably Pat. A good deal of chasing and wrestling ensued; lads rolled over on the grass, trying to pin down the leaders. Then unused to this sort of game, I chose to wrestle with the least threatening of the boys. While the whole conflict was good-humoured, the incident constituted wrestling 'for real', in so far as certain physical aims associated with wrestling were actively pursued. There was no punching or gouging, again in accordance with the rules of wrestling.

Only a couple of minor injuries were sustained on both sides during the fifteen minutes that the event lasted. This event corresponds very much to the dynamic of the last-mentioned incident, in that the theme of physical mastery prevailed. On reflection, perhaps we might conclude that it was the water fight whose form equalized the leaders more effectively than the wrestling, since their advantage of strength came out most clearly there. Thus the leader, Pat, actually initiated the wrestling, in which his physical strength and height enabled him to match the efforts of two or three lads. The young lads, through the mechanism of the game (especially the completely informal game) were able to engage the leaders in direct competitive strife on a symbolic ground of their own. The responses of Pat and the rest of the young leaders to the invitations of the boys demonstrated that the organization of roles at their command possessed an element of boyish sporting aggression in which the differences of the respective statuses of the boys and controllers were temporarily suspended, to the satisfaction of all concerned.

7 Housewives and the mass media*

Dorothy Hobson

Mass communication, in the form of radio and television, has emerged as an important aspect of the day-to-day experience of the women in the study.[1] Television and radio are never mentioned as spare-time or leisure activities but are located by the women as integral parts of their day. (The exception to this is the television viewing which is done after the children are in bed, but even then the period is not completely free for the woman because she still has to provide drinks or food if her husband wants them.) There is a separation between the consumption of radio and television, but both provide crucial elements in the experience and management of their lives.

Radio

You've got a friend, the happy sound of Radio 1. (Radio 1 jingle)

I have various people in mind. One is a man working in a small garage where perhaps there are two or three mechanics clonking around with motor cars but have the music on. And they're enjoying it as a background. And then there is this dreaded housewife figure [*sic*] who I think of as someone who, perhaps last year or two years ago, was a secretary working for a firm, who is now married and has a child. She wants music that will keep her happy and on the move. [Derek Chinnery, Head of Radio 1, in an interview published in *Melody Maker*, July 1976, quoted in *Happy Birthday Radio 1*, BBC Publications 1977]

'Dreaded' or not, the housewives in this study do listen to Radio 1 and find the experience enjoyable. The radio, for the most part, is listened to during the day while they are engaged in domestic labour, housework and child care. As Anne said, 'It's on in the background all the time.' In some cases switching on the radio is part of the routine of beginning the day; it is, in fact, the first *boundary* in the working day. In terms of the 'structurelessness' of the experience of housework, the time boundaries provided by radio are important in the women's own division of their time.

Lorna We do have the radio on all day. You know, from the time we get up till

*This is an extract from Dorothy Hobson's unpublished MA thesis, 'A Study of Working-Class Women at Home: Femininity, Domesticity and Maternity'.

the time the tele comes back on. I usually put it on at 4 o'clock for the kids' tele . . . .

Linda I listen to the radio. I put it on as soon as I get up.

Anne Six o'clock I get up (laughs), er, put on the radio full blast so that me husband'll get up . . . *

The constant reference to time during the programmes on Radio 1 also helps to structure the time sequences of the work which women perform while they listen to the radio. Programmes are self-definitional, as *The Breakfast Show, Mid-morning Programme,* which includes *Coffee Break* at 11 a.m. At the time of the study Tony Blackburn was running the morning show (9 a.m. - 12 noon), in which he had the 'Tiny Tots' spot at 11 a.m., during which a record was played for children and Blackburn attempted to teach a nursery rhyme to the children listening while the 'mums' had a coffee break. During David Hamilton's afternoon programme (2 p.m. - 5 p.m.) the 'Tea at Three' spot is included, when once more women are encouraged to 'put their feet up'. The disc jockeys (DJs) use points of reference within the expected daily routines of their listeners, and some of these references are responded to by the women in the study. The programmes which are listened to are Radio 1 and BRMB local radio, the former being the more popular. Responses to questions about radio are always given in terms of the disc jockey who introduces the programme, with the records referred to in a secondary capacity.

Pat

P. I like Radio 1. Tony Blackburn. I think he's corny but I think he's good. Dave Lee Travis I like and Noel Edmunds. Noel Edmunds, I think he's absolutely fantastic . . . .

D. So do you prefer the radio?

P. During the day, yes.

D. Would you have the radio on while you were doing housework?

P. Oh yes, yes.

D. Why do you like the people you like?

P. Erm . . their personality – it comes over on the radio. Noel Edmunds, I think he's really fantastic, you know, the blunders he makes, you know, I like (inaudible). I think he's really lovely (laughs).

D. And do you do your housework at the same time?

P. Oh yes.

Anne

A. I listen to BRMB, you know, that's quite a good programme. I like listening to the people that phone in, erm . . I like the conversations.

**Key to transcripts*

. . . or (pause)	pause
( )	non-verbal communication, e.g. (laughs)
(( ))	phatic communication, e.g. ((Mm))
. .	speaker interrupted

D. Why do you think that is?

A. Er . . I suppose it's 'cos I'm on me own.

D. Is it the music as well that you like or . . . .?

A. Yes, 'cos I find that nearly all my records are a bit old-fashioned and I like to hear a bit of the modern music. ((Yes)) I don't want to get way behind the times, you know.

The predominance of presenters or DJs in the respondents' reactions to radio programmes can be seen from various aspects. First, it is necessary for the personality of the disc jockey to be a prominent feature in the programme, since all the records which are played throughout the day on Radio 1 are the same; the only variation which exists is in the chatter between records which the disc jockeys provide. Inevitably, then, it is their ability to form a relationship with their audience which gives the disc jockeys their appeal. The disc jockeys have become personalities in their own right, as have the presenters of television current affairs programmes, and the increasing professionalism and development of the necessary features and components of the successful disc jockey could be seen as analogous with the professionalization of other television presenters. As early as the first year of the existence of Radio 1, which began in November 1967, the following point was noted: 'It soon became clear that Radio 1 DJs were going to be accorded almost as much attention by the media as the Royal Family.' (BBC/Everest 1977) The disc jockeys are prominent as a structural feature of the production process of these programmes, and it is they who direct the discourse of the radio programmes towards their known audience – in this case the housewives. Secondly, the women respond to that notion of themselves as 'feminine domestic subjects' of radio discourse which is presented by the disc jockeys. In this study I have concentrated on the reactions of the women to the disc jockeys rather than on the production process of the media messages.[2]

Within the overall picture of isolation which has emerged in the lives of the women in this study, the disc jockey can be seen as having the function of providing the missing 'company' of another person in the lives of the women. As well as helping to combat isolation, it is not too far fetched to see the DJ as also playing the role of a sexual fantasy-figure in the lives of the women who listen. Pat's comments about Noel Edmunds (above) are certainly not limited to his role as someone who breaks the isolation in her life; it includes references to his attractiveness and physical appearance, although she does not make this explicit. Nevertheless, my *reading* of the role of the DJs is that they play the role of a safe, though definitely sexually attractive man, in the lives of the women. The responses to other DJs confirm this assumption. Tony Blackburn is talked about more in terms of the content of his programme and his manner of presentation than in terms of endearment or enthusiasm. However, Blackburn himself obviously realizes the potential for fantasy relationships with his audience. When he was suffering from a throat infection, which made his voice sound rather husky, he said: 'I hope I am not turning you ladies on too much. I know your husbands have left for work, it's you and I together, kids.' (Recorded from Radio 1, autumn 1977)

Blackburn is a disc jockey whom it is impossible to ignore. Rather like *Crossroads*, the women either like him or hate him, but rarely do they remain indifferent to him. Blackburn himself provides interesting comments on his own views on radio and pop music, describing his show as 'a pleasant bit of entertainment in the background if you like – inane chatter. I think there's room for a station that comes on and is full of a lot of people talking a load of nonsense'. (*Guardian*, 9 January 1976)

Fortunately for him, he does not have to listen to his own programme for, as he says, 'It would drive me mad if I had to physically sit down and listen to David Hamilton's show, or mine, for that matter.' (ibid) And fortunately for the women in this study, they do not have to sit and listen either; they can treat the programme as background chatter. But if by chance they happen to listen to what Tony Blackburn has to say, they will be subjected to an onslaught of chatter which definitely reinforces the ideology of the sexual division of labour and places women firmly in their 'correct' place – in the home. It is in the direct comments which he makes about the records and current topics of interest that Blackburn reveals the depth of his conservatism. The 'working man', strikers, punk rockers, women involved in divorce actions, (in the wake of his own recent divorce) all warrant criticism from him. Women who are playing their traditional role as housewives and mothers constantly earn praise from him. In one programme in which he was promoting a record by Nancy Wilson (which was supposedly sung by a woman who had enjoyed a 'liberated' life, yet still yearned for the love and security of a husband and family and wanted to tell her 'sisters' of the truth of her misspent life), Blackburn fervently 'plugged' the record and consistently reminded his listeners of the 'truth' of the theme, saying, 'If you understand this, ladies, you understand everything.' In case his listeners did not fully get the message of the song, he took the trouble to explain it, using his own interpretation: 'I hope you understood these lyrics. Nothing is more important, no matter what the press and the media tell you, there is nothing more wonderful than bringing up a child, nothing more difficult either.' (Recorded from Radio 1, autumn 1977)

Perhaps Tony Blackburn does represent an extreme form of the reinforcement of the ideology of domesticity of the housebound listeners of Radio 1, but far from providing background chatter which can be ignored, he obviously intends his comments to be heard by his audience – and he knows who his audience is. The reinforcement of the dominant ideology of domesticity is definitely a function of the encoded media messages emanating from Radio 1.

The disc jockey, as well as providing relief from isolation, links the isolated individual woman with the knowledge that there are others in the same position.[3] Similarly, this can be seen as a functional effect of 'phone-in' programmes. One of the women says: 'I like listening to the people that phone in. I like the conversations . . . . I suppose it's 'cos I'm on me own.' These programmes not only provide contact with the 'outside' world; they also reinforce the privatized isolation by reaffirming the consensual position – there are thousands of other women in the same situation, in a sort of 'collective isolation'.

Radio can be seen, then, as providing women with a musical reminder of their leisure activities before they married.[4] It also, as they say, keeps them up to date with new records. Since they do not have any spare money to buy records, this is an important way in which they can listen to music. Since listening to music and dancing are the leisure activities which they would most like to pursue, radio is also a substitute for the real world of music and discos which they have lost. Also, it provides a crucial relief from their isolation. The chatter of the disc jockey may appear inane and trivial, but the popularity of radio, both in national and local terms and in the responses of the women in this study, would appear to suggest that it fulfils certain functions in providing music to keep them 'happy and on the move'. Radio creates its own audience through its constant reference to forthcoming programmes and items within programmes. As the jingle at the beginning of this section suggests, the women in this study do appear to regard Radio 1 as a friend, and they certainly view the disc jockeys as important means of negotiating or managing the tensions caused by the isolation in their lives.

Television – 'two worlds'

Linda No, I never watch the news, never!

The ideology of a masculine and a feminine world of activities and interests and the separation of those gender-specific interests is never more explicitly expressed than in the women's reactions and responses to television programmes. Here both class- and gender-specific differences are of vital importance, in terms of both which programmes the women choose to watch or reject and their definition and selection of what are appropriately masculine and feminine programmes and topics. Also, they select television programmes much more consciously than radio programmes. This must partly be a consequence of the fact that they have more freedom during the evenings, and they can make active choices because they are no longer subject to constant interruptions caused by their responsibility for domestic labour and child care. This is in contrast to their listening to the radio during the day, when radio programmes are selected primarily as 'easy listening', a background while they do their housework or look after the children.

There is an *active* choice of programmes which are understood to constitute the 'woman's world', coupled with a complete *rejection* of programmes which are presenting the 'man's world'. However, there is also an acceptance that the 'real' or 'man's world' is important, and the 'right' of their husbands to watch these programmes is respected: but it is not a world with which the women in this study wanted to concern themselves. In fact, the 'world', in terms of what is constructed as of 'news' value, is seen as both alien and hostile to the values of the women. For them television programmes appear to fall into two distinct categories. The programmes which they watch and enjoy are: comedy series *(Selwyn Froggitt, Are You Being Served?)*; soap operas *(Emmerdale Farm, The Cedar Tree, Rooms, Crown Court* and, predominantly, *Crossroads* and *Coronation Street)*; American television films *(MacMillan and Wife, Dr Welby, Colombo)*; light entertainment and quiz shows *(Whose Baby?, Mr and Mrs)*; and films. All these programmes could be broadly termed as 'entertaining' rather than 'educational and informative'. The programmes which are actively rejected deal with what the women designate the 'real world' or 'man's world', and these predominantly cluster around the news, current affairs programmes *(Panorama, This Week)*, scientific programmes *(Tomorrow's World)*, the subject-matter of politics or war, including films about war, and, to a lesser extent, documentary programmes. Selected documentaries will be viewed as long as the *subject-matter* is identified as of feminine interest. The following are extracts from responses to questions about television, and it can be seen from these that there is a clear distinction between what men and women watch and what is seen to be the *right* of the husband to watch (news and current affairs programmes).

Anne

D. What programmes do you watch on television?

A. Er. . *Crown Court, Rooms, Cedar Tree, Emmerdale Farm, Mr and Mrs.* What else is there? *Dr Welby.* Then there's a film on of a Friday.

D. This is all on ITV, isn't it?

A. (Long pause while she thinks of other programmes) Yes, er . . yes, that's another programme. *Whose Baby?*

D. There's a film on on Mondays as well, isn't there?

A. No, no . . . oh, yes, there is. It's *Mystery Movie.* I don't like, I'm not very interested in them, you know. I sort of half-watch them.

D. So it's more the short series. ((Yes.)) What do you like about the programmes that you watch?

A. Something to look forward to the next day 'cos most of them are serials.

D. Do you like them to . . Which do you like the best, which type?

A. Er, I like *The Cedar Tree* more than *Emmerdale Farm*. I'm not really keen on that. I only watch it through habit. Er, more romantic, I think, you know, there's sort of, er, family life, that is, more than *Emmerdale Farm.* I don't know, I . . . something about that isn't so good.

D. That only really takes you up to tea time, so do you watch the television at night?

A. Yes, in between half-five and eight, that's me busiest time, feed him, change him, sometimes bath him. I don't bath him very often, erm, get Richard's dinner and I always clean up straight away, the washing up, and then I get everything settled and that takes me up to about 8 o'clock, 'cos I stop at half-past six to watch *Crossroads* (laughs). And then from 8 onwards I just sit and watch the box (laughs).

D. Why do you like *Crossroads*?

A. Just that you like to know what's going to happen next, you know. I mean they're terrible actors, I know that, and I just see through that, you know.

I just, now and then I think, 'Oh my God, that's silly,' you know, but it's not the acting I'm interested in, it's what's going on. I suppose I'm nosy . . . .

D. The time then between that – do you watch the news?

A. I watch a little bit of it, erm (pause). I don't really like the news much because it's all politics, generally and British Leyland out on strike again, and this and that. I like to hear the news things if, er, – if there's been a murder, I know that sounds terrible, but I like to hear – 'Oh what's happening next, what have they found out?' That sort of news I like, you know – gossip. ((Yes.))

D. Do you ever watch documentaries?

A. Now and then I find an interesting one. I watched one the other night about people who'd got diseases.

Lorna

L. We have the radio on all day, you know, from the time we get up till the time the tele comes back on. I usually put it on at 4 o'clock for the kids' tele and they watch all the children's programmes, and it might come back off at 6 and it might not go back on again till half-past seven.

D. So you don't watch the news?

L. No, I never watch the news, never.

D. Why don't you watch it?

L. I don't like it, I don't like to hear about people dying and things like that. I think about it afterwards and I can't sleep at all. Like when I watched that thing, *World at War*, and I watched it once and all I could see were people all over the place, you know, heads and no arms and that and at night I could not sleep. I can't ask him to turn it over 'cos he likes it, so I go in the kitchen till it's finished.

It is clear that the news, current affairs, political programmes and scientific programmes, together with portrayals of war (real or in the guise of war films) are actively rejected by the women. They will leave the room rather than sit there while the news is on. The world as revealed through the news is seen to be (a) depressing, (b) boring, but (c) important. The 'news values', as realized in agendas, are 'accepted', but they have *alternative* values which the women recognize but do not suggest should form an alternative coverage. In fact, the importance of accepted 'news values' is recognized, and although their own world is seen as more interesting and relevant to them, it is also seen as secondary in rank to the 'real' or 'masculine' world. In terms of what the news is seen to present, they only select items which they *do not wish to see.* Comments or judgements are made in terms not only of what the items are but also of the effect which they have on the individual. Thus the items are not judged solely for their 'news value' but also for the way they affect the individual. There would appear to be a model for the programmes which are discussed and then rejected.

The news

Content	*Conceptualization of value of content*	*Effects on individual*
Politics War Industrial troubles	Boring Male-orientated	Depressing Causing nightmares and sleeplessness

The women's interpretation of news and current affairs programmes is an accurate reflection of the news items which are contained in these programmes. They may mis-identify the foci of some news reports, but this perhaps reinforces their claim not to watch these programmes. For instance, when Lorraine says 'It's all Vietnam, on the news', she is not necessarily identifying specific examples. In fact, Northern Ireland is much more likely to have been the exact focus of the news at the time. The general point is clear enough: 'Vietnam' has become a generic term for war.

The grouping together of the news and current affairs programmes by the women is a response to the circularity of these programmes, which is determined by the interrelation between the news and current events programmes and the prior selection of news items for their news value. A news 'story' becomes a 'current events topic', and the selection of news items according to the hierarchy of 'news value' puts political and military concerns, industrial relations and economic affairs at the head of topics for inclusion.[5] The editorial selection of these items is premised on their 'news value', and this also reflects a masculine bias in terms of the ideology of the subjects of the items included. The women find little of interest for them in the news except for any 'human interest' items, which are necessarily low in news value and rarely occur. When domestic affairs do reach the news it is often in terms of deviation or murder, and this in turn reinforces the accepted absence of these items from 'normal' news bulletins. This is illustrated when Anne says that she likes to hear news about murders (see page 111 above). It is not the fact that someone has been murdered which she finds interesting in the news but the fact that *there are elements within the situation to which she can relate.*

The ideology of femininity and feminine values over-determines the structures of what interests women. It is topics which can be regarded as of 'domestic' interest which they see as important or interesting, and it is also significant that 'domestic affairs', constructed in terms of 'news values' to include the economy and industrial relations, are not defined as 'domestic' in the categories which the women construct for themselves. 'Domestic' clearly relates to their own interests and not to the definition which is constructed through the hierarchy of 'news values'. It can be said that the majority of items which are included in news, current affairs and documentary programmes have a content which has little or no intrinsic interest for these women, and the way that they are presented means that they exclude these women from 'participation' at the point of identification with the items included. At the same time, the women accept that these are *important,* and this reinforces the split between the masculine values, which are interpreted as being important, and the interests which they see as representing their own feminine values.

The feminine 'world' of television

D. Do you like programmes that are like your life or that are entirely different?

R. I think I like things different really, 'cos if it's like me life, it's not very exciting 'cos there's nothing much really ever happens. Something exciting, different. I like watching detectives, anything creepy like ghost stories, I love ghost stories, anything creepy like that.

First, in conjunction with the programmes which women reject, there are programmes which they choose to watch and to which they obviously relate. These can be defined as those which are related to their own lives, the programmes which can loosely be termed 'realistic' – *Coronation Street, Crossroads, Emmerdale Farm, The Cedar Tree.* Secondly, the programmes which can be described as having 'fantasy content' (horror movies, or American movies or television movies), although not seen as representing 'real life' in the women's own terms, are seen as an alternative to the reality of their own lives. Finally, there are the programmes which can be categorized as light entertainment (quizzes, or competitions which often have an 'everyday' or 'domestic' theme, either because the contestants are seen as ordinary people or because of the subject-matter. In *Whose Baby?*, for example, the children of celebrity guests appear and the panel has to guess who is the famous father or mother – a direct link of parenthood between the 'famous' and the 'ordinary' viewer (in this case, the woman).

The programmes which are interpreted by the women as portraying 'everyday' or 'family' life are, in fact, far from portraying anything which has a point of *real* identification with the women's own lives. The programmes may not relate to the everyday lives of the women in the study. Within the programmes which are seen as 'realistic' there are common elements of identification. Many of the characters in the series *Coronation Street* and *Crossroads* are women who themselves have to confront the 'problems' in their 'everyday' lives, and the resolution or negotiation of these problems within the drama provides points of recognition and identification for the women viewers. It is in the 'living out' of problem areas that much of the appeal of the series is located. However, the resolution of areas of conflict, contradiction or confusion within a dramatic situation is double-edged. The woman can be confronted with the problems and also informed of the different elements which have to be considered in any 'living out' or resolution of problems. It is in the forms that the resolutions are made within programmes that the ideological basis of consensual femininity is *reproduced* and *reinforced* for women. As with the problems that are discussed in phone-in programmes and in the chatter of DJs, the very fact of recognition and *seeming* discussion or consideration by some 'outside' or 'independent' authority gives an impression that the problems have been aired. The outcome remains the same. The resolutions within either the soap opera series or the telephone conversations or talks are not revolutionary; what emerges is the reinforcement of the fatality or inevitability of the situation, without the need to change it.

It is impossible to attempt a detailed analysis of the decoding of the programmes which is made by the women because at this stage this would be only supposition.[6] What is clear, however, is that the programmes which the women watch are differentiated specifically in terms of both class and gender. Overall the programmes fall into the categories of popular drama and light entertainment, and although it is obvious that the women reject news and the political content of current affairs programmes, it would be wrong to contend that they do not have access or exposure to news or politics. Within comedy programmes, news and current affairs topics are presented in a mediated form - and often in a more easily accessible or even 'joking' or parodying manner. The news on Radio 1, which is transmitted every hour, is relatively accessible; it is also introduced by music which is recognizable, bright and repetitive and demanding of attention. The women in this study are exposed to news in this form, but they do not mention finding that unacceptable. Clearly, what is important is the definition of specifically feminine interests which women select from media output and the rejection of items which they see as specifically of masculine interest. They combat their own isolation through their interest in radio programmes during the day, and they see television programmes as a form of 'leisure' or relaxation. Radio is integral to their working day, but early-evening television is secondary to the domestic labour which they perform. The programmes which the women watch and listen to, together with the programmes which they reject, reinforce the sexual division of spheres of interest, which is determined both by their location in the home and by the structures of femininity that ensure that feminine values are secondary (or less 'real') than those of the masculine world of work and politics, which the women regard as *alien*, yet *important*.

Part Three

Media Studies

8 Introduction to Media Studies at the Centre

Stuart Hall

The Media Group is one of the longest-running Centre research groups, and Media Studies has been a focus of Centre work and interest since its inception. This area has developed through a series of stages, each taking a somewhat different focus of analysis, on the basis of a series of related but developing theoretical approaches. These are briefly resumed in this overview.

In the early days this area was heavily dominated by the mainstream traditions and concerns of 'mass-communications research', as defined largely by American empirical social science practice. This tradition was rooted in earlier debates about the relationship between 'mass communications' and 'mass society'; but these 'Frankfurt School' concerns had been thoroughly reworked by the methodologies and concerns of American empirical-based research of a largely quantitative kind, based on the audience-survey method, quantitative content analysis and a preoccupation with questions of the debasement of cultural standards through trivialization, pinpointed in the issue of the media and violence.[1] Similar concerns can, of course, be discerned in the way the influence of the media on working-class culture was analysed in Richard Hoggart's *Uses of Literacy* and in the early indications given of the Centre's interest in this question as they were outlined in his inaugural essay, *Schools of English and Contemporary Society.*[2] But in its actual practice the Centre, from a very early point, challenged the dominant paradigms and concerns of this tradition and redefined work on the media in the broader framework of Cultural Studies.

This 'break' can be summarized as follows. First, Media Studies broke with the models of 'direct influence' – using a sort of stimulus-response model with heavily behaviourist overtones, media content serving as a trigger – into a framework which drew much more on what can broadly be defined as the 'ideological' role of the media. This latter approach defined the media as a major cultural and ideological force, standing in a dominant position with respect to the way in which social relations and political problems were defined and the production and transformation of popular ideologies in the audiences addressed. This 'return' to a concern with the media and ideologies is the most significant and consistent thread in Centre media work. It has profoundly modified the 'behaviourist' emphases of previous research approaches.

Second, we challenged the notions of media texts as 'transparent' bearers of meaning – as the 'message' in some undifferentiated way – and gave much greater attention than had been the case in traditional forms of content analysis to their linguistic and ideological structuration. These two concerns – the general ideological nature of mass communications and the complexity of the linguistic structuration of its forms – has been the basis of all our subsequent work; and they were drawn together within the framework of early models of semiotic analysis which had a formative impact on our work.

Third, we broke with the passive and undifferentiated conceptions of the 'audience' as it has largely appeared in traditional research – influenced, as these had been, by the surveying needs of broadcasting organizations and advertising agencies. We began to replace these too-simple notions with a more active conception of the 'audience', of 'reading' and of the relation between how media messages were encoded, the 'moment' of the encoded text and the variation of audience 'decodings'.

Fourth, the question of the media and ideologies returned to the agenda a concern with the role which the media play in the circulation and securing of *dominant* ideological definitions and representations. This more classical set of concerns contrasted sharply with the 'mass-culture' models which underpinned much early American research and the resounding absence in that whole body of work of the question of ideology.

Early media work in the Centre rehearsed many of these emergent themes and concerns, albeit in a still provisional and unfinished form. The relation of the media to broader historical movements of social change formed the basis for the first funded media project, supported by the Rowntree Trust. This was an analysis of the popular press and social change from the mid 1930s to the mid 1960s. It was undertaken by a team of researchers (Anthony Smith, Trevor Blackwell, Liz Immirzi) and subsequently published under the title *Paper Voices.*[3] (Reference to how this project was conceived and conducted is to be found in the Introduction to this volume.) The second funded project was a study of television crime drama, undertaken by Alan Shuttleworth, Angela Lloyd and Marina Camargo Heck. This arose from the initial programme of research into television and violence which formed the basis for the foundation of the Centre for Mass Communication Research at Leicester – still the largest and most productive of the mass-communications research institutes in Britain – and was specifically designed to test some of the alternative hypotheses to those substantively derived from American research. This project concentrated on the analysis of a range of TV crime drama texts and was subsequently published by the Centre in its report form.[4] Two other projects deriving from this period deserve mention here. The first was the Ph.D on the representations of women in visual advertising undertaken by Trevor Millum and later published as *Images of Woman.*[5] This was one of the very first analyses of its kind on this subject in England, and one of the first to take visual discourse as its central point of reference. The second was a collective research project, undertaken by a large Centre group in what was the first collective 'practical research' group (1968-9), which analysed a selection of women's magazines and the way women and 'femininity' were represented there. The main focus was the large-circulation women's magazines - *Woman* and *Woman's Own* - and the analysis of the fictional story 'Cure for Marriage'. This was the first analysis of such materials in the Centre which made use of Lévi-Strauss's studies of myth and the early work of Roland Barthes. This study exists only in manuscript form, though it has had some influence on subsequent Centre work in this important area and signals a very early interest in the question of feminine representation.[6]

At this time the preoccupation with the questions of cultural trivialization and violence in mainstream research highlighted television as the privileged medium and the entertainment materials provided by the media as the most relevant for research. But, stimulated by the pioneering analysis of the treatment of the Vietnam demonstrations of 1968 in press and TV published by a team from the Leicester Centre, with its rich notion of 'inferential structures' (replacing the simplifications of 'bias'), Centre work took a lead in shifting the emphasis of Media Studies away from entertainment to the heartland of 'political communications', especially in the news and current affairs areas.[7] This was - as *Demonstrations and Communications* itself had been - a response to the 'crisis of the media' which began to develop in the late 1960s.[8] This crisis had to do with three aspects of the media which now began to command much greater attention: (a) questions of credibility, access, bias and distortion in the way political and social events of a problematic nature were represented in the media (a problem forced on to the agenda by the political movements and crises of the period); (b) questions concerning the relation between broadcasting, politics and the state, and the social role and position of the media institutions in the complex of cultural power in advanced 'electronic' societies; (c) the difficult problems arising both from attempting to understand how the media played an ideological role in society *and* from conceptualizing their complex relationship to power, their 'relative autonomy' (setting aside the simpler notions of the media as the 'voice of a ruling class', which were clearly inadequate).

Here one can find, already sketched out as a programme of study, new conceptions of the position and practices of the broadcasting institutions as 'apparatuses'; new approaches to the relation between how messages are structured and their role in the circulation of dominant social definitions; and an area of media production centrally focused on 'political communications' - on news, current affairs, the presentation of social problems and so on.

This reorientation of concerns was supported and reinforced by the employment of semiotic methods of textual analysis. In the work of Roland Barthes, for example *(Elements of Semiology, Mythologies)*,[9] which was highly influential at the time, these concerns were brought together into what was in effect a new problematic for media work in the Centre, and one which has been developed with many continuities and some breaks since then. From this period can be dated the work on news, news photographs and the 'manufacture of news', some of which appeared as the 'theme' issue of *WPCS* 3, the first report of working research on this theme published by the Centre.[10] To these can also be related the discussions of the media and political deviance (in, for example, essays by Stuart Hall in *Deviance and Social Control*, edited by Rock and McIntosh, and *The Manufacture of News*, edited by

Cohen and Young, and related papers dealing with the issue of broadcasting and the state and the questions of balance, objectivity and neutrality.[11] This early initiative in the analysis of the news construction of events has since been taken up and has come to provide a central stand in the revival of British mass-media work; for example, the Glasgow Media Group, Hartman and Husband, Golding, Schlessinger, Tracey, Chibnall.[12]

Much Centre work which has been published or has appeared in thesis form derived from this strong and sustained impetus: for example, the analysis of current affairs TV, 'The "Unity" of Current Affairs TV: *Panorama*', in *WPCS* 9; Centre theses on political communications (see the Connell extract below, pages 139–56) and on the handling of industrial relations in the media by Connell and Morley; the work reported in the British Film Institute (BFI) monograph *Everyday Television: Nationwide* by Dave Morley and Charlotte Brunsdon.[13] The latter marked a further advance from the 'high' political world and themes of programmes like *Panorama* to the more popular, more 'domestic' current affairs magazine programmes, like *Nationwide,* with more heterogeneous audiences (in both class and gender terms). These publications have both explored new methods of programme analysis and also put forward novel theses on how the complex relations between the media, politics and society could be conceptualized.

Two further developments should be noted here. The first concerns audiences. Audience-based survey research, based on the large statistical sample using fixed-choice questionnaires, has at last reached the terminal point it has long deserved – at least as a serious sociological enterprise. This has created a space in which new hypotheses may be tentatively advanced. The first, concerned with a more differentiated approach to the audience, was outlined in an early paper by Dave Morley, *Reconceptualizing the Audience.*[14] This brought together a concern with a class-based analysis of the cultural orientations of different audience groups to media materials and certain theoretical theses about how programmes were 'decoded'. The encoding/decoding propositions were first outlined in a very general form by Stuart Hall in the Stencilled Paper 'Encoding and Decoding in the TV Discourse'.[15] Both approaches have been pursued in a more disciplined framework in a project funded by the Higher Education Research Committee of the BFI and undertaken by Dave Morley, whose results are shortly to be published.

The second development has to do with the shift of interest from the encoding of 'high political themes' in the headline news and current affairs programmes to the area where television intersects more directly with, and plays a shaping and formative role in relation to, the popular, 'practical' ideologies of the general audience. This has gone hand in hand with a renewed concern for the missing dimension of *gender* in much media analysis and therefore a growing preoccupation with types and genres of TV programmes more 'popularly' addressed, and hence with a more substantial representation of women and their concerns. *Nationwide* already represented a shift in this direction. And this has been strengthened and underpinned in the recent work of the Group, which has returned – but now from a different theoretical perspective – to the area of 'popular' TV: the mass programming addressed to the popular TV audience in peak-viewing times, which functions very much under the sign not of 'information and education' but of 'entertainment and pleasure'. Work in this area has taken the TV zones of light entertainment, situation comedies, crime drama, domestic serials, quiz shows and sport as its main focus. It has also focused on a new set of preoccupations - broadly, the way 'popular' TV handles and manages the contradictions of everyday life and popular experience; the manner and effect of the intervention which such programmes make in popular common sense; and the ways in which common-sense knowledge of social structures and situations are transformed through the intervention of television. This work has been much influenced by theoretical derivations from the work of writers like Gramsci and Laclau and their concern with the ideological work of transformation, ideologies as the sites of popular struggle and 'popular common-sense constructions' as the stake in those struggles. Central to this have been the representations of gender, class and ethnicity, the importance of 'the domestic' and of 'femininity' and 'masculinity' as the privileged discourse into which other social contradictions are condensed. Much of this work is still to appear in published form, but indications as to the shift of emphasis can be found in different places in this collection: for example, in Janice Winship's article 'Subjectivity for sale' and in Dorothy Hobson's work on the media and young working-class housewives at home.

The area of film and Media Studies has become a privileged one for the construction of new theoretical approaches, and the work of the Centre in these different concrete areas of research has been considerably influenced by these developments. One can think, here, of the critique of early semiotics mounted by psychoanalysis, especially in its Lacanian version, and the rethinking of ideology substantially in terms of the way in which texts construct subject positions; of the extensive critique of 'realism' and its narrative modes - an argument already present in our work on the ideological process of naturalization and 'transparency' but since taken much further; of the rethinking of the concept of ideology in terms of Foucault's theses on 'discourse' and discursive practices - an innovation which has played some role in how our work on popular TV was conceptualized. In many of these theoretical areas feminist concerns have played a crucial role and have proved least amenable to being inserted into either existing or new frameworks. The Centre Media Group undertook a long engagement with these new theoretical positions, in the form of a critique of the theories being developed in film studies in and around the journal *Screen:* this critique will shortly be published as a Stencilled Paper. An extract from that essay, with an editorial introduction, provides the final piece in the articles presented in this section.

9 The ideological dimension of media messages*

Marina Camargo Heck

Althusser defines ideology as 'a "representation" of the imaginary relationships of individuals to their real conditions of existence'.[1] The 'imaginary' character of this relation references the distorting character of ideology. According to Poulantzas:

> This social-imaginary relation, which performs a real practical-social function, cannot be reduced to the problematic of alienation and false consciousness.
>
> It follows that, through its constitution, ideology is involved in the functioning of this social-imaginary relation, and is therefore *necessarily* false; its social function is not to give agents a *true knowledge* of the social structure but simply to insert them as it were into their practical activities supporting this structure. Precisely because it is determined by its structure, at the level of experience the social whole remains opaque to the agents.[2]

This ideological effect cannot be attributed to 'false consciousness' or a will-to-cheat by the dominant classes, but to the necessary obscuring of social realities. In short, our 'spontaneous perceptions', which take off from the distorted level (where 'surplus value' is hidden) must, themselves, be distorted. There is, therefore, a level of 'deep structure', which is 'invisible' and 'unconscious', which continually structures our immediate conscious perceptions in this distorted way. This is why, in ideological analysis, we must go to the structuring level of messages - that is, to the level where the discourse is *coded* - not just to their surface forms.

In *For Marx* Althusser argues:

> It is customary to suggest that ideology belongs to the region of 'consciousness'. We must not be misled by this appellation which is still contaminated by the idealist problematic that preceded Marx. In truth, ideology has very little to do with 'consciousness', even supposing this term to have an unambiguous meaning. It is profoundly *unconscious*, even when it presents itself in a reflected form (as in pre-Marxist 'philosophy'). Ideology is indeed a system of representations, but in the majority of cases these representations have nothing to do with 'consciousness': they are usually images and occasionally concepts, but it is above all as *structures* that they impose on the vast majority of men, not via their 'consciousness'.
>
> So ideology is a matter of the *lived* relation between men and their world. This relation, that only appears as *'conscious'* on condition that it is *unconscious,* in the

*This article is an edited extract from 'The Ideological Dimension of Media Messages', CCCS Stencilled Paper no. 10.

same way only seems to be simple on condition that it is complex, that it is not a simple relation but a relation between relations, a second-degree relation. In ideology men do indeed express not the relation between them and their conditions of existence, but *the way* they live the relations between them and their conditions of existence: this presupposes both a real relation and an *'imaginary'*, *'lived'* relation. Ideology, then, is the expression of the relation between men and their 'world', that is the (over-determined) unity of the real relation and the imaginary relation between them and their real conditions of existence.[3]

Veron, commenting on the passage from Althusser quoted above, says:

if ideologies are structures in the sense structuralism uses this expression, then they are not 'images' nor 'concepts' (we can say, they are not contents) but are sets of rules which determine an organization and the functioning of images and concepts.[4]

We can here already see the first foundation for the introduction of the notion of *code*:

Ideology is a system of coding reality and not a determined set of coded messages with this system .... This way ideology becomes autonomous in relation to the *consciousness* or *intention* of its agents: these may be conscious of their points of view about social forms, but not of the semantic conditions (rules and categories of codification) which make possible those points of view.[5]

Veron illustrates his point with an analogy: he imagines that there was a computer prepared to receive as *input* a certain type of message and to emit as *output* a classification of each message as consistent or not with a certain ideology. He concludes:

we shall call the ideological system not the input or the output of the machine, but the programme according to which the computer emits and/or recognizes ideological systems. From this point of view, then, and at this level of analysis, an 'ideology' may be defined as *a system of semantic rules* to generate messages.[6]

In many ways this perspective coincides with Eco's. Eco understands ideology to be the 'universe of knowledge of the receiver and of the group to which he belongs'.[7] He thus makes ideology more or less coterminous with 'culture in the anthropological sense'. Before this universe of knowledge is communicated, semiological analysis will not be able to detect it; it will therefore be necessary for it first to be 'reduced to a system of communicative conventions'. 'However, to achieve this, it is necessary that the *system of knowledge* becomes a *system of signs*: the ideology is recognizable when, once socialized, it becomes a code.'[8]

From this observation Veron develops his argument:

Ideology is not a particular type of message, or a class of social discourses, but it is one of the many levels of organization of the messages, from the point of view of its semantic properties. Ideology is therefore a *level of signification* which can be present in any type of message, even in the scientific discourse. Any material of social communication is susceptible to an *ideological reading.*[9]

For Veron this ideological reading 'consists in the discovery of the implicit or non-manifest organization of the message'. For the analysis of this latent organization it would be necessary to study the mechanisms of that organization - that is, the rules of selection and combination. 'From this perspective we can define ideology . . . as a system of semantic rules which express a certain level of organization of messages.' It would be only *through* the disentangling of these semantic rules that we can get to the core of a message. However, in the analysis of the ideological meanings the 'core' does not refer only to the content of the message or its 'non-manifest organization'. When a message is emitted it is not only what is *said* that has a significance but also the *way* it is said, and what is *not said but could be said.* The significations in a message are established by means of a code, and it is this code which permits the message to be organized (permits, that is, the selections and combination of the signs which actually constitute the message). The coding and decoding of a message implies the usage of the same code; that is, in cases where a message is organized and emitted in one code to a group which receives it and decodes it using a different code, the meaning of the message will differ completely. This is what Eco calls 'aberrant decoding'. These assertions refer to the denotative meanings which are the ones that are defined by the code most widely in use, while the connotative meanings are given by sub-codes or lexicons, limited to certain groups and not to others.

Barthes, in *Elements of Semiology*,[10] referring to Hjelmslev, observes that signification consists of a plane of expression (also called 'signifier') and a plane of content (or 'signified'), and that the signification is the relation of the two planes. This first system of signification he calls the plane of 'denotation'. For example, when the word *pig* (signifier) has the content of the concept, 'A very useful animal that produces meat, bacon, etc.' (signified), the relation between the signifier, pig, and the signified, 'very useful animal that produces meat', gives us the signification 'animal, pig'. In Saussure, it is not the morpheme pig, nor the actual animal in the farmyard, but the relating of the morpheme to a concept - signifier/signified - which gives us the sign.

pig
s s'
animal, pig

At a second level, the above relation between signifier and signified (that is, the whole system of 'denoted' meaning) can become the plane of expression or the signifier of a second system. For instance, in the context of the North American black movement, the word 'pig' does not mean the relation between the signifier and the concept of a material object (animal), but becomes instead the signifier of a new sign: *policeman*. This level is that which Barthes calls 'connotation'.

pig
animal pig concept:
pigness

'pig' (policeman)

As we said above, connotative meanings are defined by lexicons or sub-codes which are used within specific groups or with reference to a more delimited domain. Though a message employing this sign might be emitted and received in a common code, the connotation in *this* message – 'Off the Pig!' – would be decoded according to the lexicons only of those familiar with the language of the black ghetto. It follows that the connotation can be encoded or decoded so as to yield many different significations. Thus the same signifier, pig, with reference to the same concept, 'pigness', when read in the context of the feminist movement will connote 'male chauvinist'.

pig animal pig	concept: pigness

(male chauvinist) 'pig'

Another type of second-order system is what Barthes calls 'myth'.[11] Myth should be thought of as a special type of connotation since, according to Barthes, the mythical system is generated in the same way as connotation. The real soldier saluting the flag (signified) + the photograph of him saluting (signifier) gives us the 'denotation' = negro saluting flag (sign). At the second level, this constituted sign (negro saluting flag) + the concept of French imperiality gives us the second-order connotation, which is 'France is a great empire, and all her sons, without colour discrimination, faithfully serve under her flag'. Barthes does not make it clear why this second-order meaning, myth, is different from, rather than a special case of, connotation. We would like to suggest that the difference between myth and connotation depends on the amplitude of the lexicons from which the concepts are drawn. The connoted meaning in 'pig=policeman' and in 'pig=male chauvinist' are clearly linked to the lexicons of identifiable sub-groups. By contrast, myth seems identifiable with the lexicons of very large groups, if not of the society as a whole. Myth therefore differs from connotation at the moment at which it attempts to *universalize* for the whole society meanings which are special to particular lexicons. In the process of universalization, these meanings, which in the last instance are particular to certain lexicons, assume the amplitude of reality itself and are therefore 'naturalized'. Thus, we might say, *myths are connotations which have become dominant-hegemonic.*

In *WPCS* 3[12] we emphasized that the ideological level always refers to the connotative aspect of the message. This was one of the strong criticisms advanced by Terry Lovell in her review of *WPCS* 3 in *Screen.*[13]

Some misunderstanding here can be attributed to our failure to explain clearly enough how we were using the concept of 'denotation' (see pages 133–4 below). The concept of 'denotation' was not sufficiently clarified. By 'formal-denotative' we were following the argument by Barthes in *Elements in Semiology*, where 'denotation' is *not* given a special status as 'natural meaning', but simply refers to the first system of signification which generates a second system 'wider than the first' (which is the plane of connotation).

In part, the problem is to understand precisely what is meant by 'level of signification'. By referring to a 'formal-denotative' level, we were employing the term as an *analytic concept*, useful for distinguishing between different levels of the organization of meanings. Veron, for example, has observed that 'ideology is a level of signification which operates by connotation'. Because of our lack of clarity on this point, Lovell assumed that we therefore subscribed to the idea that 'denotation' represented a pre-ideological or 'neutral' state of the message. But, in our view, the denotative level *cannot* be identified with a 'neutral state of language': there can be no 'neutral state' because denotations also *must be produced by the operation of a code.* To distinguish between different levels of the operation of codes is not, therefore, to imply that messages can be produced without a code (see pages 133–4 below).

This point has been subject to further confusion because in the texts which followed *Elements of Semiology* (and to some extent already in *Writing Degree Zero*) Barthes appeared to subscribe to the notion of a 'zero degree of writing' and to the idea of an 'empty text'.[14] But whatever the metaphorical status of these concepts, we cannot subscribe to the idea that there is a level of 'denoted' meaning which is free of any ideological operation. In this sense, ideology is beyond and involves the whole universe of the sign as such – denotative *and* connotative. It is *inside* the coded sign that an analytic distinction can be usefully made between 'denotation' and 'connotation'. At *this* level of the message, however, the analytic distinction is important. Distinguishing two levels of analysis, or two levels of operation in the functioning of codes, does not require us to find these distinctions empirically observable in any concrete instance, since each instance will always be the product of the 'over-determination' of both levels of operation. Nevertheless, 'we believe that the method requires an *operational* distinction between two levels of organization of the sign'. From this point of view, a distinction can be made between those aspects of a sign where the meaning, produced through the operation of a code, has been *fixed* in conventional usage and is widely and *apparently* 'naturally' employed within a language community, and more fluid and open-ended significations which, through the operation of alternative codes, can be more fully exploited for their ideological signifying value. In *this* sense 'denotation' is nothing more than a useful rule for distinguishing, in any particular instance or operation, those connotations which have become *naturalized* and those which, not being so fixed, provide the opportunity for more extensive ideological re-presentations.

Barthes himself, in *S/Z*,[15] expands his concept of denotation from the definitions he offered in *Elements of Semiology*, and usefully clarifies it:

> Denotation is not the first sense, but it *pretends to be* [our italics]. Under this illusion, in the end, it is nothing but *the last of connotation* (where the reading is at the same time grounded and enclosed), the superior myth, thanks to which the text pretends to return to the nature of language . . . . We must keep denotation, old vigilant deity, crafty, theatrical, appointed to *represent* the collective innocence of language.

Semiologists contest the hierarchy of denotation and connotation, saying that any language, with its dictionary and syntax, is a system just like all others and that therefore there is no reason for reserving denotation as a privileged first level, neutral in itself, which originates all the others. Barthes, however, justifies his adoption of the distinction in an argument based primarily on Hjelmslev, a fact which demonstrates his loyalty to linguistics, at least as far as the *Elements* period was concerned.

The destruction by semiologists of the connotation/denotation distinction in its traditional linguistic sense is made through the identification of denotation with connotation and the fact that ideological meanings are present in *both* processes. Baudrillard, in *Critique of the Political Economy of the Sign,* also does this; though he distinguishes the different *degree* of ideological interference in each instance, he refuses the general distinction as it is usually used: 'Denotation is totally supported by the myth of 'objectivity' (whether concerning the linguistic sign, the analogous photographic or iconic sign, etc.), the direct adequacy of a signifier and a precise reality.'[16] And further on:

> Denotation is distinct from other significations (connoted) *by its singular function of effacing the traces of the ideological process in restoring it to the universal and the 'objective' innocence. Far from being the objective term to which connotation is opposed as the ideological term, denotation is thus, because it naturalizes this ideological process, the more ideological term* . . . . [our italics].[17]

10 Encoding/decoding*

Stuart Hall

Traditionally, mass-communications research has conceptualized the process of communication in terms of a circulation circuit or loop. This model has been criticized for its linearity - sender/message/receiver - for its concentration on the level of message exchange and for the absence of a structured conception of the different moments as a complex structure of relations. But it is also possible (and useful) to think of this process in terms of a structure produced and sustained through the articulation of linked but distinctive moments - production, circulation, distribution/consumption, reproduction. This would be to think of the process as a 'complex structure in dominance', sustained through the articulation of connected practices, each of which, however, retains its distinctiveness and has its own specific modality, its own forms and conditions of existence. This second approach, homologous to that which forms the skeleton of commodity production offered in Marx's *Grundrisse* and in *Capital,* has the added advantage of bringing out more sharply how a continuous circuit - production-distribution-production - can be sustained through a 'passage of forms'.[1] It also highlights the specificity of the forms in which the product of the process 'appears' in each moment, and thus what distinguishes discursive 'production' from other types of production in our society and in modern media systems.

The 'object' of these practices is meanings and messages in the form of sign-vehicles of a specific kind organized, like any form of communication or language, through the operation of codes within the syntagmatic chain of a discourse. The apparatuses, relations and practices of production thus issue, at a certain moment (the moment of 'production/circulation') in the form of symbolic vehicles constituted within the rules of 'language'. It is in this discursive form that the circulation of the 'product' takes place. The process thus requires, at the production end, its material instruments - its 'means' - as well as its own sets of social (production) relations - the organization and combination of practices within media apparatuses. But it is in the *discursive* form that the circulation of the product takes place, as well as its distribution to different audiences. Once accomplished, the discourse must then be translated - transformed, again - into social practices if the circuit is to be both completed and effective. If no 'meaning' is taken, there can be no 'consumption'. If the meaning is not articulated in practice, it has no effect. The value of this

*This article is an edited extract from 'Encoding and Decoding in Television Discourse', CCCS Stencilled Paper no. 7.

approach is that while each of the moments, in articulation, is necessary to the circuit as a whole, no one moment can fully guarantee the next moment with which it is articulated. Since each has its specific modality and conditions of existence, each can constitute its own break or interruption of the 'passage of forms' on whose continuity the flow of effective production (that is, 'reproduction') depends.

Thus while in no way wanting to limit research to 'following only those leads which emerge from content analysis',[2] we must recognize that the discursive form of the message has a privileged position in the communicative exchange (from the viewpoint of circulation), and that the moments of 'encoding' and 'decoding', though only 'relatively autonomous' in relation to the communicative process as a whole, are *determinate* moments. A 'raw' historical event cannot, *in that form,* be transmitted by, say, a television newscast. Events can only be signified within the aural-visual forms of the televisual discourse. In the moment when a historical event passes under the sign of discourse, it is subject to all the complex formal 'rules' by which language signifies. To put it paradoxically, the event must become a 'story' before it can become a *communicative event.* In that moment the formal sub-rules of discourse are 'in dominance', without, of course, subordinating out of existence the historical event so signified, the social relations in which the rules are set to work or the social and political consequences of the event having been signified in this way. The 'message form' is the necessary 'form of appearance' of the event in its passage from source to receiver. Thus the transposition into and out of the 'message form' (or the mode of symbolic exchange) is not a random 'moment', which we can take up or ignore at our convenience. The 'message form' is a determinate moment; though, at another level, it comprises the surface movements of the communications system only and requires, at another stage, to be integrated into the social relations of the communication process as a whole, of which it forms only a part.

From this general perspective, we may crudely characterize the television communicative process as follows. The institutional structures of broadcasting, with their practices and networks of production, their organized relations and technical infrastructures, are required to produce a programme. Using the analogy of *Capital,* this is the 'labour process' in the discursive mode. Production, here, constructs the message. In one sense, then, the circuit begins here. Of course, the production process is not without its 'discursive' aspect: it, too, is framed throughout by meanings and ideas: knowledge-in-use concerning the routines of production, historically defined technical skills, professional ideologies, institutional knowledge, definitions and assumptions, assumptions about the audience and so on frame the constitution of the programme through this production structure. Further, though the production structures of television originate the television discourse, they do not constitute a closed system. They draw topics, treatments, agendas, events, personnel, images of the audience, 'definitions of the situation' from other sources and other discursive formations within the wider socio-cultural and political structure of which they are a differentiated part. Philip Elliott has expressed this point succinctly, within a more traditional framework, in his discussion of the way in which the audience is both the 'source' and the 'receiver' of the television message. Thus – to borrow Marx's terms – circulation and reception are, indeed, 'moments' of the production process in television and are reincorporated, via a number of skewed and structured 'feedbacks', into the production process itself. The consumption or reception of the television message is thus also itself a 'moment' of the production process in its larger sense, though the latter is 'predominant' because it is the 'point of departure for the realization' of the message. Production and reception of the television message are not, therefore, identical, but they are related: they are differentiated moments within the totality formed by the social relations of the communicative process as a whole.

At a certain point, however, the broadcasting structures must yield encoded messages in the form of a meaningful discourse. The institution-societal relations of production must pass under the discursive rules of language for its product to be 'realized'. This initiates a further differentiated moment, in which the formal rules of discourse and language are in dominance. Before this message can have an 'effect' (however defined), satisfy a 'need' or be put to a 'use', it must first be appropriated as a meaningful discourse and be meaningfully decoded. It is this set of decoded meanings which 'have an effect', influence, entertain, instruct or persuade, with very complex perceptual, cognitive, emotional, ideological or behavioural consequences. In a 'determinate' moment the structure employs a code and yields a 'message': at another determinate moment the 'message', via its decodings, issues into the structure of social practices. We are now fully aware that this re-entry into the practices of audience reception and 'use' cannot be understood in simple behavioural terms. The typical processes identified in positivistic research on isolated elements – effects, uses, 'gratifications' – are themselves framed by structures of understanding, as well as being produced by social and economic relations, which shape their 'realization' at the reception end of the chain and which permit the meanings signified in the discourse to be transposed into practice or consciousness (to acquire social use value or political effectivity).

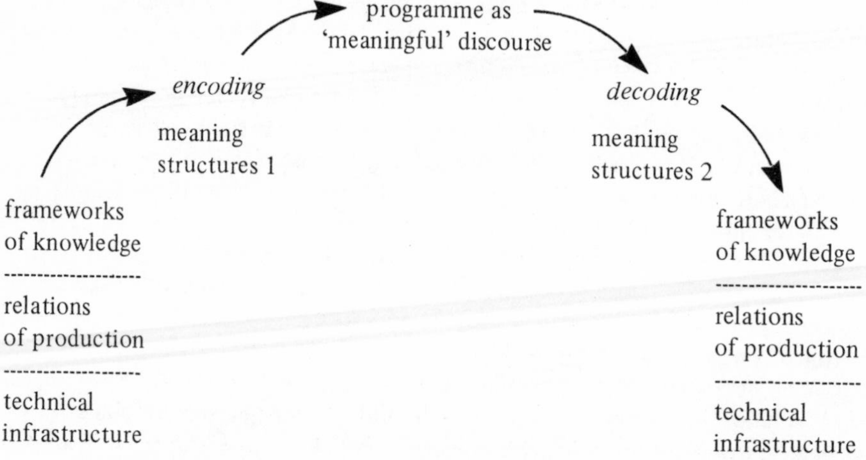

Clearly, what we have labelled in the diagram 'meaning structures 1' and 'meaning structures 2' may not be the same. They do not constitute an 'immediate identity'. The codes of encoding and decoding may not be perfectly symmetrical. The degrees of symmetry – that is, the degrees of 'understanding' and 'misunderstanding' in the communicative exchange – depend on the degrees of symmetry/asymmetry (relations of equivalence) established between the positions of the 'personifications', encoder-producer and decoder-receiver. But this in turn depends on the degrees of identity/non-identity between the codes which perfectly or imperfectly transmit, interrupt or systematically distort what has been transmitted. The lack of fit between the codes has a great deal to do with the structural differences of relation and position between broadcasters and audiences, but it also has something to do with the asymmetry between the codes of 'source' and 'receiver' at the moment of transformation into and out of the discursive form. What are called 'distortions' or 'misunderstandings' arise precisely from the *lack of equivalence* between the two sides in the communicative exchange. Once again, this defines the 'relative autonomy', but 'determinateness', of the entry and exit of the message in its discursive moments.

The application of this rudimentary paradigm has already begun to transform our understanding of the older term, television 'content'. We are just beginning to see how it might also transform our understanding of audience reception, 'reading' and response as well. Beginnings and endings have been announced in communications research before, so we must be cautious. But there seems some ground for thinking that a new and exciting phase in so-called audience research, of a quite new kind, may be opening up. At either end of the communicative chain the use of the semiotic paradigm promises to dispel the lingering behaviourism which has dogged mass-media research for so long, especially in its approach to content. Though we know the television programme is not a behavioural input, like a tap on the knee cap, it seems to have been almost impossible for traditional researchers to conceptualize the communicative process without lapsing into one or other variant of low-flying behaviourism. We know, as Gerbner has remarked, that representations of violence on the TV screen 'are not violence but messages about violence':[3] but we have continued to research the question of violence, for example, as if we were unable to comprehend this epistemological distinction.

The televisual sign is a complex one. It is itself constituted by the combination of two types of discourse, visual and aural. Moreover, it is an iconic sign, in Peirce's terminology, because 'it possesses some of the properties of the thing represented'.[4] This is a point which has led to a great deal of confusion and has provided the site of intense controversy in the study of visual language. Since the visual discourse translates a three-dimensional world into two-dimensional planes, it cannot, of course, *be* the referent or concept it signifies. The dog in the film can bark but it cannot bite! Reality exists outside language, but it is constantly mediated by and through language: and what we can know and say has to be produced in and through discourse. Discursive 'knowledge' is the product not of the transparent representation of the 'real' in language but of the articulation of language on real relations and conditions. Thus there is no intelligible discourse without the operation of a code. Iconic signs are therefore coded signs too - even if the codes here work differently from those of other signs. There is no degree zero in language. Naturalism and 'realism' - the apparent fidelity of the representation to the thing or concept represented - is the result, the effect, of a certain specific articulation of language on the 'real'. It is the result of a discursive practice.

Certain codes may, of course, be so widely distributed in a specific language community or culture, and be learned at so early an age, that they appear not to be constructed - the effect of an articulation between sign and referent - but to be 'naturally' given. Simple visual signs appear to have achieved a 'near-universality' in this sense: though evidence remains that even apparently 'natural' visual codes are culture-specific. However, this does not mean that no codes have intervened; rather, that the codes have been profoundly *naturalized.* The operation of naturalized codes reveals not the transparency and 'naturalness' of language but the depth, the habituation and the near-universality of the codes in use. They produce apparently 'natural' recognitions. This has the (ideological) effect of concealing the practices of coding which are present. But we must not be fooled by appearances. Actually, what naturalized codes demonstrate is the degree of habituation produced when there is a fundamental alignment and reciprocity - an achieved equivalence - between the encoding and decoding sides of an exchange of meanings. The functioning of the codes on the decoding side will frequently assume the status of naturalized perceptions. This leads us to think that the visual sign for 'cow' actually *is* (rather than *represents*) the animal, cow. But if we think of the visual representation of a cow in a manual on animal husbandry - and, even more, of the linguistic sign 'cow' - we can see that both, in different degrees, are *arbitrary* with respect to the concept of the animal they represent. The articulation of an arbitrary sign - whether visual or verbal - with the concept of a referent is the product not of nature but of convention, and the conventionalism of discourses requires the intervention, the support, of codes. Thus Eco has argued that iconic signs 'look like objects in the real world because they reproduce the conditions (that is, the codes) of perception in the viewer'.[5] These 'conditions of perception' are, however, the result of a highly coded, even if virtually unconscious, set of operations - decodings. This is as true of the photographic or televisual image as it is of any other sign. Iconic signs are, however, particularly vulnerable to being 'read' as natural because visual codes of perception are very widely distributed and because this type of sign is less arbitrary than a linguistic sign: the linguistic sign, 'cow' possesses *none* of the properties of the thing represented, whereas the visual sign appears to possess *some* of those properties.

This may help us to clarify a confusion in current linguistic theory and to define precisely how some key terms are being used in this article. Linguistic theory frequently employs the distinction 'denotation' and 'connotation'. The term 'denotation' is widely equated with the literal meaning of a sign: because this literal meaning is almost universally recognized, especially when visual discourse is being employed, 'denotation' has often been confused with a literal transcription of 'reality' in language - and thus with a 'natural sign', one produced without the intervention of a code. 'Connotation', on the other hand, is employed simply to refer to less fixed and therefore more conventionalized and changeable, associative meanings, which clearly vary from instance to instance and therefore must depend on the intervention of codes.

We do *not* use the distinction - denotation/connotation - in this way. From our point of view, the distinction is an *analytic* one only. It is useful, in analysis, to be able to apply a rough rule of thumb which distinguishes those aspects of a sign which appear to be taken, in any language community at any point in time, as its 'literal' meaning (denotation) from the more associative meanings for the sign which it is possible to generate (connotation). But analytic distinctions must not be confused with distinctions in the real world. There will be very few instances in which signs organized in a discourse signify *only* their 'literal' (that is, near-universally consensualized) meaning. In actual discourse most signs will combine both the denotative and the connotative *aspects* (as redefined above). It may, then, be asked why we retain the distinction at all. It is largely a matter of analytic value. It is because signs appear to acquire their full ideological value - appear to be open to articulation with wider ideological discourses and meanings - at the level of their 'associative' meanings (that is, at the connotative level) - for here 'meanings' are *not* apparently fixed in natural perception (that is, they are not fully naturalized), and their fluidity of meaning and association can be more fully exploited and transformed.[6] So it is at the connotative *level* of the sign that situational ideologies alter and transform signification. At this level we can see more clearly the active intervention of ideologies in and on discourse: here, the sign is open to new accentuations and, in Vološinov's terms, enters fully into the struggle over meanings - the class struggle in language.[7] This does not mean that the denotative or 'literal' meaning is outside ideology. Indeed, we could say that its ideological value is strongly *fixed* - because it has become so fully universal and 'natural'. The terms 'denotation' and 'connotation', then, are merely useful analytic tools for distinguishing, in particular contexts, between not the presence/absence of ideology in language but the different levels at which ideologies and discourses intersect.[8]

The level of connotation of the visual sign, of its contextual reference and positioning in different discursive fields of meaning and association, is the point where *already coded* signs intersect with the deep semantic codes of a culture and take on additional, more active ideological dimensions. We might take an example from advertising discourse. Here, too, there is no 'purely denotative', and certainly no 'natural', representation. Every visual sign in advertising connotes a quality, situation, value or inference, which is present as an implication or implied meaning, depending on the connotational positioning. In Barthes's example, the sweater always signifies a 'warm garment' (denotation) and thus the activity/value of 'keeping warm'. But it is also possible, at its more connotative levels, to signify 'the coming of winter' or 'a cold day'. And, in the specialized sub-codes of fashion, sweater may also connote a fashionable style of *haute couture* or, alternatively, an informal style of dress. But set against the right visual background and positioned by the romantic sub-code, it may connote 'long autumn walk in the woods'.[9] Codes of this order clearly contract relations for the sign with the wider universe of ideologies in a society. These codes are the means by which power and ideology are made to signify in particular discourses. They refer signs to the 'maps of meaning' into which any culture is classified; and those 'maps of social reality' have the whole range of social meanings, practices, and usages, power and interest 'written in' to them. The connotative levels of signifiers, Barthes remarked, 'have a close communication with culture, knowledge, history, and it is through them, so to speak, that the environmental world invades the linguistic and semantic system. They are, if you like, the fragments of ideology'.[10]

The so-called denotative *level* of the televisual sign is fixed by certain, very complex (but limited or 'closed') codes. But its connotative *level*, though also bounded, is more open, subject to more active *transformations,* which exploit its polysemic values. Any such already constituted sign is potentially transformable into more than one connotative configuration. Polysemy must not, however, be confused with pluralism. Connotative codes are *not* equal among themselves. Any society/culture tends, with varying degrees of closure, to impose its classifications of the social and cultural and political world. These constitute a *dominant cultural order,* though it is neither univocal nor uncontested. This question of the 'structure of discourses in dominance' is a crucial point. The different areas of social life appear to be mapped out into discursive domains, hierarchically organized into *dominant or preferred meanings.* New, problematic or troubling events, which breach our expectancies and run counter to our 'common-sense constructs', to our 'taken-for-granted' knowledge of social structures, must be assigned to their discursive domains before they can be said to 'make sense'. The most common way of 'mapping' them is to assign the new to some domain or other of the existing 'maps of problematic social reality'. We say *dominant*, not 'determined', because it is always possible to order, classify, assign and decode an event within more than one 'mapping'. But we say 'dominant' because there exists a pattern of 'preferred readings'; and these both have the institutional/political/ideological order imprinted in them and have themselves become institutionalized.[11] The domains of 'preferred meanings' have the whole social order embedded in them as a set of meanings, practices and beliefs: the everyday knowledge of social structures, of 'how things work for all practical purposes in this culture', the rank order of power and interest and the structure of legitimations, limits and sanctions. Thus to clarify a 'misunderstanding' at the connotative level, we must refer, *through* the codes, to the orders of social life, of economic and political power and of ideology. Further, since these mappings are 'structured in dominance' but not closed, the communicative process consists not in the unproblematic assignment of every visual item to its given position within a set of prearranged codes, but of *performative rules* – rules of competence and use, of logics-in-use – which seek actively to *enforce* or *pre-fer* one semantic domain over another and rule items into and out of their appropriate meaning-sets. Formal semiology has too often neglected this practice of *interpretative work*, though this constitutes, in fact, the real relations of broadcast practices in television.

In speaking of *dominant meanings,* then, we are not talking about a one-sided process which governs how all events will be signified. It consists of the 'work' required to enforce, win plausibility for and command as legitimate a *decoding* of the event within the limit of dominant definitions in which it has been connotatively signified. Terni has remarked:

By the word *reading* we mean not only the capacity to identify and decode a certain number of signs, but also the subjective capacity to put them into a creative relation between themselves and with other signs: a capacity which is, by itself, the condition for a complete awareness of one's total environment.[12]

Our quarrel here is with the notion of 'subjective capacity', as if the referent of a televisional discourse were an objective fact but the interpretative level were an individualized and private matter. Quite the opposite seems to be the case. The televisual practice takes 'objective' (that is, systemic) responsibility precisely for the relations which disparate signs contract with one another in any discursive instance, and thus continually rearranges, delimits and prescribes into what 'awareness of one's total environment' these items are arranged.

This brings us to the question of misunderstandings. Television producers who find their message 'failing to get across' are frequently concerned to straighten out the kinks in the communication chain, thus facilitating the 'effectiveness' of their communication. Much research which claims the objectivity of 'policy-oriented analysis' reproduces this administrative goal by attempting to discover how much of a message the audience recalls and to improve the extent of understanding. No doubt misunderstandings of a literal kind do exist. The viewer does not know the terms employed, cannot follow the complex logic of argument or exposition, is unfamiliar with the language, finds the concepts too alien or difficult or is foxed by the expository narrative. But more often broadcasters are concerned that the audience has failed to take the meaning as they – the broadcasters – intended. What they really mean to say is that viewers are not operating within the 'dominant' or 'preferred' code. Their ideal is 'perfectly transparent communication'. Instead, what they have to confront is 'systematically distorted communication'.[13]

In recent years discrepancies of this kind have usually been explained by reference to 'selective perception'. This is the door via which a residual pluralism evades the compulsions of a highly structured, asymmetrical and non-equivalent process. Of course, there will always be private, individual, variant readings. But 'selective perception' is almost never as selective, random or privatized as the concept suggests. The patterns exhibit, across individual variants, significant clusterings. Any new approach to audience studies will therefore have to begin with a critique of 'selective perception' theory.

It was argued earlier that since there is no necessary correspondence between encoding and decoding, the former can attempt to 'pre-fer' but cannot prescribe or guarantee the latter, which has its own conditions of existence. Unless they are wildly aberrant, encoding will have the effect of constructing some of the limits and parameters within which decodings will operate. If there were no limits, audiences could simply read whatever they liked into any message. No doubt some total misunderstandings of this kind do exist. But the vast range must contain *some* degree of reciprocity between encoding and decoding moments, otherwise we could not speak of an effective communicative exchange at all. Nevertheless, this 'correspondence' is not given but constructed. It is not 'natural' but the product of an articulation between two distinct moments. And the former cannot determine or guarantee, in a simple sense, which decoding codes will be employed. Otherwise communication would be a perfectly equivalent circuit, and every message would be an instance of 'perfectly transparent communication'. We must think, then, of the variant articulations in which encoding/decoding can be combined. To elaborate on this, we offer a hypothetical analysis of some possible decoding positions, in order to reinforce the point of 'no necessary correspondence'.[14]

We identify *three* hypothetical positions from which decodings of a televisual discourse may be constructed. These need to be empirically tested and refined. But the argument that decodings do not follow inevitably from encodings, that they are not identical, reinforces the argument of 'no necessary correspondence'. It also helps to deconstruct the common-sense meaning of 'misunderstanding' in terms of a theory of 'systematically distorted communication'.

The first hypothetical position is that of the *dominant-hegemonic position.* When the viewer takes the connoted meaning from, say, a television newscast or current affairs programme full and straight, and decodes the message in terms of the reference code in which it has been encoded, we might say that the viewer *is operating inside the dominant code.* This is the ideal-typical case of 'perfectly transparent communication' – or as close as we are likely to come to it 'for all practical purposes'. Within this we can distinguish the positions produced by the *professional code*. This is the position (produced by what we perhaps ought to identify as the operation of a 'metacode') which the professional broadcasters assume when encoding a message which has *already* been signified in a hegemonic manner. The professional code is 'relatively independent' of the dominant code, in that it applies criteria and transformational operations of its own, especially those of a technico-practical nature. The professional code, however, operates *within* the 'hegemony' of the dominant code. Indeed, it serves to reproduce the dominant definitions precisely by bracketing their hegemonic quality and operating instead with displaced professional codings which foreground such apparently neutral-technical questions as visual quality, news and presentational values, televisual quality, 'professionalism' and so on. The hegemonic interpretations of, say, the politics of Northern Ireland, or the Chilean *coup* or the Industrial Relations Bill are principally generated by political and military elites: the particular choice of presentational occasions and formats, the selection of personnel, the choice of images, the staging of debates are selected and combined through the operation of the professional code. How the broadcasting professionals are able *both* to operate with 'relatively autonomous' codes of their own *and* to act in such a way as to reproduce (not without contradiction) the hegemonic signification of events is a complex matter which cannot be further spelled out here. It must suffice to say that the professionals are linked with the defining elites not only by the institutional position of broadcasting itself as an 'ideological apparatus',[15] but also by the structure of *access* (that is, the systematic 'over-accessing' of selective elite personnel and their 'definition of the situation' in television). It may even be said that the professional codes serve to reproduce hegemonic definitions specifically by *not overtly* biasing their operations in a dominant direction: ideological reproduction therefore takes place here inadvertently, unconsciously, 'behind men's backs'.[16] Of course, conflicts, contradictions and even misunderstandings regularly arise between the dominant and the professional significations and their signifying agencies.

The second position we would identify is that of the *negotiated code* or position. Majority audiences probably understand quite adequately what has been dominantly defined and professionally signified. The dominant definitions, however, are hegemonic precisely because they represent definitions of situations and events which are 'in dominance', (*global*). Dominant definitions connect events, implicitly or explicitly, to grand totalizations, to the great syntagmatic views-of-the-world: they take 'large views' of issues: they relate events to the 'national interest' or to the level of geo-politics, even if they make these connections in truncated, inverted or mystified ways. The definition of a hegemonic viewpoint is (a) that it defines within its terms the mental horizon, the universe, of possible meanings, of a whole sector of relations in a society or culture; and (b) that it carries with it the stamp of legitimacy - it appears coterminous with what is 'natural', 'inevitable', 'taken for granted' about the social order. Decoding within the *negotiated version* contains a mixture of adaptive and oppositional elements: it acknowledges the legitimacy of the hegemonic definitions to make the grand significations (abstract), while, at a more restricted, situational (situated) level, it makes its own ground rules - it operates with exceptions to the rule. It accords the privileged position to the dominant definitions of events while reserving the right to make a more negotiated application to 'local conditions', to its own more *corporate* positions. This negotiated version of the dominant ideology is thus shot through with contradictions, though these are only on certain occasions brought to full visibility. Negotiated codes operate through what we might call particular or situated logics: and these logics are sustained by their differential and unequal relation to the discourses and logics of power. The simplest example of a negotiated code is that which governs the response of a worker to the notion of an Industrial Relations Bill limiting the right to strike or to arguments for a wages freeze. At the level of the 'national interest' economic debate the decoder may adopt the hegemonic definition, agreeing that 'we must all pay ourselves less in order to combat inflation'. This, however, may have little or no relation to his/her willingness to go on strike for better pay and conditions or to oppose the Industrial Relations Bill at the level of shop-floor or union organization. We suspect that the great majority of so-called 'misunderstandings' arise from the contradictions and disjunctures between hegemonic-dominant encodings and negotiated-corporate decodings. It is just these mismatches in the levels which most provoke defining elites and professionals to identify a 'failure in communications'.

Finally, it is possible for a viewer perfectly to understand both the literal and the connotative inflection given by a discourse but to decode the message in a *globally* contrary way. He/she detotalizes the message in the preferred code in order to retotalize the message within some alternative framework of reference. This is the case of the viewer who listens to a debate on the need to limit wages but 'reads' every mention of the 'national interest' as 'class interest'. He/she is operating with what we must call an *oppositional code.* One of the most significant political moments (they also coincide with crisis points within the broadcasting organizations themselves, for obvious reasons) is the point when events which are normally signified and decoded in a negotiated way begin to be given an oppositional reading. Here the 'politics of signification' - the struggle in discourse - is joined.

11 Television news and the Social Contract*

Ian Connell

The 'impartiality' of television news and current affairs is now widely considered a myth. This standard critique is usually presented in terms of 'bias' and 'distortion'. In this article I argue against the terms and implications of this position. In a wide variety of studies the pictures and definitions constructed by journalistic practices are said to provide 'biased' or 'distorted' accounts of an independent and objective reality; they are 'biased' or 'distorted' because they are informed by a body of ruling and dominant ideas, which are said to 'belong', in a simple way, to ruling political or economic groups. In short, television journalism is made to appear to be a kind of megaphone by which ruling ideas are amplified and generalized across all sectors of the social formation.

The material examined here is television's account of the Labour Government's attempts, since October 1974, to win, and maintain the 'voluntary obedience' of trade unions to the policy of wage restraint. This account recruited and represented the different positions constructed in and through the struggles between unions, Government and the Trades Union Congress (TUC) leadership. There was no attempt to mask the controversial reception of the Government's economic policy. Particularly during 'Phase Three' of this policy, much of the reporting concentrated on explicit trade union opposition. If television were 'biased', as the conspiracy theorists would have it, if it took its orders directly and unquestioningly from the ruling political-economic forces and if, moreover, it had no material presence and effectivity of its own, there would have been little or no representation of this opposition.

It could certainly be argued that while the positions of all those directly involved in the negotiations and struggles over and around the Social Contract were aired, not all of them had access to television in the same way. As this article attempts to demonstrate, some of the already constructed positions on the Social Contract, particularly the position which argued for a return to free collective bargaining, were subordinated in the discourse of news and current affairs. At the same time, the Government's position was taken over and constructed as the 'basis of reality' on which serious discussion was mounted. While Labour Ministers and their supporters, including, at crucial moments, the Economic Committee of the TUC, were asked whether a 'voluntary policy' would be effective, while there was speculation about whether the various limits set by the Government would hold and whether some

*This revised chapter from Ian Connell's Ph.D thesis was first published in *Screen*, vol. 20, no. 1, and is reprinted here with kind permission.

'statutory measures' would have to be introduced, television journalism did not question the basic premise that inflation was 'wages-led': on the contrary, this premise constituted the baseline of television's accounts. This form of constructing television's account does not contravene the editorial imperative to demonstrate 'due impartiality'. According to the Annan Committee's Report, 'broadcasters must take account, not just of the whole range of views on an issue, but also of the weight of opinion which holds these views'. To put it another way, the practices of television journalism reproduce accurately the way in which 'public opinion' has already been formed in the primary domains of political and economic struggle, how it has been structured in dominance there.

Television journalism does not accomplish this work of reproduction by being 'biased', as this has been defined by the conspiracy thesis. It is not accomplished *despite* the basic editorial criteria, but rather precisely in and through their practical implementation. It is because this policy is put into practice that a complex unity is forged between the accounts produced by television and these primary accounts which are constituted in the social formation as the dominant, sometimes hegemonic, definitions of political-economic antagonisms. While the basic editorial criteria are, as a matter of course, scrupulously implemented, it does not follow, as many a professional broadcaster has imagined, that television journalism is ideologically inert. Television is an ideological instance precisely because of the effectivity of these editorial criteria. This can be seen, for example, in the shaping of 'topics' by the practices of television journalism. The explanations proffered by news and current affairs programmes are made to seem the 'best sense' of a given situation. They are, in the unfolding of television's account, categorized as 'common sense', 'moderate public opinion', 'rational understanding' or 'the consensus'. The basis of these explanations are the already constructed definitions in dominance. Television actively and independently contributes to their dominance by working them into the fabric of its explanations and by granting to them the status of what 'many' or 'most' people think.

A precondition of this ideological labour is the separation and fragmentation of television's coverage from the actual events covered. Through a series of visual and verbal operations discussed below, television's account is made to seem apart from, above and beyond, the struggles over the Social Contract. It is made to seem a 'neutral' space for the serious discussion of controversies. Simultaneously, these same operations construct an 'audience position' which, like the account itself, is separated out: the audience is constantly hailed as witness of, but not participant in, the struggle and argument over issues. This is the result of the construction of a televisual space in which the struggles are dramatized through the employment of various 'actuality forms' and then framed and focused by an authoritative, informational address that offers its abstracted sense to the audience. It is here, in particular, that it is necessary to highlight how television journalism attempts the generalization of its explanations. So the main proposition which this article will elaborate is that in and through the signifying practices specific to television journalism political-economic antagonisms are contained and their development as antagonisms is neutralized. This is not accomplished by abandoning the basic editorial imperatives but, on the contrary, by fulfilling them.

The following sections consider the relation between television journalism, the Government and trade unions, not by recording and examining what broadcasters have to say about their views of this relation, but rather by examining how these views are constructed and articulated in and through the routine operations of journalistic story-telling. We will therefore be focusing upon the perspectives, themes and propositions which have been advanced by journalistic accounts. This will be done by isolating and examining key elements employed in the construction of these themes and in their organization into apparently 'adequate' and 'coherent' explanations. These same elements will also be examined to clarify the attempts made to align the explanations with the 'lived experience' of audiences.

Something of this approach has been adopted by other recent studies of television's account of political issues, studies which have worked with a notion that television is now the key 'agenda-setting' device in the sphere of public opinion. It has been argued, for instance, that beside the long-standing commitments to inform, educate and entertain enshrined in the constitutional documents of both television networks, television now plays the role, albeit unwittingly, of drawing public attention to, and shaping the understanding of, the political situations it chooses to cover. The major points of this approach can be summed up as follows. It has been argued that broadcasters possess the power to: (1) define which issues will enter the sphere of public awareness and discussion; (2) define the terms in which these issues will be discussed; (3) define who will speak on the topics that have been selected; (4) manage and control the ensuing debates and discussions. At the heart of this approach to television journalism is the notion that the professional ideologies of broadcasters – that body of 'routinized and habituated professional "know-how" '[1] – uniquely and absolutely determines all decisions concerning subject matter, speakers and treatment. This approach transfers or displaces the power to define issues from dominant political and economic forces as attributed by the 'conspiracy' theorists to the broadcasters.

As a consequence, programmes are not studied in order to specify what they reveal about the actual relations between broadcasting and other sectors. Television is regarded as an absolutely independent prime mover in the social formation; the main emphasis of studies which adhere to this position lies in determining how programmes set about effecting what Trevor Pateman has called a 'relationship of complicity' with audiences.[2] The central argument of Pateman's study leads him to suggest that the phrase 'television coverage of an election' is a misleading one. Television, he argues, can only be said to provide 'coverage of' an election, or any other political event for that matter, if it has an existence independent of it. For him the evidence of television's increased penetration of election campaigning suggests that such independence has withered away; 'we do not have television coverage *of* an election: we have a television election'.[3]

From this perspective, television journalism is not seen as taking over and conferring authority on definitions of political situations that are initially formulated elsewhere. Rather, it is seen as creating these definitions itself. In Pateman's study, as in others which hold this position, television is said, however, to mediate political events. But if we accept that television does play a mediating role, we must also accept that political events are distinct from the television events - programmes of particular kinds - which selectively represent them. The two events are certainly related: the latter consist of illustrated stories *about* the former. But they are not identical, nor can the television be said to have displaced politics - it signifies it in specific ways. The agenda of political issues, what I have called the 'primary definitions' at a given moment in time, is *not* constituted by broadcasters but rather by contending political forces and by economic forces that have pertinent effects for the conduct of the dominant parliamentary political practices. Television journalism takes its lead from political forces, the dominant ones at any rate. The process of journalistic story-telling, which will be referred to here as a process of *informed speculation*, represents and then attempts to *generalize* definitions which already dominate the political sphere.

Like others, Pateman's study is important in that it gives due weight to the specific, formal properties of this process, especially those by which generalization is attempted. He draws attention, for example, to the use of 'inflexible formats and ritual repetitions', generalizing definitions, and to a variety of other 'attention-holding devices'. The nature of such devices and their application stems largely from the taken-for-granted and therefore generally unquestioned sense of what constitutes 'good', 'telegenic' material and 'good', 'attractive' presentation - in short, from professional 'know-how'. Assessments of what makes for an attractive presentation of issues - that is, one which will win and hold the attention of an audience - are, ultimately, based upon the assumption about audiences, their interests and attitudes, which are held by professional broadcasters. The deployment of these 'attention-holding' devices has consequences for the way in which political issues and their primary definition by leading protagonists are made to appear on television. They are *transformed* in particular ways.

One consequence of the different ways in which particular programmes make their appeal to audiences is that not all the issues that are selected and presented by news bulletins subsequently become items in current affairs programmes. Nor do those which pass into the sphere of current affairs receive attention from each programme located there. Some issues are considered to be more appropriately handled by particular programmes than by others. Certain issues, however, are covered by the full range of news and current affairs programmes. At the moment such issues include the contested policies of the Government to 'curb inflation' by preventing 'excessive wage settlements', encouraging 'moderation in wage negotiations' and 'holding down' public expenditure. Issues such as these, which are classified by politicians as well as broadcasters as ones that 'affect the nation as a whole', are more or less guaranteed access to each of the regular current affairs magazines - for example, *Panorama, Tonight, Weekend World* and *Nationwide.*

There are other types of issues which are not granted this universal access. Some issues (crime, for example), while receiving extensive routine surveillance in television news bulletins, rarely set in motion the full current affairs apparatus. They will typically be handled by investigative documentary reports and by some of the magazine programmes, such as *Tonight*, which, over a period of time, have come to include higher proportions of 'social problem' issues. For a 'crime issue' to receive the more intensely speculative forms of coverage which, over a period of several years have come to be regarded as the province of *Panorama*, it would have to have passed through certain additional thresholds of definition by accredited witnesses in the primary domains of the political and the economic. An example could be a run of particularly violent crimes which were said to represent a whole social pattern of events, or something which was seen to be a more general crisis in the legal apparatus as such. We cannot speak of a universal journalistic mode of appropriation and transformation of these primary definitions. The same content, already formed in the primary domains, will be transformed in different ways depending upon the televisual 'slot' to which they are directed.

This can be briefly illustrated by reference to the peculiarities of *Nationwide*. Political issues of the type regularly featured by *Panorama* occupy an exceptional and subordinate position in *Nationwide*'s repertoire of topics. When such 'heavy' political items do appear there they are typically marked out by some variation on the basic phrase 'and now we turn to more serious matters'. The following statement from the programme indicates more clearly the basis upon which selections and placings are made: 'Whenever we can on *Nationwide* we try to bring you the brighter side of life, to counter all the gloom and despondency around us. And tonight we have a success story . . . .' Similar statements about the programme itself pepper its presenters' narratives; they fulfil a meta-discursive function, reminding audiences of the status of the programme's transformations and, simultaneously, marking their difference from the others paradigmatically possible within the field of television journalism.

This cast to the programme's transformations is carried through to the handling of issues demarcated as 'heavy'. In general terms, it leads to a quest for the 'ray of hope' or the 'good news' amidst the 'bad'. So prevalent is this orientation that the mere presence of contradictory forces within the events covered by the programme can be elevated as a 'sign of hope'. Thus, for example, having failed to produce any measure of conciliation in the course of interviewing representatives of the 'men' and 'bosses' at Chrysler's Coventry plant at a time when the company was seeking Government assistance to continue operating in this country, Michael Barrett wound up the interview thus: 'Well, at least you're sitting together here on a very cold night tonight, and let's hope that kind of spirit moves on' (*Nationwide*, 19 February 1976). In short, the mere presence of the 'representatives' in the discourse is mobilized to suggest that conciliation which was manifestly absent from the interview's account.

These kinds of transformations have mainly to do with generalizing, though they unquestionably structure the forms of appearance of issues. They are, however, *secondary* aspects of journalistic story-telling in the sense that they can only be engaged on condition that the 'real' has already been constructed. The *fundamental* aspects of the process of informed speculation are those which articulate the 'real', the processes and means by which primary definitions in the political and economic spheres are recruited to, and incorporated within, the overall fabric of television journalism's accounts. Television journalism does *not* initiate definitions of political and economic issues. These definitions originate in the struggles between contending political and economic forces. Television does not take on board each and every definition in exactly the same way. I want now to examine this differentiating process of appropriation in some detail.

I have referred to the process of journalistic story-telling as one of informed speculation. This is a process common to all the slots in the news and current affairs sector, though the precise form of its accomplishment will vary according to the particular slot. It is comprised of two relatively distinct stages. During the first the main concern is to *establish* the topic and its 'basis of reality'. Between the first and second there is a transitional stage during which questions or points of interest are formulated. It is these which organize the second speculative moment in the process. Broadly speaking, it is possible to identify a repertoire of elementary televisual forms which are mobilized in the work of informed speculation. Together they constitute the formal paradigm of this sector of broadcasting – a basic set of formal possibilities from which selections are made and combined together in particular ways. This repertoire of possible forms has been developed and modified over time, but since the mid 1950s to the present it has remained essentially stable.[4] It contains the following elements:

A live studio 'piece to camera'
B live studio report
C live studio interview
D live studio debate
E actuality film sequence
F actuality film sequence with commentary over
G actuality film sequence with captions superimposed
H actuality extract
I actuality 'piece to camera'
J actuality report
K actuality interview
L graphics with commentary over
M stills with voice/captions over
N credits/titles with music over

The repertoire of communicative roles in journalistic television includes: (1) presenter; (2) commentator; (3) reporter; (4) chairperson; (5) interviewer; (6) interviewee; (7) expert; (8) protagonist in debate; (9) man/woman-in-street (ordinary person). These roles are not abstract essences; they exist and are differentiated only in and through discursive practice. The elementary forms can, of course, be broken down into smaller units. The live studio debate, for example, a form used throughout the field but only within the speculative stages, can be broken down into lower units of 'transaction', 'exchange', 'move' and 'act'. However, it can be regarded as elementary in the sense that each mobilization of this form contains certain necessarily fixed syntagms at each level of organization.

Not all the forms and roles I have mentioned are mobilized in the 'informational' stage of journalistic story-telling. News bulletins do not, for example, employ live studio debate. Though the selections and combinations vary with the nature of the primary definitions, any item in a news bulletin would include, at the very least, *A* and *B* (live studio report). A not-infrequent combination is: *A–B–E–F–K–A*. This combination gives to the work of appropriation its manifest informational cast. There is a dialectical relation between the elements *A, B* (live studio 'piece to camera', live studio report) and *E, F, K* (live studio report, interview, debate) in which the latter appear to ground, license and authenticate the former. Conversely, the statements made in *A* and *B* function as metalanguage; they appear to highlight, to set in place for the audience, the 'truth' of statements made in *K* especially. Although manifestly informational, the work of establishing topics is not ideologically inert. The heavy reliance on 'actuality' forms, particularly when pre-definitions of an issue have already constituted it as having 'grave-consequences-for-the-nation-as-a-whole', masks the extent to which the issue is framed and focused by the broadcasters themselves. The work of framing and focusing accomplished by the discourse of *A*, *B* and the commentary over in *F* establishes, for the audience, a certain orientation or 'point of view'. But this is grounded in the events and statements depicted in the actuality forms – 'the real events out there'. The use of the actuality forms sustains a 'transparency-to-reality' effect which makes the constructed orientation appear 'natural' – the only one possible.

To begin to demonstrate how this part of the process works and the nature of the orientations constructed, here are two examples from television news coverage of certain key moments in the proceedings of TUC Conferences. The first example is taken from the coverage of the TUC Conference in September 1974, at which the Labour Government's Social Contract was 'officially' endorsed; the second, from the TUC Conference in September 1977 which rejected a further year of pay restraint but agreed to hold to the Government's twelve-month rule. Each employs *H* (actuality extracts) extensively to recruit the Government's definitions to television's account.

1

Actuality scenes of delegates applauding. Voice over:
The Prime Minister gets a standing ovation from the TUC at Brighton after a speech that is seen as reinforcing the prospects of an October election.

In studio, newsreader talking direct to camera:
Mr Wilson in a forty-five minute address outlined the achievements of a Labour

Government, attacked Conservative policies and praised the Social Contract on which, he said, Labour's policies and hopes for a better future depended. Mr Wilson also attacked those whom he said had already been fighting the next election campaign for several months.

Wilson seen addressing delegates:
Britain's ability to fight inflation and our trade gap have been inhibited by the fact that from the moment a minority Government was formed there were those in the political world, and in the press, in finance and in some of those well-heeled activities on the fringe of productive industry, who have been more concerned with fighting the next general election. All right, they'll have their chance. We must be prepared though for an all-out effort on their part for, say, a few more weeks (laughter and applause).

2

Actuality scenes of delegates applauding. Voice over:
A standing ovation for the Prime Minister from the TUC after telling them some hard facts about the economy.

In studio, newsreader talking direct to camera:
Good evening. The Prime Minister today delivered to the trade unions his plea for moderate pay deals and for maintaining twelve-month intervals between pay rises. He said he believed the moderate increases and reduced taxation were the best way forward. He refused to go back on what he called the absurd inflation of 1974/1975. Instead he hoped to see inflation below 10 per cent. Mr Callaghan believed this was possible with moderation and the Government could respond by stimulating the economy. He hinted at a mini-Budget later this year, saying, 'I certainly do not rule out measures during the autumn.' For half an hour Mr Callaghan spoke forcefully to TUC delegates in Blackpool who tomorrow will vote on the twelve-month rule. He argued that there were dangers in pay flexibility and free collective bargaining and he regretted that a third year of pay code was not possible.

Callaghan seen addressing delegates:
As I say I would have liked, eh, a third year, but, ehm, all right, I'm told it's not on. Well, other things won't be on either. And this is, I think, the situation that the movement as a whole has got to discuss. We believed, I still believe, that despite all the difficulties, a combination of moderate earnings increases and reduced taxation is the best way to safeguard the interests of your members. I dare say some of your members don't believe it. Well, that's a situation we all have to face because this is a democracy. I understand. I would agree that there is a case, a very important case, for flexibility. It's the argument, if you like, against a statutory wage policy, which I am not in favour of. But flexibility implies that differentials will be allowed to grow. You can't have an inflexible flexibility. And if we get into the situation in which, as a result of one excessive claim and settlement, others use that to make a back and leap-frog over it, Madam Chairman, there's nothing the Government can

do then to stop you all being back in the situation you were glad to escape from in '74, '75, when wage claims made at twelve-month intervals eventually became wage claims made at nine-month intervals and, if it had gone on, some of them were being made at six-month intervals and if you had continued, it would have been at six-week intervals and three-week intervals and you would have been in hyper-inflation (shouting up, but remains at the level of general background noise). Well, I don't believe, indeed I would say with certainty, that the majority of your members and their wives do not want a return to that situation. (BBC *News*, 6 September 1977).

The extracts presented here from these early-evening television news bulletins do not exhaust the accounts. In both cases the accounts, after the actuality quotes, are passed over to the Industrial Correspondent, who begins to fill in more details of the speeches and the response to them. His comments will be considered in a moment. In both cases the establishment of the topic relies heavily on the use of actuality forms of television journalism: direct verbal and verbal-visual quotes. Thus the accounts have the appearance of simple reports which do little more than give the main points of the Prime Minister's speeches. The use of these actuality forms is the practical mode of demonstrating the objectivity of television journalism. They are ritualized means of affirming that what has been selected from the available pool of definitions has not been invented by the broadcasters. They are, then, the key means by which the 'transparency' effect of television is realized, an effect which denies the productivity of television's specific practices. Undoubtedly, the broadcasters are appropriating a topic which has already, in some measure, been prestructured, articulated in the political discourses. The often extensive use of actuality forms masks the specific structuring accomplished by the broadcasters. They are not simply engaged in restating what has already been said; their appropriation of the topic represents it as a televisual event.

What is particularly interesting here is that the process of authentication relies upon – and constantly reaffirms – the veracity of journalistic discourse as such. The process requires both modes of television: direct, live recording/transmission from the studio (marked principally by direct address to camera) and the transmission of recordings of events that have already happened (marked principally by the *lack* of direct address). Each requires the other; together they function to validate one another's order of truth and to pose the former as the authoritative and predominant mode. The temporal register, marked by the system of address to camera, not only locates the studio-based discourse in the here-and-now but simultaneously reduces the actuality discourse to its content. The 'elsewhere' of activity and participation is, in and through the juxtapositioning, made to appear as the simple substance of the 'here-and-now' of witnessing.

The moment of appropriation is one in which television can be said to be dominant over politics but without obliterating the latter. The articulations produced in the political discourses continue to exercise determination on television's mode of appropriation. Between the prime ministerial speeches and what the journalists have to say about them, there is a *reciprocity of perspectives.* To put it another way, the journalists' accounts not only provide details of the speeches, they are also positioned within the terms of reference of the speeches. The propositions and interpretations contained in the speeches are reproduced by the journalists' accounts and, because these assume the form of straight reports, are made to appear as 'facts'.

The clue to this lies in the opening remarks of the accounts. In both examples these remarks function as headlines; that is, they announce, in summary form, a focus or an orientation to what follows in the main body of the account. The orientation provided by the headline in each example is contained in the statement that each speech received a 'standing ovation from the TUC'. This observation is taken to convey that what the Prime Minister had to say was 'well received'. In the case of example 2 this point was underscored by the current affairs coverage of the speech later in the day. Opening an interview with Ken Gill, General Secretary of TASS (Technical, Administrative and Supervisory Section of the Amalgamated Union of Engineering Workers) and Allen Fisher, General Secretary of NUPE (National Union of Public Employees), Robin Day said:

> First of all gentlemen, your verdict generally on the Prime Minister's speech today, which was received quite warmly and, indeed, with standing applause at the end. Mr Fisher?
> *Alan Fisher:* Well, I wouldn't have put it warmly. I would have thought it was respectfully by the Congress, and I think that's usual with the TUC and the Labour Prime Minister. I wouldn't think it was warmth. (*Tonight*, 6 September 1977)

What Allen Fisher's redefinition of the standing ovation indicates is that journalists had given not just *an* interpretation of the reception, but one which was favourable to the Prime Minister's position. That this account was positioned within the Prime Minister's terms of reference was also indicated by its calling the Prime Minister's interpretation of the causes of and remedies for inflation 'hard facts about the economy'. There is little questioning in this example of the Government's proposition that excessive claims and settlements over wages brought about inflation and that 'the best way forward', therefore, lay in 'moderate increases and reduced taxation'. What there was concerned how effective the Prime Minister's presentation of his case would be 'at shop floor level in the months ahead'.

This direction was developed in the 'news analysis' section of the account which followed the run-down of the Prime Minister's speech and the details of its immediate reception. News analysis, typically provided by the specialist correspondents, represents a kind of half-way house between 'straight reporting', the informational stage of informed speculation, and 'comment and analysis', contained in the second speculative stage of the process. The object of news analysis is to provide a preliminary contextualization of the themes contained in the report section of the account. As in this example, this typically means providing an assessment of the responses made by important people involved in the situation. On this occasion the BBC's Industrial Correspondent began by noting that 'there was nothing new in what the Prime Minister had said . . . though the style of delivery of the economic analysis seemed rather more determined . . . and he told delegates squarely that so-called free collective bargaining had not produced social justice'. From here he moved to the main concern of this part of the account, 'union leaders' reactions', which were said to vary 'according to the stance taken on the twelve-month rule and on moderation in pay settlements'. (Notice here that the yardstick by which union leaders are positioned is provided by the Government's case and not their own.) This was presented by means of extracts from video-recorded interviews with two union leaders, Clive Jenkins, who was presented as 'a militant exponent of free collective bargaining', and Tom Jackson, who was presented, in an unqualified way, as 'a supporter of incomes policy'. The questions asked of them set up a situation in which their replies were confined to an assessment of the effectivity of the speech and also prevented any detailing of the alternative case.

The labels applied by the Industrial Correspondent to the alternative economic strategy that had been adopted by the TUC on the previous day in the form of 'an orderly return to free collective bargaining' and to its proponents further reproduced a sense of the Government's case as 'hard fact'. Although an alternative case is announced, it does not form the basis of the journalists' account, nor is its logic developed. Indeed, in being marked out as the exclusive property of 'militants', it is made to appear as though it had no logic. The overall effect of this disposition of the available cases is to render the Government's strategy - adherence to the twelve-month rule, moderation in wage bargaining and possible cuts in taxation - the only plausible one.

This presentation of the Government's strategy, the pursuit of a third round of 'pay restraint', in the informational stages of journalistic story-telling was by no means novel nor exclusive to this particular bulletin. By the time of this particular broadcast it had become a familiar and recurrent theme in the news. It began to emerge in the accounts provided of Denis Healey's Budget of 29 March 1977, which, among other things, had made promises about cuts in taxation if another round of restraint could be agreed with the unions. It also was one of the fundamental organizing themes of the news coverage of the various trade union conferences between April and July. Throughout this coverage the case on which the Government's strategy was based, namely that 'excessive' wage settlements were the cause of inflation, was as such only infrequently dealt with.

The 'transparency-to-reality' effect is, then, not simply accomplished in and through the juxtapositioning of the formal modes of television journalism to which attention has been drawn. It also requires an ideological alignment between the definitions constituted in the journalistic accounts and those already constituted as dominant in the discourse of the political-economic sphere. The 'reality' of television journalism is not immediately identical with the 'reality' of the political-economic discourse, nor does the former in some simple way reflect the latter. Rather, the reality of television journalism must be formed in such a way that it *corresponds* to the reality that has been formed by the political-economic discourse.

I want now to examine, in more detail, the specific journalistic practices by which this correspondence is attained, and to do so with reference to the television coverage of the trade union conferences held in the months before the TUC Conference of September 1977. In so doing, I hope to make it clear not only that between this coverage and the Government's account there was a shared ideological problematic, but also that the signifying practices of television journalism actively constituted the dominant definitions as normal and self-evident. From earlier sociological studies of television journalism we know that it is centrally concerned with those actions which have been pre-signified as 'unexpected' – that is, with actions which break from the meaningful and consonant,[5] to use Galtung and Ruge's terms. It is the latter, the meaningful and consonant, the expected, which operates as a yard-stick for determining the 'unexpected'. The expected, if it is manifested in the utterances of television journalism at all, does so as 'what everyone knows' and, therefore, does not need to be spelt out. During the period we are concerned with here the Government's proposition that inflation was wages-led was only rarely mentioned, let alone explicitly articulated. At an earlier moment, during the first months of 1975, after Healey had announced that 'it is far better that more people should be in work even if that means accepting lower wages on average . . . that is what the Social Contract is all about', the proposition was explicitly articulated and speculated on. It is not possible here to go into details of the form that the articulation assumed in television news. It can only be pointed out that it was prompted by a reversal in the position adopted by the Labour Party during the latter part of 1974, when the whole question of wages was subordinated for the purposes of gaining the assent of the TUC and winning the October 1974 General Election.

By 1977 the proposition that inflation was wages-led had become a taken-for-granted in television news – an apparent 'fact of life' – and the form of the coverage actively reproduced it as such. Though rarely mentioned in the course of television's monitoring of the trade union conferences held between April and September 1977, it nevertheless functioned as a premise, as the 'always-already-there' of the explicit articulations concerning the conferences. The substance of many television news items in this period was conference debates about wages. Only rarely were debates on other topics featured. The following is a typical example of how the wages debates conducted by the 'minor' unions were represented:

Newsreader talking direct to camera:
The National and Local Government Officers' Association voted decisively for another phase of pay restraint today. The resolution before them was against restraint but they threw that out by 448,000 to 139,000. So that means that the fourth largest union in the country with 700,000 members and the largest of the white collar unions is behind the Government. (*Independent Television News,* 15 June 1975)

The account does not simply provide information about the vote: it gives the vote a particular significance. The narrator transforms this, and indeed other votes in other unions, into evidence of support for the Government. It is made to be of interest only in terms of the relation to 'another' phase of pay restraint.

Throughout this period then, the facticity of wage restraint was constantly reproduced. What television news constructed as the 'unexpected', what bulletins articulated, was the question of whether the unions were going to deliver. Certain conferences were expected not to deliver - for example, the Scottish TUC's Conference in April 1977. Both the BBC's and the ITN's coverage elected to feature prominently the speech of the Scottish Secretary (Bruce Millan) to that conference. The BBC's news analysis of the speech ran as follows:

Industrial Correspondent, in studio, direct to camera:
Mr Millan came to Rothesay to try to impress upon this pretty left-wing gathering the advantages of continuing pay restraint after July and of preserving the Social Contract between Government and trade unions, no less than the Prime Minister will be doing much the same thing at the Welsh TUC later this week - but again for the benefit of a much wider audience.

Mr Millan's message was that the next phase of the pay policy would not be an easy one to work out. How far and how quickly it was possible to return to normal collective bargaining without throwing away the benefits from the last two years in a general free-for-all. A wages explosion, he predicted, would push prices and unemployment even higher still and could bring down the Government.

At this point there was a direct actuality extract depicting Millan setting out what he thought the consequences of a Conservative Government for Scotland would be.

In this section of the transcript we see some of the key devices employed for handling not only the expected opposition of the Scottish TUC, but also other unions already known to be likely to oppose the Government's policy. The narration, following the lead set by Millan and the Government Ministers, forms this likely opposition into a call for a wages explosion. In this case the advocates of opposition are presented as a 'pretty left-wing gathering', which in the register of television news talk has the effect of marking them off from 'the moderates', that 'much wider audience' spoken of in the narrative, which might just be seduced by decisions taken at this conference.

Following the actuality quote, the Industrial Correspondent set about contextualizing the decision that the Scottish TUC might take on the issue of pay restraint. To convey the significance of the decision he said:

Tomorrow the Scottish miners will lead the opposition to interference of any kind in free collective bargaining. If this move gains majority support, as it might, although there is some doubt tonight, it will really be the Scottish TUC doing its usual militant thing; opposing incomes restraint. And the foreign exchange markets were well-advised to ignore this. A couple of union leaders up here from London pointed out to me that issues like the Social Contract and pay policy are subject to discussion between the Government and TUC - the British TUC, not the Scottish TUC. (*BBC News,* 19 April 1977)

The perspective on the Scottish TUC is, from the evidence of the final remarks, again licensed. It is not wholly the invention of the Industrial Correspondent, since he reproduces the statements of 'a couple of union leaders up here from London'. Nevertheless, the perspective is supplemented by the reference to the possible majority support for free collective bargaining as the Scottish TUC 'doing its usual militant thing' and by opening this part of the account with a reference to the 'Scottish miners'. It is a massively reassuring perspective; it is tantamount to saying that the opposition is mere ritual and, moreover, will have little impact on the eventual outcome of 'national' negotiations.

When, on the following day, the move to oppose any form of wage restraint was 'narrowly defeated', the Industrial Correspondent back-pedalled somewhat on his previous estimation of the significance of the decision. He said:

This is not a conference of any real significance in the decision-making process. But at this stage in the attempt to work out a phase three of pay restraint, the Government might be quite relieved that even the unions up here haven't voted for a free-for-all. *(BBC News,* 20 April 1977)

In the course of advocating 'terminating the Social Contract' at the Scottish TUC, Mick McGahey had argued that the main reason for doing so was that 'the Government had not fulfilled its pledges within the Contract'. An earlier item in the same bulletin in which this was quoted could have been seen to have provided some evidence to support McGahey's case. The opening item of the bulletin, read out in the studio direct to camera, announced:

As the debate on pay policy continues, figures out today show that the rate of increase in earnings continues to fall. It's now well below the current rate of price inflation. Average earnings in February were 11½ per cent higher than at the same time last year. The increase in prices over the same period was just over 16 per cent.

Although the item on the Scottish TUC followed on immediately, *no* explicit connections were made, for to have done so would have run contrary to the plot structure of television's accounts.

The proceedings of the Scottish TUC, as represented by television, are of interest only because of the potential threat they posed to the Government's strategy. The predominant feature of the plot adopted was to determine 'how well' the Government was doing, a feature which was retained throughout the following months. In May the information that 'the rate of inflation was back where it was nearly a year ago. It's now 17.5 per cent' (*BBC News,* 22 May 1977) did not lead to any fundamental revision of the plot. Rather, it was transformed into a misfortune, a test of the Government's fitness. The account noted that 'at a time when the Government is trying to win a third year of pay restraint, the relationship between pay and prices is not helping'. But later the Government was redeemed. The narrator (BBC Industrial Correspondent) pointed out that 'the Government sticks by its forecast of inflation falling to 13 per cent by the end of the year', and that 'the best that can be said about the figures is that they were expected by the Government, who made it clear before today that inflation won't start coming down until the second half of the year'. That the figures were expected, known about, implies that the Government also knew how to deal with them.

Later in the year, as the major unions, particularly the National Union of Miners and the Transport and General Workers' Union, rejected the Government's economic strategy, the plot was modified, but again not fundamentally revised. The Government was still allocated the part of hero and the unions the part of villain. There was, however, a marked shift from a heroic to a tragic orientation.

In the coverage of the Transport and General Workers' Union Conference the centrepiece was again made to be the consequences of their discussions on pay for the Government's economic strategy. The *BBC News* bulletin of 5 July 1977 represented that union's leadership's attempts 'to keep Britain's largest union firmly in line with TUC objectives', and in so doing emphasized that the leadership believed 'that if there were a wages free-for-all, it could damage the long-term prospects for the British economy'.

While this part of the account employed actuality forms to ground the narration, these were not employed in representing the 'considerable ground swell of opposition to these policies'. This opposition was formed up entirely by means of the newsreader's direct address to camera:

> And as Mr Jones and his executive left the conference hall tonight, they took with them copies of a motion that will also be put to the delegates tomorrow which calls for an immediate return to unfettered collective bargaining and the total ending of phase two on 1 August of this year – a call which, if it is heeded, would finally shatter what remains of the Social Contract.

The articulation of the 'considerable ground swell of opposition' in this union considerably raised the stakes. The narration transformed that opposition into an act of destruction which threatened not only the remains of the Social Contract, but also the long-term prospects of the British economy. This signification of this union's actions was massively re-enacted on the following day after its vote 'against an orderly return to free collective bargaining'. We have, then, the lowering of wages represented as 'orderly' – a term bringing into play such semantic equivalents as 'obedient', 'not unruly', 'well behaved'. The representation of the union's vote against this opened with the statement that delegates had 'defeated the moderate motion against the advice of their General Secretary, Jack Jones', thus associating wages restraint with moderation. There then followed an actuality extract from a speech against 'the moderate line':

> Brothers and sisters, we've been conned [cheers]. The pensioners and lower paid workers are worse off. The social services have been cut to ribbons, and we're in the grip of the talons of the international money-lenders. Of course we do not want a Tory Government. But if this Government does not reverse these disastrous policies and introduce the measures advocated by the Labour Party Conferences, that is, a socialist alternative, we'll get Margaret Thatcher at the helm as sure as little apples. Recent election results have shown this. Wages a major cause of inflation? They never have been. The last two years have proved that. Another period of marking time? We've had enough. Mr Healey, you're not on. (*BBC News*, 6 July 1977)

It would have been possible, as on other occasions, when acuality quotes had been included from the speeches of Cabinet Ministers, to provide background information on the speech. But this did not happen. Instead, the journalists opted to emphasize that the 'militants . . . dominated the whole debate', and that the debate had been 'noisy, emotional'. From here on the account concentrated on the defeated executive's line and then included an interview with Jack Jones, 'the architect of the Social Contract' – a constructive image which contrasts sharply with the destructive images constructed for the opponents.

The interview once again returns to constituting the destructive effects of the motion that had been carried. Jack Jones was asked, first of all, 'whether the threat of a wages explosion now threatened the Labour Party's own ability to govern', and then, following an affirmative reply, ('I think that is a danger . . .'), he was asked if he thought that 'now, after this decision this afternoon, the political stability of the country is not threatened as a result of what has happened, that the Government may indeed not be in a position to govern any longer?', which again received an affirmative response when Jack Jones said: 'Well, the political stability could be threatened if the Liberals decided to withdraw support. . . .' The transformation of the act of opposition into an act of destruction is consummated by the interview. It is not only authenticated; it is also rendered authoritative by the affirmations of the architect of the Social Contract.

The television news bulletins which we have been examining here are not the 'windows on to reality' that they are made to seem by professional ideologies of broadcasting and by the extensive use of actuality forms (of which more shall be said in a moment). The point to be stressed is that we do not see 'through' the bulletins to an objective and independent 'reality' beyond. We see only that reality which has been jointly produced by the journalistic practices of signification and by the other practices of signification employed by journalism's accredited witnesses in the political-economic sphere. In this respect, the simple 'bias' thesis is inadequate, based as it is on an untenable assumption of a separation between images and ideas on the one hand, and objective, material reality on the other. Within the terms of the 'bias' thesis we have no option but to regard television journalism as a mere (and inadequate) reflection of material reality rather than an active material process, itself intimately bound up in the construction and articulation of reality. This thesis takes at face value the journalistic practices of signification. The construction and articulation of 'reality' as seemingly independent, as natural, is inscribed in the most basic practices of television journalism. The organization of the visual discourse, for instance, which shows little variation between networks or across the period from 1974 to the present, is such that it produces this effect. Newsreaders and correspondents are always to be seen talking direct to camera (seemingly 'to us'), while those placed in the drama of news as protagonists are always to be seen talking at an angle to the line of vision of the camera (seemingly 'to others'). The depiction of protagonists in this manner constructs a potential sense of distance between them and viewers. This is a *sense of witnessing* (that is, of being present at, but not directly involved in) a 'reality' which is, in and through this visual mode, made to seem 'out there', separate from and independent of those positioned as witnesses. The relation in which the 'audience' is cast by this visual mode is that of *onlooker*: the proceedings of protagonists are 'looked in on'. Whether the social beings who watch television news programmes, who are themselves sites of intersection of a multiplicity of discursive practices, actually assume this position is, of course, another matter. The point to be stressed here, however, is that the mode of vision currently in dominance presents the relation in this form – that is, as a relation between the 'involved' and the 'uninvolved'.

The exposition and interpretation of the actions of those cast as the 'involved' falls to the narrators, newsreaders or specialist correspondents. Their direct address is a posture which recreates certain of the conditions of interpersonal communication. Often, following their initial exposition of the pro-televisual action of the involved, newsreaders will turn from the camera to look at the monitor in the studio, signifying that they, like the viewer, are similarly detached, uninvolved onlookers. The direct address has, then,the potential effect of including the viewer in the process of communication. The viewer is positioned as a partner in the exchange: the direct look of the newsreader/reporter/specialist correspondent implicates the audience. So while the audience is set apart from the protagonists, it is lined up with the media personnel in the studio.

These forms of vision of television news bulletins are based on, and contribute to the reproduction of, an already given political ideology. The visual disposition of the role of audience as onlookers in relation to what is shown of protagonists by actuality sequences and as partners to the exchanges initiated by media personnel reproduces the notion that the 'nation as a whole' is divisible into 'activists' and the 'rest', who are involved in problematic situations only in as much as they are affected by them. Within this *lived* view of the polity, with its assumption of a fundamental division between those who 'do' and those who are 'done by', the studio appears as the vantage point of the latter. It seems the site upon which those who are 'done by' – 'the public', 'the majority', 'most people', 'consumers', 'taxpayers' and so on – gain an insight into the actions of 'doers' – 'the unions', 'politicians', 'militants'.

This apparently fundamental division is further refined in what is said of the issues and activists featured. It is clear from the extracts above that not all those signified by television as 'activists' are spoken of in the same way. Some are verbally defined as 'representative individuals'; they are not only named but have the authority to speak, their 'representative' credentials presented: 'The Prime Minister, Mr Callaghan . . .'; 'the union's General Secretary, Mr Jones . . .'. Others are referred to only as a collective – 'the militants' motion . . .'. Not only are they presented without credentials but their representativeness is either heavily qualified or denied. Those opposing the policy of wage restraint within the Parliamentary Labour Party were presented as a localized grouping, as 'the left wing of the Labour Party'. In the coverage of the Scottish TUC Conference the Scottish TUC was not only localized but also presented as having 'no real significance in *the* decision-making process'.

It is principally the verbal discourse which accomplishes the classification of activists, a classification which separates out the legitimate and acceptable activists from the illegitimate and unacceptable. As we have already suggested, these classifications are the effects of the adoption of a certain political perspective: that is, a certain way of understanding already given political positions. Any classification of positions is possible only on the condition that a system of classification already exists. The system of classification by which television news identified and placed the forces involved in the economic struggles of the last few years did not spring uniquely from the broadcasters' professional 'know-how'. Nor did it emerge 'from the outside', a wholly independent perspective. It is, rather, the reproduction of a system of classification already ingrained in the institutional procedures for the management of the clash of opposing activists.

The perspective adopted by the news bulletins was, as we have said, that of the Government and the TUC in as much as they were its principal advocates. The adoption and reproduction of this perspective did not result, however, from a conspiracy between broadcasting, the state and the hegemonic organs of civil society, such as the TUC. Television journalists do not have to be explicitly instructed, as a rule, in how to classify appropriately the protagonists of a given situation and the positions they advance. As we have seen, the Government's interpretation of the causes of inflation was accepted without question. It was a premise of the coverage, and the proposed solution, wage restraint or the lowering of 'real' wages, was thus made to appear a 'natural' consequence. Only the opposed interpretations were questioned and made to appear 'unreasonable', the product of 'militant' self-interestedness. In part, the unqualified acceptance of the Government's logic proceeded from its status as the 'elected representatives of the people'. But this is not a sufficient condition; the Government's handling of inflation was questioned and probed, especially in the current affairs programmes, though not in a fundamental way. Its position was accepted, principally, because the broadcasters *shared* its logic. For both broadcasters and the Government it seemed 'obvious' that the prices of commodities are determined or regulated by wages. It was the acceptance of this 'antiquated fallacy' which placed the broadcasters, the Government and the TUC on the same side.

12 Recent developments in theories of language and ideology: a critical note*

Stuart Hall

In recent years the two journals *Screen* and *Screen Education* (sponsored by the Society for Education in Film and Television) have provided the base for the development of a set of challenging hypotheses about the relationship between language, ideology and 'the subject'. Though principally relating to film texts and practices, this theory has far-reaching implications for the analysis of all signifying practices, as well as for the debates on the problem of language/ideology and representation. This body of work (hereinafter, for convenience, 'screen theory') draws extensively on recent French theoretical writing in a number of different fields: film theory (early semiotics, the work of Christian Metz, the debates between the journals *Cahiers du Cinēma* and *Cinētique*), the theory of ideology (Althusser), the psychoanalytic writings of the Lacan group, and recent theories of language and discourse (Julia Kristeva, the 'Tel Quel' group, Foucault). It has also been strongly influenced by the critique of 'realism', defined as the dominant filmic practice in the cinema: this critique originates in Brecht's work and the Brecht–Lukācs debate and, to some extent, in the Russian formalists. It has recently much developed in both the theory and the practice of *avant-garde* cinema. 'Screen theory' has reworked and expanded these theories through a series of wide-ranging articles. The problematic which they have been elaborating now constitutes the dominant point of departure in film studies and in the debates around the relation of discourse and ideology.

'Screen theory' originates in the break which the structural linguistics of Saussure first made with earlier theories of language and which was developed into a general paradigm for the study of signifying systems by Lēvi-Strauss and the early Barthes. This is the point of departure for early semiotics. But the real theoretical distinctiveness of 'screen theory' arises from the further break between what, for convenience, may be called semiotics 1 and semiotics 2 (for an elaboration of this distinction, see pages 36–7). Crudely, the argument is that semiotics 1 was correct in its attempts to identify signification as a practice for the *production* of meaning, as against earlier theories which assumed that 'reality' was somehow transparently reflected in language. It also advanced the field considerably by dethroning the position of the integral Cartesian subject – the authorial 'I', assumed to be both the source and the guarantor of the 'truth' of any enunciative statement – in favour of an analysis

*This article is based on a forthcoming critique of recent theoretical developments by the Media Group, 1977–8.

pitched at the level of the relations between elements and the rules governing their combination in signifying systems themselves (Saussure's *Langue*). However, 'screen theory' argues that, in itself, this break with empiricist theories of language is inadequate, since (in Lēvi-Strauss's 'myth', Barthes's 'codes' and Althusser's theories of ideology) the whole question of 'the subject' is left as an empty space. The Cartesian subject has been displaced: but what replaces it has not been adequately theorized.

In semiotics 2 this gap is filled by drawing extensively on the psychoanalytic writings of Lacan. Three converging lines of argument sustain this attempt to deploy Lacan to rectify the inadequacies of semiotics 1. First, Lēvi-Strauss made much of the 'entry into culture' as the founding moment of signification and symbolic representation, but he located this outside 'the subject', in the cultural and social system itself. Lacan's work retains the structure of Lēvi-Strauss's explanation but now locates this as the entry into the 'symbolic' - the moment when 'the subject' enters into/is constituted in language, the network of signifiers. In Lacan the moment of the 'symbolic' is given a psychoanalytic interpretation, based on a re-reading of Freud and linked with the unconscious processes and stages through which the unformed infant becomes a 'subject', as these are outlined in Freud's work. This, however, is no longer the integral and homogeneous 'subject' of Descartes, since it is constituted by unconscious processes; it is not the unitary individual but a set of contradictory 'positions', fixed by those processes in a certain relation to knowledge and language.

Second, these propositions were substantially reinforced by Althusser's later writing on ideology, especially where (in the 'Ideological State Apparatuses' essay) he argues that all ideologies 'work' by and through the constitution of the subject and then gives to the process by which ideological discourses constitute and 'hail' subjects the term 'interpellation' - a concept which has an ambiguous provenance in Lacan.

The third element is harder to pin down exactly, but it arises from the fact that in Lacan's reading Freud's theory of the formation of 'the subject' is a highly linguistic one, and the processes of that formation are especially linked with visual analogues (for example, the 'mirror phase', narcissism, voyeurism, Lacan's work on the 'look' and the 'gaze', the castration complex as a 'scenario of vision', founded on the presence/absence and the 'recognition'/denial through which it is resolved and so on). These have made it especially easy and tenable to forge a connection between the 'primary' psychoanalytic processes through which subjects-as-such are constituted and the related processes of representation and identification in visual discourses and texts (especially those of the cinema). Metz's article 'The imaginary signifier'[1] is a *locus classicus* of this move from semiotics 1 to a Lacanian psychoanalytic framework, and its republication in *Screen* marked the passage of that journal from the earlier debates on 'realism' to a full-blown Lacanian position.[2] It ought to be said that 'screen theory' is far more than an attempt to supplement existing theories of language, representation and ideology by developing the neglected area of 'the subject'. In effect, all preceding theories have been substantively reworked and/or displaced by the deployment of Lacan's propositions. The premises of historical materialism, for example, which attempt to relate ideologies to political and economic practices, to their functioning and effectivity in specific social formations and in specific historical conjunctures, have been translated on to the terrain of 'the subject'. We would argue that this is accomplished through a series of reductions: the unconscious process through which 'the subject' is constituted is also – it is proposed – the process which constitutes 'the subject' *in language*. It is also the same as that which constitutes 'the subject' for ideology. First a series of homologies, then a series of identities give these apparently distinct (if related) levels a single and common source and foundation. The 'politics' of ideological struggle thus becomes exclusively a problem of and around 'subjectivity' in the Lacanian sense.

'Screen theory' is therefore a very ambitious theoretical construct indeed – for it aims to account for how biological individuals become social subjects, *and* for how those subjects are fixed in positions of knowledge in relation to language and representation, *and* for how they are interpellated in specific ideological discourses. This theory is then lopped back to the earlier concerns with 'realism'. Most filmic texts are held to operate within the conventions and practices of 'realism': they are said to be governed by the rules of *the* classic realist text (in the singular). The classic realist text sets the viewers in a position of transparent and unproblematic knowledge in relation to their representations of 'the real', which they actually produce but which they appear only (naturally) to reflect. They therefore depend on an empiricist relation to knowledge. But – so the argument runs – this is because the rules and conventions of the classic realist text recapitulate and replay the basic positions of 'the subject', already fixed by unconscious processes in the early stages of its formation.

This theory gives texts a central place. Texts do not express a meaning (which resides elsewhere) or 'reflect reality': they produce a representation of 'the real' which the viewer is positioned to take as a mirror reflection of the real world: this is the 'productivity of the text', discussed more fully below. However, this 'productivity' no longer depends in any way on the ideological effectivity of the representations produced, nor on the ideological problematics within which the discourse is operating, nor on the social, political or historical practices with which it is articulated. Its 'productivity' is defined exclusively in terms of the capacity of the text to set the viewer 'in place' in a position of unproblematic identification/knowledge. And that, in turn, is founded on the process of the formation of the subject. Within this framework, then, the functioning of language, the practices of representation and the operations of ideology are all explained by reference to Lacanian psychoanalytic theory. It follows that all ideological struggle must take place, also, at the level of 'the subject' (since this is where the relation of 'the subject' to ideology is constituted and is the mechanism through which ideology functions) and is confined to disrupting the forms of the discourse which recapitulate those primary positions.

This ambitious theory, with its aim to resolve a host of problems unsatisfactorily dealt with in classical Marxist theory, has been forcefully advanced and expounded with considerable sophistication. Nevertheless, it is open to a number of criticisms which have not so far been adequately met. These may be briefly summarized as follows.

1 The theory is substantiated by, first, establishing a series of homologies - 'ideology is structured like a language', 'the unconscious is structured like a language' and so on - which are then declared to be not just 'like' each other but actually 'the same': constituted in the same moment by the same unconscious mechanisms. This movement from homology to identity is a dubious procedure and has not so far been adequately defended.

2 These processes are all declared to be 'the same'. But *one* of them is given exclusive explanatory power over all the others. It is the psychoanalytic process by which 'the subject' is constituted in the 'symbolic' which explains how language/representation function (in any/every other instance). Specific discourses or representations appear to require no other conditions of existence or further premises to be explained and have no other determinate effectivity. But this form of psychoanalytic reductionism seems to 'resolve' the problems of semiotics 1 simply by inverting them. What in Saussure was explained by practices wholly exclusive *of* 'the subject' is now - by a simple inversion - explained exclusively *at* the level of 'the subject'. Except in a largely ritual sense, any substantive reference to social formation has been made to disappear. This gives 'the subject' an all-inclusive place and Lacanian psychoanalysis an exclusive, privileged, explanatory claim.

3 This relates to the 'in-general' form of the argument. The mechanisms which Freud and Lacan identify are, of course, universal. All 'subjects' in all societies at all times are unconsciously constituted in this way. The formation of 'the subject' in this sense is trans-historical and trans-social. It is a theory of the universal 'contradictory' subject - different from 'the subject' of classical philosophy in being intersected by contradiction and unconsciously constituted, but similar to it in the transcendental/universal form in which it is predicated. It is, of course, difficult, if not impossible, to square this universal form of argument with the premises of historical materialism, which requires us always to attend to the pertinent differences - Marx's *differentia specificae*, which *differentiate* one modality of individualism from another - which historicizes the different forms of subjectivity and which needs a reference to specific modes of production, to definite societies at historically specific moments and conjunctures. The two kinds of theory are conceptually incompatible in the form of their argument. This has not prevented 'screen theory' from claiming that its theory of 'the subject' is a 'materialistic' one and satisfactorily resolves the problems posed by historical materialism.

4 Further, suppose that we were to accept the validity of Lacan's theory of the constitution of the subject, as well as the 'screen theory' argument that we cannot

have an adequate theory of language/ideology without taking the functioning of 'the subject' into account. It does not follow that a theory of how the 'subject-in-general' is formed offers, *in itself,* without further determinations, an adequate explanation of how historically specific subjects, already 'positioned' in language-in-general, function in relation to particular discourses or historically specific ideologies in definite social formations. The theory of 'the subject' as advanced by 'screen theory' *may be* a necessary part, but *it is not yet a sufficient explanation of* particular discourses or specific ideologies and their functioning. The practices of language, discourse and ideologies may have other determinations, only some of which can be fixed at the level of 'the subject'. Thus other premises, relating to further conditions of existence and having determinate effects, would have to be introduced in order to move the explanation – as historical materialism requires – from the level of the 'in-general' (compare 'production-in-general' – what Marx described as 'a chaotic abstraction') to the more concrete, historically determinate level (that is, specific modes of production under determinate conditions). 'Screen theory' seems here to have fallen prey to the temptation to treat the most abstract/ universal level of abstraction as the most pertinent – indeed, the only 'truly theoretical' – level of explanation.

In its present, all-embracing form 'screen theory' refuses to countenance any propositions about discourse or ideology which are not reducible to, and explicable by, the Lacanian theory of 'the subject'. Thus it claims to explain how 'the subject' is positioned in relation to patriarchal ideology-in-general. But it cannot explain the pertinent differences between different patriarchal ideologies in different social formations at different times. Even less can it explain how patriarchal ideologies may be broken, interrupted or contravened: since, according to the theory, 'the subject' cannot help but enter the 'symbolic' under the patriarchal sign, for it is this which, in imposing the 'Law of Culture' (the 'Law of the Symbolic'), establishes the rule of difference on which language itself is founded. 'The subject' is then, by definition, always already inside patriarchal language/ideology. Thus all ideology is, by definition, the dominant ideology – the *doxa*. This reproduces all the problems earlier identified in the 'functionalism' of Althusser's 'Ideological State Apparatuses' essay; only now the 'functionalism' of the dominant ideology appears to be given, not at the level of social formation, but at the level of 'the subject'.

5 It is, therefore, conceptually impossible to construct, from this position, an adequate concept of 'struggle' in ideology, since (for example) struggle against patriarchal ideology would be a struggle against the very repressive conditions in which language as such is itself constituted. No alternative model has been proposed as to how 'the subject' might be positioned in language without also being positioned in patriarchal ideology. 'Screen theory' has attempted to deal with this problem by advancing the strategy of 'deconstruction' (for example, deconstructing the practices and positionings of classical realism). But although deconstruction may provide a significant strategy of resistance, especially for the unmasking and interruption of dominant discourses, it certainly does not identify the conditions for the production

of alternative languages and discourses. What it appears to do is to establish a simple alternation between being 'in language' (and therefore, inescapably, in ideology) or 'against language'. But a non-patriarchal language cannot be conceptualized in terms of a revolution against language *as such:* this is a contradiction in terms. One effect of this, however, has been that a rather simple and unproblematic identity has been forged between the practices of struggle in ideology and the practices of the *avant-garde.* Julia Kristeva has taken this implied premise to its logical conclusion in her theory of the revolution in language. But this has not proved an adequate resolution of the problem, which arises because the argument has collapsed a theory of the functioning of specific ideologies into a theory of the conditions for language as such.

6 We have taken patriarchal ideologies as our example in the foregoing criticism because 'screen theory' has advanced particularly strong claims in this area (in contrast to classical Marxism), has been deeply influential for feminist theory and film practice - and yet seems to encounter particular difficulties precisely on this ground. For in Lacan the differences and distinctions which make language and representation possible (a condition of the 'symbolic') are rooted in the marking of sexual difference - the latter providing the paradigm for, as well as the supporting structure of, the former. But the key mechanism which sustains this passage into the 'symbolic' is the resolution of the castration complex. However, this is a highly phallocentric theory, and its effect appears to be to consign women, not just in this culture but forever - and as a condition of having access to representation at all - to a negative entry into language, which is already and always marked by patriarchal dominance. If the 'Law of Culture' is, by definition and always, the 'Law of the Father', and this is the condition of language and the 'symbolic', then it is difficult to see why patriarchy is not - psychoanalytically rather than biologically - a woman's necessary and irreversible destiny.

These debates are by no means yet resolved: they have been vigorously and often contentiously pursued: and they continue to define a central terrain of theorization and argument in this area of work. Consequently, in 1977-8 the Media Group spent the year making itself familiar with this difficult body of work and with the bodies of theory on which it is based. It attempted to identify the central thesis and premises of the 'screen theory' problematic, as well as demystifying a little the forbiddingly arcane language and abstract formulations in which a great deal of the transcriptions from French theory have been cast. It attempted to develop a serious critique of 'screen theory', at the same time revaluing its own premises and practices in the light of that work. This critique is due to be published in its longer form. What follows (pages 163-73) is an extract from that longer argument, referring specifically to the question of how to think the relations between texts, subjects and readers/viewers. It develops a particular critique of 'screen theory' positions on this theme (similar points have begun to be formulated recently in the pages of *Screen* itself) and begins to advance alternative propositions, which, however, significantly modify earlier arguments as a result of the encounter.

13 Texts, readers, subjects*

Dave Morley

One major problem with the dominant theoretical position advanced by *Screen* is that it operates with what Neale has characterized as an 'abstract text–subject relationship'.[1] The subject is not conceived as already constituted in other discursive formations and social relations. Also, it is treated in relation to only one text at a time (or, alternatively, all texts are assumed to function according to the rules of a single 'classic realist text'). This is then explicated by reference to the universal, primary psychoanalytic processes (Oedipus complex, 'mirror phase', castration complex and its resolution and so on), through which, according to Lacan's reading of Freud, 'the subject' is constituted. The text is understood as reproducing or replaying this primary positioning, which is the foundation of any reading.

Now, apart from the difficulty of trying to explain a specific instance of the text/reader relationship in terms of a universalist theory of the formation of subjects-in-general, this proposition also serves to isolate the encounter of text and reader from all social and historical structures *and* from other texts. To conceptualize the moment of reading/viewing in this way is to ignore the constant intervention of other texts and discourses, which *also* position 'the subject'. At the moment of textual encounter other discourses are always in play besides those of the particular text in focus – discourses which depend on other discursive formations, brought into play through 'the subject's' placing in other practices – cultural, educational, institutional. And these other discourses will set some of the terms in which any particular text is engaged and evaluated. 'Screen theory' may be assumed to justify its neglect of the interplay of other discourses on the text/reader encounter by virtue of its assumption that all texts depend on the same set of subject positions, constituted in the formation of the subject, and therefore that they need be accorded no other distinctive effectivity of their own. Here, however, we wish to put in question this assumption that all specific discursive effects can be reduced to, and explained by, the functioning of a single, universal set of psychic mechanisms.

Pêcheux has provided us with the useful and important concept of *interdiscourse*.[2] As explicated by Woods, he argues that:

The constitution of subjects is always specific in respect of each subject . . . and this

*This article was originally based on work undertaken with Charlotte Brunsdon to extend the theoretical terms of the argument in *Everyday Television: 'Nationwide'* (BFI 1978), particularly in relation to the problem of audiences. This version incorporates material from the 1977–8 Media Group's longer, forthcoming critique on recent theories of discourse and ideology. It also incorporates comments from Dorothy Hobson, Adan Mills and Alan O'Shea, and was extensively revised for publication by Stuart Hall.

can be conceived of in terms of a single, original (and mythic) interpellation – the entry into language and the symbolic – which constitutes a *space* wherein a complex of continually interpellated subject forms interrelate, each subject form being a determinate formation of discursive processes. *The discursive subject is therefore an interdiscourse, the product of the effects of discursive practices traversing the subject throughout its history.*

The important point about this formulation is the distinction it holds between the constitution of 'the subject' as a general (original and mythic?) moment – constituting 'a space' – and the (second) moment when the subject-in-general is interpellated in the subject forms (the discursive subject positions) which are provided by the existing complex of discourses that make up the discursive formation (the interdiscourse) of specific social formations. Pêcheux therefore opens out what precisely 'screen theory' is at pains to close up – the space, the difference, between the formation of subjects-for-language and the recruitment of specific subjects to the subject positions of discursive formations through the process of interpellation. Thus whereas 'screen theory' poses the problem of the 'politics of the signifier' (the struggle over ideology in language) exclusively at the level of 'the subject', Pêcheux locates it at the intersection between constituted subjects and specific discursive positions – that is, at the site of interpellation. This is a critical distinction.

In 'screen theory' there can be no struggle at the site of the interface between subject and text (discourse), since contradictory positions have already been predetermined at the psychoanalytic level. Pêcheux takes over some part of this theory of the formation of the subject without, however, assuming that the struggle over meaning/interpretation in any subject/text encounter is already determined outside the conditions of 'reading' itself. To put this in Althusserian terms, whereas 'screen theory' assumes every specific reading to be already determined by the 'primary' structure of subject positions, Pêcheux treats the 'outcomes' of a reading as an over-determination. The two structures involved (constitution of 'the subject'/interpellation into specific discursive positions) are articulated, but are not identical, not mere replications of each other.

This links closely to the argument advanced by Laclau concerning the centrality of interpellation to the functioning of ideological discourses and the struggle in ideology to disarticulate/rearticulate the interpellative structure of particular discourses. The term 'interpellation' itself is an ambiguous one and has been subject to variable formulations. Althusser introduced it in the 'Ideology and Ideological State Apparatuses' essay, as a sort of 'loan' from Lacan, without making clear the status of the borrowing in relation to Lacanian theory.[3] That is, Althusser did not clarify to what extent he accepted the argument as derived from Lacan: that interpellation could be explained exclusively by reference to the 'primary' psychoanalytic processes. Althusser proposed, in the controversial second part of his essay, that 'there is no ideology except for concrete subjects', adding that ideology always functions through 'the category of the subject'. But he gave the constitution of that category not to the psychoanalytic level but to the functioning of ideological discourses themselves – that is, at this stage in his argument 'the subject' is a *discursive* category: 'at the same time and immediately I add that the category of the subject is only constitutive of all ideology in so far as ideology has the function (which defines it) of "constituting" concrete individuals as subjects'. And when, later, he advanced the more Lacanian proposition that the 'individuals' hailed by ideological discourses are always-already in ideology – 'individuals are always-already subjects' – he still leaves somewhat ambiguous the degree of determinacy accorded to this proposition. The unborn child already has an 'ideological' destination and destiny awaiting him/her: but Althusser only goes so far as to say:

> it is clear that this ideological constraint and pre-appointment, and all the rituals of rearing and then education in the family, *have some relationship* [our italics] with what Freud studied in the forms of the pre-genital and genital 'stages' of sexuality . . . But let us leave this point, too, on one side.

Laclau is more openly agnostic than Althusser when he adopts the term 'interpellation'.[4] He never refers the 'subjects' of interpellation to the psychoanalytic level, and he makes no reference to the Lacanian hypothesis. Instead, following Althusser's lead, he locates it at the level of the discourse: 'what constitutes the unifying principle of an ideological discourse is the "subject" interpellated and thus constituted through this discourse'. Certainly, Laclau cannot mean that this structure of interpellations is already pre-constituted at the moment when the infant becomes a 'subject' in the Lacanian sense, because the whole thrust of his argument is that these interpellations are *not* given and absolute but conditional and provisional. The 'struggle in ideology' takes place precisely through the articulation/disarticulation of interpellations: 'how are ideologies transformed? The answer is: through the class struggle which is carried out through the production of subjects and the articulation/disarticulation of discourses'. The position, then, seems to be that Pêcheux adopts part of the Lacanian argument but treats the constitution of 'the space of the subject' as only one, predetermining, element in the functioning of specific ideological discourses. Laclau locates interpellation exclusively at the level of the play in and struggle over discourses. Both locate ideological struggle at the level of the interplay between the subject and the discursive.

The concept of contradictory interpellations can be employed to clarify and modify the sociological approach of Parkin and others,[5] who refer to workers who grant legitimacy to a 'dominant ideology' in the abstract but inhabit a 'negotiated' or 'situationally defined' ideology at the level of concrete practice. That is, it can be used to clarify the problem of contradictory ideological positions, and specifically forms of corporate or sectional class-consciousness, without recourse to the premises of 'false consciousness'. Parkin refers to this evidence as showing 'split levels of consciousness'. However, if we introduce the concept of interpellation, we get rid of the presumption that there is a prescribed, unitary, homogeneous form of class-consciousness. This allows us to specify the articulation of different, contradictory subject positions or interpellations, to which the same individual worker (a contradictory subject, traversed by different discursive practices) is 'hailed': for example, he/she can be interpellated as 'national subject' by the television discourses of the dominant news media, but as 'class/sectional' subject by the discourses of his/her trade union organization or co-workers. In this approach the relative dominance of these contradictory interpellations and the political practices with which they are articulated are not given elsewhere (for instance, at the level of the formation of the subject) but vary with the conjuncture in which the subject is interpellated.

This stress on contradictory interpellations emphasizes the unstable, provisional and dynamic properties of positioning, rather than falling (as Parkin does, with his conception of 'split levels of consciousness') towards a static sociological ascription. The latter simply separates out into fixed proportions - where the subject identifies with the dominant discourses, and where he/she is in potential opposition to them. Again, Laclau's conception of the ideological work of disarticulation - especially his argument about the way discourses can convert opposition and contradiction into mere difference, thereby neutralizing a potential antagonism - is of crucial relevance. The stress now falls on the ideological process and struggle itself, thus making once more problematic a prescribed text/reader/subject relation.

By 'interdiscourse' Pêcheux appears to mean the complex of discursive formations in any society which provide already available subject positions (the 'pre-constructed') as a necessary category of their functioning. It is clear that the concept of interdiscourse transforms the relation of one text/one subject to that of a multiplicity of texts/subjects relations, in which encounters can be understood not in isolation but only in the moments of their combination.

A further consideration, not taken into account in 'screen theory', is that subjects have histories. If it is correct to speak not of text/subject but of texts/subjects relations with reference to the present, it must also be the case that past interpellations affect present ones. While these traditional and institutionalized 'traces' (to use Gramsci's term) cannot in themselves determine present interpellations, they do constitute the well established elements of the interdiscourse and frame successive new encounters. Gramsci speaks of the weight of traditional elements and Laclau of the 'relative continuity' of popular traditions. Indeed, Laclau may not have gone far enough in examining how these elements of the 'pre-constructed' may help to delay and impede the process of articulating/disarticulating the existing interpellative structures of ideological discourses. Consequently, he may offer a picture of too 'open' a struggle between discourses which is not sufficiently attentive to the weight of traditional elements.

Since 'screen theory' does not make any distinction between how the subject is constituted as a 'space' and specific interpellations, it deduces 'subjects' from the subject positions offered by the text and identifies the two. Thus the 'classic realist text' recapitulates, in its particular discursive strategies, the positions in which the subject has been constituted by the 'primary' processes. There is a fixed identity and perfect reciprocity between these two structures, which in 'screen theory' are, in effect, one and the same structure. The 'realist text' is therefore not so much 'read' as simply 'consumed/appropriated' straight, via the only possible positions available to the reader – those reinscribed by the text. This forecloses the question of reading as itself a moment in the production of meaning. In the 'screen theory' account this moment is doubly determined – by the primary subject positions which inscribe the subject in a relation of empiricist to knowledge/language and by those positions as they are reinscribed in the text through the strategies of realism.[6] Since these are posed as very general mechanisms, 'screen theory' is not required to address either the possibility of different, historically specific 'realisms' or the possibility of an inscribed realist reading being refused.[7] Readers here appear merely as the bearers or puppets of their unconscious positionings, reduplicated in the structure of the realist discourse (singular). But this runs counter to two of the most important advances previously established by structural linguistics: the essentially polysemic nature of signs and sign-based discourses, and the interrogative/expansive nature of all readings. In many ways 'screen theory', which insists on the 'productivity of the text', undermines that concept by defining the 'realist text' as a mere replay of positions established elsewhere.

In contradiction to this argument, we would still want to retain some of the ideas expressed through the concept of 'preferred readings'. This suggests that a text of the dominant discourse *does* privilege or prefer a certain reading. We might now expand this to say that such texts privilege a certain reading in part by inscribing certain preferred discursive positions from which its discourse appears 'natural', transparently aligned to 'the real' and credible. However, this cannot be the *only* reading inscribed in the text, and it certainly cannot be the only reading which different readers can make of it. The theory of the polysemic nature of discourse must hold to the possibility of establishing an articulation between the 'encoding' and 'decoding' circuits, but it should not adopt a position of a 'necessary correspondence' or identity between them. Vološinov[8] insists that it is the 'multi-accentuality of the sign' which makes it possible for discourse to become an 'arena of struggle'. What we may call the 'reality effect' is not the product of the required reduplication of the empiricist subject in the discourse of realism but the effect of an achieved alignment between subjects and texts which the discourse itself accomplishes. 'The ruling class tries to impart a supraclass, eternal character to the ideological sign, to extinguish or drive inward the struggle between social value judgements which occurs in it, to make the sign uniaccentual'.[9]

Even in the case of the 'classic realist text', the subject positions inscribed by the text, as a condition of its intelligibility, may be inhabited differently by subjects who, in the past (as the result of interpellations by other texts/discourses/institutions) or in the present, are already positioned in an interdiscursive space. It does not follow that because the reader has 'taken the position' most fully inscribed in the text, sufficient for the text to be intelligible, he/she will, for that reason alone, subscribe to the ideological problematic of that text. The text may be contradicted by the subject's position(s) in relation to other texts, problematics, institutions, discursive formations. This means that we must establish a distinction between inhabiting inscribed subject positions, adopting an ideological problematic and making a dominant reading of a text. We cannot, then, assume that one text inscribes a required subject, but only that specific text/subject relations will depend, in part, on the subject positions given by a multiplicity of texts that produce (and have produced) contradictory 'subjectivities' which then act on and against each other within 'the space of the subject'.

Neale draws an important distinction between ideological problematic and mode of address.[10] His examination of the two Nazi propaganda films *Der Ewige Jude* and *Jud Suss* suggests that they both share broadly the same ideological problematic but differ in their modes of address. 'If *Der Ewige Jude,* then, can be seen to share with *Jud Suss* a common problematic in terms of race, order and their representation, it nonetheless articulates that problematic in a different way: it has a different mode of textual address'. Neale extends this argument to take into account the effect of the interdiscursive; thus

> address is not synonymous with textual address . . . although the latter can be analysed and has an effectivity; particular positions and modalities of position are a product of textual address in conjunction with the immediate discourses that necessarily surround it within the apparatuses that support it, and . . . these in turn owe their character, the particular modalities of position that *they* produce in interaction with a text, to ideological practices – the state of ideological struggle – within the conjuncture as a whole.[11]

Ideological problematic, here, must be understood not as a set of contents but rather as a defined set of operations: the way a problematic selects from, conceives and organizes its field of reference. This is constituted by a particular agenda of issues and themes, premises and propositions which are visible/invisible; or a repertoire of questions (proposing answers) which are asked/not asked. This matrix of propositions constitutes it as a relatively coherent space of operations. A problematic can define the dominant or preferred themes of a text. But texts may also be structured by more than one problematic, though one or a restricted set will tend to be in dominance.

Neale employs 'mode of address' specifically with reference to the positioning of the subject:

> To speak of representation in discourse in relation to ideology is also to speak of subject positions: each discursive representation constitutes a subject position, a place for the production and configuration of meaning, for its coherence, or, occasionally, for its critical rupture . . . .

but, he adds, 'they are not necessarily marked by a single, specific mode of address'.[12] The term may, however, be more usefully defined in relation to all those discursive operations which seek to establish and define the form of the text/reader relation. But we must beware of arguing that the positions of knowledge inscribed in the textual operations are obligatory for all readers. We must also distinguish between the positions which the text prefers and prescribes in its discursive operations and the process by which concrete individuals, already constituted as 'subjects' for a multiplicity of discourses, are (successfully or inadequately) interpellated by any single text. Individuals are not merely 'subjects' for/by leave of a single text. A successfully achieved 'correspondence' must be understood as an accomplishment, not a 'given'. It is the result of an articulation: otherwise it could not be disarticulated.

'Screen theory' constantly elides the concrete individual, his/her constitution as a 'subject-for-discourse', and the discursive subject positions constituted by specific discursive practices and operations. These need to be kept analytically distinct, otherwise we will fail to understand the relation subjects/texts within the terms of a 'no necessary correspondence'. Of course, specific combinations - for example, between specific problematics and specific modes of address - may exist historically as well secured, dominant or recurring patterns in particular conjunctures in definite social formations. These may be fixed in place by the institutionalization of practices within a particular site or apparatus (for example, Hollywood cinema). Nevertheless, even these correspondences are not 'eternal' or universal. They have been secured. One can point to the practices and mechanisms which secure them and which reproduce them, in place, in one text after another. Unless one is to accept that there is no ideology but the dominant ideology, which is always in its appointed place, this 'naturalized' correspondence must constantly be deconstructed and shown to be a historically concrete relation. It follows from this argument that there must be different 'realisms', not a single 'classic realist text' to which all realist texts can be assimilated. And there is no *necessary* correspondence between these realisms and a particular ideological problematic.

Individuals, subjects, 'subjects'

In an important contribution Paul Willemen has identified an unjustified conflation, in a great deal of 'screen theory', between the *subject of the text* and the *social subject.* He argues:

> There remains an *unbridgeable gap between 'real' readers/authors and 'inscribed' ones, constructed and marked in and by the text.* Real readers are subjects in history, living in social formations, rather than mere subjects of a single text. The two types of subject are not commensurate. But for the purposes of formalism, real readers are supposed to coincide with the constructed readers.[13]

Hardy, Johnston and Willemen also mark the distinction between the 'inscribed reader of the text' and the 'social subject who is invited to take up this position'.[14] More recently Christine Gledhill has opened up this question of the psychoanalytic and the historical 'subject';[15] in response Claire Johnston, who retains a firm base in the psychoanalytic framework, has also called for

> a move away from a notion of the text as an autonomous object of study and towards the more complex question of subjectivity seen in historical/social terms. Feminist film practice can no longer be seen simply in terms of the effectivity of a system of representation, but rather as a production of and by subjects already in

social practices, which always involve heterogeneous and often contradictory positions in ideologies.[16]

In their earlier paper Hardy, Johnston and Willemen proposed a model of 'interlocking' subjectivities', caught up in a network of symbolic systems, in which the social subject

always exceeds the subject implied by the text because he/she is also placed by a heterogeneity of other cultural systems and is never coextensive with the subject placed by a single fragment (i.e. one film) of the overall cultural text.[17]

The subjects implied/implicated by the text are thus always already subject within different social practices in determinate social formations – not simply subjects in 'the symbolic' in general. They are constituted by specific, historical forms of sociality:

this subject, at its most abstract and impersonal, is itself in history: the discourses . . . determining the terms of its play, change according to the relations of force of competing discourses intersecting in the plane of the subject in history, the individual's location in ideology at a particular moment and place in the social formation.[18]

Nowell-Smith rightly points to the particularity of Neale's approach, *breaking, as it does, with the ahistorical and unspecified use of the category of the subject.* In his summary of Neale's position Nowell-Smith points out that '[propaganda] . . . films require to be seen, politically, in terms of the positionality they provide for the socially located spectator.'[19] This is 'on the one hand, a question of textual relations proper, of mode of address'; but it is also a question of 'the politico-historical conjuncture', because 'the binding of the spectator takes place' (or, we would add, fails to take place) 'not through formal mechanisms alone but through the way social instructions impose their effectivity at given moments across the text and also elsewhere'.[20] This argument has consequences for how both 'texts' and 'subjects' are conceptualized. It gives the level of the discursive its proper specificity and effectivity; but it does not treat the text as autonomously signifying, nor does it accord signification an all-inclusive effect. It qualifies what can be meant by the term 'the productivity of the text'. As Gledhill has recently observed, at a more general level:

Under the insistence of the semiotic production of meaning, the effectivity of social, economic and political practice threatens to disappear altogether. There is a danger of conflating the social structure of reality with its signification, by virtue of the fact that social processes and relations have to be mediated through language, and the evidence that the mediating power of language reflects back on the social process. But to say that language has a determining effect on society is a different matter from saying that society is nothing but its languages and signifying practices.[21]

It follows that the meaning produced by the encounter of text and subject cannot be read off straight from its 'textual characteristics' or its discursive strategies. We also need to take into account what Neale describes as 'the use to which a particular text is put, its function within a particular conjuncture, in particular institutional spaces, and in relation to particular audiences'.[22] A text should, also, not be considered in isolation from the historical conditions of its production and consumption – its insertion into a context of discourses in struggle, in discursive formations cohering into different strands of ideology and establishing new condensations between them (cf. Laclau); also its position in the field of articulation secured between the discursive and economic/political practices. Both the text and the subject are constituted in the space of the interdiscursive; and both are traversed and intersected by contradictory discourses – contradictions which arise not only from the subject positions which these different discourses propose, but also from the conjuncture and institutional sites in which they are articulated and transformed.

The meaning(s) of a text will also be constructed differently depending on the discourses (knowledges, prejudices, resistances) *brought to bear on the text by the reader.* One crucial factor delimiting this will be the repertoire of discourses at the disposal of different audiences. Willemen notes that

> individuals do have different relations to sets of discourses, in that their position in the social formation, their positioning in the real, will determine which sets of discourses a given subject is likely to encounter and in what ways it will do so.[23]

Willemen here returns to the agenda – but now from a position within 'the discursive' – a set of questions about the relations between the social position of 'the reader' and discursive formations. These questions, in a more 'sociological' form, were at the centre of Bernstein's early work and that of Bourdieu and Baudelot and Establet.[24] Their disappearance from the discussion is, no doubt, attributable to that general critique of 'sociological approaches' common in 'screen theory'. Though basically correct, this has sometimes been taken to extreme lengths, where the mere ascription of the qualifier 'sociological' is enough to consign a text so stigmatized to the scrap-heap of theory.[25] Bernstein did invite criticisms by the overly deterministic way in which the relation between class and language was posed in his early work. The position was extensively criticized, and there has been some modification on his part since then.[26] The terms of the argument can be extensively faulted. But the questions addressed are not without their 'rational core'. Willemen argues that 'the real determines to a large extent the encounter of/with discourses'.[27] Neale observes that 'audiences are determined economically, politically and ideologically'.[28] The basic problem with the sociological formulations is that they presumed a too simple, one-to-one correspondence between social structure and discourse: they treated language as ascribed by and inscribed in class position. Thus, as Ellis remarked, 'it is assumed that the census of employment category carries with it both political and ideological reflections'.[29] This position cannot be defended or sustained. It is based on a too simple notion of how classes are constituted, and on the ascription of fixed ideologies to whole classes. There is no conception of signifying practices, their relative autonomy and specific effects.

The weaknesses in the position need not be elaborated at length. Class is not a unitary category with effective determination at the level of the economic only. There is no simple alignment between the economic, the political and the ideological in the constitution of classes. Classes do not have fixed, ascribed or unitary world views. In Poulantzas's phrase, they do not carry their world views around like number plates on their backs.[30] Laclau argues that even 'ideological elements, taken in isolation, have no necessary class connotation and this connotation is only the result of the articulation of those elements in a concrete ideological discourse'[31] and the articulation of these discourses with class practices in specific conjectures.

Much the same problems beset Parkin's formulations, which on other grounds were highly suggestive.[32] Parkin's dominant, negotiated and oppositional 'meaning systems' provided a useful point of departure for early work on 'decoding'.[33] But his framework, too, can be faulted on the grounds outlined above. Simply, he proposed that a given section of the audience 'either shares, partly shares or does not share the dominant code in which messages are transmitted'. He related these fairly unproblematically to class position, defined in a sociological manner. This formulation was useful in the preliminary work of establishing, in a hypothetical-deductive manner, the presence of different and variable 'decoding' positions. (These, of course, then required further refinement and concrete exemplification.) Now the definition of a range of possible 'decoding' positions is *not* undermined by the objections advanced earlier. What *is* undermined is the simple ascription of these positions to classes as such or, alternatively, the deduction of them from socio-economic positions in some *prior* manner. Parkin did himself identify the category of 'negotiated code', the amplification of which has potentially fruitful uses in the analysis of sectional or corporate class-consciousness. He also identified the possibility of 'contradictory' meaning systems. But he did not take this finding, which undermined the ascriptive nature of his basic framework, far enough. In fact, there are no simple meaning systems but a multiplicity of discourses at play in a social formation. These discourses have varied sources of origin – they cannot be attributed to classes as such. There is no unproblematic link between classes and meaning systems. Different discursive positions need to be analysed in terms of their linguistic and discursive characteristics and effects.

However, the essentialism and class-reductionism which tends to characterize this position has generally been countered by its simple opposite or inversion: the premise, in essence, of an absolute autonomy, and the assumption that any relationship between discursive formations and class formations must be, by definition, 'reductionist'. This is not acceptable either. The problem can only be resolved if we are able to think through the full implications of two apparently contradictory propositions: first, discourses cannot be explained by or reduced to classes, defined exclusively at the level of the economic; second, nevertheless, 'audiences *are* determined economically, politically and ideologically'. The first proposition suggests that classes, understood economically, will not always be found 'in place' in their proper discursive position. The second proposition, however, insists that the economic and political constitution of classes will have some real effectivity for the distribution of discourses to groups of agents. (We deal here exclusively with the question of the reduction of discourses to classes. But it must be remembered that other structures and relations – for example, those of gender and patriarchal relations, which are not reducible to economic class – will also have a structuring effect on the distribution of discourses.)

In short, the relation classes/meaning systems has to be fundamentally reworked by taking into account the full effectivity of the discourse level. Discursive formations intervene between 'classes' and 'languages'. They intervene in such a way as to prevent or forestall any attempt to read the level of the operation of language back in any simple or reductive way to economic classes. Thus we cannot deduce which discursive frameworks will be mobilized in particular reader/text encounters from the level of the socio-economic position of the 'readers'. But position in the social structure may be seen to have a structuring and limiting effect on the *repertoire* of discursive or 'decoding' strategies available to different sectors of an audience. They will have an effect on the pattern of the distribution of discursive repertoires. What is more, the key elements of the social structure which delimit the range of competences in particular audiences may not be referable in any exclusive way to 'class' understood in the economic sense. The key sites for the distribution of discursive sets and competences are probably – following some of the leads of Bernstein and Bourdieu – the family and the school – or, as Althusser (following Gramsci) argued, the *family-school couplet*.[34] This is the key institutional site or articulation for the distribution of 'cultural capital', in Bourdieu's terms. Other formations – for example, gender and immediate social context or cultural milieu – may also have a formative and structuring effect, not only on which specific discourses will be in play in any specific text/reader encounter, but also in defining *the range and the repertoire of performance codes.* The distribution of the discourses of the media and other cultural apparatuses will also have a structuring effect on the differentiated discursive competences of socially structured audiences.

This proposition now requires to be elaborated at a more concrete level. But the direction in which further work must proceed is already clear. In effect, what is required is to work through more fully the consequences of the argument that the discourses mobilized by 'readers' in relation to any 'text' cannot be treated as the effect of a direct relation between 'discourses' and 'the real'. It must be analysed, instead, in terms of the effects of social relations and structures (the extra-discursive) on the structuring of *the discursive space* – that is, of the 'interdiscourse'. These structured relations cannot produce 'a reading' (and no other) in any specific instance. But they do exercise a limit on (that is, they 'determine') the formation of the discursive space, which in turn has a determinate effect on the practice of readings at the level of particular text–reader encounters. This approach undermines any notion of the automatic or 'unquestioned performance of the subject by the text' – an approach which merely replaces a sociological determinism by a textual one. It provides the theoretical space in which the subject may be placed in some relation to the signifying chain other than that of a 'regulated process'.

Part Four

Language

14 Introduction to Language Studies at the Centre

Chris Weedon, Andrew Tolson, Frank Mort

This section deals with Language Studies at the Centre. It is organized in four chapters. This introduction traces the development of interest in theories of language and signifying practices and attempts to summarize the key questions which have been the focus of attention in the Centre's work over recent years. In Chapter 15 we are reprinting an extract from past work on language theory. Chapter 16 deals with aspects of more recent work on theories of language, and Chapter 17 is an extract from a recent piece on a specific signifying practice: advertising in women's magazines. Within the constraints of time and space, we have not dealt with recent Anglo-American discourse analysis.

It has often been argued that questions of language are central to Cultural Studies, that all cultural phenomena include some linguistic component and that processes of linguistic perception are involved in cultural analysis. Yet the study of language as such has frequently been marginalized, both in empirical research and in the Centre's theoretical concerns. This is a confusing situation, not least because of the several distinct theoretical approaches to language currently defining the field. It was with the double aim of establishing the theoretical importance of language and clarifying the different traditions of linguistic theory and research that a 'Language and Ideology' study group was established in October 1975.

At first sight, the marginalization of linguistic concerns in the Centre's early work seems strange, After all, it might have been expected that the Centre's early development out of English Studies would have been conducive to the study of language. In Richard Hoggart's own work there is a recognition of the significance of spoken discourse. In Chapter 2 of *The Uses of Literacy* Hoggart examines distinctive patterns of working-class speech, such as popular phrases, proverbs and aphorisms. He insists on the importance of 'the degree to which working-people still draw, in speech and in the assumptions to which speech is a guide, on oral and local tradition'.[1] Moreover, there was a theoretical attempt to come to terms with the significance of language within the 'culture and society' debate. The early work of Raymond Williams, for example, which had provided the Centre's first theoretical grounding, included specific interest in language and communication:

We have many ways of describing, both by learned rules . . . and by certain kinds of response, in gesture, language, image . . . This vital descriptive effort – which is not merely a subsequent effort to describe something known, but literally a way of seeing new things and new relationships – has often been observed by artists, yet it is not the activity of artists alone. The same effort is made not only by scientists and thinkers, but also, and necessarily, by everyone. The history of a language is a very good example of this, for the ways in which language changes, to amend old descriptions or accommodate new ones, are truly social, in the most ordinary business of living.[2]

Language is seen as important in Williams's definition of culture as 'a whole way of life'. Yet in a sense it is precisely this way of defining culture as a 'vital descriptive effort', a 'way of seeing . . . things and . . . relationships', that has hindered the development of a specific theoretical interest in language and signifying practices within Cultural Studies which would pay attention to the way meaning is constructed and communicated. In both Hoggart's and Williams's early work we find a shared problematic: culture is inherently meaningful, and meanings are rooted in practical social experience. What this principally involves is an expressive theory of language in which, while linguistic meanings can be referred to the reality they 'describe', they remain rooted in essentially subjective acts of perception and creativity. In this view, linguistic utterances can be read back, or 'interpreted', in terms of their founding 'structures of feeling', as in Hoggart's argument that:

We have to try to see beyond the habits to what the habits stand for, to see through the statements to what the statements really mean (which may be the opposite of the statements themselves), to detect differing pressures of emotion behind idiomatic phrases and ritualistic observances.[3]

It is in this 'seeing through' to the real meaning that the linguistic level or signifier of the utterance disappears: it becomes *transparent*.

Our criticism here of the absence of attention to the specificity of modes of signification within the early work of Hoggart and Williams is intended as one explanation of the development of interest in semiological approaches to signifying practices at the Centre. This has run alongside, and is separate from, ethnographically based work on the cultural tradition, popular culture and subcultures. We recognize that both Hoggart and Williams have done much valuable work on the historical analysis of specific signifying practices, in a way which raises important questions absent from much of the structuralist-based theory which we go on to look at in this chapter. We intend therefore to return to problems of theory and historically specific analysis in our conclusion.

Early work on semiology

It was in the context of Media Studies that questions of language and signification were first posed at the Centre. Following the publication of Roland Barthes's essay, 'The rhetoric of the image',[4] the Media Group devoted some time to a study of news photographs, a study which appears in several articles in *WPCS* 3, particularly Stuart Hall's 'The determinations of news photographs'. Here the concern with written forms of signification is not central, but it is necessary, as Barthes and Hall refer to the 'linguistic anchorage' of the news photo in a headline or caption. According to this analysis, the necessity for a 'linguistic anchorage' arises out of the polysemic nature of the visual sign (that is, its openness to a variety of readings). Its meaning is impossible to pin down, partly because a photo contains a plurality of signifiers. Our attention must therefore be directed to those sets of significations 'preferred' in the editorial practice of the newspaper. For example, Barthes discusses the generalized qualities of 'Italian-ness' signified by a French advertisement for pasta, and Stuart Hall develops this theme:

> In any particular instance, then, the item – photo or text – perfectly indexes the thematic of the ideology it elaborates. But its general sphere of reference remains diffuse. It is there and yet it is not there. It appears, indeed, as if the general structure of a dominant ideology is almost impossible to grasp, reflexively and analytically, *as a whole.*[5]

Here 'linguistic anchorage' both indicates what, in the image, we are supposed to be looking at and defines the ideological field, in this case 'nationalism', through which visual meaning is produced. The written text effects an ideological 'closure' in relation to the polysemic visual sign: 'It is therefore common to find a loosely coded expression in a photo used in a "closed" way – the closure being effected by an anchoring text, caption or headline.'[6]

This theory of linguistic function, developed in early issues of *Working Papers in Cultural Studies,* is based on Barthes's early semiological work, which takes its primary linguistic impetus from the work of Saussure and Jakobsen. Its key principles are contained in two texts by Barthes: *Elements of Semiology* (1967) and *Mythologies* (1972), in particular the essay 'Myth today' in this latter text. The analysis of 'Myth today' operates with a twofold distinction. First, following Saussure, a distinction is made between the signifier (sound image) and the signified (concept), which come together to form the sign. These two parts of the linguistic sign are related in an arbitrary fashion – that is, there is no natural connection between them and no immediate dependence of the signified on its material referent. Second, within the theory of myth itself Barthes establishes a distinction between 'language' and 'metalanguage'. Metalanguage takes, as its signifier, an already constituted linguistic sign. Barthes's famous example is a photo in *Paris-Match* of a black soldier saluting a French flag. Here the 'myth' of French imperialism, the subservience of the colonized races, operates as a second-order signifying system on the basis of the recognized image.

As Barthes defines it in *Elements of Semiology*, this distinction between the levels of signification refers to two related levels of 'denotation' (we see a black soldier) and 'connotation' (the implied reading of his act at an ideological level):

> the first system is then the plane of *denotation* and the second system (wider than the first), the plane of *connotation*. We shall therefore say that *a connoted system is a signifying system whose plane of expression is itself constituted by a signifying system.*[7]

It is, of course, the case that connotations are linguistic (as metalanguage they are constituted through language), but Barthes's theory of the language system is confined to the denotative level: 'the common cases of connotation will of course consist of complex systems of which language forms the first system (this is, for instance, the case with literature)'.[8] In other words, this form of semiology tends to reduce the functions of language as a system to the plane of denotation, either in its function as a first-order signifying system or, as we have seen with news photographs, providing the 'linguistic anchorage' which defines and 'closes' the connotative visual sign. The denotative quality of the linguistic sign implies its having a given, fixed meaning within the closed order of language, which does not, however, rely for its meaning on the external referent in the 'real'. The denotative model of language is subsequently modified by Barthes in his later work, where language becomes chains of connotation.

The kinds of criticisms which have been made of Barthes's work fall into two general categories. First, there have been criticisms of the linguistic model itself. Is the Saussurean concept of the linguistic sign – the relation between signifier and signified – theoretically viable? Does semiology warrant a formal distinction between two orders of signification (denotation and connotation)? Is it indeed useful to analyse language at the level of the system (*langue*) rather than within actual speech acts (*parole*)? These are questions which will be taken up in the final section of this chapter. However, Barthes's analysis was not initially criticized within the Centre on these theoretical grounds. Rather, a second type of criticism was directed at the semiological project as such; that is, at the attempt to construct and define the social function of myths on the basis of a purely formal analysis of their internal systems.

Barthes's principal aim in *Mythologies* was to provide a basis for a critique of the 'naturalizing effect' of ideology, its quality of *vraisemblance*. For example, even though she or he may be critical of its connotations, the reader of *Paris-Match* nevertheless believes its denoted 'truth': this event took place, it has a real history and so, in a sense, the soldier's behaviour is 'only natural'. Barthes locates this 'very principle of myth' in the relations between his two orders of signification. The denoted signified establishes the reality of the ideology; it allows myth to be innocently consumed:

> If I read the negro saluting as a symbol pure and simple of imperiality, I must renounce the reality of the picture, it discredits itself in my eyes when it becomes an instrument. Conversely, if I decipher the negro's salute as an alibi of coloniality, I shatter the myth even more surely by the obviousness of its motivation. But for the myth-reader, the outcome is quite different: everything happens as if the picture *naturally* conjured up the concept, as if the signifier *gave a foundation* to the signified: the myth exists from the precise moment when French imperiality achieves the natural state: myth is speech justified in *excess*.[9]

Barthes's method of analysis in *Mythologies* has been criticized for interpreting the apparent 'realness' of ideology entirely in formal terms: in the internal relation of language and metalanguage, signifier and signified. Although he is concerned to distinguish between language and myth, there is a sense in which Barthes reduces all signification to language, or at least to a formal system derived from linguistic theory. This is the criticism put forward by Iain Chambers in 'Roland Barthes: structuralism semiotics'. Chambers argues not only for a principled distinction between language and myth but, further, that different signifying systems must be seen in terms of the social practices *of their production*:

> The point to note here is that Barthes equates all signs with language objects. Even if all systems of signification are 'languages' (the 'language' of film, the 'language' of dance), there is still a reductionist argument at work here. If pictures and writing are to be related without distinction, equally as signs, constituting 'one just as much as the other', then the specificity of the practices that produced them is lost. Associated with that loss, the intentionality inscribed in those practices, as they exist within the universe of practices, is bracketed out under the blanket phrase 'bourgeois ideology'.[10]

Chambers criticizes what he sees as an 'idealist' and 'ahistorical' character of all semiology and of Barthes's work in particular. The idealist tendency is inherent in the formalist linguistic model which fails to recognize the effectivity of social practices in the structuring of different signifying practices. Chambers proposes an analysis of the ideological sign, which recognizes its socially determined, not wholly 'arbitrary', character and which argues for a historically specific study of language. However, there is a tendency in Chambers's analysis to reduce the 'materiality' of ideological signification to a simple dependence on the referent in the real:

> The difference between the linguistic and the connotative sign is not between 'intentional' and 'non-intentional', but a difference founded on the varying degrees of openness operating in the different planes' systemic organization . . . They are both dependent on awareness of the extra-systemic referent to which both systems ultimately refer in the decoding of their respective signs and the realization of the *meaning* of those signs.[11]

The theoretical weakness of this position is that it seems to return to a pre-semiological concept of meaning as a transparent reflection of a taken-for-granted 'material world'. As John Ellis points out in a brief reply to Chambers:

> In this formulation, language is a mere doubling of the real world, coextensive with it and expressing it without problems. . . . To concentrate on 'concrete' objects like this is an oversimplification that even intelligent idealists find hard to bear . . . a word like 'labour' or 'struggle' does not have such a clear, self-evident meaning, and in such cases it is obvious that the 'referent' and the signifier are equally caught in a process of conceptualization.[12]

Chambers's position is actually contradictory, since he is at times himself working within a semiological problematic. In some of his formulations the 'material world' is not simply 'out there', to be reflected in a signifying system. It is, rather, part of the constitution of signifying practices themselves. This perspective seems to recognize a material construction of ideologies, within social institutions, which require socially defined subjective 'interpretations'. As Chambers puts it:

I would suggest it to be extremely naïve to understand ideology as something imposed from above. Ideology has to negotiate a path through the differential social totality in order to win consensus, and it arises *within* social relationships and particular practices. For instance, whilst waiting at the barber's, I am given a copy of *Paris-Match* to read. This is not a pure moment, but occurs in the 'common-sense' world of everyday experiences that forms the framework for my interpretations. My perceptive and cognitive faculties, which are not neutral, but socially and culturally acquired, recognize a French soldier saluting a French flag. Thus my perception of that photograph is grounded in norms of societal expectancies. Secondly, my 'reading' of it is further demarcated. It is not any photograph but the cover of *Paris-Match*; a specific practice with its own ideological configurations ('newsworthiness', captions, touching up photos, etc.). It is in the space between the sedimented perceptual appropriation and the contextualized reading that the hegemonic ideology passes 'as though behind men's backs'.[13]

Here Chambers is developing the analysis of the 'social practices of news production', which was initiated by Stuart Hall and the Media Group.[14] In this analysis the formal linguistic processes of signification are situated within social practices, involving complex configurations of commercial, technical and editorial criteria ('news values'). Although this relies on a concept of language as denotation, where the meaning of the ideological signifier is fixed *a priori* within the linguistic chain, we can recognize here the beginnings of a wider theory of 'signifying practice', within a theory of ideology, related to other material practices in the social formation:

Newspapers trade in stories. But though the need to harness a multitude of different stories and images to the profitable exchange of news values is 'determining in the last instance', this economic motive never appears on its own. The ideological function of the photographic sign is always hidden within its exchange value. The news/ideological meaning is the *form* in which the sign-vehicles are exchanged. Though the economic dialectic, here as elsewhere, determines the production and appropriation of (symbolic) values, it is 'never active in its pure state'. The exchange value of the photographic sign is, thus, necessarily over-determined.[15]

It was in the context of this work on denotation and connotation in relation to the media that a 'Language and Ideology' Group was formed in 1975. It took as its object theories of language since Saussure. This included formalist linguistics, Barthes's early work on myths, Benveniste, the neo-semiology of the 'Tel Quel' group (later Barthes, Kristeva, Sollers) and Lacan's psychoanalytic theory of language which underpins much of the work of the 'Tel Quel' group. It also included Derrida's critique of Saussure, Marxist theories of language and ideology (Marx, Stalin, Vološinov, Althusser) and historically specific approaches to language through Foucault's theory of discursive formations.

Saussure's theory of language and the analytical model of denotation/connotation, which Barthes developed on the basis of Saussure's system, were seen as posing two main problems for an adequate theorization of language. These were, first, the question of the way in which meaning is fixed within language (can we assume already constituted denotative signs which are then subject to multiple connotations?). This question is part of the wider issue of the degree of autonomy which we would wish to ascribe to the language system as such: can it be abstracted out from speech acts, and how far has it, even as a system, a historically specific character? Is it, indeed, theoretically viable to posit a level of denotative meaning in the analysis of language? The other main problem, which had a strong political as well as a theoretical dimension, was the question of the role of the speaking subject within language and, by extension, within ideology and politics, including sexual politics. The socio-linguistic tradition had posed the question of the speaking subject within a phenomenological framework – that is, the subject was seen as an intentional consciousness, the source of speech acts which are negotiated, in terms of meaning, through social interaction with the other intentional conscious subjects. Within the Marxist tradition the subject had been treated as an empty space, as the bearer (*Träger*) of social relations and ideologies. The development by Lacan of a psycho-analytic theory of language, which insisted on the importance of unconscious as well as conscious meaning, and its appropriation by the 'Tel Quel' group in its work on language and the politics of subjectivity (with its strong Maoist and feminist tendencies), together with a shift away from economistic models of ideology, primarily in the work of Althusser and in feminist theory, had placed the question of 'the speaking subject' on the theoretical and political agenda. It was a central question in the group's work on the various theoretical approaches to language. Both the question of how meaning is fixed and the role of the speaking subject in language will be dealt with in detail below.

Initially, however, different positions on language were defined in relation to two distinct theoretical tendencies, which, it was argued, were mutually opposed. The first derived from a 'forgotten tradition' of Marxist linguistics which had surfaced in a new translation of V. N. Vološinov's *Marxism and the Philosophy of Language.*[16] The second was associated with the neo-semiology of the 'Tel Quel' group in Paris. Vološinov, writing in the 1930s in the Soviet Union, had developed his theory in opposition to Saussurean linguistics. He insisted on the importance of actual utterances, not just the language system, and he conceived of the sign as 'multi-accentuated', by which he meant that it is open to different meanings when seen from different, class-based, subjective positions. In Vǒlosinov's theory linguistic meaning is negotiated through class-based, social interaction and it reflects and refracts an underlying material reality: socio-economic relations. Thus, while insisting on the study of language through specific utterances, Vǒlosinov develops a social psychological approach to language and social interaction in which he maintains a theoretical level of denotation through his notion of the neutrality of the word *vis-à-vis* any particular ideological field.

Work on the other important theoretical tendency, the 'Tel Quel' group and psychoanalytical approaches to language, was developed initially within the Language Group around the problematic of subjectivity. This work, which was initiated by Rosalind Coward and John Ellis, is best represented by their book *Language and Materialism*.[17] (It is represented here by John Ellis's piece on ideology and subjectivity, extracted below.) Theoretically, the 'Tel Quel' group reject both a conception of subjectivity as rational consciousness and a denotation/connotation model of language, which relies on a rationalist theory of representation (the *a priori* fixing of meaning within the language system). Drawing heavily on Lacan's work, they re-theorize language as unconscious chains of signifiers, in which the ideological effect of meaning is achieved retrospectively through the closing of the chain of signifiers by means of the *positioning of subjects* within language. This theoretical approach will be dealt with in much greater detail in Chapter 16.

We should point out here that the extract reprinted below represents only one brief moment in a much longer and wider-reaching debate. Questions of ideology, both in Cultural Studies generally and in Language Studies in particular, have been widely debated in this country and abroad in the seventies, both in and outside academic institutions. Theoretically, the debate has been influenced, on the one hand, by Althusserianism and Marxism and, on the other, by feminism.[18]

Althusser's influence stems from his theoretical challenge to economism, in which he argues for a more adequate theory of ideology which would not reduce it, in any simple way, to economic contradictions at the level of the mode of production. His model of the social formation,[19] which specified the relative autonomy of the ideological level, created the space within Marxism for serious consideration of the importance of signifying practices. It also helped to bring the question of subjectivity and its importance in the working of ideology to the fore. Thus, for example, in his essay 'On Ideology and Ideological State Apparatuses' Althusser introduced into his theory of ideology the concepts of *misrecognition* and the *interpellation* of the individual as subject within ideologies.[20] These concepts were drawn from Lacan's theory of the constitution of the subject in language. Whereas in Lacan's work they are an integral part of a full-scale theory of subjectivity, Althusser uses them to *describe* the *mechanism* by which ideology functions. Subsequently they have been used in a similar way by Laclau, in his analysis of popular-democratic ideologies.[21] Although Althusser himself does not develop theoretically the question of subjectivity and the process of internalization and rejection of ideologies by the individual subject, he does point the way towards a serious consideration of psychoanalysis in relation to these questions (see, for example, 'Freud and Lacan').[22] Since Althusser's essays were published psychoanalysis has been taken up as the potential basis for a materialist theory of language and ideology – as, for example, in the work of Julia Kristeva, Rosalind Coward and John Ellis. The theoretical viability of such a move has been one of the key questions informing the work of the Language Group.

The other important influence on the debate of theories of language and subjectivity has been feminism. The Women's Movement's focus on lived experience of oppression has encouraged feminists to attempt to theorize the area of the subjective internalization of ideology. The problem of sexual ideologies and their relation to the construction of individual identity has directed attention to the question of subjectivity. Here again Lacanian psychoanalysis, with its theory of the constitution of the gendered subject in language, seemed to offer a way of theorizing this area. Thus, for example, psychoanalytic theory has been used as a basis for explaining the structures of femininity and masculinity,[23] but it has also been central to language theory, the question of masculine and feminine discourses and women and language. Here Julia Kristeva's work on different forms of discursive practice, particularly artistic and literary discourses, is central, as are attempts to look specifically at women's language as a function of their positioning within discourse and the symbolic order of socio-cultural relations. These aspects will be considered in detail on pages 206–8, and on pages 217–23 we are including an extract from Janice Winship's work on advertising in women's magazines, which attempts to use semiology and psychoanalytic concepts, within a materialist framework, to analyse the effectivity of sexual ideologies within a specific, materially located signifying practice: advertising.

15 Ideology and subjectivity*

John Ellis

One development of semiology no longer deals with systems of signs; it deals with the formation of the subject in language, with the internalization of social contradictions and of their contradiction with the superstructure. It constructs a science of human nature, surpassing the traditional division of Marxism between humanism (advanced by those, with Markovic, who believe in a given human nature) and anti-humanism (proposed by those, with Althusser, who account for the individual as constructed by ideology and by social structures).

This work is being carried out in various ways by the 'Tel Quel' group (Sollers, Kristeva, Barthes and others in Paris), the *Screen* group in England and others. It owes much to Lacan's seminal reading of Freud, which demonstrates the social construction of the individual subject through the crucial medium of language.

First, the misrepresentation and misunderstanding of the work is briefly examined, for the ideas and assumptions it mobilizes both on the Left and on the Right. The way in which these coincide is fascinating; they reveal a common way of reading texts and of thinking about the subjective, internal, psychological moment of the social process. (The three repetitive adjectives are necessary to show that this is no longer a question of 'subjectivism', 'behaviourism', 'personal politics' and so on; it is a matter of the overdue politicization of psychoanalysis and, equally, the encounter of Marxism with the concerns of psychoanalysis.) The normal ways of thinking revealed in this section are ultimately deeply damaging to any Marxist political movement. This the following sections demonstrate.

The second section deals with certain crucial notions of the superstructure and its relation to the base. It takes into account the way in which ideology is concerned with the reproduction of the relations of production, the way in which ideology enters into contradiction with economic and political practices. It then examines the way

*This extract was originally published in *WPCS* no.9. It was written in reply to a reading of Vološinov's *Marxism and the Philosophy of Language* by Charles Woolfson and his application of this reading to the analysis of working-class speech (*WPCS* 9, pp. 163–98). Given the object of this chapter, and the constraint of a tight word limit, we are reprinting an edited version of John Ellis's text, which concentrates on the theoretical approaches to language, ideology and subjectivity, developed by the 'Tel Quel' group, and their importance to Marxism. The edited text also deals briefly with Vološinov's book, which in some senses prefigures the 'Tel Quel' group's later concern with the importance for Marxism of a theory of subjectivity. The third section has had to be heavily cut, but we hope it will stand as a brief statement of Volosinov's position and the importance of his critique of formalism.

in which subjectivity is constructed within this process, how external social contradictions articulate themselves internally; and what the effects of this process can be.

Misrepresentation

There are five major themes in the offensive against these recent developments in semiology. The first is to dub it 'structuralism', and then to trot out the traditional criticism which claims that it is incapable of dealing with process, transformation or change (the diachronic). This still happens in the face of almost a decade's work from people like Barthes, Kristeva and Lacan, whose project has been to dissolve the distinction synchrony/diachrony (for example, Barthes's recently translated *S/Z*).[1]

Second, this system of thought is then seen as anti-humanist, probably because it is considered as dealing with structures at the expense of the human. It will be seen that, far from doing this, the exact value of this 'Marxism of the subject' is to interrogate what hitherto had remained hidden under the category of 'human nature' or had disappeared in accounts of the operation of social structures. A common problematic can be found in both Left and Right critiques of semiology (besides the anti-French chauvinism often displayed). Seemingly disparate, they all perpetuate the old division between subjective and objective. It is not possible, according to this thinking, to treat both at once: it is assumed that the work cannot be Marxist because it deals with the subjective (many Marxists also hold this view, considering the subjective as a mere chimera, constituted entirely of the objective, and insubstantial in itself). It seems more palatable for the Left to accept the idea that individuals are caught within structures and simply produced by them (crude Althusserianism) rather than the notion that a person and his/her unconscious is formed at every point by his/her history in society, and that this formation – particularly the unconscious – can operate according to its own logic and come into conflict with economic needs. In the West this problem has been opened on to by psychoanalysis in the form of Lacan's reading of Freud, a subject that interests many Marxists, including Althusser. In the East the Chinese have faced this problem during the struggle between two lines and the Cultural Revolution. These two developments are central for any understanding of ideology, its specificity and its power. Without an account of the subjective moment of the social process, Marxism is unable to account for Fascism or political apathy in terms which could prevent the same political mistakes from being repeated.

The superstructure and the subjective moment

The Cultural Revolution is a revolution 'of men's minds'. It demonstrates the importance of ideology, considered not just as a system of ideas, a 'behavioural ideology' or a 'socializing force' but as the practice that constructs what is often taken as given – that is, human nature. Ideology is seen as a force which enters into the very constitution of the individual and is therefore the area in which changes of attitude are generated. The subjective moment is thus seen as vital for the political struggle.

It is stressed again in Mao's conception of the ideological struggle: 'Ideological struggle is not like other forms of struggle. The only method to be used in this struggle is that of painstaking reasoning and not crude coercion.'[2]

What is at stake in the Maoist understanding of the superstructure? Three things: its sometimes determining role; the need for creative thinking within a party, a movement; a vigilance against a return of attitudes typical of capitalist societies.

The Cultural Revolution is the fruit of Mao's understanding of the role of the superstructure in the social totality. This understanding is vital for a Left movement taken by surprise by the events of 1968, a surprise which is often expressed but rarely learned from. The implications for Marxist political practice are clear. Contradictions are produced between the changing nature of the relations of production and language and thought, which often lag behind; these contradictions can become antagonistic, as in the case of the events of May 1968. There is a space, therefore, and a necessity to activate these contradictions within superstructural formations. The need is for a genuine politicization which acts as a geniune corrective to all forms of leadership.

Macciocchi quotes Mao summing up this thinking of the superstructure and showing exactly what is being challenged – the habitual attitudes, the self-orientation of ordinary people:

> 'It is thus,' says Mao, 'that the contradiction between the forces of production and the relations of production, and their contradiction with the superstructure will continue to exist in all human societies as long as there exists a mode of production. Inside a mode of production there are reproduced the relations of authority and subjection, of leadership and obedience within which the capitalist relations of production are reproduced.'[3]

A superficial glance might see this as far from the work of Althusser and of people like Kristeva and Sollers. Their references to the Chinese experience have even been claimed to be 'assertions, tacked on for rhetoric's sake'. However, this work is absolutely central if the Chinese experience is to be learned from. For the implications of this attitude for analyses of social structures are very clear: any analysis that is 'characterized by the breach between the subjective and the objective' is inadequate to the political tasks it sets itself. It remains hardly more than a destructive exercise unless completed by an analysis of the mass psychology involved: the psychological processes by which individuals are subjected to the social structures, the drives whose repression these social structures accomplish only to have to deal with their (partial) return.

We see the beginning of the exploration of this process in Althusser's *Lenin and Philosophy*.[4] At least until the late sixties he had been very aware of the importance of Mao's work, and in 'Ideology and ideological state apparatuses' he begins his notes for an investigation by developing Mao's emphasis on the crucial role of ideology in the *reproduction* of the relations of production.[5] The essay then goes on to deal with the *external* aspects of this reproduction, without however dealing with the *internal* aspects. The questions often asked of this essay are: 'what is a subject?'; what constitutes this point (carefully not called person, individual) at which the active production on a day-to-day basis of the structure-in-dominance actually takes place? The answers are not given in this piece but in a very divergent (and in many ways inadequate) essay 'Freud and Lacan', which he was 'correcting' whilst writing about ideology.[6] In Althusser, the reconciliation of the discoveries of Marx and Freud does not take place: they are marked as parallel, both oriented around a 'decentredness'. His timidity comes, perhaps, from the outcast nature of psychoanalysis, which he describes at the beginning of the essay. The work which deals with the subject in ideology is to be found elsewhere, in the developments from formal semiology that have taken place since 1966 in Paris. The work has met with exactly the misrepresentation and/or rejection that Althusser describes. In order to explain it, I will use Kristeva's examination of the sensitive point in Marxist theory, the concept of practice.[7]

Kristeva begins by pointing out that Mao's emphasis in his essay 'On practice' is that practice is personal and concerned with direct experience. In this light she then examines the process of generation of new concepts: 'a sudden change (leap) takes place in the brain in the process of cognition'.[8] Common sense describes this as 'It all fell into place', 'It suddenly dawned on me'. But a dialectical materialist understanding of the process has to begin from a different point. It is precisely the contradiction between the superstructure and the forces and relations of production that creates the conditions in which this can happen. But the presence of the objective conditions is no guarantee that anything will happen: an account of the subjective moment is needed. However, Marxism does not usually examine this moment, assuming a subject which is unified and outside the objective process. To think the objective without the subjective is to leave the subjective free to reproduce the same old orientations. But the concept of practice that Kristeva is explaining, a conception which pays attention to the 'leap of understanding', can only be grasped by using the Freudian notion of the formation of the human subject through the dialectic of drives (*Triebe* is more often, and incorrectly, translated as 'instincts') and social constraints. This is not to posit a pre-given 'instinctual' being since, according to Freud, everything occurs across social formations. It is a conception, then, which posits a human subject formed by what is refused entry into consciousness; that is, through the formation of the unconscious. A brief exposition of this theory of the construction of the subject will now follow, which can do no more than situate certain features of it.

The human child is not born with a predetermined sexual identity, according to Freud. The child is composed of many diverse drives which could join each other, 'never reach their goal, find another goal, dry up, overflow and so get attached to something quite different'.[9] This alteration of drives to form the normal 'sexed' infant takes place, according to Lacan, through the dialectic of need, demand and desire. The subject has to find the constituting structure of his desire in the structure of signifiers (language), which are already established in the other person to whom the infant's demand is addressed. In other words *desire* is formed through the subject's relation to language. Both Lacan and Kristeva take account of the development of modern linguistics, particularly from Saussure, which establishes language as a series of difference. They posit the 'endless tautology' of language, with meaning only established retrospectively: that is, deep structures such as the logical, semantic or intercommunicational are articulated only in so far as language is used by a subject who intends meaning. Meaning occurs only through the function of a subject, not through the fixed position of a sign.

This formulation is not to be interpreted as some form of idealist subjectivism: it proposes *the necessary positionality of the subject to enable communication.* This is close to some of Vološinov's formulations. The mechanism by which this positionality occurs is the refusal of entry into signifying positions of certain signifiers. This is one of the fundamental mechanisms of the unconscious as identified by Freud: metaphor. Lacan recognized that this notion of the 'metaphoric' construction of meaning in language is exactly the same model as that of repression. Primal repression, for Freud, exists at the level of the constitution of the unconscious. By this certain signifiers are barred entry into consciousness, and the subject has to recognize himself in the organizing structures of the signifier. The unconscious is seen to be constructed in the same process as that by which the individual acquires language: it results from the capture in the web of signifiers of the structuring of need, demand and desire. In Lacanian theory (too complex to be done justice in this space)[10] certain key signifiers organize the structure of the unconscious. These are, for example, what Lacan calls 'the name of the father' (that is, the organization of desire according to patriarchal social formations in which the phallus is a central term). These signifiers ensure the positions for the reproduction of the species through the establishment of sexual difference. It is not only in these moments that consciousness is constructed out of unconscious formations; the logical structures of language and thought arrange themselves through the same process as the construction of the unconscious. Thus, consciousness itself is affected by the movement in which signifiers are altered, disturbed or put into crisis by the contradictions between the superstructure and the relations and/or forces of production, when they become antagonistic. This experience is one of consciousness encountering an external process which it has not yet organized into language, has not yet symbolized.

Faced with the laws of a developing historical process, for example with the structure of capitalist society, the rejected drive either invests and recognizes itself within these laws, making symbolic theses from them and blocking itself; or, by a violence that no theses can hold back, it rejects all stoppages and produces a symbolization of the objective process of transformation, according to the constraints which impose themselves on the movement of the drive: it then produces a revolutionary 'discourse', which only testing (cf. Mao's practice-truth-practice) puts in correspondence with objective movements and necessity.[11]

It is necessary to explain certain terms: the practice of 'making symbolic theses' from a historical process means constructing a conscious understanding in the terms given by the process itself (that is, in conformity to its ideological practice); this is opposed to an energy which has been constructed in such a way that it can no longer be organized by the web of symbolic theses, an energy which goes on to produce new concepts, whose validity is then shown in practice.

In explaining the way in which this production of new ideas takes place, Kristeva uses the term 'rejection' (*le rejet*), which indicates the drive which meets the external organization of language and has to structure itself accordingly or restructure that external system. The result is an internal disorganization in which the subject is thrown into process, into questioning and crisis. This state of the subject-in-process comes about because of the impact of social contradictions. The subject, hitherto able to think himself unified, feels disoriented. Social contradictions articulate themselves within the composition of the person by an investment of drives; but these drives are themselves formed by both social and personal history, and this investment throws into flux the composition of the conscious and unconscious.

> Ex-centring the subject, the rejection brings about a confrontation between the atomization of the subject and the structures of the natural world and of social relations, runs up against them, repulses them and is displaced. At the moment of this rejection, which implies the period of the annihilation of an old objectivity, a linkage component which is symbolic, ideological and therefore positive intervenes in order to constitute in language the new object which the subject in process, whilst rejecting, produces across the moment of rejection. So practice contains, as its fundamental moment, the heterogeneous contradiction which places a subject thrown into process by a natural or social exterior that is not yet symbolised, in struggle with old theses (that is, with systems of representation which differ from the rejection and blunt its violence).[12]

This describes the way in which the conflict is resolved: the signifying practices intervene to constitute a new understanding.

It is vital for Marxism to take into account this process of the unconscious, whose effects are heard and felt in the conscious. If not, the psychology at work in propaganda and political action remains mechanistic, a simplistic causality. It ignores the process by which social contradictions articulate themselves subjectively, the way in which they can produce a reactionary stance – in short, the contradiction between ideological practice and economic and political practices.

The conversation that Charles Woolfson analyses in *WPCS* 9 provides a means of illustrating this argument. One worker (Worker 6) attempts to provide a political intervention into the conversation of several other workers. His approach shows exactly the practical effects of a lack of psychology in politics. Far from challenging 'the whole basis of authority' (as the analysis claims), Worker 6 rests his whole intervention on himself as authoritative, on conceiving discussion as a matter of winning or losing. Looking at the speech of Worker 5, however, we see that his speech is anti-authoritarian in a confused and by no means conscious way. This appears dramatically in his verbal slip which Woolfson has carefully recorded: 'workers are their own worst enemies – they expect the union – the, eh, I beg your pardon – the gaffers, you know, the employers – to be fair and just . . .'.[13] It's clear that at some level the terms 'union' and 'gaffers' are more interchangeable than he is prepared to admit. He has a profound unease about ideas of authority, which expresses itself consciously in an annoyance with Worker 6, a 'gut' opposition to the display of superiority. This unease demands to be politicized. This is not to put a positive value-judgement on Worker 5 as 'confusedly political' or to condemn Worker 6 as 'authoritarian' in any simplistic way. It is to propose a different political attitude, which sees the points at which Worker 5's conscious confusion (and bloody-mindedness) are the expression of a multitude of contradictions which demand to be politicized. This can be achieved by generalizing the themes he situates himself within; by producing an awareness of contradiction to enrich his critical thinking. It shows that it is he who holds the idea of authority as problematic, that he has a deep unease in the region where Worker 6 finds a firm basis for his political style. Such a reading does not pay attention to the 'manifest content' of the speech so much as to its production, the way in which it comes out, the way in which speakers are orienting themselves. It is an analysis based not on classification but on listening symptomatically for what is being said underneath what is said.

Vološinov and formalism

Vološinov, along with M. M. Bakhtin and P. N. Medvedev, was a member of the Bakhtin group, constituted in the late twenties to produce an 'immanent critique' of formalism. Kristeva reviews Bakhtin's work on literature in an important article in which she shows that part of the breaking with formalism was constituted around an inquiry into history, the history of meaning systems, *genres of discourse.*[14] It is symptomatic that Woolfson's analysis takes no account of the particular form of conversation (as opposed to debate) which 'frames' the interchange he deals with. However, this is the least of the matter. The real point of difference is that his whole reading of Vološinov excludes the book's fruitful concern with the subjective and ideology which is expressed in such prevarications as this:

> *Anti-psychologism is correct in refusing to derive ideology from the psyche.* But even more than that is needed: the psyche must be derived from ideology. Psychology must be grounded in ideological science. Speech had first to come into being and develop in the process of the social intercourse of organisms so that afterward it could enter within the organism and become inner speech.
>
> *Psychologism is also correct, however. There is no outer sign without an inner sign.* An outer sign incapable of entering the context of inner signs, i.e. incapable of being understood and experienced, ceases to be a sign and reverts to the status of a physical object.[15]

Here ideology is treated as a material force in the constitution of the social subject in the first section; yet, in the second section there are distinct indications that this subject could be considered relatively autonomous (with its own laws and history) and is also in some sense constitutive of the social reality that constructs it. There is, in other words, a sense in which Vološinov's text tends to treat the subjective moment as by no means entirely subservient to, dominated by, objective forces. But it was not possible for him to go further. Already at odds with Soviet orthodoxy, he also did not have the necessary linguistic understanding of Freud (given by Lacan) in order to read him other than as a biological determinist. As Kristeva puts it:

> The formalists did not question the assumption that the work must be a system of signs, an objectal surface on which pre-existing elements are combined, a structure in which the transcendental sense is mirrored and maintained by the transcendental consciousness of the ever-present language-users. These were the necessary postulates of a reasoning entrapped in representation. Could anyone go beyond such postulates at a time when the Freudian breakthrough was not an accepted part of language theory, and when linguistics, in the process of becoming structural, could not foresee transformational methods? The facts of history show that no one could.[16]

The work of the Bakhtin group was precisely in these areas. By studying the history of meaning systems, they began to break open the transcendental sense. Through attention to the subjective that characterizes Vološinov's book they began to look at the form of the transcendental subject. For a Marxist paying attention to the psychological the constitution of the subject is a vital question. Human beings are composed of shapeless drives which are constructed into sociality by a *necessary* (that is, it is the prerequisite of social organization) *repression* (a shaping whose effect is one of blocking-and-returning-elsewhere rather than a mere channelling, as Reich might put it). This means that social structures, particularly as expressed in the family, enter into the very dynamic of the construction of the individual. The individual is not seen as unified, an expression of essence, but as crossed by contradictions (as in Althusser's more mechanistic formulation) and *producing* contradictions. The tasks of Marxism are, then, to unite the subjective and objective factors to change the material conditions of existence and afterwards, by a continuous criticism, to transform self and society in the same movement. Philippe Sollers has summed up the divergences between these two politics:

> Whilst idealism, as Lenin saw, 'develops' the subjective and works on it to the point of drowning in it . . . materialism completely ignores internal causality. Here we see the intersection of a double misrecognition of the dialectical process, whose result is the same refusal of the verifiable workings of psychoanalysis and the politics of passivity. That thinking of the subject that either sees it as diffracted everywhere or denies it does not permit any link between external causality and internal causality, any marking of the aspect of constant transformation, of plurality of contradiction (antagonistic and non-antagonistic contradictions, principal and secondary aspects of contradictions, etc.). This situation enables the perpetuation of that greatest of false debates between humanism and anti-humanism, which is completely surpassed by both the Freudian perspective and the historical conjuncture; it also provokes the perpetuation of a break between the politics of the subject (to be posed *in* language) and that of the masses.[17]

Cultural Studies should occur at precisely the site of this break between the individual and the masses; its task is to elaborate a theory which overcomes this gaping chasm in our understanding. Failure to do this will leave the Left powerless against Fascism, mouthing some variant of the conspiracy theory of history or the coercive theory of ideology. Our choice is clear: either to be correct dogmatically, or to be correct historically. We cannot do both.

16 Theories of language and subjectivity

Chris Weedon, Andrew Tolson, Frank Mort

In the first two chapters of this section, we looked at semiological theories of language through the work of Saussure and the early Barthes, where language is conceptualized as a system of arbitrary signs. These signs are neither transparent reflections of referents in the 'real' world, nor more complex, class-based reflections or refractions of an 'underlying material reality', as in Vološinov. Signs are, however, representational, since they have fixed meanings, at Barthes's level of denotation, prior to their articulation in any particular speech act. These meanings are fixed within the language system itself through the arbitrary linking of signifiers (sound images) to signifieds (concepts). The meaning of the individual sign lies in its difference from all other signs in the language chain. Saussure's theory of language relies implicitly on a rationalist theory of meaning and consciousness, since it rests on a notion of signs as representing ideas which precede any actual utterance and are, consequently, timeless and context-free. It is this aspect of Saussure's theory, with its implicit reliance on a notion of unified, fixed, rational consciousness, which is subject to criticism by John Ellis (Chapter 15). His critique comes from the perspective of psychoanalytic theory, which offers a radical alternative to rationalist-based theories of language and the speaking subject.

In this chapter we intend to look in greater detail at the questions of representation and subjectivity. We begin with Saussure and with Derrida's critique of Saussure and all rationalist-based theories of language. Derrida's alternative theory displaces the centrality of individual consciousness, the speaking subject and spoken language. We then move on to consider Lacan's parallel, psychoanalytic critique of language theory, based on a concept of unified, rational consciousness and the 'Tel Quel' group's reformulation of the problem of representation on the basis of Lacan's theory. We look at the work of Julia Kristeva, who formulates a text-based approach to language on the basis of psychoanalysis, in which the speaking subject is constantly in process. Finally, we reconsider the problems inherent in these general theories of language when it comes to the historically specific analysis of signifying practices. In the light of this we turn to the questions of language and subjectivity in an alternative theoretical approach – that of Michel Foucault – which insists on historical specificity.

The arbitrary nature of the sign in Saussure's theory

In the *Course in General Linguistics*[1] Saussure's principle of the arbitrary nature of the sign has two important implications. First, the 'identity' of the sign is relatively independent of its material conditions. The 'Geneva to Paris express', for example, does not refer to one fixed locomotive and one set of carriages but to any train located within, and defined by, certain conditions which make it the 'Geneva to Paris' express. The sign 'does not constitute a purely material entity, it is based on certain conditions that are distinct from the materials that fit the conditions .... Still, the entities are not abstract since we cannot conceive of . . . a train outside its material realization'.[2] The linguistic sign does not refer to the material entity as such but to the 'concept' of that entity. The second implication of the principle of arbitrariness refers to the internal structure of the sign itself. There is no natural, *a priori* connection between the concept (signified) and the sound image associated with it (signifier). Saussure sometimes refers to this as the 'unmotivated' character of the signifier: 'I mean that it is unmotivated, i.e. arbitrary, in that it actually has no natural connection with the signified'.[3] Thus the linguistic sign does not simply 'reflect' (or 'refract') reality. According to the principle of arbitrariness, it formulates a 'concept' – a 'signified' – which is itself complexly articulated with a particular sound image (signifier).

However, there are several theoretical difficulties implicit in making the principle of the arbitrary nature of the sign the starting-point for a general theory of language. First, it is not clear how 'meanings' are established within language. Saussure himself recognizes this problem, which he defines as the 'limiting of arbitrariness' – for, as he puts it, 'the irrational principle of the arbitrariness of the sign . . . would lead to the worst sort of complication if applied without restriction'.[4] It is to avoid the confusion of purely arbitrary associations that Saussure attempts to introduce some regularity to his system. In his attempt to resolve the problem of arbitrariness Saussure concentrates his attention entirely on the internal composition of the sign, ignoring the question of the relation of language to its material conditions of existence. He suggests that the arbitrariness of the sign is qualified by the language system through the links which are made between differential chains of concepts and sounds. These links, which Saussure visualizes as a series of vertical cuts in a 'signifying chain', produce 'combinations' between signifiers and signifieds, which take on 'values' as positive terms. Thus:

> when we consider the sign in its totality . . . we have something that is positive in its own class. A linguistic system is a series of differences of sound combined with differences of ideas, but the pairing of a certain number of acoustical signs with as many cuts made from the mass of thought engenders a system of values, and this system serves as the effective link between the phonic and the psychological elements within each sign. Although both the signified and the signifier are purely differential and negative when considered separately, their combination is a positive fact. . . .[5]

The question, which Saussure is unable to answer satisfactorily, is how these 'positive facts' of the language system are established. He has a general answer for this – they are 'social facts' or 'social conventions' – but his concept of the social institution of language is ambiguous. Saussure recognizes that language does not come from individual, intentional subjects and cannot be changed by any one individual (that is, that it 'eludes the individual or social will'),[6] and that individual speakers are 'largely unconscious' of its laws.[7] Yet when referring to speech acts Saussure is consistently forced to contradict this general principle and to define language as a kind of 'social contract', mutually recognized and adopted by a 'speech community'.[8] Implicitly, he assumes a network of self-conscious speaking subjects: '[Language] is both a social product of the faculty of speech and a collection of necessary conventions that have been *adopted* by a social body to *permit* individuals to exercise that faculty' [our emphasis].[9] However, the language system, with its fixed meanings, precedes individual speaking subjects, and we are left with the problem of the untheorized social nature of meaning: 'No longer can language be identified with a contract pure and simple . . . it furnishes the best proof that a law accepted by a community is a thing that is tolerated and not a rule to which all freely consent'.[10]

We can understand Saussure's ambiguity here if we refer back to his attempt to limit the arbitrariness of the sign. As we have seen, Saussure opts for a formal resolution: his 'domain of articulations' – between signifiers and signifieds, which makes it possible for language to 'signify' – is internal to language itself. Yet it is impossible for language to function autonomously. In order that signifiers and signifieds may 'articulate' as signs, Saussure is forced to hold to a concept of meaning already established within the signifying chain which the speaking subject articulates.

When we hear an unfamiliar language we are at a loss to say how the succession of sounds should be analysed . . . But *when we know* the meaning and function that must be attributed to each part of the chain, *we see* the parts detach themselves from each other and the shapeless ribbon break into segments [Our emphasis].[11]

Given Saussure's resolution of the problem of arbitrariness, he is ultimately forced to contradict the principle itself – he must presuppose a speech community which already 'knows' and 'recognizes' the meanings it will hear.

Derrida's critique of Saussure

A similar critique of Saussure has been made by the contemporary French philosopher Jacques Derrida. In *Speech and Phenomena* he offers a thorough-going critique of the tradition of rationalist and logical theories of language through a critique of Husserl.[12] In his essay 'Differance' in this volume and in *Of Grammatology*[13] he addresses himself directly to Saussure's problematic of the sign. Derrida argues that Saussure is self-contradictory because, in spite of his principle of the arbitrary nature of the sign, he remains attached to the nationalist, 'logocentric' tradition in Western metaphysics, which presupposes the *a priori*, fixed meaning of concepts. In this tradition language is intrinsically related to the self-consciousness of rationality. It is what allows the subject to present her/himself to her/himself. He argues that this entire rationalist discourse, which includes Saussure, is founded on the concept of language as speech – speech which comes from conscious, rational minds. His own radically different approach is founded on a reformulation of the object of linguistics.

Derrida starts from the Saussurean distinction between language as speech and as writing: 'Language and writing are two distinct systems of signs; the second exists for the sole purpose of representing the first. The linguistic object is not both the written and spoken form of words; the spoken form alone constitutes the object.'[14] His main point is that Saussure's theory of representation here contradicts his principle of the arbitrary nature of the sign, since if this is a general principle, the relations between phonemes (minimum significant units of sound) and graphemes (minimum significant written elements) must themselves be arbitrary. Thus there can be no 'phonetic writing'. Furthermore, Derrida points out that Saussure privileges the phonic level, as constituting the 'true' object of linguistics: in his theory the graphic level must always be secondary. In short, the phonic level is elevated to a transcendental position. It becomes the 'transcendental signifier' or concept, which writing exists solely to 'represent'. Derrida makes clear connections between this incidence of 'phonocentrism' (the privileging of the spoken word) and the 'logocentrism' (reliance on *a priori* transcendental meaning) of Saussure's theory as a whole.

Derrida's argument is, of course, extremely complex, and we cannot do justice to it here.[15] We can only indicate briefly the theoretical value of his critique of Saussure and some of its potential limitations. Its value, for us, consists in what Derrida has to say about the concept of 'representation' in general and the connections between this concept and Saussure's logocentrism. The point which Derrida makes is that the 'logocentric' perspective *requires* a 'naive representivist' concept of writing. However, as Derrida points out, the very tone of the 'logocentric' discourse, in its desire to separate out the inner meaning from its external 'clothing', puts us on our guard:

> One already suspects that if writing is 'image' and exterior 'figuration', this 'representation' is not innocent. The outside bears with the inside a relationship that is, as usual, anything but simple exteriority. The meaning of the outside was always present within the inside and vice versa.[16]

What is at stake here is not simply a relationship between speech and writing; it is the very status of the signified and signifier in Saussure's concept of the sign. For if writing affects speech, and if writing is to speech as a signifier is to a signified, then it follows that the signifier is constitutive of the signified or, conversely, that the 'transcendental signified' itself is at risk. In fact, Derrida argues that the concept of the signified falls with the critique of representation because 'this reference to the meaning of a signified, thinkable and possible outside of all signifiers, remains dependent upon the onto-theo-teleology (logocentrism) that I have just evoked'.[17]

The significance of Derrida's argument is that it makes possible a critical perspective on the whole problematic of the sign. It enables reconsideration of the semiological tradition, which derives its method from Saussurean linguistics and is based on a concept of representation. For example, Barthes's distinction between 'language' and 'metalanguage' (or myth) is premised on the assumption that the latter 're-presents' the former. In the reality effect, which Barthes attempts to theorize, myth works on the basis of the primary linguistic sign, the level of denotation, which has the implicit status of a transcendental signified to which myth refers. The point which can be drawn from Derrida's critique is that if the mechanisms of representation are at work in the production of ideology, these mechanisms are themselves ideological. There can be no primary denotation, no unified sign to be represented, except in logocentric discourse.

Derrida replaces the *a priori* fixed signifieds of Saussure's theory, which writing represents, by a concept of 'differ*a*nce'. He uses the term to signify the double meaning of the French word *differénce*: the differing and deferring of meaning. It is the shared principle by which both speech and writing function and, as such, enables spoken language to be reformulated in written discourse and vice versa. In Saussure's theory meaning functions according to the principle of the difference between signs in the language chain. This difference is between fixed signifieds which stand in a relation of non-identity to one another. Derrida transforms and extends this principle. Meaning is no longer a function of the difference between fixed signifieds. It is never fixed outside any textual location or spoken utterance and is always in relation to other textual locations in which the signifier has appeared on other occasions. Every articulation of a signifier bears within it the *trace* of its previous articulations. There is no fixed transcendental signified, since the meaning of concepts is constantly referred, via the network of traces, to their articulations in other discourses: fixed meaning is constantly *deferred.*

There is, currently, a reading of Derrida which would go so far as to reject any concept of 'representation' to describe all types of discourse. Undoubtedly, some of Derrida's own formulations encourage this kind of reading – in particular, his insistence on the total autonomy of texts, which may refer to one another but not to things outside themselves. This autonomy of textual discourses rests theoretically upon Derrida's critical strategy of 'reversal', where he makes not speech but writing primary – not the signified, but the signifier. A set of problems seems to follow from this. In Derrida's work the signifier itself sometimes appears to have assumed a transcendental position. It provides its own guarantee: 'the condition of its ideality, what identifies it as signifier, and makes it function as such'.[18] Similarly, the whole of history seems to be determined by the movement of the trace, taking the autonomy of language to the extreme.

Our conclusion must be that Derrida has certainly re-established the radical significance of Saussure's principle of the arbitrary nature of the sign, and this must be taken to exclude any *a priori* fixing of signifieds. It is therefore illegitimate for semiology simply to assume a primary level of 'denotation', to be represented in myth/ideologies. If denotations exist, they must be secondary impositions, a retrospective 'fixing' of signifiers, which is an effect of the ideological mechanism itself. This position is, in fact, argued by Barthes in his later work, where denotation is used to describe the last in a chain of connotations which are ideologically closed off. Conversely, however, it would be equally untenable to argue that the principle of arbitrariness simply 'appears' at every level of signifying practice. Clearly, there are secondary mechanisms which fix and sustain 'representation effects' and the illusion of a transcendental signified, both within specific social practices and at the level of individual subjects. This is, however, to return to our previous question of the social determinations acting upon language in general, as the linguistic signifiers enter the social and historically specific realms of discursive practice. We need to go beyond Derrida's critique for an answer to these questions.

Derrida's move away from representational theory of language based on speech to a theory of language located in written texts (grammatology) displaces the importance of the speaking subject in language. In rationalist discourse the fixed concepts, which precede any actual speech act, have to be articulated via the conscious intention of the individual speaking subject and the speech community at large. In abandoning the notion of transcendental fixed signifieds and focusing on traces of meaning within written texts, Derrida opens the way for a reconceptualization of the speaking subject, not as the intending originator of speech acts but as an *effect* of the structure of language.

This decentring of the subject, which is a mark of Derrida's departure from rationalist discourses, is shared by the other major contemporary theory of language which challenges the primacy of rationalist consciousness. This is Lacanian psychoanalysis, which insists on the importance of meaning in unconscious thought processes. Whereas Derrida's theory decentres but does not retheorize the speaking subject, Lacan offers a general theory of the constitution of the speaking subject in language and it is this theorization that we now go on to look at in detail. In the light of both Derrida's and Lacan's work, other writers (notably Julia Kristeva) have attempted an analysis of texts which rests on a concept of the subject 'in process' – that is, as an effect of language (see below). Kristeva and other members of the 'Tel Quel' group, in particular Barthes, work with the concepts of 'traces' and 'intertextuality', whereby meanings recur in different texts and connote other meanings which have been established in other texts. This textual theory has a theoretical underpinning in Lacan's theory of language, the unconscious and the subject. Kristeva also attempts to establish the compatibility of Lacan's theory of subjectivity with a Marxist approach to social relations. Her theory is offered as an alternative to an essentialist, humanist conception of the subject, usually alienated by capitalist social relations on the one hand, and the subject as empty space or bearer (*Träger*) of ideologies and social relations on the other. Here no attempt is made to theorize the structure of subjectivity. We will look at this attempt to unite psychoanalysis and Marxism later. We continue now by looking in greater detail at psychoanalytic theory of language.

Freud's approach to language

At various points in his writing Freud uses different theoretical models of the psyche. These include the biological, dynamic-energy model; the structure of the id, ego and superego; and the division of the psyche, via censoring mechanisms, into the unconscious, preconscious and conscious. The unconscious is the site of repressed ideas, and the preconscious consists of memories not currently present to consciousness but to which it has ready access. It is within the framework of this latter model of the psyche that language assumes a fundamental importance. The unconscious is, in this approach, the seat of *not* the drives but rather of their ideational representatives. By this Freud means the ideas to which the words become attached and thereby find psychical expression. The unconscious is the site of meaningful representations which can be consciously appropriated through language. Language, like all human activity, is ultimately motivated by the desire for pleasure.

Unconscious ideas (experiences, fantasies and so on) are governed by what Freud calls the primary processes (the mechanisms of condensation, displacement, representation and secondary revision). These processes are fundamental to the functioning of the psyche and govern Freud's method of dream interpretation, dreams being the 'royal road to the unconscious'. Every dream has a manifest and a latent content. The manifest content of the dream is what the dreamer can remember on awakening. The much more extensive latent content consists of the whole range of repressed thoughts which analysis can unravel and to which the manifest content is connected via the primary processes: 'The dream thoughts and the dream content are presented to us like different versions of the same subject matter in two different languages.'[19] The most important of these mechanisms are condensation and displacement, and in Lacan's reading of Freud they become the very mechanisms of language itself. Through condensation one idea comes to represent a number of chains of meaning in the unconscious. Displacement is the mechanism whereby an originally unimportant idea is invested with the energy which is due to another drive-motivated idea (in Freud's terminology, an idea 'cathected' with psychic energy). The two ideas are linguistically linked by associative chains of meaning. The psychoanalytic method enables the recovery of the repressed idea, from which psychical energy has been displaced. This method relies on the patient's own words, on her or his account of dreams, memories and fantasies and on free association. It is the principle of free association which makes language as a system central for Freud. It is the key to unconscious as well as conscious thought.

It is this aspect of Freudian theory which Lacan privileges when he sets out to develop a full theorization of 'the unconscious structured as a language' and of the constitution of the subject in language. In the context of post-Freudian developments in psychoanalysis Lacan's point of departure is a critique of those theoretical developments which have taken a biologist direction (Klein, Horney *et al.*) or developed in the form of ego psychology (Erikson) and of prevailing forms of Freudian psychotherapy, where the analyst assumes the role of expert, interpreting experiences to the patient. Underlying both these criticisms is Lacan's insistence on the primacy, within Freudian psychoanalysis, of the unconscious, understood as a site of *meaningful* thoughts and of language (in practice, the patient's own language) as the sole means of access to unconscious thought. Since thought and meaning are not the exclusive province of consciousness, the philosophical principle of man's unified, intentional consciousness as the source of meaning (found in rationalist and phenomenological approaches to language) must necessarily be challenged. It is the fundamental discovery of the unconscious as a site of meaning that, Lacan claims, other post-Freudian theorists have distorted or repressed. He identifies Freud's work on dreams and parapraxis as the key texts for psychoanalytic theory and practice, and he sets out to re-read these texts in the light of Saussurean linguistic theory. We intend here to look briefly at the way Lacan takes up Saussure within the context of a general, psychoanalytic theory of language and subjectivity, and at the claims made for this theory as the basis for a materialist theory of language.

The unconscious structured as a language

Lacan's theory is a general rather than a historically or culturally specific theory of the acquisition of language and gendered subjectivity. In its universality it draws on Lévi-Strauss's attempt, in structural anthropology, to identify the universal features of human culture. For Lévi-Strauss the principal feature is the Oedipal structure of relationships, which is linked to exogamy and the exchange of women. Lacan, like Lévi-Strauss, posits the Oedipus Complex as a general structuring principle of human culture.

In Lacan's theory the unconscious is formed via the organization of the drives at the resolution of the Oedipus Complex. This organization is structured so that demands for satisfaction are channelled in the direction of non-incestuous, heterosexual love objects. In the psychosexual development of the child the resolution of the Oedipus Complex is achieved in a gender-specific way through the differential male and female effects of the fear of castration. In the male mode this is a real fear of castration by the real father, who is identified with the symbolic position of power and control. In the female mode it involves acceptance of having already been castrated and of standing in a negative relation to the symbolic position of control of the laws of human culture with which the father is misidentified. This position of power and control, which Lacan calls control of the phallus (the phallus being the signifier of desire) from the position of the 'Other', is not actually occupied by anyone but is the structuring principle of the positions which individuals can occupy within the symbolic order of human culture. It is culturally identifiable, for example, in the power of the 'Name of the Father' in Judaic and Christian cultures. Desire to control the laws of human culture (to occupy the position of control of the phallus by the 'Other') is the structuring principle of language.

The moment of the acquisition of language as a total structure is the point in psychosexual development when the resolution of the Oedipus Complex is achieved and the individual is able to assume a gendered position within the symbolic order. The symbolic order is the realm of conscious human thought, laws and culture, and its structures are embodied in the very structures of language itself, which designate positions from which one may speak. Language exists prior to any individual speaking subject, and it is through language acquisition - that is, by taking up the position of speaking subject within language - that the human individual acquires gendered, conscious subjectivity. The basis of language is desire, and signification is a continual attempt by the subject to control desire by striving to occupy the position from which meaning and the socio-cultural laws controlling the satisfaction of desire come. This is what Lacan calls occupying the position of 'Otherness' (identifying, in an *imaginary* way, with the 'Other') - the position of control which structures one's own ability to speak and to obtain satisfaction.

Thus desire is the structuring principle of the psyche, of langauge and of subjectivity. It is the manifestation of the *lack* experienced by the individual because she or he is not the source of the laws of human culture and does not control them but is subjected to them and to the subject positions they make available. The lack of control is manifested in the individual through the gap between need, demand and satisfaction. Desire, which marks this gap, can, in principle, never be satisfied, since this would involve occupying the position of the 'Other' and becoming the structuring principle of human culture. Language, which involves the symbolization of this lack, is a never-ending attempt to control it. However, desire as a structuring principle, like 'differance' in Derrida's theory, has the effect of constantly deferring meaning through chains of signifiers, which are never fixed once and for all, as this fixing could only come from the source of meaning and control, the position of the 'Other'.

Since desire is not merely an abstract theoretical principle, like 'differance', but a theoretical principle in Lacan's theorization of the acquisition and structuring of subjectivity and language, which has a psychosexual basis in child development, we need now to look at this process of psychosexual development. The pyschosexual theory is also important to an understanding of the way parts of Lacan's theory, in particular the 'mirror' phase, have been taken up and incorporated in materialist theories of ideology.

Lacan's theory of the psychosexual development of the human infant follows Freud's closely, but with the important addition of the 'mirror' stage. The first stage that the infant goes through after birth is the pre-Oedipal, when it is concerned with the exploration of sensory perception; its main feature is auto-eroticism. At this stage the infant is unable to distinguish between things associated with its own body and the external world. It has no sense of its physical separateness from the rest of the world, nor of its physical unity as an organism. Its predominant sensation is one of fragmentation. The automatic satisfaction of need which it experienced in the womb is no longer a constant factor. Satisfaction in the form of the mother's breast, warmth and physical comfort is sometimes absent, and the child can neither control the satisfaction of its needs nor attempt control through language.

The initial conscious recognition by the infant of the distinction between its own body and the outside world comes at about six months, with the beginning of the 'mirror' stage. The child, which experiences itself as a fragmented mass of unco-ordinated limbs, identifies with a visual (mirror) image of a complete, unified body. This identification, which is the child's first intelligent act, is the basis of what Lacan calls 'imaginary relations'. Identification with the physical form of another gives the child an imaginary experience of what it must be like to be in control of its body and of its own needs – to be able to control their satisfaction. However, the child is as yet unable to distinguish between the form it identifies with and itself. This form, which is seen as unified and distinct from the rest of the world, is seen by the child as itself. In this sense the identification is based on *misrecognition*; it is 'imaginary'. Thus, for example, children at this stage of development cannot distinguish between themselves and their object of imaginary identification (their imago): 'A child who strikes another says he has been struck; the child who sees another fall cries.'[20]

The structure of misrecognition laid down in the imaginary relations of the 'mirror' stage remains important even after the child has entered the symbolic order and has become a speaking subject on the resolution of the Oedipus and castration complexes. Thus, when speaking, the subject identifies herself or himself with the 'Other' – that is, with the source of meaning – as if meaning came from her/him, in an act of misrecognition. It is this structure of misrecognition which has been taken up by Althusser, Laclau and others as one of the mechanisms at work in ideology. It is seen as the basis of identification by the subject with a particular ideological position, through what is termed the 'interpellation' of the subject in ideology. Other Marxists have gone further than this, claiming the whole of Lacanian theory as a valid materialist theory of subjectivity and the internalization of ideology (see below).

It is during the 'mirror' stage that the child begins to acquire language. This results from the child's attempts to express and to come to terms with its experience of the presence and absence of satisfaction. Absence of satisfaction creates a sense of anxiety in the child, and both Freud and Lacan see the attempt to master this anxiety (and ultimately to control desire) as the impetus behind the acquisition and use of language. Lacan cites Freud's example of a child playing with a cotton reel. The child's repeated action of throwing away and retrieving the reel to the accompaniment of the words 'fort' ('gone') and 'da' ('here'), enabled the child to symbolize control over the presence and absence of objects, the primary object being the child's mother, and thus symbolically to control the source of satisfaction. Throughout the 'mirror' stage all identifications are imaginary. This is marked by the child's use of language, by her/his inability to distinguish between the positions of I, you and she/he. The child refers to itself and others in the third person. Full mastery of language does not occur until the child is able to assume a gendered position with the *symbolic* order of socio-cultural relations after the resolution of the Oedipus Complex. Language is the key to this positioning within the symbolic order, in the sense that it is through language that consciousness and the unconscious are structured around Oedipal relations and social relations more generally are laid down.

It is in language that the 'I' of the imaginary order is transformed into a fully conscious, thinking, speaking subject, able to distinguish between itself and others. The 'I' becomes a full speaking subject through its incorporation into the cultural structures of linguistic communication, where it becomes the subject who speaks and from whom knowledge apparently comes. Yet by virtue of being in the position of speaking subject, the 'I' is subjected to the laws of language and, by extension, society - laws which precede it and give it the power to speak. Subjectivity is thus a function of language, not a pre-given, fixed human characteristic, as rational philosophy presupposes. As such it is continually 'in process', in the sense that it is reconstituted every time we use language, whether to ourselves or to others.

Thus language forms the structure of both the unconscious and the symbolic order. Lacan looks to Saussure and to Jakobsen for a way of theorizing the actual mechanisms of language. From Saussure he derives the concepts of a linguistic chain and the concepts of signifier and signified. From Jakobsen he takes the concepts of metaphor and metonymy, which he sees as homologous with Freud's concepts of condensation and displacement (see below). In Lacan's theory language consists of interlinked chains of signifiers rooted in the unconscious. Lacan insists on the term *signifier* because it is a principle of his theory that meaning cannot be fixed, *a priori*, in a particular signified; that is, there can be no such thing as denotative meaning. Meaning lies in the relation between signifiers. These relations can be structured according to the principles of either metonymy or metaphor. Language could be denotative (could contain *a priori* fixed signifieds) only if the speaking subject were its source rather than its effect. Fixed meaning could come only from the source of the laws of human culture, the position of the 'Other'. Since the pre-given structure of language is the precondition for signification by the speaking subject, and since signification is motivated by desire and the wish to control its satisfaction, which the individual subject can never do, fixed meaning is constantly subverted.

Metaphoric relations, which correspond to Freud's concept of condensation, function according to a principle whereby, under the force of repression, a signifier is replaced by a new one. In so far as the new signifier stands in place of the previous signifier and represents it, the first signifier acquires the status of a signified. In effect, it has become a signifier in a repressed chain of signification. A conscious idea may well be linked, via metaphor, to a number of unconscious chains of meaning, and it is the associated chains of repressed signifiers which make metaphoric relations so powerful in conscious language. The other mode of language operation is metonymy (cf. Freud's concept of displacement). Metonymy describes the relation of a signifier to the rest of the signifying chain - that is, to a relation whereby meaning is constantly deferred and can only be said to reside in the relations between elements of the signifying chain as a whole. The metonymic movement of language is motivated by desire, which is constantly striving for satisfaction. While there are no fixed signifieds in language, signification within the symbolic order is made possible by the privileging of certain key signifiers to which the drives, organized around non-incestuous heterosexual sexuality, become attached. Lacan calls these key signifiers *points de capiton* (raised buttons on a mattress) in an attempt to give a visual image of the structure of the unconscious. They act as nodal points which link signifying chains to one another and prevent an indefinite sliding of meaning.

Via their attachment to the drives, which have been organized in a culturally acceptable way, these nodal points structure the unconscious in terms of the positions from which any individual can speak. These positions are organized in terms of gender.

In Lacanian theory the mode of entry into the symbolic order and positioning within language is gender-specific. Speaking subjects are always gendered, and sexual identity relies on possible, imaginary modes of access to the control of the satisfaction of desire, which Lacan calls possession of the phallus. It is only men who, on account of their penises, can realistically imagine themselves possessing this power. For women the imaginary control of desire can only be mediated through the position of the mother bringing forth a male child. In relation to language it is through the primary difference penis/no penis and the ensuing resolution of the Oedipus Complex that incestuous and homosexual attachments are repressed - a conjunction which acts as the unspoken condition of signification within the symbolic order. The eternal privileging of the penis/phallus in the structure of the symbolic order and the unconscious makes Lacanian theory necessarily patriarchal, like that of Lévi-Strauss, on which, to some extent, it draws. It has been argued that Lacan's phallus is theoretically a neutral signifier, and that the linking of phallus and penis is cultural and arbitrary.[21] From this position phallic power - the control of the satisfaction of desire - could equally well be linked, under different cultural conditions, with another signifier of difference (for example, the breast). If this were so, it would free Lacan's theory from the criticism of being necessarily, eternally patriarchal and would make it more acceptable as the basis of a general theory of language, consciousness and ideology. However, we would argue that this position is untenable, in that Lacan's theory of language, which relies on a key structuring signifier of difference, is rooted in the psychosexual development of the child, while Lacan, like Freud before him, privileges the penis as the primary and sole organ of sexual difference, which is apparent from birth onwards.

Feminist appropriations of Lacan

As we indicated earlier in this chapter, a key political and intellectual influence on the recent development of theoretical debate around psychoanalysis in relation to ideology and subjectivity has come from feminism. While Althusser's appropriation of Lacanian concepts in a Marxist theory of ideology remained at the level of the mechanism of subject interpellation or positioning on the basis of misrecognition, feminist theorists have attempted to make Lacan's theory the basis of a materialist theory of ideology which could deal with the structure of gendered subjectivity. The insistence on the importance of gender and sexual ideologies in the constitution of subjectivity and on the structure of language and signifying practice within the symbolic order has resulted in three main strands of development of Lacan's theory.

First, there are those positions which deny the necessary eternal, patriarchal structure of Lacan's and Lévi-Strauss's general theory. For example, Juliet Mitchell[22] or Rosalind Coward and John Ellis[23] insist that the penis/phallus equation, and the power structures which go with it, are not necessarily universal but culturally and historically specific and therefore changeable, even within the terms of Lacan's theory. Then, informing much of this British work on Lacan, is the writing of Julia Kristeva, who has attempted, if only in principle, to fill in the theoretical *lacunae* in Marxist theorizations of the social formation in relation to language and subjectivity with Lacanian theory. Her theory involves a conception of a symbolic order governed by a set of dominant, masculine, patriarchal discourses to which some available discourses (for example, those of art, literature and irrationality) are marginal. These 'feminine' discourses draw on areas which the patriarchal symbolic order represses. Women's position within language and culture is defined by their negative entry into the symbolic order, an entry which, Kristeva insists, occurs via the social structuring of the unconscious. This notion of negative positionality within language has led to discussion of the need for the development of a separate language for women and the development of an alternative symbolic order. These ideas have become most important in the third line of post Lacanian theoretical development, by which the Lacanian problematic is reversed. A concept of an essential femininity, different from and superior to masculinity and founded in women's physiology, has led to attempts to develop a women's language and an alternative symbolic system through forms of separatist politics. We look now in more detail at Kristeva's work, since she has most to say about the area of language and subjectivity.

Kristeva develops a notion of signifying practice, 'significance', that covers both the symbolic order of rational language and the marginal, repressed, feminine discourses of poetry, irrationality, art and so on, which draw directly on repressed unconscious thought and which she calls 'semiotic'. All signifying practice involves both aspects of 'significance' but, depending on the type of discourse, one side or the other will predominate. Thus, for example, rational discourse is predominantly symbolic, whereas poetic discourse is governed by the semiotic side of language and draws on repressed signifiers which, under patriarchy, are predominantly feminine in character. Kristeva calls the unconscious basis of language the 'semiotic chora'. It results from the organization of the drives prior to the acquisition of language, an organization which Kristeva, unlike Lacan, insists is determined by historically specific familial and wider social relations. The 'semiotic chora' poses a constant challenge to symbolic communication. It makes itself felt through rhythm, intonation and lexical and syntactical transformations.

The semiotic challenge to symbolic relations occurs on the site of the individual subject. After entry into language, subjectivity is not constituted as fixed and conscious to itself once and for all. It is constantly in process and is differentially reconstituted within language every time an individual speaks. There is no essential subjectivity, and the individual subject, as a function of language, is as much a potential site for revolution as social structures. The two sites are linked by the effective role of social relations in the organization, within each individual, of the 'semiotic chora'. In this way, Kristeva attempts to link what she calls the mode of sign production with the mode of socio-economic production. The problem with this theory is the assertive nature of the link made between forms of psychoanalytically based theory of language and subjectivity and wider social structures. Kristeva's work is centred on textual analysis carried out within an amended Lacanian problematic. It lacks the theoretical underpinning of a detailed analysis of how desire is organized via historically specific social relations, rather than (as in Freud, Lacan and Lévi-Strauss) via the eternally given, patriarchal mechanism of the resolution of the Oedipus Complex. It illustrates the fundamental problem involved in attempting to bring together a psychoanalytic theory of language, in which desire is the founding principle, and a materialist theory of social relations. If, as we would maintain, a theory of language and subjectivity based on Lacanian psychoanalysis is intrinsically incompatible with a materialist, feminist approach to language and ideology, on account of the universal, patriarchal status of its concepts, which do not allow for a historically specific perspective, this does not mean that we do not have much to learn from it. At this stage we would indicate that a possible line of development in the attempt to construct a materialist psychology would involve rendering Freudian concepts historically specific. That is to say, what is needed involves the task of tracing concretely specific structures of unconscious subjectivity in their relation to concrete social and cultural practices and institutions in a way that preserves the specificity of the psychoanalytic instance.

We would argue, however, that for our present purpose of understanding the importance and effectivity of the structures of language and subjectivity within social ideologies and practices, at the level both of the discourses emerging from institutional sites and of popular consciousness and common sense, we do not necessarily need to wait for the development of a materialist psychology. Thus, while not disregarding the desirability and eventual importance of historically specific analysis of the structures of unconscious subjectivity, we should not fall into the trap of making a theorization of the structuring of unconscious and conscious subjectivity and the process of internalization and resistance to ideology the *necessary* starting-point in any consideration of language and subject positionings within language. This would be to preclude a politically useful analysis indefinitely.

Both the semiological and the psychoanalytic theoretical traditions which we have explored in this chapter offer, as they stand, general theoretical frameworks which have a universal rather than a historically specific status. However, the questions which they embrace – the move away from transparent readings and a concern for the specificity of signifying systems, as argued for by the semiological tradition, plus, we would insist, their material location: the importance of the construction of subjectivity within language and the effectivity of subject positioning within ideologies – are those questions which we can and must begin to address in a more adequate, historically specific way. It was with this in mind that the Language Group turned to the work of Michel Foucault. We saw Foucault's work as forming a thematic continuity with the central questions about language which emerged from the theoretical perspectives examined above. It also provided a number of possible movements forward.

Foucault's theory of discursive practices

Foucault outlines his position in relation to language in his most explicitly theoretical text, *The Archaeology of Knowledge*.[24] He constructs it through the historical location and critique of various dominant theories of language and linguistics. Foucault groups and identifies these theories in terms of the categories of *formalization* and *interpretation*, which are the two forms of analysis with which he takes issue. Significantly for our own argument, both these elements are central to the various theories of language and signification which we have considered in this chapter, and there are ways in which Foucault's own critique has formalized certain of the problems encountered by the Language Group in this area.

Foucault maintains that within the 'formalist system', language is conceived of as an autonomous structure, with its own laws of construction and application. The system may be constructed as total - that is to say, all possible specific uses are embraced by the system's general concepts, as, for example, in Saussurean or Derridaean linguistics. Alternatively, the system may be understood in terms of a set of more partial or particularized concepts, which describe the specific ways in which language functions. Foucault gives as examples of these latter concepts the 'sentence', the 'proposition' and the 'speech act', as conceptualized in Anglo-American discourse analysis. The totalizing and the particularized concepts share common criteria for specifying language as an analytical object through the identification of certain uniform and general features. These features are formal and universal, in that past and future uses of the language system in speech acts can be determined from the formal concepts. Hence within a formalist theory of language the conditions of appearance of a particular speech act are explained in terms of general theoretical concepts, as is the case in Saussure, Barthes, Derrida and Lacan. In Foucault's view this approach denies or ignores the historical specificity of the particular linguistic act and the historical determinations which may influence its appearance.

Interpretation, which Foucault defines as the second dominant feature of general theories of language, rests on a methodology which divides up the written or spoken in terms of the dualism of its 'internal' and 'external' aspects. It assumes that 'beneath' the external forms of language there is to be found an element which is fundamental and determinate in the construction of the linguistic system. Formalist theories are often implicitly premised on the belief that something is concealed within language which it is the task of interpretative analysis to discover and decipher. Foucault maintains that this 'silent' level can be conceived of as 'sovereign subjectivity', or the denotative moment (with its signifier in 'the real world') or, in philosophical terms, as the *logos* of reason.

In both elements of his critique Foucault stresses that the possibility of an analysis of the particular historical conditions under which individual linguistic formulations have appeared is ignored or suppressed in these general theories of language. It is this insistence that language owes the forms of its appearance to particular and not general conditions which forms the defining principle of Foucault's approach. In effect, the consequence of this position is an insistence that no total, exhaustive account of the domain of language is possible. Equally, it suggests that there can be no theoretical concepts which delineate language in general.

In contrast, Foucault insists that, in terms of analysis, it is possible (and necessary) to isolate a certain level at which, within a historically given moment or continuum, there exists a radical and marked connection or difference between individual linguistic elements. Foucault's basic concern, particularly in *The Archaeology of Knowledge*, is to conceptualize the way in which certain of these elements, referred to as *statements*, are linked by a coherence to form and define a distinct field of objects (for example, 'madness', 'illness', 'criminality'), a particular repertoire of concepts, a specific 'regime of truth' (that is, what can be said and what must be left unsaid) and a definite set of subject positions. Such coherent formations are defined by Foucault as *discursive practices.* He maintains that the coherence of a specific body of statements constituting a particular discourse is governed and defined by the principle of *regularity*. This is emphatically *not* a regularity based on formal rules of construction – a formal understanding of regularity would imply an idealist, self-generating structure. Regularity in the Foucauldian sense attempts to account for the ways in which statements are combined and coexist under determinate historical conditions. It attempts to define the conditions of formation under which specific types of statements are consistently distributed and dispersed over a given series of places within the discursive field.

In similar terms, Foucault's understanding of the position occupied by subjects within language and discourse marks a quite radical departure from the theorization of subjectivity in the linguistic, semiological and psychoanalytic traditions. As we have indicated, those respective traditions all rely on a general theory of the subject in relation to language which forms the basis for the analysis of individual speech acts. Though the understanding of the way in which subjects are positioned within language varies considerably across the different problematics (for example, a conscious, active subjectivity in the culturalist tradition, as opposed to a psychoanalytic approach in Freud and Lacan), all these theoretical traditions attempt to construct general principles of subjectivity and language which are assumed to remain constant over time and across cultures. Foucault's approach, in contrast, again emphasizes the historical specificity of the positions occupied by subjects within particular discursive practices, the historical conditions of their appearance and their relation to the body of linguistic statements which constitute a discourse.

As is the case with Foucault's remarks on language, it is difficult to 'abstract out' any general theory of subjectivity, or the subject from a mode of analysis, which is directed principally against the construction of general theoretical or universalist concepts. Foucault's most significant statements on the position occupied by subjects within discourse are to be found in the practical historical analysis of the emergence and constitution of particular discursive practices: that is, primarily in his analysis of the shifts in the organization of punitive systems in *Discipline and Punish*[25] and his work on an investigation of 'modern' sexuality in *The History of Sexuality*.[26] However, it still remains important to distinguish the principal features of Foucault's understanding of 'subjectivity' and to locate the nature of his theoretical differences from the earlier traditions we have examined.

In *The Archaeology of Knowledge* Foucault acknowledges the recent part played by psychoanalysis and linguistics in the deconstruction of active and sovereign subjectivity, 'in relation to the laws of. . .desire, the forms of. . .language, the rules of. . .action. . .sexuality and. . .[the] unconscious. . .'.[27] Moreover, he insists that a specific discursive practice provides a number of available subject positions from which it is possible for a specific individual to formulate or enunciate linguistic statements. Within discourse analysis it is necessary to distinguish who is qualified to speak and who must remain silent, and to locate the institutional sites or terrain on which subjects are constituted.[28] However, Foucault is insistent that the subject who formulates a statement 'should not be regarded as identical with the author of the formulation'.[29] Given the explicit critique of conscious (or unconscious) speaking subjectivity, Foucault maintains that statements should no longer be situated in relation to a 'sovereign subjectivity': 'The analysis of statements operates therefore without reference to a cognito. It does not pose the question of the speaking subject, who reveals or who conceals himself in what he says, who, in speaking, exercises his sovereign freedom.'[30] The various forms of speech and the modes of speaking which are possible within a given discourse (what Foucault calls the 'enunciative modalities') are not referenced to an original, unified subject but are defined according to the principle of discursive regularity, which distributes and disperses subjects across a variety of sites and positions within a discourse. 'Subjectivity', in the Foucauldian sense, is always discursive: that is to say, it refers to the general subject positions, conceived of as empty places, or functions, which can be occupied by a variety of particular individuals in the enunciation of specific statements. We should be aware that a Foucauldian understanding of 'subjectivity' is not in any sense concerned with the relation between discursive subject positions and the particular individuals who occupy them – that is, the area which has been theorized primarily by Freudian and Lacanian psychoanalysis and variants of social psychology. For Foucault the subject of a linguistic statement is 'absolutely general', 'in so far as it can be filled by virtually any individual when he formulates the statement; and in so far as one and the same individual may occupy in turn, in the same series of statements, different positions, and assume the role of different subjects'.[31] Foucault is able to maintain this position precisely because the enunciation of a discursive statement is not dependent on the subject/author as its cause or origin but rather on 'the prior existence of a number of effective operations that need not have been performed by one and the same individual . . .'.[32]

Further, Foucault's theorization of the enunciative subject is importantly linked to his understanding of the operation of power within a discourse. For Foucault the exercise of power relations should not be seen as *external* to a particular discursive practice; that is, it should not be sought 'in the primary existence of a central point, in a unique source of sovereignty from which secondary and descendant forms would emanate'.[33] Rather, power should be seen as 'immanent' or implicit in the constitution of discourse. Power, for Foucault, defines the type of relations of force which operate within a specific discursive practice and, more specifically, it can be seen to distribute and hierarchize the various discursive subject positions within a field of unequal relations. Given Foucault's understanding of the constitution of subjectivity, power cannot be said to be 'held' or exercised by particular individuals; it does not result 'from the choice or decision of an individual subject'.[34]

Foucault's recent historical studies, *Discipline and Punish* and *The History of Sexuality*, focus centrally on an analysis of the conditions for the emergence and constitution of specific forms of discursive subjectivity within penal discourse and discourses addressing sexuality respectively. *Discipline and Punish* traces the transformations in the conception of the criminally deviant individual in the late eighteenth and early nineteenth centuries. Foucault sees these transformations as linked to the general shift in the forms of the exercise of power, in the movement from a primarily juridical form of regulation of the rule of law, to the growth of a 'disciplinary society', in which the forms of punishment and surveillance are associated with the growth of a variety of practices (economic, juridico-political and scientific). Foucault's documentation of this transition traces the emergence within legal and penal discourse of a new type of criminal subject (with an aetiology, 'instincts, anomalies, infirmities, maladjustments, effects of environment or heredity'),[35] to whom the innovatory forms of regulation are addressed.

Similarly, in the investigation of the expansion constituting a distinctly 'modern' sexuality in *The History of Sexuality* Foucault locates the emergence of a number of new discursive subject positions – most significantly, 'the mother', 'the child' and 'the pervert'. Foucault identifies a defining characteristic of the modern regime of discursive sexuality in the consistently causal link made between sexuality and the formation of individual identity: 'it is through sex . . . that each individual has to pass in order to have access to his own intelligibility . . . to the whole of his body . . . to his identity . . .'.[36] For example, the sexually deviant individual of the nineteenth century emerges with a particularized history, biography and aetiology, and possibly a differentiated physiology. In fact, for Foucault an understanding of the historically specific construction of sexuality within discursive practices extends to include an insistence that the physical pleasures extracted from, and intensified in, the bodies of individual subjects are also a product of discourse. *The History of Sexuality* is not premised on a trans-historical constant of the body, which can be universally defined through physiology and anatomy, as is still partly the case in Freud's theory of the unconscious in its relation to instinctual drives. Rather, what we should seek to understand are the innovatory ways in which the body is constituted within discourse to form a distinctly modern politics of biology, population and welfare.

Foucault's theorization of the field of language and subjectivity, in their relation to particular social and cultural practices and institutions, has provided the Language Group with a series of new approaches to the problems in this area of Cultural Studies. Most significantly, it is Foucault's general and consistent stress on the *historical specificity* of the emergence of particular forms of linguistic statements and specific subjectivities which has marked a radical intervention in the language-subjectivity debate. That is to say, the conditions of possibility for the emergence of a particular body of discursive statements and subject positions will be dependent on the overall state of the discursive field, together with the structure of related practices and apparatuses in any given historical instance. Although Foucault's theory of discourse analysis does necessarily rely on a series of methodological and theoretical protocols, it is defined against the notion of a general theory of language and subjectivity, which is the principal focus of the other theorists we have examined. Foucault's mode of analysis is consistently historical in a sense that, for example, Freud's, Lacan's or Saussure's is not. For Foucault concepts are formulated in relation to the analysis of a historically specific object or continuity – they are not the formally derived concepts of a general system or theory.

Further, his theory of discourse analysis alerts us to the specificity of power relations within a particular practice or institutional site. In his critique of particular variants of Marxism Foucault insists that the conditions of possibility for the emergence of a particular discursive practice, together with the power relations which are integral to it, are not derived from any single or primary cause. We cannot, for example, 'read through' the structure of the field of medical discourses, or discourses addressing sexuality (that is, their particular manifestations of subjectivity, and the organization of their linguistic statements) to any single contradiction at the level of the mode of production. Foucault's understanding of discourse analysis, though it implies attention to particularization and specificity, is not a methodology which excludes the possibility of tracing articulations and effects from one discourse to another or examining the relation of specific discourses to other social and cultural practices and institutions. An attempt to locate the conditions of formation for the emergence of a particular discursive practice would, for Foucault, involve an examination of the overall state of the discursive field in its relation to other practices and institutional sites, rather than a search for the causal and determinate relation between the constitution of a discourse and the 'basic' political and economic class contradictions.

However, despite certain real advantages to be gained from the use of Foucauldian concepts in historically specific analyses, his theory of discourse analysis does present major difficulties which have particular implications for an adequate theory (and a politics) of the role of language and subjectivity in ideologies. First, we would insist that, despite Foucault's general protocols for defining a discursive practice, it nonetheless remains unclear how the boundaries or parameters of a discourse are delimited and, more specifically, how a given body of statements are assigned a place within a particular discursive practice. Thus discursive analysis seems most pertinent in examining those bodies of knowledge which are relatively tightly defined as theoretical disciplines (for example, medicine, psychoanalysis, political economy) and where there is little possibility of statements remaining ambiguous in relation to their discursive location. Yet even here we may be in danger of merely taking over and reproducing the traditionally defined boundaries of a consistent body of knowledge rather than reading for any underlying problematic. The problems become acute if the terrain of analysis is shifted to include written or verbal statements which do not clearly belong to a discursive practice – for example, statements which are formulated within the field of popular culture, common sense and so on – and which may in fact be the matrix or point of condensation of a number of social and cultural practices – linguistic, educational, familial, religious. In such an instance a theory of discourse analysis presents itself as rather too 'pure' to address the multi-accentuality of statements within what Laclau, in a different though related context, has referred to as 'popular ideological discourse'.[37]

A similar set of problems is raised by the more general question of the relationship between a Foucauldian understanding of the discursive and the 'non-discursive'. There is a sense in which Foucault's specifications for the constitution of discursive practices can tend to produce a type of 'history from above': that is, a history of 'official' practices, institutional sites and academic bodies of knowledge, which are understood to be operational without the possibilities of struggle and contestation. Foucault is insistent that 'where there is power there is resistance', in that resistances 'are the odd term in relations of power' within a discursive formation.[38] Further, at points in his historical analyses, particularly in *Discipline and Punish*, Foucault does attempt to trace the effectivity of popular and localized points of resistance to traditional forms of the exercise of power in influencing the formation of the new penal code (particularly in the account of the spontaneous resistances to the power of the king at public hangings and executions). However, the point of focus specified by discourse analysis – that is, the regularity of its organization and its field of effects – tends to militate against any examination of the interrelation between the emergence and continuity of a discourse and forms of resistance, struggle and contestation. We still need a more complex model for conceptualizing the possible field of relations and effects between the discursive and the non-discursive, which holds, in something of the Gramscian sense,[39] to an understanding of the continual formation and recomposition of power relations in a process of struggle.

Finally, Foucault's understanding of discursive subject positions can lead to the assumption that discourse constructs passive and unresisting subjects, who are only interpellated within the discursive realm. It presupposes a neat and functional relation between the empty discursive subject positions and the individuals who occupy them, rather than allowing for the possibility of resistances to those subject constructions, which could draw on a history of previous interpellations from other discursive or non-discursive social and cultural practices. There are, for example, moments in *Discipline and Punish* where Foucault's theory of discursive subjectivity has many of the same problems as 'labelling theory' in the sociology of deviance or Althusser's theory of 'subjectification' in the essay 'On Ideology and Ideological State Apparatuses'.[40] Subjects are 'automatically' assumed to consent to their subjugation:

> He who is subjected to a field of visibility and who knows it, assumes responsibility for the constraints of power, he makes them play spontaneously upon himself; he inscribes in himself the power relation in which he simultaneously plays both roles; he becomes the principle of his own subjection.[41]

Conclusion

So far, discussion of the place of language within Cultural Studies has largely been conducted through an exposition and analysis of the major theories which constitute the field. In conclusion, we feel that it is important to pose questions of language more specifically: that is, to indicate the possible ways in which the theoretical works which we have examined relate to the problems encountered in concrete, historically specific studies of language. We attempt here to outline a possible framework for a type of cultural analysis which would be more attentive to the centrality and specificity of linguistic structures.

In the range of work which constitutes the field of cultural studies it is apparent that language is most often awarded a privileged place in text-based research, which addresses itself to the structures of signification in literature, film and televisual discourses. Media Studies, together with developments in literary criticism and English Studies, is the principal area in which questions relating to the organization of language, authorship and subjectivity are encountered, and where theoretical attempts have been made to move away from transparent readings of texts, using aspects of the semiological theory outlined above. In other areas of work, where we would insist that questions of language are no less central, these theoretical issues are often largely ignored. Much social and oral history, for example, reads language 'transparently', as a source of empirical and factual evidence, with little attention to the structural determinations exercised historically by specific linguistic forms (though we should be aware of the exceptional quality of E. P. Thompson's work in this area). Also, work in the field of ethnography often takes an unproblematic view of the constituted subjectivity of individuals who are interviewed, relying implicitly on a phenomenologically based interactionist theory of individual acts and utterances (though here the work of Paul Willis on the culture of working-class schoolboys presents a far more sophisticated approach).[42] Similarly, work examining the operation of various institutional sites - particularly the apparatuses of the state - has, as yet, paid little attention to the structures of language and modes of signification which play a crucial role in the construction of official discourses. (For example, in the analysis of government policy, language is read transparently as the medium through which particular ideological discourses are constructed.)

The sort of theoretical approaches which have been applied to work on literature, film and television have included formalist, linguistic approaches, the denotation/connotation model and the form of semiology developed by the 'Tel Quel' group as an alternative to holding to an *a priori* level of denotation. Here, as we have seen, subject positionality becomes crucial, as, for example, in Barthes's later work on literature (*S/Z* and *The Pleasure of the Text*)[43] or as in the sort of film analysis developed in the journal of the Society for Education in Film and Television, *Screen*, over the last few years. The main problem with these forms of textual analysis, from our perspective, has already been indicated: their failure to pay due attention to the material, social practices which help to structure different forms of signifying practice. We would argue, as a general principle, that consideration of these factors is an important element in any attempt at the historically specific analysis of signifying practices.

It can be argued that the roots of semiological approaches in Saussure's general linguistic theory, with his primary division of language into the language system (*langue*) and the spoken utterance (*parole*), has enabled the development of forms of textual analysis which propose to tackle ideology purely at the level of general theoretical systems. If, with Foucault, we are critical of the notion of general theories and would insist on historical specificity at all levels of analysis, what then constitutes the specificity of language as a relatively autonomous structure? We certainly cannot simply reverse the problem and reduce language to the social practices within which specific forms of signification are located (for example, the technical determinants on film or televisual discourses).

In attempting to think about what constitutes the specificity of language structures, located within historically specific, social practices, it seems to us that we have much to learn from the forms of general theory outlined in this chapter. The most we can do here, is indicate what we consider to be important starting-points and why we think so, since the choice of theoretical models - though governed, we would argue, by criteria of adequacy in terms of their analytic and explanatory power - are also necessarily the subject of a political choice. Thus, for example, we would insist on the inadequacy of transparent readings of language. Such readings mask both the socio-ideological determinants of signification and the linguistic specificity (in terms of subject positionality and the fixing of meaning) whereby discursive practices operate and common-sense ideologies are 'lived' and represented in a variety of cultural practices. Such cultural practices consist of apparently 'spontaneous' forms of consensual shared meanings and values, which appear, to individual speaking subjects, to be given as *a priori*, denotative meanings but which are, in fact, socially and historically constructed. We would argue that the questions of subject positionality and representation (that is, how meanings are ideologically fixed in language) are central; but that also there is a need for attention to language in cultural analysis which goes beyond general positions on subjectivity and representation. Here we feel the need for a form of sociolinguistics which would pay attention to both language *structure* and *usage* in historically specific locations, thereby opening up the area of the language of continually repositioned, speaking subjects within the symbolic order, thought historically to be a particular formation of social practices and discourses. Thus while decentring the subject as the source and guarantee of meaning, we would want to look at the range of socially and institutionally constructed possible subjectivities available to individuals; and here, we would argue, close attention to forms of language within discursive practices is central.

Just how much an adequate sociolinguistics could learn from the established Anglo-American tradition we do not feel able to gauge abstractly here. However, we consider this whole area to be one which needs urgent attention, in the light of the general theoretical positions which we have defined for ourselves, through our engagement with semiological and psychoanalytic theories of language and with the work of Foucault, which we consider to be of central importance.

17 Sexuality for sale*

Janice Winship

Despite its glorifying display of commodities, advertising represents a *moment of suspension* in their production and circulation: production - the sweat and exploitation of work - is over and hidden in its verbal and visual persuasion: the consumption of someone else's (or your own) objectified labour, to which you, the as-yet-passive spectator, are invited, has not begun. Yet in monopoly capitalism advertising has become integral to these circuits of production and circulation: it sustains the movement of commodities, from their social production to their *individual* but socially repeated consumption, which eventually ensures the reproduction not only of the individual but of capital too.

> The individual produces an object and, by consuming it, returns to himself, but returns as a productive and self-reproducing individual. Consumption thus appears as a moment of production.[1]

By concealing the production process, advertising similarly covers up class distinctions between people, through a form of fetishism: 'the definite social relation between men . . . assumes here, for them, the fantastic form of a relation between things'.[2] It replaces them with the distinctions achieved through the consumption of particular goods. As Judith Williamson points out:† 'Instead of being identified by what they produce, people are made to identify themselves with what they consume'.[3] However, in order to cement identification with consumption, ads move away from capital's terrain proper; we individually consume *outside* the production process:

> in consumption, the product steps outside this social movement [of production and distribution] and becomes a direct object and servant of individual need, and satisfies it in being consumed.[4]

In confirmation of consumption outside economics, ads rarely exhort us to *buy* the commodities, but merely to *use* them, hence glossing over the capitalist moment of exchange - the purchase with money. Further, they never simply sell us the use values of commodities; they sell them as 'exchange values'[5] for qualities in our private relationships with people that are unattainable through the capitalist produc-

*This chapter is an extract from 'Advertising in women's magazines, 1956–74', CCCS Stencilled Paper (forthcoming).

† I would like to acknowledge my debt to Judith Williamson, whose own analysis has generated many of the ideas I have taken up here.

tion process. For example, a commodity cannot 'buy' you love (with a man), but ads give just such an illusion of capital's ubiquitous power: 'Your face is your fortune: look after it with Outdoor Girl.'

Addressing us in our private personae, ads sell us, as women, not just commodities but also our personal relationships in which we are *feminine*: how we are/should be/ can be a certain feminine woman, whose attributes in relation to men and the family derive from the use of these commodities. Femininity is recuperated by the capitalist form: the exchange between the commodity and 'woman' in the ad establishes her as a commodity too. In ads addressing women this process is insidious: it is the modes of femininity themselves which are achieved through commodities and are *replaced* by commodities. A woman is nothing more than the commodities she wears: the lipstick, the tights, the clothes and so on are 'woman'. Here the ads not only conceal the labour which produces the commodity; they also, contradictorily, omit the *work* of femininity which women carry out as they use commodities, yet always sell commodities for that purpose. This is in striking contrast to ads directed at men, in which the terrain of activity which is appealed to is that of *leisure* - leisure defined in relation to *completed* work for *capital.* Women, on the other hand, are sold commodities for their work: the *patriarchal* work of domesticity and child care; the work of beautification and 'catching a man'.[6] This work, like that of social production, is collapsed in the ad into mere consumption of commodities by us as individual women. To consume the commodity (even just to consume the ad itself) is already to have accomplished the tasks of femininity until, at its extreme, it appears almost as if the commodity can replace femininity, can take on femininity without female intervention.

We can conceptualize ads therefore as representing a particular articulation of capitalist production and consumption. But in that articulation they also particularly, if not exclusively, operate through ideological representations of femininity. This *ideological work* relies on, but also constructs, an ideology of femininity which is completed through our *collusion* as we read and consume the ads. We are never just spectators who gaze at 'images' of women as though they were set apart, differentiated from the 'real' us. Within the ads are inscribed the images and subject positions of 'mother', 'housewife', 'sexually attractive woman' and so on, which, as we work to understand the ad, embroil us in the process of signification that we complete. Yet we do not come 'naked' to the ads or to any ideological representation and simply take on those representations. We already have both a knowledge of images of women from other discourses and an acquaintance with 'real' women in our everyday lives. The signification of an ad only has meaning in relation to this 'outside' knowledge of the ideology of femininity. Even when it appears that ads are producing a *new* representation (for example, 'Dress to kill'), not merely reproducing an idea of femininity found elsewhere, the signification is not completely autonomous but anchored by the patriarchal and capitalist relations in which we as individuals already have a history and which we already know about.

The signifier 'woman' always signifies woman: we recognize ourselves in *any* representation of woman, however 'original', because we are always already defined by our gender. Having recognized ourselves in the ad, we are then 'freshly' positioned as specific feminine subjects in an identification achieved through a misrecognition of ourselves – the signifier 'woman' can never in fact represent us as individual women. It is through this process of misrecognition that ads are effective in producing and reproducing the particular ideological modes in which we live.

The discourse of ads contradictorily places us both in relation to other discourses and, more particularly, in relation to those economic and political positions which, through feminist struggle, begin to challenge patriarchal relations. If we are to sustain and further those material gains, we have also to recognize ideological fields as a terrain for women's struggle. As Coward argues, 'the struggle for power within discourses becomes an issue of political importance for the Women's Movement'.[7] To be able to engage politically at that level we need first to understand the processes of signification which are at work.

In ads, as elsewhere, femininity is contradictorily constructed. Ideologies of 'motherhood', 'domesticity', 'beauty', 'sexuality' and 'feminine independence', as they are cut across by an ideology of the 'free' individual, are all separately and sometimes jointly mobilized and constructed anew. In this extract, however, I want only to consider some elements of an ideology of sexuality.

To make yourself passively attractive is, by the mid 1960s, to make yourself specifically *sexually* attractive and *available*: as if, it is represented, the act of beautifying yourself is *already* to engage in sexual relations – it is not just the promise of it. This is always implicit: 'Girls are coming back warm lipped', says Yardley. 'So come out of the cold and into the warm. Be lit up. Alive. All girl.' Or: 'Lips are too sensitive to withstand the sensation of harsh lipstick contact and much too important to expose to experimentation. Super Jewelfast 22 Special is a *new experience itself* . . . Soft and gentle and kindness itself. . . .' (my emphasis). Or you are perhaps prepared for sex: 'Your lips have never looked this wet before'; 'You're getting warmer . . . three new bronzed lip-polishes wetter than wet. The warmest colours you ever saw. Each one spiced with excitement.'

This ideology of sexuality in the ad context admits both to a *passive*, virginal and innocent sexuality – waiting for men, typified by the image of a young woman in long white robes and flowing blonde hair ('A Clairol Summer Blonde') – and to an *active* experience of sexuality. However, the active experience of sexuality only takes place in a fetishistic mode (in the Freudian sense of fetish). Women are invited by the ads to respond to themselves through the imagined fetishes of men – the tights/legs, the lipstick/lips which fragments or distortion of them stand for all of their womanness.[8] Yet since men are absent, there is an ambiguity: is it a sexual experience with men that is inferred, or are women 'masturbating' with 'phallic substitutes' or through masculine fantasies? 'Your lips have never looked this wet before': we see just a woman's red lips, open, a lipstick resting against them, alongside an army of big shiny, erect and partially encased lipsticks.

This ambiguity extends to the more obviously narcissistic representations in which pleasure is self-induced rather than being reliant on men. 'Imagine the clinging soft caress of stockings' – a girl, nude, gently holds her ankles almost suggestively, caressing herself and looking out at us (or at men?); or 'A touch of Fenjal Silky' (see below). As John Berger discusses and Ros Coward takes up, the naked woman is always a *nude* woman, 'framed in the beautiful photograph', a representation comparable with soft-porn photos, potentially to be gazed at by men even if it is women who look at it.[9] Thus women not only *see* themselves as men see them but are encouraged in these ads to enjoy their sexuality through the eyes of men. It is a narcissism which, at the moment of self-masturbation and scopophilia (looking, in this instance, at one's *own* body), is also exhibitionist, inviting voyeurism from men.[10]

There is a further narcissism which affirms women's self-indulgence and involvement but plays down the sexually exhibitionist elements. 'Only drink it if you never bathe before noon. Freezomint Crème de Menthe. Green, cool and slightly wicked.' It is an independence of sensual pleasure, however, which we can translate into more heterosexual terms through the visuals of the ad: the virginal white of the woman's dress; the abundant *fertile,* as well as fresh, green of the plants.

This ideology of sexuality is therefore disparate and contradictory for women, though nevertheless contained within patriarchal relations: active/passive; heterosexual/narcissistic; dependent on men/independent of men; fetishistic, masturbatory. And it is set firmly apart from 'motherhood' and 'domesticity', which admit to no sexuality even though premised on reproductive sexuality.

The three examples described below have been chosen to illustrate

(a) The construction of an 'original' femininity which we did not know about until we read the ad
(b) its containment within patriarchal relations
(c) the 'penetration' of femininity by masculinity – the 'masculinization' of femininity by the commodity form to create a dependence both on men and commodities
(d) the contradictory modes in which we, as readers, are inescapably ensnared in the signification processes and in those modes of femininity

Pittard's gloves (*19*, March 1968, p.1 – colour)

The caption, 'Dress to kill', draws on two opposing ideological referent systems,[11] 'femininity' concerned with 'dress' and a form of 'masculinity' concerned with 'aggression', which are brought together. Visually, the condensed signifier also embraces this contradiction: a woman, partly shown, her one eye looking at us, has her arms round a man whose back is towards us. She is 'killing' her man – but with her 'dress' (in fact, her gloves) and not with the gun which the gloved hand holds; she is 'killing' him in order – we know 'outside' the ad – to catch him. The power of the gun has slipped over into the *red* gloved hand. That colour is a signifier in a discourse organized around blood, killing and danger, but it is also associated with a chain of meaning organized around the danger of *sexuality*. Simultaneously, the gloves are both tough, 'killing', almost masculine weapons and feminine – 'soft' and 'supple' and daringly sexy.

She is in control of the situation, has power over the man who, vulnerably, has his back towards us (imagine us with that gun/those gloves). She looks at us, almost winking, woman to woman, knowing about men and how to catch them. She controls him as if he were just another rather dangerous *object*: 'Don't be caught barehanded. Whether you're dealing with a man or a Mauser.' However, she does not have this power independently: she needs the gloves, not to be '*bare*handed' (my emphasis). Paradoxically, 'dressing' herself, she becomes *more* sexual: she has 'the Pittard swing ticket'. Ostensibly the 'swing ticket is your guarantee of washability' but in the underlying sexual discourse it guarantees you a man: Pittard's gloves 'buy' you a man.

The reciprocal emptying and exchange of meaning between the signs 'dress' and 'kill' create a new sign which conflates into a new referent - an 'aggressive femininity'. Even though such a masculinization of femininity exists 'outside' the ad, the means of signification permissible in the ad allows a *heightened* signification (the gun as signifier) not possible in the 'real' relations between a woman and a man: it is, in this sense, an 'original' construction. Nevertheless, the ad must be seen as participating in those relations by 'voicing', making explicit and setting the terms within which 'femininity' operates. 'Masculinity' retains its dominance, even while being subverted - woman is 'aggressive' precisely for the feminine aims of catching a man.

Fenjal bath oil (*Cosmo*, May 1974, p.146 - colour)

Narcissism, here, is very private; almost without men, but with a public edge, directed at men. On the one hand, it is a representation of woman that is typical of soft porn: there is a movement in the ad from the 'natural' petals of the pink carnation at her breast, to the caption, down to the carnation's reappearance with the product and finally to 'A touch of Fenjal Silky' - a reference by this time both to the product and to the woman's sexuality, signified by her pubic area, her hair, which hides the site/sight of her female genitalia, her 'petals', the 'heart' of her sexuality within patriarchal relations.

Thus the text and visuals can be read as suggesting that you bathe in Fenjal to await a *man's* touch. But we also have to recognize that the ad is directed to women and we can therefore read a contrary meaning: she is touching herself in the photo, privately, behind the mistiness; eyes directed at herself, she is self-sufficient, though dependent on the commodity: 'As you lie in a Fenjal bath you can feel the gently cleansing action beautifying your skin and when you step out one touch tells you how effective the Fenjal moisturiser has been. A touch of Fenjal Silky.' Even though that kind of pose is a sign in a patriarchal discourse - and since we still live within patriarchal relations, its meaning must over-determine and carry over into any oppositional signification - we should not refuse to recognize it as also, contradictorily, establishing a *difference* from that patriarchal representation. We must, however, be wary of our assessment of it. As Griselda Pollock, writing of feminist attempts to create 'an alternative imagery outside ideological forms', relevantly argues:

The attempt to decolonize the *nude* female body, a tendency which walks a tight rope between subversion and reappropriation, often serves rather to consolidate the potency of the signification rather than actually rupture it.[12]

It is finally as a 'reappropriation' of feminine sexual independence within patriarchal and capitalist relations that we must understand this ad.

Guinness (*Honey,* November 1974, p.99 - colour)

Concisely and illustratively, this ad not only brings together many of the tendencies in the representation of 'femininity' in ads but also poses the limits to such a representation. It constructs and works through fetishistic relations in both Freudian and Marxist forms.

The ad is surreal, its surrealism constructed by the camera: a close-up shot obscures the shape and dimensions of the face, merging it into the foam of the Guinness, so that the vivid, glossy, red lips stand out above the flattened, labelled glass of dark Guinness. It is a condensation involving *absence* and *contradiction* which 'Ladylike - Guinness' *denies* but also demands that we necessarily decipher. When we set in play the signifying chain we move from the 'inside' to the 'outside' of the ad; we 'fill' the absences and recognize the contradictions. The absences concern 'femininity' and 'masculinity' which *we already know about*, which the ad presupposes and which are in contradiction with each other. The one bit of woman, the vivid red lips, signifies the whole of 'femininity' (woman) through a metonymic relation - in that sense the 'lips' are 'ladylike'. But metaphorically their colour and texture and shape signify daring, excitement, sexuality, in contradiction to the sober connotations of 'ladylike'; 'masculinity', in its difference from these red lips, is signified by the dark drink. We participate in a 'joke': the red lips are *not* 'ladylike', although it says they are; Guinness is not ladylike either, but the ad dares the *impossible* and declares that it is. Unlike the Benson and Hedges ads, for example, which rely on a similar joke that is fantastical because there is no way in which the ad can bring about what it signifies (that is, a Benson and Hedges packet can never be a pyramid, a fountain pen nib, and so on), Guinness *can* be 'ladylike'; the ad may generate 'Ladylike - Guinness' because women will drink it. Benson and Hedges remains at the level of a joke, at the level of signs; Guinness, on the other hand, potentially *intervenes* in the reality to which initially it only refers - 'femininity'.

Reading the ad as women, we are constantly caught in its contradictions, oscillating between 'ladylike'/'not ladylike' (masculine), and not drinking Guinness/ drinking Guinness, but are finally ensnared within its imaginary unity: not either/or but *both* - the dare of 'ladylike' and drinking Guinness which empties 'ladylike' of its referred meaning and fills it with the product, Guinness. However, that engagement with the meanings of the ad involves *submitting* ourselves to the means of signification - to fetishistic relations. First, the 'human' element of face, to which the lips belong, has been obliterated; yet we understand those lips as representing *women's* lips, even if they are only a thing - painted lips, a sign of women, like a lipstick. It is another 'thing', the commodity Guinness, which is the sign for masculinity. The relation between 'femininity' and 'masculinity', in its particularity of the gender-organized social conventions of drinking, is set up for us to see as 'the fantastic relation between things':[13] a pair of lips and a glass of Guinness, which appear 'naturally' to have the characteristics of 'femininity' and 'masculinity'. Marx writes:

> The mysterious character of the commodity-form consists therefore simply in the fact that the commodity reflects the social characteristics of men's own labour as objective characteristics of the products of labour themselves, as the socio-natural properties of these things.[14]

But here both capitalist commodity production and patriarchal ideological construction are hidden.

Furthermore, we have to engage with the representations of a fetishistic sexual relation structured in masculine dominance. The (closed) lips represent a displacement from the genital area of the lips of the vagina, a displacement which does not bring to light the absence of a penis and women's castration. According to Freud,[15] the fetish is substitute for the penis which the little boy believes his mother has and the absence of which he refuses to take cognizance of when he observes her lack. However, he both retains the belief and gives it up: he affirms and disavows castration of women by appointing a *substitute*, which takes over his sexual interest, while avoiding the site/sight of female genitalia for which he has an aversion. In the ad the fetish is obviously not a literal one in the sense Freud meant it; nevertheless, the signification of the ad works in a mode very similar to the operation of these fetishistic relations for men. The ad depends on our knowledge that women do not usually drink Guinness - they are 'ladylike' (and castrated): it depends on the *difference* between women's 'lack' and men's plenitude - the full glass of Guinness. However, that difference is *disavowed* in the condensation of 'Ladylike - Guinness': women can and do drink Guinness but remain 'ladylike'. But the future pouring of the commodity Guinness between the as-yet-closed lips - the as-yet-'ladylike' lips - is also a metaphor for the sexual act: man's penetration of the lips, the vagina, which provides affirmation of women's 'castration'. We are dared to drink Guinness, but our daring, after the grounds of 'femininity' have slightly shifted, continues to place us firmly within the conventional bounds of patriarchal relations.

Part Five

English Studies

18 Literature/society: mapping the field*

The Literature and Society Group, 1972–3

The revival of interest in the literature/society theme

As a glance at the bibliography in this issue will confirm, there has been, in recent years, a remarkable growth of interest in the literature/society problem. To place this changing visibility properly, in all its complex significance, would require a critical review of the whole map of intellectual culture. Any attempt to explicate the current shift in attention must take account of the following:

1 The continuing force of the Leavis/*Scrutiny* tradition, both in English studies and in education generally. The central elements in this position are summarized below.

2 The growth of an interest in 'culture', often from a base within English studies. The work of Hoggart and Williams is paradigmatic here.

3 A disenchantment with the pragmatic, empirical, anti-theoretical nature of Anglo-Saxon literary criticism; a growing interest in literary theory.

4 The availability, in English, of some of the key texts of European theorists and writers (Lukács, Goldmann, Marcuse, Benjamin, Brecht, Adorno), especially the Marxists, whose work had hitherto been known, if at all, only at second hand.

5 The expansion in the use of *linguistics* in literary and cultural studies. There are, of course, many kinds of linguistics. What is important here is the apparent promise that a more rigorous and 'scientific' approach can be discovered through a linguistics-based study of literary work rather than through the intuitive and interpretative procedures of literary criticism.

6 The intellectual impact of French structuralism and semiology. (Though the coverage in English is still extremely limited, there are, *inter alia*, translations of Lévi-Strauss, Barthes, Foucault, Lacan, Althusser.)

7 The application of semiology, structuralism and ideological criticism to the new media and a general revival of interest in aesthetic and formal questions. Here the English development lags well behind the French, German and Italian debates. (But some discussion has emerged in magazines like *Screen* and *Monogram* and in Wollen's widely read *Signs and Meaning in the Cinema*.)[1]

There are also three important, though less immediately related, factors:

8 The so-called 'cultural revolution' which has manifested itself in Western societies since the early 1960s. These extremely heterogeneous movements have

* This chapter is an extract from *WPCS* 4 (1973).

yielded, among other things, 'theories' attempting to deal with 'the politics of culture' and to relate art/life, literature/politics, *avant garde*/politics, culture/ideology. This climate has been exceedingly favourable to a renewed interest in the social and political dimensions of art and literature.

9 A shift in the whole intellectual universe of the social sciences away from positivistic and quantitative approaches and towards phenomenology, structuralism, Marxism, 'critical theory' and so on. This has promoted, in turn, a renewed interest in such hitherto marginal fields as 'the sociology of literature', 'the sociology of art', 'the sociology of culture'.

10 A quite remarkable general interest in theory, marked especially by the slow, uneven, but significant way in which Marxism has penetrated English intellectual life in recent years. This intellectual shift parallels political and historical tendencies which cannot be further developed here. One convenient signpost is the translation into English of some key Marxist theoretical texts (for example, Marcuse's early essays, Goldmann's *Human Sciences and Philosophy*, Gramsci's *Prison Notebooks,* Althusser's *For Marx* and *Reading Capital,* Korsch's *Marxism and Philosophy,* Sartre's *Problem of Method,* Reich's *Mass Psychology of Fascism,* selections from Marx's *Grundrisse*).

Approaches from within literary criticism

The dehistoricizing of the text has had a specific influence on literary-critical concepts of literature as a social phenomenon, yet within that tradition equally sophisticated positions can retain enormous differences of emphasis. As instances we cite Northrop Frye's essay on 'The social context of literary criticism', and F. R. Leavis's 'Literature and Society'.[2] Both, it should be noted, define themselves explicitly against the Marxist approach (thereby negatively confirming the argument advanced by Tom and Elizabeth Burns that 'the genesis of the concern with literature . . . as a social institution, lies in Marxism').[3] Frye acknowledges that this is a serious issue in criticism; and, after reviewing a number of approaches and finding them unsatisfactory, he remarks: 'I wanted a historical approach to literature, but an approach that would be or include a genuine history of literature, and not the assimilating of literature to some other kind of history.' Via such concepts as 'conventions', 'genres' and then 'archetypes' and 'myths', Frye finds his way to an

> historical overview, on the basis of what is inside literature rather than outside it. Instead of fitting literature deterministically into a prefabricated scheme of history the critic should see literature as, like a science, unified, coherent, and autonomous created form, historically conditioned but shaping its own history, not determined by external historical process.

In this argument the 'social context' of the literary text is both acknowledged and at the same time reinserted into the framework of 'literary activity', which is 'autonomous'.

Leavis has always affirmed that the critical act of reading, interpretation and judgement is, fundamentally, a *social* act – while limiting the kinds of people, the sorts of mind, equipped to engage in this critical dialogue. His famous prescription for this dialogue – 'This is so, is it not?' – is one to which only an embattled civilizing minority can profitably subscribe. Perry Anderson has pointed out that his interrogative statement demands one crucial precondition: 'a shared, stable system of beliefs and values'.[4] The less evident the existence of this morally and culturally unified set of uncommon 'common readers', the more relative this universalized practice of criticism becomes and the more explicitly elitist his prescription, the more one-dimensional his lament for the loss of an 'organic reading public'. But Leavis, too, acknowledges that 'if the Marxist approach to literature seems to me unprofitable, that is not because I think of literature as a matter of isolated works of art, belonging to a realm of pure literary values'. He never aims for the degree of 'closure', the squaring of the circle, which satisfies Frye: indeed, it is Leavis's ability to hold, at one and the same moment, to the specific quality of the 'words on the pag while using the 'felt experience' organized in language as a representative index of the 'quality of life' of a whole culture, which makes his work so pivotal to the whole argument. Leavis always tries to 'go through' from the close response to the text to the 'qualities' which lie behind its specific organization.

> Without the sensitizing familiarity with the subtleties of language, and the insight into the relations between abstract or generalising thought and the concrete of human experience that the trained frequentation of literature alone can bring, the thinking that attends social and political studies will not have the edge and force it should.

We find here the sources of the paradox that those critics within the Anglo-Saxon tradition who have tried to think the literature/society problem in a rigorous way have usually taken their point of departure from Leavis, while at the same time breaking from the way he has formulated the problem.

The 'break' with traditional literary-critical practice

The most significant 'break' within traditional literary criticism to a new way of formulating the literature society problem is to be found in the work of Raymond Williams, in whose major theoretical writing[5] literature becomes one specially privileged level or instance of a 'cultural totality', itself composed of many different levels, several 'particular histories'.[6] The art and literature of a society are aspects of its culture: and culture is understood as the crucial meanings and values which distinguish the 'way of life' of one particular society from that of another. Culture, in this sense, is expressed and carried not simply in literature and the arts but in every level and activity which go to make up the social totality. It is there 'in institutions and ordinary behaviour, in implicit as well as in explicit ways'. Literature is one of the specially privileged ways in which such key meanings are expressed, clarified, discovered and transmitted.

The key question is how this privileged activity and its product, the literary text, are related to other activities in the totality. Here Williams dispenses with a formulation which would give prior determination to any one level or activity – for example, the economic '*base*' which art, in a simplified Marxism, reflects as part of the '*superstructure*'. He argues that, if literature really is a part of the 'whole', there is 'no solid whole, outside it, to which . . . we concede priority'.

The art is there, as an activity, with the production, the trading, the politics, the raising of families. To study the relations adequately, we must study them actively, seeing all the activities as particular and contemporary forms of human energy.

If 'culture' can be said to 'relate' in any sense, then it is as an expression of the way in which *all* the activities hang together – 'the theory of culture is the study of relationships between elements in a whole way of life'. The same pattern or structure, then, might be revealed as active in very different, apparently unrelated levels within this totality. Thus the study of literary texts, provided it was undertaken in this 'many-sided' way, could 'stay in touch with and illuminate particular art works and forms' while at the same time being connected to the 'forms and relations of more general social life'.[7] Williams's work represents a long, sometimes displaced critical engagement with the Marxist tradition on these questions. In his early substantive work (*Culture and Society*) Marxism is discussed in terms of English Marxist literary theory of the 1930s – an engagement with traditional literary criticism which, Williams argues, *Scrutiny* won and deserved to win. In the theoretical sections of *The Long Revolution* Marxism provides the hidden 'sub-text' of the argument but the key terms and concepts are retransplanted and reshaped. This applies, above all, to the problem of base/superstructure, which, despite the reshaping, emerges from Williams's work as *the key problematic of the whole field.* Base/superstructure is the classic framework within which the relationship of 'being' and 'consciousness', of 'ideas' to their 'social base' has been formulated in Marxist thinking. In 'From Leavis to Goldmann' Williams acknowledges that some way of conceptualizing the relations of determination – 'the economic base determines the social relations which determine consciousness which determines actual ideas and works' – is not only 'near the centre of Marxism' but 'indicates an appropriate methodology for cultural history and criticism and then of course for the relation between social and cultural studies'. But his own way of handling this problem is to substitute for some sophisticated version of the base/superstructure framework 'the more active idea of a field of mutually if also unevenly determining forces'.[8]

The key concept, for Williams, in his attempt to 'think' the relationship of ideas or works of art and literature to the social totality, is *structure of feeling*. This concept locates both the internal order and values of a literary text and the pattern of experience at a given historical moment. The pattern of experience, however, is not defined in terms of a set of explicit beliefs – for example, an ideology – but in terms of the implicit structure which social life exhibits at the level of *experienced values*: thus 'structure/of/feeling', an apparently paradoxical concept. The literary text is one concrete instance of the 'structure of feeling' in a particular society at a particular moment. In practice (and often, it seems, somewhat at odds with his theoretical position), Williams does seem to treat literature as qualitatively different from other activities. This is partly because he stresses the active, creative process by which society organizes 'received meanings' and discovers 'possible new meanings'. This, indeed, is change – the 'long revolution'. This process depends on the ability to communicate these new meanings, to find a language and form as a description for new experiences. Every social individual takes part in this process – 'culture is ordinary': but – it follows – the moments of the most intense exploration, those embodied in art, are a very special aspect of a common activity. Williams's engagement with Marxism only begins with these subtle formulations. His work poses the whole question of whether 'culture' can be simply and easily assimilated into the Marxist notion of ideology, or whether it requires new terms, concepts, ways of establishing its relationship to its social base. In his most recent work Williams seems to have discovered, via the work of Goldmann and Lukács, a more direct and sympathetic route between his own thinking and the Marxist tradition. Though this has not yet borne fruit in substantive terms, he has gone so far as to pinpoint certain key convergences between his own work and Lukács and Goldmann: (a) the concern, in both, with the notion of the 'social totality'; (b) the search for homologies or correspondences between a work and its social base at the level of *structure* (rather than of content); (c) similarities between Williams's 'structure of feeling', Lukacs's 'potential consciousness' and Goldmann's 'world vision'.

Reformulating the 'break'

Much of what has been said indicates the absolute centrality of Marxism to the literature/society problem. Many who explicitly dissociate themselves from Marxism implicitly acknowledge its centrality by the very form of their disavowal. Williams's work progressively reveals the complex tension it maintains with Marxist concepts and problematics. In this section we must now address these questions *directly*. Whichever variant of the Marxist problematic we take, we are always led back to the central formulation, *base/superstructure*. From the early 1844 manuscripts, through *The German Ideology* to the *Critique of Political Economy* and the *Grundrisse*, whenever Marx wanted to refer to the ways in which economic structure, social relations and the 'ideological forms' cohere to form a distinctive social formation he tended to employ some variation on the idea of a 'basis' and 'the superstructures'. The nature, degree and mode in which one level determined the other was variously expressed in Marx's own writings and was the subject of key reformulations in Engels's later correspondence.

This argument is too complex to trace through in detail here. Marx always insisted *both* that 'the formation of ideas' should be explained 'from material practice' *and* that art was related to material production by an 'uneven development'. The 'transformations' which connected 'the economic foundation' with 'the whole immense superstructure' were, clearly, not simple, transparent or unmediated.[9] We know that by 'economic foundations' he meant something as complex as 'the material production of life itself . . . the form of intercourse connected with this and created by the mode of production (i.e. civil society in all its stages)' – 'the totality of these relations of production constitutes the economic structure of society, the real foundation'. We know he thought it crucial

> to distinguish between the material transformation of the economic conditions of production, which can be determined with the precision of natural science, and the legal, political, religious, artistic, or philosophic – in short, ideological forms, in which men become conscious of the conflict and fight it out.

But in the absence of the promised volumes on the state, politics and art, it remains an unfinished project for Marxism to 'think' rigorously how the 'correspondences' between these levels are to be understood. That is the reason why (a) in Marxism a proper 'theory of the superstructure' still awaits elaboration; (b) it is difficult to base a Marxist theory of literature as a social phenomenon squarely on the existing texts and concepts; and, paradoxically, (c) the study of the literature/society problem, in a Marxist framework, is not a marginal enterprise, but absolutely central to the development of historical materialism as a science – because, within that problem, a critical absence in the theory can be, progressively, clarified.

Despite the confused state of Marxism in this whole area, two things at least are clear. First, the 'vulgar Marxist' way of conceptualizing the base/superstructure relation is not likely to take us very far. It conceives this relation in narrowly reflexive ways and tends always towards a reductively economistic kind of analysis. Second, Marxism nevertheless *does* require the analyst rigorously to confront the question of *determinations* – more especially, the 'determination of the economic level in the last instance'.[10] We may usefully break this question down into several, related questions:

(a) how to 'think' a social totality or social formation – the 'ensemble of social relations' – in a different way;
(b) how to 'think' *what is specific* about each of the levels, activities or 'practices' which compose or 'produce' this complex totality;
(c) how to 'think' the different *modes* in which social activity in history (what Marx, in *The German Ideology*, defined as praxis and Williams translates as 'human energy') appears – for example, in economic life and production; social relations; institutional life and the state; consciousness, ideas, ideologies and beliefs; artistic and symbolic productions, including language;
(d) how to 'think' the relationships of determination and 'relative autonomy' *between* the different levels in this totality.

We may identify *two variants or problematics* in this area within Marxism. The first follows from Marx's notion that 'definite forms of social consciousness' correspond to the 'totality of relations of production'. It attempts to elaborate and clarify just what that notion of *correspondence* entails. The theorists who belong to this variant all reject some simple notion that the superstructures *directly reflect* the base. They therefore explore the mediations, the transformation, the refractions, which establish or reveal the dialectical links between 'ideas' and 'society'. These writers address the base/superstructure problem head-on and deal with literature as a 'superstructural' phenomenon. Lukács and Goldmann (but also, from another position, Adorno and Marcuse) belong within this problematic.

There is, however, a second line of theorizing. This stems rather from Marx's equally important injunction that 'consciousness must be explained from the ... conflict existing between the social forces of production and the relations of production'. The base/superstructure problem is seen not so much as a two-tiered model but in terms of a complex, differentiated totality. Thus literature is regarded less as a *refraction* of the base through the superstructures and more as a specific kind of activity (praxis), as a certain *kind* of practice, even as a form of *production.* To this alternative tradition belongs Brecht, with his stress on the 'mounting' of the work of art, his concern with 'effect'; Benjamin, with his attention to the new 'productive forces' in artistic work; perhaps, in an *intermediary position,* Sartre, who is concerned with praxis and project, but for whom the work of art is the production not of a text (object) but of certain kinds of signified meanings - artistic production as a form of *signification*; and the structuralist and semiotic schools, for whom the primary mode of artistic production is the production of signs through language and sign systems. We should also include here the 'Althusserians', who, though they have not produced a 'theory of literary practice' as distinct from their discussion of ideology, have given a most rigorous and fruitful definition of the term *practice* which could be developed into a 'regional theory' for art and literature.[11] In Althusser the two sides - base/superstructure and practice-production - come together in a useful way. Althusser accepts the value of the base/superstructure distinction. He also accepts Engels's notion that in capitalism the economic level is 'determining in the last instance'. But since he sees any complex social formation as a base/superstructure complex, he argues that it is never actually possible to find one level (the economic, say) appearing on its own without the other levels (social relations, political practice, ideology, theory). Thus instead of a simple determination, he speaks of relations of 'contradiction and over-determination' defining how any one level relates to another 'within a structured whole'.[12] Althusser therefore does not believe that there are simple correspondences or homologies between the different levels (the Hegelian problematic): each level is produced by its own kind of practice, or 'production', and may stand in an 'uneven relation to other practices'. Thus we are required by him to think what is specific to, 'relatively autonomous about', each level, as well as the relations of similarity and difference which govern social formation. The notion of *practice* is useful here in clarifying what might be meant by speaking of literature as a *form of production.*

Althusser has proposed that by *practice* we should mean 'any process of transformation of a determinate raw material into a determinate product, a transformation effected by a determinate human labour, using determinate means (of 'production')'.[13] The overall perspective of this view of art as a production, of literature as a 'practice' is that the determination of art within society appears not (as with Lukacs and Goldmann) at the level of general relations between the structures of being and consciousness (the way Marx formulated the problem in *The German*

Ideology); but rather at the level of the specific character of the moment, materials and activity of artistic production. Such a perspective recognizes art as an activity within a determinate social world – but, more significantly, as always in certain specific relations to other 'practices' at work within the same historical moment. Art is seen as a practice which employs certain specific 'means' to transform some set of objects or concepts or perceptions into something else – the specific structure of the literary text or the work as a symbolic-social object. However, what it is that literary practice transforms, what distinguishes its means, materials and 'mode' of production, what and how this practice is 'determined by' or 'relatively autonomous from' other practices, and so on, are problems in this approach which have not, so far, been rigorously exposed.

19 Recent developments in English Studies at the Centre*

The English Studies Group, 1978–9

Theoretical developments

In this section we review some theoretical work which has seemed to us important since the publication of *Mapping the Field* (1973). First we extend the previous map by noting, in the work of Raymond Williams and Terry Eagleton, an English appropriation of the two problematics reviewed; that is, literature as a part of the superstructure or as a form of production. Then in two further sections we look at the implications of thinking literature as production, institution or formation; and at attempts to think about 'reading'.

Williams and Eagleton

In Williams's move from his 'Base and superstructure' article[1] to *Marxism and Literature*[2] questions of consciousness and determination are sophisticated by way of Gramsci's thought. Gramsci's concept of 'hegemony' is brought nearer to Williams's own account of dominant and subordinate cultures (both residual and emergent), which might be oppositional or alternative. This is combined with an analysis of determinations, though the stress on 'the whole social process' threatens to evacuate the concept altogether, and again with a forceful stress on creativity – the 'active struggle for new consciousness'. Eagleton, in *Marxism and Literary Criticism* and *Criticism and Ideology*[3] has inflected Brecht's and Benjamin's thinking on literature as practice/production, through Althusser and Macherey, to develop a highly schematic account of 'the literary mode of production'.

Eagleton's almost parricidal attack on Williams in *Criticism and Ideology* is interesting, not just because it presents an extreme version of the split between what have been called 'culturalist' and 'structuralist' Marxisms[4] but because two radically different views of what constitutes critical practice are brought out. In *Marxism and Literature* Williams starts by stating that it is 'impossible to carry through any serious cultural analysis without reaching towards a consciousness of the concept

* This chapter is based on work and comments by Janet Batsleer, Rob Burkitt, Hazel Carby, Tony Davies, Michael Denning, Michael Green, Rebecca O'Rourke, Michael O'Shaughnessey, Roger Shannon, Stephen Shortus and Michael Skovmand.

itself: a consciousness that must be, as we shall see, historical'.[5] Most of Williams's work has been informed by this 'reaching towards a consciousness of the concept' (the most obvious example being *Keywords*), attempting both an historical clarification of shifts in the meaning of words such as culture and base/superstructure and a redefinition of such words/concepts for his own argument. This search for adequate concepts has produced such hybrids as 'cultural materialism' and 'structure of feeling', to name two of the central ones. The acid test of the usefulness of the concepts, to Williams, lies in their confrontation with the 'experiential', an attitude which Eagleton, half-admiringly, describes as 'this passionate premium placed upon the "lived" '.[6] This constant movement between the concept and 'the experience' produces its own contradictions, as when Williams insists that 'it is not "the base" and "the superstructure" that need to be studied, but specific and indissoluble real processes',[7] from which point he moves to a discussion of the concept of 'determination'.

Whereas in Williams we find a recurrent emphasis on the critical idiom as in some way partaking of the reality it signifies, in Eagleton critical practice involves the construction of a discourse consciously at a distance from the object of inquiry. Criticism, according to Eagleton, must 'situate itself outside the space of the text on the alternative terrain of scientific knowledge'.[8] 'Its task is not to redouble the text's self-understanding, to collude with its object in a conspiracy of eloquence.'[9] Agreeing with Williams on the insistence on art as 'material practice', he proceeds to 'set out in schematic form the major constituents of a Marxist theory of practice';[10] a hierarchy of concepts, beginning with 'the general mode of production' and ending with 'the text'. The function of criticism, for Eagleton, is 'to refuse the spontaneous presence of the work – to *deny* that "naturalness" in order to make the real determinants appear'.[11] He is concerned with 'the *destruction* of corporate and organicist ideologies'.[12] Much of Williams's work has been in areas of cultural practice hitherto marginalized or unconnected, whereas most of Eagleton's critical practice aims at subversion within the traditional definition of literary criticism.

Literature: production, institution or formation?

In the 1859 *Preface* Marx included art among those 'definite forms of social consciousness' that rise as a 'superstructure' upon the 'real foundation' of the productive relations. The notion of art as a 'form of consciousness' – whose relation to the productive basis might be variously conceived as correspondence, reflection, representation, homology, relative autonomy – dominated the classical period of Marxist aesthetics. But in the *Grundrisse*, while retaining the concept of 'forms of consciousness', Marx had already suggested another way of envisaging art – as a *production*:

> Certain forms of art, e.g. the epic, can no longer be produced in their world epoch-making, classical stature as soon as the production of art, as such, begins . . . . Greek art presupposed Greek mythology, i.e. nature and the social forms already reworked in an unconsciously artistic way by the popular imagination.

Here art is seen not as a superstructure standing in a secondary relation to a productive foundation, but as itself a form of production with its own materials and means.

The concepts of art as production was developed in two pioneering essays by Walter Benjamin;[13] but outside his native Germany Benjamin's writing seems to have had little impact on literary theory. More influentially, for us at least, artistic production – as against consciousness, creativity, subjectivity – has been strongly argued within an Althusserian critique of humanism. For Pierre Macherey[14] literary criticism's talk of 'creation', 'genius', 'great literature' belongs to a discredited tautological humanism whose 'purest product' is its aesthetics, its 'religion of art'. Against this he asserts the wholly objective character of literary production:

> Art is not man's creation, it is a product (and the producer is not a subject centred in his creation, he is an element in a situation or system) . . . all considerations of genius, of the subjectivity of the artist, of his soul, are *on principle* uninteresting.

In a similar vein, Terry Eagleton has offered an ambitious theorization of a 'literary mode of production' as a structure of forces and relations both determined by the productive process in general and capable of considerable autonomy of form and development:

> The social relations of the LMP (literary mode of production) are in general determined by the social relations of the GMP (general mode of production). The literary producer stands in a certain social relation to his consumers which is mediated by his social relations to the patrons, publishers and distributors of his product. These social relations are themselves materially embodied in the character of the product itself.[15]

Of course, the insistence on determinate conditions and relations of production must be central to any materialist analysis of writing and reading. But for Eagleton, as for Macherey, it seems that the writer (and, implicitly, the reader) can hardly be *more* than an element in a system (Macherey) or structure (Eagleton) that allows no space for movement, contestation, change. Only the privileged (Marxist) critic somehow eludes the grim necessities of the system:

> An attentive criticism of the work which defines the conditions of its production, is altogether different from a reading. [Macherey]

> The task of criticism, then, is not to situate itself within the same space as the text, allowing it to speak or completing what it necessarily leaves unsaid. On the contrary, its function is to install itself in the very incompleteness of the work in order to *theorize* it. [Eagleton]

If the work is a 'tissue of fictions' exhibiting a 'false conformity', the critic's task must be to expose it, to denounce it, to reduce it to a guilty silence in the awesome presence of 'theory'. But why? For whom? Where, in what conditions, and with what political effect? No one would expect political effects to flow immediately under the pressure of a theoretical insistence; but the absence of these questions from some recent work suggests that the voice of confident and peremptory theory booms the louder for the resonant emptiness of the space assigned to it by the intellectual division of labour of the dominant order – the university.

The extent to which much Marxist criticism remains within not only the institutions but also the conceptual terms of 'bourgeois aesthetics' may have something to do, too, with the fact that such theories of literary production rarely attempt any historical account of the ideological concept of 'literature' itself. By contrast, Renée Balibar has argued that literature exists not as an absolute, 'out there', but as a constructed element within a specific ideological apparatus – education – where it both legitimates and disguises the reproduction of linguistic inequality.[16] Thus 'literature' is both an agent and an effect of ideological class struggle within the dominant institution of the bourgeois state. More recently, within a similar theoretical field, a case has been made for literature as *itself* an institution.[17] As a concept, insitution is perhaps preferable to apparatus, since it enables the sense of 'being instituted', and thus the possibility of resistance and transformation. In practice, though, the two have often been virtually synonymous, with the emphasis on structure rather than on process, thus reproducing the functionalism, as well as the inhibiting political inertia, of Althusser's 'Ideological State Apparatuses'.

If, as this implies, both the *production* and *institution* of literature are too monolithically and 'objectively' determined and determining, directly reproducing the productive relations in ways that can be critically exposed in postgraduate seminars (but never, seemingly, transformed by political activity), the equally influential work of Michel Foucault raises a different problem: his version of 'superstructures' gives no account of material determination at all. Foucault has not written directly about literature, but it would not be difficult to argue that literature and literary ideology constitute one of those relatively discrete structures of knowledge that he calls *discursive formations*: sets of related statements, objects and institutional sites that together compose the 'episteme' or field of practical knowledge at a particular moment. His analysis of the relations and rules of transformation of discursive practices is suggestive, but its effect, in spite of some throw-aways about 'non-discursive practices', is to imply that such formations are virtually independent of the production process, of class struggle, of politics. Prisons, hospitals, universities emerge as structures of *statements*. Power appears as a function not of classes, nor of the state, but of discourse itself.

Raymond Williams has recently commented on these theoretical difficulties in a highly interesting, if too general, way.[18] Of institutions he notes that

> it is an underestimate of the process to suppose that it depends on institutions alone . . . it is never only a question of formally identifiable institutions. It is also a question of *formations* . . . which may have a variable and often oblique relation to formal institutions.

But, conversely,

many of those in real contact with such formations and their work retreat to an indifferent emphasis on the complexity of cultural activity. Others altogether deny (even theoretically) the relation of such formations and such work to the social process and especially the material social process.

Williams has arrived at these concepts and these criticisms by his own, often lonely, route. For a while his work was partly eclipsed by the prestige of more 'rigorously' theoretical accounts. As that prestige wanes or is qualified by a sense of sharpening political urgencies, his work looks more and more compelling: not least for its persistent emphasis on literature and culture not as a 'structure' (whether institution or formation) but as a productive practice and a political struggle.

Reading

If we can agree, with Macherey, that literary criticism is not 'an art, completely determined by the pre-existence of a domain, the literary work, and finally reunited with them in the discovery of their truth, and, as such . . . has no autonomous existence', but is rather the 'study of the conditions and possibilities of an activity',[19] then the starting-point for a literary theory of reading must be to find ways of adequately conceptualizing the conditions and possibilities of this activity. Marx's insistence that 'a product becomes a real product only by being consumed'[20] may seem to offer a methodological starting-point for such a theory. Yet, while sometimes paying lip-service to this and similar formulations, theories of literary production have evinced no comparable body of work on the consumption, reception or just plain *reading* of texts. As Dubois has noted, 'the tradition [of Marxist aesthetics] has a tendency to consider the reader as a neutral pole, a "man [*sic*] without qualities" '.[21] Thus the recipient of the text too frequently remains, as in much bourgeois criticism, a cipher, assumed and untheorized. Two tendencies play into this: a notion of the reader as wholly and inflexibly constituted elsewhere, and a contrasted but, in effect, similar view of the reader as a mere effect of the text. Neither position is worthless, but neither will do as it stands, since both reduce the process of reading to the mechanical reproduction of elements always already composed, in either the text or the 'subject'.

One of the central concepts, and one of the most subject to vagueness or confusion, is the concept of the 'reader'. The distinction offered by Naumann between (1) recipient - the actual historical reader, (2) addressee - the author's conception of whom s/he is addressing/will be read by, and (3) reader - a formal, textual-defined entity,[22] may provide a conceptual basis for considering how existing theories attempt to think the text-reader nexus.

On the face of it, Althusser's notion of interpellation, as elaborated by Laclau, seems to encompass all three versions of the 'reader': the recipient constituted as addressee through the interpellation or 'hailing' of ideological discourse. It provides what looks like an overall theory of discourse, in so far as Laclau writes: 'what constitutes the unifying principle of an ideological discourse is the "subject" interpellated and thus constituted through the discourse'.[23] Furthermore, Laclau's insistence on the plurality of ideologies, and hence of interpellations, is valuable. Individuals are not interpellated as subjects once and for all, but rather dispersed across a range of successive and simultaneous interpellations (legal, familial, political and so on). Literary texts certainly allude to these ideologies and so evoke interpellative transactions negotiated elsewhere. But the real problem of employing the notion of interpellation in a theory of reading lies in the danger of equating literature as a specific cultural practice with the concept of 'ideological discourse' (which, of course, neither Althusser nor Laclau actually does). The notion of interpellation as applied to a theory of reading provides no distinction, but rather a conceptual slide between, the concept of the 'subject interpellated' and thus constituting 'the unifying principle of an ideological discourse'[24] and the historical subject involved in the practice of reading. Furthermore, the notion of interpellation fails to come to grips with the specificity of literary practice as a second-order system of signification whose raw material is language and which is therefore, in a sense, constituted by its own 'problematic'.

It is, however, significant that attempts to erect theories of reading on the basis of a notion of literature as a specific, basically self-referencing, conventionalized form of linguistic practice will tend to see reading as the performance of a 'literary competence',[25] or to envisage literary criticism as the 'reconstruction of a horizon of expectations':[26] theories in which the reader is little more than an extrapolated ensemble of literary sensibilities. Thus, according to Culler,

> the question is not what *actual readers* happen to do but what an *ideal reader* must know implicitly in order to read and interpret works in ways which we consider acceptable, in accordance with the institution of literature.

Historically, one of the reasons for shifting the emphasis from 'text' to 'reading' derives from the preoccupation with 'polyvalence' or 'indeterminacy' which has undermined the view of literary criticism as the quest for the one irrefutable meaning, the essential 'truth' of the text. In the work of Iser the notion of interdeterminacy is actively appropriated and promoted to being a criterion of what constitutes the 'truly' literary text. To Iser, it is the

> virtual dimension of the text that endows it with its reality . . . expectations are scarcely ever fulfilled in truly literary texts . . . we feel that any confirmative effect . . . is a defect in a literary text. This virtual dimension is not the text itself, nor is it the imagination of the reader: it is the coming together of text and imagination.[27]

It is indicative of the anti-materialist tendency of such notions of 'competence' or 'imagination' that, for Culler, the road forward would be in the direction of 'an aesthetics based on the pleasure of the reader', while for Iser the direction is towards individual self-discovery, 'the chance to formulate the unformulated'.

It is perhaps in the work of Manfred Naumann and of other East German 'reception theorists' that a Marxist theory of reading may find a serviceable basis. Naumann's central notion of the text as *'Rezeptionsvorgabe'*, a determining element in the process of reception (an idea that draws on the *Grundrisse* concept of productive consumption), combined with the Brechtian notion of the 'active subject', seems to provide a productive formulation which retains the specificity of literary practice while at the same time seeing that practice as inherently social, as a field of multiple determinations structured in dominance. For Naumann the relation between the text and the reader 'represents only in appearance the basic relation through which a social practice is mediated. In fact, it represents the abstraction of a plurality of multiple determinations'.[28] It is only 'from the social and historical totality, of which the institutional practices of literature are a part, that the practices of "active subjects" can be made concrete'. Naumann insists that the practice of reading cannot be thought of as constituting a causal relation between text and reader, however widely defined, as theories of 'effect' or 'uses and gratifications' would imply. His description of literature as an 'area of experiment for social imagination',[29] while clearly addressed to internal East German polemics, includes both Lenin's view of literary practice as 'partisan' and Brecht's emphasis on emancipation, the movement from the 'self-evident' to the 'evident'. Reading, accordingly, is seen as both the end-point and the starting-point of a complex of social, psychological and aesthetic processes and practices. These practices, and the institutions from which they are inseparable, are both the 'stake' and the 'site' of struggle. As Brecht programmatically put it, 'our critics must study the conditions of struggle and develop their aesthetics from them. Otherwise their aesthetics is of no use to us, for we are in the struggle.'[30]

Contexts for recent work

In this section we look outside of these theoretical discussions to some other developments by which our own work has been influenced.

One way of evoking the issues would be to say that an important stage, the moment of *Mapping the Field* itself, in which there was a considerable and almost wholly theoretical excitement about the study of literature, has begun to be left behind. For good reasons, the result is not yet (and may never be) an equivalently confident map of major names and tendencies. *Mapping,* after all, occurred at the intersection of four developments: (1) a confident rejection of the disdain for contemporary life which marked the late work of Leavis and his followers, the dominant grouping in the field; (2) the extension of work by Williams, in particular, to a point where a body of English social and cultural thought seemed near to its limit and open to movements in other directions; (3) the arrival, in translation, of a variety of European Marxisms, welcomed at a time when both liberal gradualist reforming energies and orthodox received Marxisms seemed to be in stalemate; (4) a sense of possibilities within the academy for the rethinking of disciplines and the opening up of interdisciplinary work.[31] Literature then became a test case for the excitement of thinking the cultural:

> the antispeculative bias of [the liberal] tradition . . . continues to encourage submission to what is by preventing its followers from making connections . . . . [It is time to] acquire the rudiments of a dialectical culture . . . . [Literature] offers a

privileged microcosm in which to observe dialectical thinking at work.[32]

In England Williams noted at the time that the drive of such work towards the difficult yoking of theory to practice seemed also to demand 'alternative procedures and styles, as one of the few practical affiliations that could be made at once and by an act of will'.[33] Later, much restlessness has come from a strong sense of unfulfilled promises and expectations.[34] This has not been because that work in its English development has been dense, difficult and abstract (though it has been all these to a degree, rendering it vulnerable to misunderstanding and neglect) but because of its own lack of connection with cultural and more general movements inside its own decade. At one level its distance both from the bidding for a widespread popular conservatism in the 1970s and from other energies and demands evolving since the late 1960s has been very great.[35] More concretely, and in this respect quite unlike most previous literary analysis of any real substance, it has neither actively informed and helped to constitute an artistic practice nor inaugurated a new set of directions for teachers in different areas of education. Further, even before *Mapping*, the women's movement accorded a centrality to autobiographical and fictional forms, and to the awareness of sexism in textual representations,[36] in ways from which too much theoretical work, uninterested in gender, has stood separate.

Here we look briefly at three sets of questions: (1) the development of literary theory in relation to the uneven and divided situations of those teaching at different levels of the education system; (2) the rapid development of new kinds of cultural practice scarcely yet described, let alone assessed; (3) the uniquely strong position of feminist work within the contradictory space between educational work and cultural practice.

Education and English studies

It has been an important paradox that while 'English' has inevitably been caught within the ever-extending processes of certification and qualification dominating the post-war growth of the state education system, it has also been at all levels the most open and ambiguous disciplinary space. But definitions and aims have diverged sharply and now make up a peculiar pyramid.

At its apex, the university 'discipline' of English has remained nearly inviolate. Since the founding days of Sussex, contemporary or interdisciplinary work has scarcely been contemplated by universities able to claim financial stringencies or to shelter under the convenient doctrine of the 'binary' system. In English departments the intellectual consequences of a now eroded confidence in untheorized readings ('we feel that . . . .') have gone little beyond a skirmish with linguistics. Mainstream criticism no longer treats the great tradition as a unique repository of moral values, but it gets by in practice (despite an overall impression of directionlessness, combined with a modishly brisk, colloquial manner) with an eclectic pluralism of approaches (the sociological, the psychological, the biographical, the formalist, the bibliographical, and so on, *ad nauseam*), which, because they lack a thorough literary historical grounding, make literary texts appear to be arbitrarily selected out of, or 'naturally' given by, the 'literary tradition' itself. Other work has remained isolated, carelessly under-organized, except in the productive literature/ society conferences at Essex, or politely absorbed: 'context' and 'new directions' often remain old 'background' writ large. And as Rée remarked in another context: 'British philosophy still exists . . . . *Radical Philosophy* relates to it decreasingly; it is uninterested; and the feeling is mutual.'[37]

In the polytechnics there has been an effective movement away from the great tradition, by way of combined or integrated degrees or by routes into degrees in Communications, Media or Cultural Studies. The results have included a much wider range of texts thought worth study, detailed historical work in connection with the analysis and a greater openness to theoretical questions, even though 'readings' and debates rooted in the literary field have remained central. This work, if still corralled by the general vulnerability of the polytechnics, has had a considerable effect upon its first generation of graduates. In its wake a range of new journals (*Literature and History, Screen* and *Screen Education* but also *Ideology and Consciousness, Wedge* and *Red Letters*) have come to be something of a second intellectual network, with a potential capacity to develop further towards other issues, audiences and ways of working.

However, it has been in secondary schools and with the 'least able' pupils of conventional euphemisms that modes of English teaching have become the most flexible site for an expanded set of interests: in ways of communicating (from spoken languages to film and video); in textual representations (including those of race and gender); in questions or democratic organization of the media, of teaching and learning themselves. Encouraged by the Mode 3 CSE examinations, which are teacher-influenced, and by a wider definition of English in television programming for schools, this work has been a decisive advance within the crucial 'progressive' practices of post-war teaching. *Teaching London Kids*, the new *English Magazine*, *Radical Education, Socialist Teacher* and others have articulated its development. Precisely this work stands to lose most, if it can survive at all, in the attempted restructuring of the educational field around 'standards' and 'the needs of industry'.

Divisions of labour in educational work have in these ways become advanced and carefully patrolled since the 1944 settlement: the expansion and diversification of degree work in higher education has ironically coincided with uncertainty and a loss of momentum in secondary teaching as 'progressive' practices have faced internal and external criticism. In addition, Leavis's *Education and the University*[38] was a considered and far-reaching challenge to the place occupied by universities, to which there has been no adequate reply or successor. Instead, university workers have often remained arbiters and authorities, at worst in charge of systems of examination, at best as referees of the practices of others, 'standing above society'. Even the best exploratory work of theory has then been defined, potentially, as oppressively academic rather than as a resource or a contribution, since a communality of purpose, even of shared debate within English studies, exists in only the most fragmentary ways. Our own aim would be to develop work at least partly of interest to, and for use in, schools, though not ourselves above reciprocally learning from and about the development of school English practices in this century. It was Balibar's *Les Français Fictifs* and then our own work on the literary formation in the 1930s which began to make connections for us between the teaching of English and the relations of the 'literary' canon to the marginalized 'non-literary'.[39]

Cultural practices

Ken Worpole has cited figures which, in his view, 'represent a scale of alternative, or oppositional, publishing probably not seen in this country since the growth years of the Chartist movement in the 1830s'.[40] The development of feminist and Left theatre groups and the prominence of committed playwrights in major institutional spaces (the National Theatre, peak-time television drama series) has been similarly striking. To understand the emergence of these and many other new kinds of cultural practice requires us to take stock of the uneven histories of diverse activities. We should be particularly hesitant about describing such cultural developments as concomitant reflexes or as in any way parallel to new moves in 'theory'; initiatives such as Socialist Centres may have more to do with a legacy and history of regional political activities than with the exegesis of Gramsci on counter-hegemony.[41] There are several histories, of a complex and broken kind, which relate to the politics of specific cultural practices and should not be conflated: ideologies and ways of working which both converge and diverge; different histories, different funding, different practices, different politics.

At one pole there have been the efforts of ex-students (but also of working-class people and of other groups) in pioneering local initiatives, often deliberately ephemeral, working in and with the resources and potential of a particular place and moment; at the other, a large increase in official funding for the arts, including regional associations and sub-panels, and in more direct local authority initiatives. In one direction the enormous fissure between these activities and the operations of the major culture/leisure industries (with their stock-exchange citations and their capacity to create international and multi-media selling patterns and spin-offs) is still there:

> the great problem now is to see the extent to which (self-organizing, self-stating initiatives) can for long coexist with or eventually replace what is still a very powerful sort of minority culture . . . actually a few very large scale institutions which really do capture the big audiences and have become skilled in supplying them.[42]

In another, at the level of form, strategic questions about the use of traditional forms (recognizable, starting 'where the audience are') or of experimental forms (making and claiming imaginative space) remain open: Trevor Griffiths's television work was a striking case for hard arguments about the constraints of realism; attempts to locate Brechtian work in a post-war British context reverberate in Left drama groups.

There are two particular areas of contradiction, where the limits of potential work are blurred or open. One is found at the interface between 'community' and the local state. Many emerging practices have clustered around the notion of 'community' in various forms: engendering community 'spirit' (often 'as it used to be') by Tenants' Associations, sometimes with a radical critique of local government politics; the relocation of resources back in supposedly 'culturally deprived' inner-city areas and council estates (community workers and theatre groups, children's drama, community artists); the active recovery of forgotten or moribund cultural forms (Centerprise in Hackney, and many others). The development of interest by the local and national state in the promotion of new forms of community life has had two very different effects: the grafting of a new stratum of employees into local authority pay, to supervise working-class cultural activities (with parallels in the work of community development projects, intended perhaps as 'soft policing' but becoming, until terminated, quite other than that); and a mobilization of historically bypassed cultural practices. A host of complex interconnections have surrounded attention to the reconstitution of 'community' in specific areas: a major redefinition of the meaning and boundaries of artistic work; paranoia about inner-city 'idle time'; the continuation of ideologies of 'cultural deprivation'; the intervention of groups working in a cultural/political strategy. Community arts hang between alternative and oppositional practice and test the simplicity of the dichotomy, connecting both with attempts at more sophisticated modes of control and with more democratic and participatory models.[43]

Second, in Britain and several other European countries an alternative publishing network has been powerfully forged in the last five years. Worpole has cited, for Sweden, a project set up by organizations equivalent to the WEA and the Co-operative Society, which has achieved 40,000 sales for novels by working-class writers; also a Writers' Book Machine, a state-subsidized

> resource centre in Stockholm. It works on the principle that authors have access to free use of a typewriter and small printing press and that they pay half the origination costs of a limited edition . . . sent round to all the book-reviewing agencies . . . perhaps re-commissioned with a much bigger print run.[44]

In England new journals have helped with the creation of a distribution co-operative and small presses have been prolific. It remains to be discovered (and Lane's book may help illuminate)[45] whether there is a point already (or soon to be) reached at which such a network critically lacks capital and other resources with which to develop further by comparison with mainstream institutions. The state's role, characteristically, has so far been to support otherwise untenable lame ducks: in this area the Royal Opera House and the National Theatre. The case for stronger state intervention, in the creation of spaces for non-commercial bookshops, for many kinds of cultural production and distribution, is just being heard again for the first time since Williams's remarks in *The Long Revolution.*[46]

Again, in the whole area there has been an absence of relevant supporting work (analysis of the theoretical underpinnings of strategies, historical and also critical) within higher education. The general issue broached here is the paradox of an aggressive commercial development of the cultural field, and yet also the variety of experimental alternatives attempted in the last few years.

Feminism and gender

Feminist criticism has an active relationship with the political practices of feminism by which it was generated. Feminism's critique of sexism and its stress on woman-centredness through the concept and practice of sisterhood has led to the existence of what can now, with reservation, be termed a women's culture. By this we mean that some forms of organization (for study, creative and cultural production, participation or for entertainment) are by, for and about women and designed for their support and pleasure. Any reservations about calling this a women's culture arise because of the way certain tendencies within the women's movement exclude men from their lives, as a result of a political analysis in which women's oppression is seen to stem solely and directly from men as the agents and bearers of patriarchy, and because of problems about the extent to which an alternative or oppositional culture can be envisaged as flourishing within a dominant culture which opposes or contradicts it. The relation should be thought as one in which a feminist politics of cultural struggle can transform the dominant culture.

Despite these reservations, there is still much to be said about the positive and engaged situation of feminist cultural practice within which feminist criticism is a dimension, particularly when compared with the characteristic situation of male socialist literary critics. The most striking distinction between feminist and other criticisms is that feminist criticism has created and has maintained an active involvement with past and present women's writing, which often takes a celebratory form. This differs radically from mainstream criticism where the critical object is increasingly given by theoretical questions deriving from structural linguistics rather than by traditions of writing. But it also differs in kind from some contemporary Marxist criticism, which exhibits aggressive embarrassment at the text's failure to dissolve itself as the consequence of its own redundancy. Feminist criticism, in working against the marginalization and misrepresentation of women's writing, has a far greater investment in actual *writing* than do other criticisms. This relationship with writing informs the constitutive concern with the recovery and revaluation of women's writing and is, importantly, not restricted to the writing of critical and theoretical texts. Since much women's writing was (significantly) unobtainable and out of print, the development of *Virago* and *The Women's Press* has been of enormous usefulness, not just in furthering critical work in the context of higher education but also in the creation of a feminist reading public, demonstrating the active interest which some forms of fiction have for women. In addition to feminist presses publishing and republishing fiction by and for women, a feminist distribution service has recently been established whose centre, Sisterwrite in London, stocks British and overseas work by women. A similar enterprise, though without the bookshop base, is the Women's Liberation Bookbus which (when money allows) tours areas of Britain badly provided by bookshops and in which feminist work is hard to obtain. These developments clearly indicate that traditions of women's writing are being rediscovered, revalued and made available in ways extending well outside the formally academic.

The model of feminist critical work offered by North America, that of an individual, professionalized academic activity, has not been possible to adopt in this country, given a smaller and male-dominated higher-education sector. Consequently, the principal mode of British feminist work has been in collectives, either outside or in a self-consciously problematized relation to the traditional ethos of academic work. Such collectives, still few in number and often based in London, are a response to the isolated position in which feminists have found themselves. Among the better known are the Women's Research and Resources Centre, the Feminist Archive, the Women's Arts Alliance, the Feminist Theatre Group, the writing collectives which produced *Tales I Tell My Mother* and *Licking the Bed Clean* and the Marxist-Feminist Literature Collective, a study group which organized a workshop in 1979 aiming to stimulate contact between women working on or interested in literature through conferences and a newsletter. In addition, there are local study groups and a growing number of women's study courses.

Feminist criticism now takes as its critical object women's writing rather than the identification of sexism in male writing, which had been a politically useful starting-point. Only recently, with a developing interest in the representation of sexual ideologies involving work on masculinity as well as femininity, have feminist critics begun to look again at male writing. The most consistent concern has been with recovery – the rediscovery or rescue of individual works and authors through work that aims to establish women's presence in particular genres, to the current situation in which whole traditions of women's writing are being recovered. Women's writing has also been read as giving access to or illustration of historical processes in which women have been central, and this work has sometimes used biographical material in an interesting way to mediate the distance between history and the literary text. This is important in providing positive self-images for women, but the celebration of these literary women can also draw out more general social and historical shifts concerning women. Last, women's writing has been read for its thematic representation of particular systematic concerns: patriarchy, androgyny, domesticity, feminism and others. This approach often appears in conjunction with a reading which locates thematic ideas in their social and historical context. It can also be used as part of an argument against historical definitions of women's subordination. Heilbrun[47] and Spacks[48] argue respectively that ideas of androgyny and the presence of a female imagination exist across time, outside historical determinations, and can be discerned in women's writing.

In addition to the development of feminist critical approaches to women's writing, there have been recent moves towards a more theoretical work of feminist criticism. Three areas should be considered: work following Julia Kristeva in the psychoanalytic and semiotic account of sexed subjectivities; the relation to writing of feminist theories of kinship and reproduction; the theorization of gender determination, predicated on gender difference as socially constructed and ideologically maintained, as it affects the writing and the reading of fictional texts.

Our own current work, which has involved us in the recovery and revaluation of women's writing, is directed towards analyses of the concrete historical, understood as gender-differentiated at every level. Gendered reading here becomes as central as gendered writing or as the representations of gender within writing.

Work in the Centre

Our own recent work, from which the next two sections are drawn, has developed in response to issues raised within these three areas as well as to theoretical work reviewed earlier. So far it has been uneven, and there are some lines of research which we (and we hope others) will wish to develop over the next few years. These include the priorities set by feminist concerns at the centre of our project; a knowledge of alternative and oppositional practices of writing and reading in this century; and work on popular cultural forms, not only as a way of challenging the Hegemony of Literature but also because they form the ground from which the new forms of a future culture must develop.

University-based research can easily be disabled by the constraints of a division of labour which separates the 'criticism' of the university from the 'literacy' of the school or the 'practice' of cultural workers. We have been involved in a preliminary attempt to break with received practices of research (individual author, individual 'supervisor', one bound library copy of a thesis). At present we experience the strength given by a way of working that is collaborative, involving joint writing and mutual support and criticism. But the move towards collective work is still, inevitably, highly contradictory and full of problems, for we remain hedged in by powerful material and institutional determinations. Access to, and appropriation of, knowledge is still caught within unequal social relations of gender, status and age. The potential loneliness of the individual research moment, with its detailed grasp of a particular area, is an uneasy partner to the stimulus of work in groups. New definitions of 'adequate work' are being struggled for, but the shifts in register of a collective text such as this may be more open, or simply more incoherent, than the worked-up argument of an individual author. Finally, to say that both women and men may consider questions of gender is not to say that the questions which feminism poses may readily be jointly worked on. But we are committed to joint work which combats received academic practices and their social relations.

'Work in progress 1' (pages 249–56 below) draws on work in 1977–8, part of which issued in a paper at the Essex '1936' conference. The work began with an attempt to deconstruct a received ideology of the 1930s (constructed in the heyday of the Cold War), which emphasized an unsuccessful involvement of writers with Left politics. 'Writers' proved to be a particular male coterie, and the work broadened to look at the literary formation of the period as a whole, with its 'popular' genres, a distinctive 'middlebrow' set of texts and much other women's and working-class writing which was marginalized. We tried to show the ways in which kinds of writing were at once constituted through different kinds of schooling, through publishing and in relation to particular ideologies such as the political ideology of 'citizenship', and articulated against each other. A cluster of women writers were taken as a detailed case for these concerns and began (in discussion of Gibbons's *Cold Comfort Farm*) to open up questions to do with gendered reading.

'Work in progress 2' (pages 256–68 below) draws on work in 1978–9 concerned with the relations between popular fiction and popular culture, in which the issue of common sense became important. Bromley's characterization of masculine and feminine romance was extremely suggestive,[49] and we turned to women's romance, especially Cartland, for a detailed case.

Feminism has been central to the work throughout, and while we began by looking at English in education (under the shadow of Balibar and Althusser) for its institutional role in constructing readerships, the work on popular fiction has begun to take up the 'extra-curricular', to look at new kinds of 'educative' fiction emerging oppositionally in the construction of an adequately 'popular culture'.

Work in progress 1

Women, feminism and literature in the 1930s

The juxtaposition of literature and history, of text and society, in order to ground a historical analysis of literature has been a central achievement of Marxist work. It broke with traditional literary history's uninterrupted ideal ordering of great books across the ages, though not far enough to question the inevitable 'greatness' of these works. Much Marxist literary analysis has attempted to theorize more clearly the relationship between literature and history. The signposts in the debates – causal determination, reflection, homology, correspondence, over-determination, mediation, relative autonomy, reproduction – can be seen as permutations derived from the central juxtaposition. However, the terms of debate which these various concepts represent continually make it difficult to consider two very important issues – the relation of gender to writing and the relation of literature to other non-literary fictions. Our aim has been to produce an account in which the specific and different histories of various kinds of fictions are acknowledged and which enables an analysis of the class, gender and ethnic determinations of the social and cultural relations of literary production.

In a project on the 1930s[50] it became clear that literature must be thought of not simply as possessing certain special qualities which either reveal or occlude real historical processes to which the text refers, but as constituted *within* history across a range of social institutions and practices, such as the education system, publishing, libraries, book reviews and the broadcasting media. The literary canon of great writing, for instance, is sanctioned and reproduced by a process of selection from a diverse matrix of fictional writing. The role of *Scrutiny* here is an unusually vivid example. Although fixity is a feature of the literary tradition, complete stasis is considered undesirable, particularly in relation to the school curriculum. That literary traditions are sites of struggle is highlighted by the contemporary cases of black and women writers. The advantages of students being brought into contact with such work have to be seen clearly within the limitations which the form of contact can impose. For example, would the reasons why Woolf is so much better known than Holtby be in themselves challenged by replacing *To the Lighthouse* with *South Riding*[51] as an A-Level book?

The construction of literature does not just involve the inclusion of certain 'great' works in a canon of writing. In the same process, all other fiction is categorized and defined. Other books are not merely 'not literature' – they may be named 'popular fiction', 'general fiction', 'women's writing', 'middlebrow', 'lowbrow' or, as is the case with working-class writing, may be marginalized to the extent of appearing to be non-existent.

In the extract which follows we discuss the conditions which formed the limits of the possible for women as writers in the thirties and look very briefly at one novel and its place in the field of literary production.

The critique of received literary histories and the deconstruction of their assumptions about the literature and history of the 1930s – and, indeed, the whole making and remaking of 'the thirties' in itself – made it imperative to rethink the scope of the term 'the literary field'. In terms of writing, we defined the terrain at first by using terms derived *from the period* (highbrow, middlebrow, lowbrow) but did not use the terms evaluatively. We added a category 'marginalized' to cover those works which, either because of their political content or because of the class position of their authors, were outside the mainstream of literary production and distribution and had very clearly defined readerships (for example, among the labour movement). We then attempted to determine how the 'brows' were constructed in the ideologies and practices of particular institutions – through the education system, with the definitions of 'literariness' in higher education and of levels of literacy in the schools, and through production, marketing and distribution of books as 'literature', 'general fiction' or 'romance' in publishing, libraries and book clubs.

However, it is important not to reduce texts to their social location, and we also attempted to think of literary production in terms of the hailing or interpellation of readers by texts. In terms of the ideological function of the text, we associated 'lowbrow' with the dominant positioning of the reader through identification with one or two characters; 'middlebrow'/the publishing category 'fiction' with the interpellation of the reader in the position of the literary ideology itself (as defined, chiefly through higher education) – judgement, discrimination. We also used interpellation as a method of analysing the positioning of subjects within ideologies which exist outside and are represented within literary texts. It is this concern with both the institutions which structure the field and the ideological practice of reading/writing which is meant by 'exposing and understanding the social and cultural relations of literary production'.

Examining the processes of the exclusion and marginalization of women in their literary and social histories and their specific response at the time is one important aspect of our overall work on the construction of a decade and its literature. Another aspect is reading women's writing for the presence of sexual ideologies and the effects of gender discrimination in access to literary production. This further complexifies the relations between institutional determinations and textual processes which we seek to elucidate. Such analysis is new and difficult, and this piece is marked by that difficulty. We do, however, attempt to show how obstacles which women encounter in the family, in education, in work and in politics appear in one novel, *South Riding*, in a quite specific way. The novel is placed in an ambiguous, though clearly critical, relation to both the literary and the political fields of the period. As we will show, Holtby's self-identification as a middlebrow writer is not simply an individual choice taken between literary kinds but is determined by her political commitment to a feminist politics grounded in the concept of equal citizenship. We also want to begin to redress two distortions relating to women's history in the 1930s. In general, we aim to challenge the misrepresentation of women in history, the way in which they are not simply located as a forgotten half but relegated to a domestic sphere, painted as an eternal backcloth to the 'real', man's world of historical activity. Secondly, we question the common assumption that there is a hiatus in women's organization which stretches from suffrage to the present day. We did not take our own form of feminist politics as the acid test for all previous contenders. Instead, we began to uncover the forms of women's understanding at the time as to what they were doing and to the available forms of politics generally. The substance of this work can only be indicated here through a brief listing of some key organizations, groupings and publications: *Time and Tide* (1920s, 1930s); the Women's Publicity Planning Association (1940s); the Woman Power Committee of 1942; the Feminine Point of View Conference of 1952; *The Woman's Side*;[52] *What Fools We Women Be*;[53] *The Lesser Half*;[54] *Mainly for Men.*[55]

Women's place: institutions and ideologies

From our work on social institutions in relation to women and literary production we aimed to uncover the important developments and shifts in sexual ideologies and forms of resistance to them. These formed the material conditions of existence for women's access to 'literary' culture and for women's writing in general in the period. We intend here to give a brief and provisional account of these developments in relation to gender difference. What follows does not make any claims to be a definitive statement about women's position in the thirties. It is of an illustrative nature. We hope to indicate through it areas of importance in any attempt to approach literary production in this way.

We would argue that women's position in the family is a necessary starting-point for any analysis of their relation to other social institutions and to the sphere of literary production. While we ourselves would not see the family as a natural, given object of study but rather as an institution socially structured through a range of ideological practices, it is important to examine how the family was seen in the thirties.

The nuclear family was ideologically constructed as the *natural* basic unit of social organization. Whether we looked at the ideology of the Conservative Party or at that of the Labour Party, we found women's position to be over-determined by an unquestioned primary location of women within the nuclear family. Although legally equal to men as citizens after the granting of full adult suffrage in 1928, they were seen as having a different role to play from men and were subject to discrimination as women irrespective of whether, in the aftermath of the First World War, they were able to marry and have children. Women's primary location was often, and was always seen to be, in the family. The effects of this were manifold: for example, inequality in education, pay and employment. In 1931 domestic service still provided a quarter of all employment for women. The conditions of employment for these women in waged work in the personal sphere of the home (albeit not their own home) highlighted the ideological contradiction between and within waged work and housework, which women 'naturally' did without need for recompense. For example, although kitchen maids were trained in government training centres to alleviate unemployment, they were not covered by the national insurance scheme and were thus excluded from unemployment benefit.

We found another example of the over-determining ideological importance of women's primary location within the home in the panic which the fall in the birth rate provoked and its direct effect on the demands made on women. In 1933 the birth rate touched its lowest point in any peacetime year before or since. It might be expected that fewer pregnancies and the reduced burden of child care would begin to give women more freedom outside the home. Instead of this, MPs began to demand that women return to their duty, to provide 'citizens of the right breed' for 'the countries of the British Empire'.[56] Similarly, the publication of *Twilight of Parenthood* by Dr Enid Charles in 1934, arguing that the decline in the birth rate was a threat to national security, caused widespread concern. In these debates on women's role from the perspective of eugenics we can glimpse the continuation of the ideological nexus connecting the family, the nation and the Empire, and the subordination of women with that of other races and nations.

By the mid thirties this panic had virtually silenced arguments about the importance of birth control. There was a concurrent shift towards pressure for family allowance schemes (that is, better provision for child rearing) and there were developments in education for 'scientific motherhood' and domestic science.

The implicit contradiction between the vital importance of women fulfilling their 'natural' role and the stress on training for it was contained within educational practice in the 1930s by the notion of education for citizenship, to which all, as citizens, were entitled but which was different in nature for girls and boys. After the First World War the state education system underwent a gradual and regionally uneven process of restructuring and transformation, which included some expansion in the secondary sector. Behind these shifts lay ideas of equal educational opportunity for all, which were both a labour movement ideal and, more generally, a part of the ideology of the rights of citizenship. There were two main strains of educational theory – multilateralism, which corresponded to comprehensive education policy today (Tawney, the National Union of Teachers and the Trades Union Congress), and a system including a range of secondary schools with selection at the age of eleven on the basis of intelligence testing. This second strand, advocated by the psychologist Burt, influenced official Government policy in the Spens Report (1938). Whatever their differences, both were aimed at diversification within education according to the ability of the individual child and specialization along *traditional gender lines*. Equality served as a formal criterion beneath which the dominant modes of gender differentiation established in the home were reinforced. Thus diversification of the educational programme entailed for girls the teaching of subjects deemed suitable for their 'natural' profession as wives and mothers. In relation to the teaching of English, it is significant to note that 'literature' is categorized by Burt as a subject that girls are good at. This coincides with a move in the teaching of literacy from the use of literature to the English subjects (history, civics and geography) through which literature becomes marginalized within non-grammar school curricula.

For the small majority of girls who had the opportunity of secondary and further education, teaching was geared towards the requirements of the expanding female professions of, for example, secretarial work, nursing and teaching. Access to other professions was limited, and women were barred from teaching and the Civil Service upon marriage. University education was still unavailable to most women, and in the field of literary production men occupied the positions of power within the universities and publishing. Openings for women were, on the whole, limited to journalism and jobs as literary agents, which were low-status professions within literary production. However, while marriage continued to be regarded as the only true and natural profession for women, to which they should devote their energies exclusively, there was an increase in the number of professional women, if not a revaluation of their status. 'It may be love that makes the world go round, but it's spinsters who oil the wheels.'[57]

Citizenship and feminism

For the purposes of this extract we are focusing on just one ideological element in relation to women - that of *citizenship*. It is a theme which spans a range of social practices, is present in some women's writing and plays an important role in delimiting the ground of feminist practice in the thirties. Citizenship is a concept which suggests equality of rights and opportunity under the law. As such it refers to both men and women, although, as we have shown, wherever it occurs within ideological practices in the thirties it is applied in a gender-specific way. Feminists, however, did not accept that citizenship was necessarily a gendered concept, and much of the feminist struggle at the time was aimed at establishing rights of citizenship for women on the same basis as for men:

> while the inequality exists, while injustice is done and opportunity denied to the great majority of women, I shall have to be a feminist with the motto Equality

First. And I shan't be happy till I get . . . a society in which men and women work together for the good of all mankind, a society in which there is no respect of persons, either male or female, but a supreme regard for the importance of the human being.[58]

The granting of full female suffrage in 1928 and women's determination to use their hard-won constitutional rights located women's politics within parliamentary boundaries. The numerous struggles that followed were directed towards social change through legislation under the broad heading of equal rights for women, *as citizens*, to material welfare, equal pay and opportunities. Much attention was paid to the new female voter, both in the form of propaganda from the three main political parties and in a spate of 'New Voter's Guides'. The struggle for sex equality moved into existing political parties, especially the Labour Party Women's Section, the Co-op Women's Guilds, the Independent Labour Party and the Communist Party. For example, Stella Browne conducted her campaign for contraception and abortion through the political institutions of the labour movement. These campaigns did include consideration of women's special needs and offered some challenge to existing social structures on the grounds of their blindness to those needs.

In the writings of such feminists as Winifred Holtby and Vera Brittain and in the programme of women's organizations, struggle is focused on the realization of equal citizenship. The Six Point Group demanded:

abolition of the present solicitation laws and the passing of the Public Places Order Bill – equal moral standards: more women police: peeresses in the House of Lords: the right of married women to engage in paid work if they want to . . . [women should be] separately assessed and taxed and free to retain their own nationality. And all this to be established by International Feminism – through an Equal Rights Convention of the League of Nations.[59]

Citizenship is clearly not a narrowly political concept but rather one which embraces a vision of a new world for women. The Utopian belief that full equality might be granted by a government or the League of Nations should be understood in part through the Fabian ideology of the neutrality of the state but also in the context of aspirations for peace after the First World War and movements such as the Peace Ballot in which women played a considerable part.

In turning now to *South Riding* we do not intend to suggest that the novel simply contains or reflects the various historical elements we've outlined. Rather, as we said at the outset, it is situated within and determined by them. One means of seeing these determinations at work is to start from the author's biography as an instance of mediation between text and history. Thus Winifred Holtby's career as novelist, journalist, part-time teacher and lecturer occurred in this context of increasing access to such professions for educated women. The reception of her work in the thirties and since is an index of the ambiguous relation of such 'new women' to the literary establishment. Holtby's writing includes political journalism, poetry, a women's history, parody and satire, short stories and two long realist novels, *Mandoa, Mandoa!* and *South Riding*. Like other 'middlebrow' novelists of the time (George Orwell, J. B. Priestley, Howard Spring), she consciously distanced herself from 'art':

People who write very rare things like Virginia Woolf have a far higher standing than professional journalists like myself. I have no illusions about my work. I am primarily a useful, versatile, sensible and fairly careful artisan. I have trained myself to write quickly, punctually and readably to order over a wide range of subjects. That has nothing to do with art. It has quite a lot to do with politics.[60]

The realist narrative of *South Riding* distances itself both from the self-consuming uncertainties of the modernist text and from the simple certainties of the popular romance's 'luxurious descriptions of feminine underwear, the conflicts of vice with virtue'.[61] Although it takes the political ideology of citizenship as its subject, the concluding imperative is one clearly spoken from a position of feminism:

Don't let me catch any of you at any time loving anything without asking questions . . . . Question the Kingsport slums, and the economies over feeding schoolchildren, and the rule that makes women have to renounce their jobs on marriage . . . . But questioning does not mean the end of loving, and loving does not mean the abnegation of intelligence.[62]

This narrative statement of position is achieved out of textual contradictions and conflicts. The representation of this is both thematic (the pull against an independent life for women which romance represents) and formal (the text, at significant moments of stress, is transformed into something other than that which it appears to be). These slippages often reference things outside the text. For example, the competing themes of romance and feminism provide the main narrative tension, which is ultimately resolved by recourse to a humanity larger than, and ultimately encompassing, both. In the presentation of romance and the novel's romance interest the reference to traditions of romantic literature is one of qualification – 'She became vulnerable, afraid, disarmed before a hostile world . . . . I won't think of him, Sarah was vowing to herself. My work needs all of me . . . . I'll look to the future – to the world outside'[63] – and of ironization:

Sarah saw the harsh face above her illumined by the smile which had won his wife, chained Mrs. Beddows and given Carne of Maythorpe a reputation for popularity. It was, she decided afterwards, only a physical accident, a trick of bone and muscle, a flash of white teeth, a widening of long lashed eyes: but it had its effects.[64]

In this way romance – the granting of time and importance to personal and sexual relationships – is never treated romantically. Its overall presentation confirms the novel as characteristically middlebrow in keeping with the guide-lines indicated earlier in the text: 'She has observed and she can describe . . . . You've got imagination Lydia, of course, but you've got sense too.'[65]

The commitment to a feminist politics in which human equality is the ultimate referent is also affirmed by the text: 'We all pay, she thought; we all take; we are members of one another. We cannot escape this partnership. This is what it means –

to belong to a community; this is what it means, to be a people.'[66] The romance/feminism conflict, while focused on Sarah Burton, is not represented as an individual psychological one. It extends to other characters in the novel and is itself always understood in terms other than its own: 'Beyond her personal troubles lay the deep fatigue of one whose impersonal hopes do not mark time with history.'[67] Nor is it the central narrative conflict. Romance/feminism are cast in terms of the private/public opposition which underlies the whole narrative structure: '[what fascinated me was] the complex tangle of motives prompting public decisions, the unforeseen consequences of their enactment on private lives'.[68]

The conflicts and competing concerns of the text, public and private, are held together by the idea of community, with responsible citizenship as its basis, and the fictive resolution is dependent upon the ideological repertoire of citizenship which we have discussed earlier. Just as citizenship in political discourse has ambiguous and sometimes contradictory connotations, so in the novel the community of citizens, which at its end connects Kingsport with the nation, is a resolution able to hold in harmony the unstable and contradictory elements in the text and to stabilize the narrative points of view, specifically those centred on romance and gender. The particular female cast to those lives and problems is both subordinated to and offered transcendence by the idea of an identity defined communally rather than sexually:

> She was not outside it. What she had taken from life, they all paid for. What she had still to give, was not her gift alone. She was in debt to life and to these people; and she knew that she could repay no loan unaided.[69]

The nature of this article - overviews and extracts - limits what can be said. Therefore we conclude this section by indicating briefly the fuller analysis from which this extract is taken. In the first instance, although *South Riding* gives a particularly vivid representation of thirties' feminism, it is not typical of, or equivalent to, *all* women's writing of the period. As we have indicated, it occupies a particular relation to the literary field, and our fuller analysis considers women's writing and the literary field in more general detail. Second, there are aspects of *South Riding* which are not dealt with here - for example, thematic representations of family and motherhood, which pursue a feminist axis in the absence of secure nuclear families and a citizenship axis in subordinating families to communities and stressing the accountability of 'the nation' to responsible, questioning citizens.

Work in progress 2

Popular fiction: reproduction and common sense in feminine romance

In each of the main traditions of popular/mass cultural analysis there have been both affirmations and denunciations of that culture. Is it the authentic art of the people, to be set against 'high' or 'elite' culture, or is it a degraded form of deception and distraction, to be distinguished from a critical and deconstructive art? If popular culture is contradictory, then it is not surprising that analyses of it seem contradictory too. We may take as an example Walter Benjamin's claim that his affirmative account of the liberating potential of film complemented rather than contradicted Adorno's critique of popular music: 'I tried to articulate positive moments as clearly as you managed to articulate negative ones.'[70]

There have been four main conceptualizations of popular/mass culture: as the product of a culture industry; as coterminous with working class culture; as myth; and as an ideological apparatus of the state.

The 'culture industry' analysis sees cultural products as commodities, dominated by the structures of propaganda, advertising and consumerism. Writing during the Second World War, in reaction both to Fascism in Europe and to the impact of American mass culture, the 'Frankfurt School' (Adorno, Horkheimer, Marcuse) pioneered work in which mass culture was seen as the degeneration of earlier folk-art forms, involving a numbed sensory perception. Alongside this negative strain a more positive version was offered, not only by Benjamin but also, in his later work, by Marcuse, who came to see within popular culture repressed and disguised Utopian energies and desires.

A second version of popular/mass cultural analysis has been developed from a revaluation of aspects of working-class culture and leisure which sees them as an integral part of the lived experience of the class as forms of resistance or adaptation, to be analysed with the attention and the methods of literary criticism. The work of the early British New Left (Hoggart, Williams, Thompson, Hall) focused on traditional British working-class culture and was sympathetic to the social-democratic aspirations of the labour movement. That these writers were not unaware of 'negative moments', however, can be seen in Hoggart's vision of the potential degeneration of popular working-class forms into a new classless - and worthless - mass art.

A third tradition has extended the structuralist and semiotic analysis of myth developed by Lévi-Strauss into the study of popular/mass culture. The texts of such a culture can be seen, in the same way as myths, as formal attempts to resolve social contradictions in the imagination. Thus the analysis of popular/mass culture can offer a privileged view of collective fears and fantasies. But other work, beginning with Barthes's *Mythologies*, has claimed that the formal organization of popular artefacts obscures and mystifies social relations, affirming and 'naturalizing' the existing social order. This work, emerging from the *avant-garde* literary culture associated with the magazine *Tel Quel* and heavily influenced by the counter-culture of the 1960s, has led to a powerful critique of realism that points to its role in confirming, rather than challenging, the position of the audience or readership as passive spectators.

Finally, a fourth tradition sees popular/mass culture as a site of ideological struggle within and around what Althusser has called an 'ideological state apparatus' - the popular media, or 'cultural ISA'. In the following section our analysis of the narrative-ideological structure of certain popular fictions draws heavily on Althusser's account of the naturalizing and reproductive function of ideology and also, in its attempt to relate that structure to the linguistic practices of the school, on his assertion that the dominant ISA of capitalist societies is the apparatus of state education. But in the course of that analysis we have become increasingly conscious that such an account is too simple and unproblematic. Popular fiction is, in varying degrees, as unstable and ambiguous as the popular politics described by Gramsci and, more recently, Laclau: fertile ground for reactionary and chauvinistic connotations, but also, in different circumstances, for potentially progressive ones. In this we have been influenced by the revival of Gramscian notions of the national-popular and of popular culture as a terrain of the struggle for hegemony – a revival itself linked to the emergence in recent years of a distinctive 'Eurocommunism' that has increasingly distanced itself from the cultural politics of orthodox Leninism and has developed instead a strategy of broad democratic alliance between the 'popular classes'. So we conclude this chapter by outlining Gramsci's concept of common sense and its uses in the analysis of popular fiction.

Narrative 'grammars' have sought hitherto to relate the structure of narratives to some underlying and permanent 'structure of signification', a trans-historical general grammar.[71] Here we attempt something rather different: to suggest analogies between certain narratives – the novels of Barbara Cartland – and a particular grammar practised within an historical institution: English teaching from the 1930s to the 1950s. School grammars across the period classify sentences into two types: the simple sentence (subject:verb:object), with its straightforward aggregate, the compound sentence (simple sentence + simple sentence), belongs to elementary English. The complex sentence, with its articulation of principal and subordinate clauses, stands at the threshold of a more advanced literacy; beyond lie the richer pastures of composition, interpretation, literature itself. Thus a standard formal typology of the sentence corresponds rather closely to a basic structure of the English educational system.

It is not a question of popular narratives being composed entirely of simple sentences. We have argued elsewhere for a formal relation between certain 'middle-brow' fictions of the 1930s and specific contemporary practices of English teaching.[72] And as secondary English stands in a special relation in the curriculum to history and civics in the formation of educated, responsible social-democratic 'citizens', so elementary English has, for girls, an intimate connection with 'domestic science' and education for motherhood.

> Girls who from circumstance, lack of training or low intelligence find themselves in repetitive jobs are mainly interested in the prospect of marriage . . . . Such girls form the majority of 15-year-old school leavers, and all of them are future home-makers. Their own happiness, as well as the good of the community, requires that they should be much better equipped for this particular career than many who undertake it at the present time.[73]

The relation of popular narratives to elementary English is not primarily grammatical but formal and ideological. The narratives of popular female romance are so composed as to 'boil off' all narrative elements of a subordinate kind, to reduce potentially complex narrative sentences to a set of functions that corresponds as closely as possible to the subject:verb.object of the elementary sentence. But this distillation or reduction of effective functions may actually produce, at climactic moments, a simple sentence:

'I love you,' he said a little unsteadily. 'And now tell me, my darling, what you feel for me.'
'I love . . . you! I love . . . you!' Romara cried.[74]

'Aren't you going to answer me?' he asked . . . .
'I love you,' she whispered.[75]

If these exchanges seem more suggestive of the classroom than the bedroom, it may serve to remind us not only that in every case the experienced male is instructing the inarticulate female in the grammar of domesticated rapture, but also that Cartland's texts assume, for their readers, an important educational function. The climactic enunciation of the marital sentence is only the culminating lesson - a literal 'matriculation' - in an extensive and purposeful sentimental education whose nodal emphasis is not sex but motherhood and domesticity. For the male hero the romantic epiphany coincides with his realization of the potential *maternity* of the heroine and so serves to resolve the narrative dilemma typical of female romance, the problem of the 'other woman'.

'How could you possibly have loved anyone who looked as I did?' Romara asked.
'But I did fall in love with you,' he said. 'when I came into the salon and saw you holding the baby in your arms at the window.'[76]

Somehow he had never thought of children in connection with Lynette . . . with Moida it was an aching need - it was a desire almost as great as his desire to possess her and make her his - their children who would be part of him and part of her.[77]

Housekeeping and domesticity are closely related. Marriage, children and home form the thematic unity towards which all the narrative codes and functions converge (' "I want a wife," he said simply. "I want a home and children." ')[78] The hero of *Blue Heather* recognizes in the heroine the future mother of 'children who would grow up here at Skaig and belong, even as he had always known, from the time he could think at all, that he belonged . . . .',[79] and the recognition enables him to discard the fiancée whose unsuitability has already been registered in terms less of love than of real estate.

'I want you to love Skaig, darling,' Ian had said to Lynette before he left.
'I'm sure I shall love it, if you do,' she answered, but he felt her reply was said too lightly . . . .
'I'll make you love it,' Ian said fiercely.[80]

Hence the central importance of houses: notionally aristocratic country houses, actually, in their domestic atmosphere and distinctive family form, *petit bourgeois* suburban. Houses tend to be introduced with the breathless reverence of the property pages of *Country Life*:

With its huge porticoed front and elegant winged sides . . . its background of green trees and a lake in front . . . exactly, she thought, the sort of country house she had always dreamt about.[81]

A perfect Queen Anne red-brick house, standing on the summit of a small hill, with lawns and terraces sloping away to a great lake of silver water.[82]

The castle had been joined neatly onto the ruins . . . the new castle was in its own way almost as romantic . . . it was imposing, and, as Ian well remembered, a schoolboy's idea of what a Scottish baronial castle should be.[83]

Or rather, an estate agent's, perhaps. This last passage, with the old ruins 'neatly' joined to a new house 'in its own way almost as romantic', can stand as a metaphor for the incongruous union in these texts of aristocratic decor and *petit bourgeois* domesticity. 'Elegant', 'imposing', 'perfect', the houses are also reassuringly domesticated, cosy, suburban.

It impressed me, in spite of all its splendours, treasures and air of luxury, as being a warm, happy place, the kind of house one could easily live in and make a home.[84]

He remembered how his mother had loved her rose-garden. He had not really appreciated how many improvements she had made in the garden and house until she was no longer there.[85]

The simple sentence of female romance condenses the thematic unity of marriage, home, children into a timeless moment. All subordinate elements that might tend to qualify, ironize or historicize that moment are progressively neutralized or eliminated. History itself, in a genre that is frequently 'historical', is invoked only to testify to its own unreality, to the eternal and unchanging reality of 'love':

I sat crouched in front of the fire, wondering first about Philip Chadleigh in 1939, then about the Philip of 1727. Had women loved him too?[86]

Yet violence and murder, treachery and bitterness, were not the only memories that lived in Holyrood . . . . If he had never known it before, he knew now that love is eternal, unquenchable, a part of the Divine. For love in Holyrood had survived the mortal hearts which created it, and it still lived on.[87]

The close association evident here between love and religious sentiment links it to the related motif of self-sacrifice: the voluntary self-subordination of the woman.

'Look at it this way,' he said. 'The key-note of Nada's last years was her great, overwhelming love for Philip. That was what was of importance in her life . . . . What matters then is love, not for yourself or for your own peace of mind, but for Philip. Think of him, it is he that matters.' I was silenced; there was nothing more to say.[88]

'I was silenced': the subordination of the woman to the narrative-ideological syntax of home and children is strikingly visible in the progressive extinction of her powers of articulate speech. The heroine of *Lord Ravenscar's Revenge*, bold and independent enough at the outset to speak her mind to her sister's tyrannical seducer, is reduced at last to mumbling inarticulacy, as well as to depersonalizing conformity to the 'eternal feminine':

'That is . . . what I . . . felt,' Romara said, 'but I never . . . thought, I never . . . dreamt, that you would . . . feel . . . the . . . same.'
'You seemed in so many ways to be like my mother,' Lord Ravenscar said.[89]

But the process of reduction and simplification can perhaps be seen most clearly in the texts' handling of a central motif, found across a wide range of women's writing – the 'other woman'. This unstable combination can be resolved in a number of ways (which certainly need to be analysed historically as well as formally): by the death of the heroine (*The Mill on the Floss*) or of the man (*Daniel Deronda*) or, perhaps most typically, of the other woman herself (*Jane Eyre*). The other woman may be dead but still potent in memory, so that a second, symbolic death is necessary (*Rebecca*). It may be resolved in a comic peripeteia which reveals that there never really *was* another woman (*Emma*); or it may be fractured altogether by the presence of powerful new elements, as in *South Riding*, where traditional formulaic resolutions (mad wife, death of the man) are rendered virtually redundant by the determination of the feminist heroine not to marry in any case. In all these instances the working out of the motif generates some degree of narrative complication and a residual disturbance or ambiguity. Cartland's texts are notable for the ease with which the triangle is resolved and the potential narrative discomfort neutralized. In both *Blue Heather* and *Lord Ravenscar's Revenge* the other woman is painlessly married off to a conveniently unattached minor male, thus forming a simple sentence of her own. And in one interesting example, *The Black Panther*, which can be fruitfully compared with both *Rebecca* and *Deronda*, she is literally incorporated into the heroine by the unexpected but useful device of reincarnation.

The silencing subjection of the woman and the accompanying closure of narrative codes; the exclusion of irony in the rigorous simplification of the narrative 'grammar'; the prominence of a sententious vein of common sense: all serve as a reminder that these texts are far from ideologically inert – mere 'entertainment'. Every element of the textual common sense articulated and enlivened by the play of the narrative speaks directly to the ideology of the subordinate classes and (in Cartland's case, at least) of the lower middle classes in particular: pride and anxiety of ownership, fear of history, professional insecurity, female domesticity. The nature of this ideological work can be understood in terms of *reproduction*.

The reproduction of the social relations of production requires, in class societies, the continual production of specifically classed and gendered individuals within an ideological field that naturalizes existing classes and genders. In the broadest sense, the work of ideologies is to represent historical contradictions as *natural*: as immutable *differences* (between men and women, blacks and whites, 'them' and 'us', the 'successful' and the 'idle'); as rich or amusing *variety* ('it takes all sorts', '*vive la différence*'); as mutual *dependency* ('different but equal', social contract, a share of the profits); or as mere appearances subsumed in a larger *unity* (the family, the British people, 'we're all human beings'). All these and many other forms of naturalization are at work in developed social formations, not only in those institutions of the superstructure (school, church, family) that directly 'manufacture' ideology, but also in the most intimate interstices and very atmospheres of public and private life.

If we identify certain basic structural features of popular female romance, we can begin to see how these features closely tie in with the texts' predominant concern, reproduction through the heterosexual family. They compose a cluster of assumptions concerning the natural inevitability of love and marriage. In fact, a conflation of the two takes place, with an ideology of 'romantic love', infused with religiosity, becoming the guarantor and site of reproduction. Romantic love leads to the family and children. Romance and reproduction are harnessed together. Popular female romance enacts a closure as the knot is tied by the collapsing of emotional commitment into marital inevitability.

In this passage from unreproductive femininity to potential familial reproduction an attenuation of the woman's public identity takes place, leaving her to explore the 'external values' of love and emotion only within the privatized and servicing cage of the family. The needs of the male (often represented as a displaced or exiled aristocrat) to continue his family's line and to assume symbolic manhood by settling down in his ancestral home are the centre of the text. It is this cluster of traditional assumptions concerning heterosexual relations and romantic love as the guarantor of secure reproduction that demarcates the span of the connection between popular female romances and 'common-sense' popular culture, but it also pinpoints the particular terrain on which such romances work. There are alternatives offered, but only on this terrain. For example, the alternative of marrying for money is roundly defeated by the dominant form of marrying for love.

But these texts are not to be read simply as ideological (in that, by various magical ways, a happy ending is achieved and is equated with marriage and abnegation before the husband). For in the course of these novels the various contradictions between love and money, independence and marriage are staged, and disruptive and forbidden elements (for example, sexuality) make their absences known (as in, for example, the Gothic novel). So too the 'confinement' of the romance to the realm of personal experience and emotional relationships has been seen as the suppression of 'real relations', as outside history or as a 'feminine' (that is, trivial) concern. This is due to the invisibility, both to the Left and to the Right, of the domestic sphere and the unacknowledged domestic labour involved in day-to-day and generational reproduction.

Nevertheless, in their overriding attention to marriage as a natural and inevitable form for sexual relations and reproduction, to domesticity as the only and proper space for women, to the social, emotional and sexual servicing of the woman to the man, popular romances are located within the structures and relations of capitalist and patriarchal hegemony. A process of naturalization recruits and secures the consent of the dominated classes and groups to the conditions of their own subordination by supplying crucial connections and articulations between the coercive institutions of civil society and the common-sense intuitions and assumptions of everyday life. In the chronic instability of mature capitalist societies it can seem to offer a 'safe space', a reassuring refuge from the bewildering proliferation of institutions that seek to police the deepening crisis. This is the terrain of the popular media, which should be seen, therefore, neither as entirely institutional (a 'cultural ISA' or 'culture industry'), since reading, watching television, going to the cinema - unlike going to work or school - are 'private' activities, nor as altogether private, since they are forms of cultural commodity production, with specific ideological conditions and effects.

If naturalization, the representation of dominant ideologies as a self-evident, if contradictory, common sense, is the site and raw material of the popular media, how can this be seen with the necessary specificity in a particular form of popular literature? First, we have already suggested that in spite - or because - of its exclusion from the literary-linguistic practices of formal education, popular fiction has itself an important educative function. The formal coherence and intelligibility of a popular narrative hangs upon an active assent to certain key propositions, sometimes implicit, more often standing out of the surrounding narrative with the gnomic assurance of common sense itself:

> Money, titles, possessions - what did they matter in reality? What mattered was if a man and a woman could come together in love and know that the emotions they felt for each other were part of the Divine pattern of creation.[90]

But, as this implies, popular fiction is also a *form,* and its effectiveness depends less upon such direct 'interpellations' (which accomplish little in themselves) than upon the negotiations and resolutions of narrative functions, which in turn derive their meaning from their power to articulate connotations of an already familiar common sense. An adequately full analysis of even a single text would need to be more extended than we can attempt here. In any case, it is decidedly not our purpose to offer yet another 'method' for analysing texts. But unless the formal distinctiveness of popular fiction is recognized as a specific practice of writing and reading the texts will continue to dissolve into the ideologies that constitute them.

The hero of Barbara Cartland's *Blue Heather* returns to his ancestral home in the Highlands to find it already occupied by strangers: a young woman and her nephew and niece. He seeks the advice of his cousin, an eccentric duke who has recently achieved his lifelong ambition of breeding a strain of blue heather. The young woman claims the hero's home and his family title as the rightful inheritance of her nephew. While the claim is being investigated, the heather disappears. The ensuing search throws the hero and the young woman together, and their realization that they love one another, which coincides with the recovery of the heather and the satisfactory resolution of the inheritance, enables the hero to discard his glamorous careerist fiancee, who painlessly transfers her affections to the duke, thus aptly supplementing her suspect femininity with an equally defective masculinity (he has a 'drooping moustache'). The three major narrative strands show a close formal correspondence. In each three terms must be reduced to two: a false claimant must be eliminated and the true one revealed. In the marriage narrative the wrong woman is neatly removed, to be replaced by the right one. In the property narrative the false heir gives way to the true one but is reincorporated by becoming virtually the hero's son. In the heather narrative the plant is 'stolen', then recovered for its true owner, and potential unpleasantness is avoided by the discovery that it was not stolen at all, but merely removed inadvertently by a child, whose working-class mother is satisfyingly abject and deferential. As the title suggests, the first two narratives are mediated by the third, not only because the pursuit and recovery of the heather actually provides the conditions for their successful outcome, but also because at the level of formal functions it suggests the metaphorical mechanism by which that outcome is accomplished: hybridization.

The text accords a surprising and seemingly irrelevant prominence to *nationality*: Scottish, English, American. Each is variously nuanced, but it is not difficult to see that problematics of gender, of ownership and domesticity, even, marginally, of class are all condensed into the central motif of nationality. A textual schema might look like this:

pure Scots	*pure English*	*pure American*
hero's grandfather (dead)	grandfather's mistress (dead)	
hero's uncle (dead)		
	hero's father (dead)	hero's mother
heroine's father (dead)	heroine's mother	
child's father (never appears)	child's mother	
		rich neighbour
	'hybrids'	
	hero (Scots-English-American)	
	heroine (Scots-English)	
	nephew and niece (Scots-English)	
	child (Scots-English)	
	old castle/new castle	
	the blue heather itself	

From this it can be seen that the inevitable rightness of the narrative resolution is already composed, from the beginning, in the terms of a sub-narrative ideology of hybridization. The cross-breeding of elements that may in themselves be decayed, effete or crass produces a stronger, purer stock – an alliance of aristocracy and petty bourgeoisie, of English-speaking nations, above all of man and woman, children and home: the authentic need that the text evokes and the crucial site of reproductive common sense.

'I love you,' she whispered, 'I love you, darling, with all my heart.'

And this time Ian knew it was true and he had found the blue heather which all men seek and so few discover.[91]

The narrative ideological closure is, or seems, complete. But it is precisely at such a point that we should remind ourselves that neither narrative form nor common sense itself is ever fully closed. Romance's concluding affirmation of a world without contradictions can be seen as close to the Utopian element in popular religion and may thus provide a clue to its possible antagonistic uses.

Thus do ideas of equality, liberty and fraternity [we might add, ideas of love and happiness] ferment among men; among those strata of mankind who do not see themselves as equals nor as brothers of other men nor as free in relation to them.[92]

In Britain the use of Gramscian concepts for the analysis of literature has been developed by Raymond Williams in a theory of 'cultural materialism',[93] by Colin Mercer[94] and, most specifically, by Roger Bromley in two essays on the analysis of popular fiction.[95] Although we have disagreements with Bromley's use of Gramscian concepts, it was his work which in many ways set us in a new direction. He draws analogies between the forms of narrative and characterization in the popular fiction of the 1930s and the crisis of hegemony and the reformation of the class alliance in the ruling bloc which was occurring at the same time the texts were written. It seems to us, however, that to see characters in texts standing in for social classes is too fast and easy a leap from text to society, as well as creating a curious blindness to non-class representations in a text. For example, Bromley sees woman characters as representatives of the petty bourgeoisie, not particularly as caught in patriarchal relations. However, the basic thesis that popular fiction has a particular work to do in the maintenance and struggle for hegemony is important. Gramsci insists that hegemony is struggled for in every sphere of society, even in those areas which seem most private and removed from the incursions of politics or the state.

One of the ways in which Gramsci analyses the presence of domination and subordination in unlooked-for areas of social life is his discussion of what he calls 'spontaneous philosophy', and particularly his delineation of common sense. 'Spontaneous philosophy' is a term rather similar to Williams's 'structure of feeling': it does *not* mean that ideas come from nowhere, spontaneously, into the minds of the subordinate classes. It holds in tension the idea of 'philosophy', a developed body of ideas (rather like an earlier meaning of the term *ideology*), and the recognition that our ideas do seem to be our own, that we speak as much as we are spoken by language and that the words we use *do* address the real situations in which they are spoken.

Gramsci calls *common sense* the philosophy of the non-philosophers. It is not a single, unique conception, identical in time and space. It is the folklore of philosophy and, like folklore, it takes countless different forms. The personality formed within common sense is

strangely composite: it contains stone age elements and principles of a more advanced science, prejudices from all past phases of history at a local level and intuitions of a future philosophy which will be that of a human race united the world over.[96]

This fragmentary, proverbial view of the world is the inheritance of the subordinate classes; it has been formed in a long history of struggle for domination and can be seen as the negotiated terms of consent which we give to our continuing subordination. It is partly because common sense has been formed over a very long period that it presents itself as timeless knowledge. Ideologies of previous historical moments, at one time generated and enshrined in institutions, have become embedded in a set of assumptions about 'the way things are'. The explanations of subordination may be contradictory, containing both pragmatism and fatalism: 'God helps those who help themselves.' Gramsci suggests that at moments of heightened struggle common sense crystallizes into a more critical, coherent and oppositional 'good sense'.

It was initially certain striking similarities between the romances and thrillers we were reading and Gramsci's characterization of common sense which suggested that the two might fruitfully be thought together. First, popular female romances are characteristically formed from an amalgam of modern and pre-capitalist elements. The simplified characterization, the withdrawal from society on the part of reader and romance heroine, the happy ending, the strongly enforced code of conduct are all continuing formal elements of romance as a genre which predate capitalist society. Second, Gramsci points to an analysis of language as part of an analysis of 'spontaneous philosophy', language determined by, and carrying the signs of, culture and 'not just words grammatically devoid of content'. The simple, didactic, clichéd language of Cartland's novels does share the proverbial 'written on stone' quality of common sense. Third, the persistent moralizing of popular fiction suggests a relation to the *content* of common sense - for example, true love never runs smoothly, money can't buy you happiness (but it helps). Last, and most tentatively, there may be a similarity between Gramsci's definition of popular religion as a more systematic fragment of common sense providing 'a unity of faith between a conception of the world and corresponding norm of conduct' and the work of narrative form in popular fiction. The narrative organizes a plot, produces coherence, leads the reader from confusion and disarray to a happy ending and links the happy ending with the triumphs of one common-sense conception over others. It is the tendency of popular fiction to be linked with the production of moral norms which suggests the analogy with popular religion. The similarity may also point to the Utopian elements in popular fiction, in so far as it promises, in the end, a world without contradictions.

We are *not* saying that popular fiction is the same as common sense. But whereas previously we defined popular fiction solely by its relation to the institutions which structure the field of literary production and consumption, 'the literary field', we would now see popular fiction as also placed between highly developed ideologies/philosophies, the language of common sense and the experience of subordinate groups and classes. When a fiction addresses each of these we call it *popular*.

Popular fiction's relation to the literary field, and particularly to education, is one of exclusion. Girls' magazines, 'confessions' books, romantic novelettes or Superman comics are not normally legitimated by schools, let alone by the cultural gatekeepers of universities. They are part of the 'mass civilization' against which the 'minority culture' defines itself and 'exist within social and cultural relations which are different from and antagonistic to those represented in the school curriculum'.[97]

Yet, however antagonistic the literary establishment appears to be to popular fiction, the case of romance makes it clear that popular fiction is not oppositional in any simple way. 'Romance' as a category in literary criticism connects novels as dissimilar as Richardson's *Pamela*, Du Maurier's *Rebecca*, Cartland's *Blue Heather*. Also, the themes of love and of the true nature of womanhood which permeate Cartland's fiction can be seen as the popularization of an elaborate ideology/philosophy of womanhood, developed in response to the nineteenth-century women's movement and crystallized by John Ruskin in the doctrine of separate spheres.[98]

If romance is placed in this way in relation to 'high' literature and philosophy, it also addresses the linguistic practice of common sense (the simple sentence?) and is read within popular culture. The words 'I love you', which are the culmination of romantic fiction, are spoken daily as part of the lived experience of women and men within different class cultures, different age groups and different familial positions, and they have a range of connotations depending in part on when and by whom the magic words are uttered. It is because popular female romances occupy this contested space between highly developed ideologies, common sense and women's lived experiences that we have turned our attention to them.

To paraphrase Gramsci once more, a socialist feminist analysis of popular fiction initially aims to demonstrate that everyone is a reader and a writer. 'It is not a question of introducing from scratch a scientific form of thought'; it is a question of renovating and making critical an already existing activity, drawing out the historical forms and contradictory status of already existing practices of reading and writing. It is not altogether easy to draw a distinction between the two practices involved: the rereading of old stories quickly becomes a rewriting (from current feminist rereadings of fairy stories to Brecht's rereading of *Coriolanus*). Feminist analysis or reinterpretation of popular female romance would bear the following in mind: (1) the sphere of feelings and love is a particularly powerful arena for femininity and, as such, an important site of feminist political struggle and historical analysis; (2) romance, with its representation of the natural inevitability of woman's position in reproduction, presents us with a literary history of patriarchal relations; (3) romance has been displaced by the hegemonic fictional form of realism. It is therefore fruitful ground for the presentation of an alternative form of writing to realism and for an investigation of why women's writing has been marginalized.

The renovation of the writing of popular fiction has begun in the work of worker-writer groups:

It is usually young women writers who have adopted the short-story form based on the life of the streets and the complex adolescent world of courting and dating. Chelsea Herbert's *In the Melting Pot*, Stella Ibekw's *Teenage Encounters*, Colleen

Skeate's *Love Trouble*, all explore ironically and understandingly this milieu: what I would guess is that these writers have in fact taken the form from the numerous romantic short stories which are published in all the teenage magazines and converted the settings into local ones and added their own realism to the form and used it for quite different purposes from those inherent in the commercial stories.[99]

If this analysis of the specific contested space which popular fiction occupies is anything like correct, then the first implication is that books cannot be called popular simply on the basis of a reading of them or on the basis of an analysis of their interpellative structures/strictures. A complete analysis would have to include not only textual analysis but also an account of what writing exists and is read within popular leisure/culture (that is, the culture of subordinated groups and classes). The site of analysis would no longer simply be the relation of these books to other books but their relation also to languages of lived experience, and such an analysis would have to grapple with the structural class and gender relations which frame the field.

The renovation or reclaiming of popular fiction means asking which practices of reading and writing, and how transformed, can become part of:

a new common sense and with it a new culture and a new philosophy which will be rooted in the popular consciousness with the same solidity and imperative quality as traditional beliefs.[100]

20 Selective guide to further reading and contacts*

Our concern here is to provide a link with the section on developments in the 1970s (pages 235–68) by giving a guide to the main arguments and further reading in each area we discussed: feminism; Marxist literary theory; popular culture and reading. We also include relevant bibliographies. Finally, we include a resources section in which journals, bookshops and organizations are listed.

Feminism and literary criticism

Barrett, M. (ed.), *Virginia Woolf: Women and Writing* (The Women's Press 1979). A useful collection of Woolf's writing on women and fiction, with an introduction situating her work.

Batsleer, J., *et al.*, 'Women, literature and feminism' (CCCS Stencilled Paper, forthcoming). Examines women's fictional writing in the thirties and relates it to an analysis of women's position and women's politics at the time.

Elbert, S., and Glastonbury, M., *Inspiration and Drudgery* (WRRC 1979). A consideration of literature and domestic labour in the nineteenth century in England.

Ellmann, M., *Thinking About Women* (Virago 1979). A reprint of a work first published in 1969. Its subject is the representation of women in the critical and fictional writing of men.

Harrison, Rachel, '*Shirley*: relations of reproduction and the ideology of romance', in Women's Studies Group, *Women Take Issue* (CCCS/Hutchinson 1978).

Marxist-Feminist Literature Collective, 'Women's writing 1848: *Jane Eyre, Shirley, Villette, Aurora Leigh*', in F. Barker *et al.* (eds.), *The Sociology of Literature: 1848* (The University of Essex Press 1978). Categories from Marxist and psychoanalytic thought are used as a means of understanding class and gender determinations within women's writing.

Millett, K., *Sexual Politics* (New York: Doubleday 1969). One of the founding texts of contemporary feminist criticism and feminist theory. It develops a theory of patriarchy and examines its effects, as sexism, in some fictional male writing.

Moers, E., *Literary Women* (The Women's Press 1978). A literary history of women's writing in America, England and France.

Mulvey, L., 'Women and representation: a discussion', in *Wedge*, no. 2 (1978). A discussion of feminist film practice and theory, with particular reference to

Riddles of the Sphinx. It discusses theoretical issues of relevance to work on fiction and representation.

Showalter, E., *A Literature of Their Own* (Virago 1977). A literary historical account of British women's writing from the mid nineteenth to the mid twentieth centuries, which argues that women's writing is best understood using a sub-cultural model.

Taylor, H., 'Class and gender in Charlotte Brontë's *Shirley*', *Feminist Review*, no. 1 (1979). Argues that *Shirley* has been repeatedly misread in criticism because of the failure to see her concern as being with class and sexual politics, rather than the one being a metaphor for the other.

Marxism and literary criticism

Balibar, R., *Les Français Fictifs* (Paris: Hachette 1974). An account of the process by which certain writings are recognized as 'literary' in the context of the development of the French national language and education system in the nineteenth century.

Balibar, R., 'An example of literary work in France: George Sand's "La Mare au Diable"/"The Devil's Pool" ', in F. Barker *et al.* (eds.), *The Sociology of Literature: 1848* (University of Essex Press 1978). An essay (in English) demonstrating literature's relation to literacy, social class and education, which Balibar developed theoretically in *Les Français Fictifs*.

Barrett, M., *et al.* (eds.), *Ideology and Cultural Production* (Croom Helm 1979). A collection of papers presented to the 1978 Annual BSA Conference on culture. Various concrete studies locate and outline the main problems and issues within cultural studies.

Bennett, T., *Formalism and Marxism* (Methuen 1979). A taut, clear and useful account of Russian formalist criticism and of recent Althusserian Marxist criticism, concluding with attractive suggestions for future work.

CCCS English Studies Group, 'Thinking the thirties', in F. Barker *et al.*(eds.), *The Sociology of Literature: 1936* (University of Essex Press 1980). An analysis of the social relations of literary production, which suggests an analysis of fictional writing in terms of a literary formation. It addresses a number of theoretical issues: periodization, gender determination and the question of reading/s.

Davies, T., 'Education, ideology and literature', in *Red Letters,* no. 7 (1978). Seminal first thoughts on Renée Balibar's work in relation to English education and the English language.

Dubois, J., *L'Institution de la littérature* (Brussels: Fernand Nathan 1978). A 'sociological' but very useful review of ways of thinking the literature/society relation, whether or not the concept of the literary institution is found convincing.

Eagleton, T., *Marxism and Literary Criticism* (Methuen 1976). An introduction to and account of the development of Marxist literary criticism, which outlines its main theories and issues.

Eagleton, T., *Criticism and Ideology* (New Left Books 1977). An important theoretical account of literature's relation to ideology within an Althusserian framework.

Jameson, F., *Marxism and Form: Twentieth Century Dialectical Theories of Literature* (Princeton University Press 1972). A full and suggestive meditation on the work of Adorno, Benjamin, Lukács, Sartre and others, 'towards a dialectical criticism' of literary form.

Lane, M., *Commerce Against Culture* (Pluto Press, forthcoming). A history and analysis of changes in the structure of publishing since 1945.

Macherey, P., *A Theory of Literary Production* (Routledge and Kegan Paul 1978). A work of theoretical analysis which developes the Althusserian theory of ideology in relation to literature.

Macherey, P., 'Literature as an ideological form: some Marxist theses' (CCCS Stencilled Paper, forthcoming).

New Left Books, *Aesthetics and Politics* (New Left Books 1977). A collection of essays by Lukács, the 'Frankfurt School' and Brecht, outlining the main positions in the realism/modernism debates. Each group of essays is introduced, and there is a concluding afterword by Fredric Jameson.

Solomon, M. (ed.), *Marxism and Art - Essays Classic and Contemporary* (New York: Vintage 1974). A reader designed to present a wide range of Marxist critical opinion on the theorization of literature, art and culture. Currently out of print, it is to be republished in America - a project financed through public subscription.

Williams, R., *Marxism and Literature* (Oxford University Press 1977). A fully considered bringing together of Williams's own body of work with a suggestive review of central Marxist concepts.

Williams, R., *Politics and Letters* (New Left Books 1979). Taped intellectual and political autobiography, immensely resonant and important.

Popular culture

Braden, S., *Artists and People* (Routledge and Kegan Paul 1978). A study of the role of art in the community and of community artists.

Bromley, R., 'Natural boundaries: the social function of popular fiction', in *Red Letters,* no. 7 (1978). An analysis of popular fiction using a broad theory of ideology and culture which develops the concept of masculine and feminine romance.

Brunsdon, C., and Morley, D., *Everyday television: 'Nationwide'* (British Film Institute 1978). An analysis of the way *Nationwide* addresses itself to both a national audience, united in the diversity of regions, and an audience of ordinary individuals, grouped in families.

Horkheimer, M., and Adorno, T., 'The culture industry: enlightenment as the mass deception', in *Dialectic of Enlightenment* (New Left Books 1979). The central text in the 'Frankfurt School's' account of mass culture in terms of the structure of the commodity and reification.

Jameson, F., 'Ideology, narrative analysis and popular culture', in *Theory and Society,* no. 4 (1977). A review of recent work on popular culture utilizing recent concepts of ideology and developments in narrative theory.

Laclau, E., *Politics and Ideology in Marxist Theory* (New Left Books 1977). Contains an account of interpellation through ideology which others have tried to use in relation to literary texts.

Mercer, C., 'Culture and ideology in Gramsci', in *Red Letters,* no. 8 (1978). A useful account of Gramsci's and Althusser's work, developing a reading of interpellation.

Nowell-Smith, G., 'Common sense', in *Radical Philosophy,* no. 7 (1974). A short but pointed essay on Gramsci's use of common sense.

Open University, *Popular Culture,* Course Unit U203 (Milton Keynes 1978). Papers by Bennett, Eagleton, Hall and Williams on various approaches to popular culture.

Palmer, J., *Thrillers* (Edward Arnold 1978). Examines the origins and development of the thriller as a distinctive popular genre.

Screen Education, no. 22, 'Popular culture and education' (1977).

van der Will, W. (ed.), *Workers and Writers* (University of Birmingham German Department monograph 1975).

Worker Writers and Community Publishers, *Writing* (Centerprise Publications 1978).

Worpole, K., 'Politics and writing', in *Radical Education*, no. 12 (1979).

Reading

Althusser, L., 'Ideology and ideological state apparatuses', in *Lenin and Philosophy and Other Essays* (New Left Books 1971). A key essay for materialist criticism, which introduces the notion of interpellation in relation to ideology.

Bathrick, D., 'The politics of reception theory in the GDR', in *Minnesota Review,* no. 5 (1975). A useful survey of the theories of reception aesthetics.

Cohen, R., *New Directions in Literary History* (Baltimore: Baltimore Press 1974). A selection of articles from the journal *New Literary History.* Its selection of works pertaining to reception theory and reading is particularly useful.

Escarpit, R., *Sociology of Literature* (Frank Cass 1971). One of the most thoroughly researched examples of empirical sociology of literature.

Hohendahl, P., 'Introduction to reception aesthetics', in *New German Critique*, no. 10 (1977).

Mehlman, J., 'Teaching reading: the case of Marx in France', in *Diacritics*, vol. 6, no. 1 (1976). An account of some of the theoretical and political effects of Althusser's notion of symptomatic readings.

Naumann, M. (ed.), *Gesellschaft-Literatur-Lesen* (Berlin: Aufbau-Verlag 1973). An East German attempt to develop a Marxist literary 'reception aesthetics', drawing on *Grundrisse* and Brecht; it includes an interesting critique of theories of reading. A translation of the main body of ideas can be found in *New Literary History,* no. 8 (1976).

Bibliographies

Fairbanks, Carol, *More Women in Literature: Criticism of the Seventies* (NJ: Scarecrow Press 1979).

Lawford, P., *Marxist Aesthetics: A Short Bibliography* (Keele University Department of Sociology and Social Anthropology Occasional Papers 1977).

Lazere, D., 'Mass culture, political consciousness and English Studies: a selected bibliography', in *College English*, vol. 38, no. 8 (1977).

Myers, Carol Fairbanks, *Women in Literature: Criticism of the Seventies* (NJ: Scarecrow Press 1976)

Resources

CCCS Occasional Papers, CCCS, University of Birmingham, PO Box 363, Birmingham B15 2TT. Empirical and theoretical discussion of issues within and areas of cultural analysis.

Compendium, 234 Camden High Street, London NW1. A bookshop with an extensive range of work relating to politics and sexual politics, good for pamphlets, booklets and journals.

Cultural Correspondence: Dorrwar Bookstore, 224 Thayer Street, Providence, Rhode Island 02906, USA.

Federation of Worker Writers: E Floor, Milburn House, Dean Street, Newcastle, NE1. Encourages and publishes working-class and socialist writing; acts as an information and resource centre for locally based writing groups.

Feminist Archive, Orchard House, Shepton Mallet, Somerset. Recently established, the archive hopes to develop a library of significant feminist documents which would be available to its subscribers.

Feminist Review, 14 Sumner Buildings, Sumner Street, London SE1. A journal of women's studies and women's liberation. It publishes articles covering a wide range of issues relevant to women, including questions of culture.

Feminist Theatre Group, 95 Barnsbury Street, London NW1. A co-ordinating group for women working in mainstream and alternative theatre, film and TV.

Grassroots, 1 Newton Street, Manchester M1 1HV. A thriving bookshop which also acts as a focal point for political and community action. Carries a wide range of pamphlets, journals and papers as well as books.

Ideology and Consciousness, 1 Woburn Mansions, Torrington Place, London WC1. A forum for work and debates within Marxist theories of ideology.

Literature and History, Department of Humanities, Thames Polytechnic, Wellington

Street, London SE18. A journal committed to interdisciplinary materialist criticism and discussion.

M/F, 69 Randolph Avenue, London W9 1DW. A Marxist feminist journal which aims to develop political and theoretical debate within the women's movement.

Minnesota Review, Box 211, Bloomington, Indiana 47401, USA. A journal of poetry, fiction and Marxist literary theory and criticism.

New German Critique, German Department, University of Wisconsin, Milwaukee, Wisconsin 53201, USA. An interdisciplinary journal of German cultural studies which publishes important translations.

New Left Review, 7 Carlisle Street, London W1V 6NL. Carries the work of continental Marxist theorists, as well as British Marxist debate, including aesthetics.

News from Neasden, available by mail order from Grassroots. A comprehensive catalogue of new radical publications, it is mailed free to bookshops.

Praxis: A Journal of Radical Perspectives on the Arts, 2125 Hearst Avenue, Berkeley, California 94709, USA. A wide-ranging journal of radical cultural practices.

Publications Distribution Co-operative, 27 Clerkenwell Close, London EC1. Distributes left and feminist books and magazines.

Radical Publications Group, 27 Clerkenwell Close, London EC1.

Red Letters, 16 King Street, London WC2 8HY. The literature journal of the Communist Party.

Schooling and Culture, ILEA Cockpit Arts Workshop, Gateforth Street, London NW8

Science Fiction Studies, Department of English, Indiana State University, Terre-Haute, Indiana 47809, USA. A journal which, in addition to the analysis of particular SF texts and authors, has developed a radical analysis of SF as a popular genre. Angenot, Jameson, Le Guin, Russ and Suvin are regular contributors to it.

Sisterwrite, 190 Upper Street, London N1. A bookshop run by and for women, recently opened. It has an impressive stock and women-only meeting rooms and a café above the shop.

Socialist Review, New Fronts Publishing Co., 4228 Telegraph Avenue, Oakland, California 94609, USA. The leading American independent socialist journal, it carries much work on culture and ideology.

Social Text, 700 West Badger Road, Suite 101, Madison, Wisconsin 53713, USA. A journal devoted to problems of theory, particularly in the area of culture and ideology.

Stand, 19 Haldane Terrace, Newcastle NE2 3AN. A journal concerned with political writing, it carries reviews and debate articles but its main space is given to poetry and prose.

The British Film Institute, 81 Dean Street, London W1V 6AA. The BFI runs a distribution service, publishes its own pamphlets and books and finances research into film practice and film studies.

The Journal of Women's Studies in Literature, Eden Press Women's Publications, 3 Henrietta Street, London WC2E 8LU. Recently launched, the journal aims to publish work on 'women writers and characters who belong in the mainstream of the literature of the English-speaking world'.

The Leveller, 57 Caledonian Road, London N1. A monthly magazine with regular coverage of socialist and feminist cultural activities.

The Oxford Literary Review, 2 Marlborough Road, Oxford OX1 4LP. A journal focusing on recent developments in literary theory.

The Society for Education in Film and Television, 29 Old Compton Street, London W1V 5PL. The Society publishes two journals, *Screen* and *Screen Education. Screen*'s primary concern is film theory, *Screen Education*'s with the teaching of Media Studies. Their theoretical articles and discussions are useful in other areas besides film studies.

The Women's Art Alliance, 10 Cambridge Terrace Mews, London NW1. Provides rooms for the practice, exhibition and performance of women's art.

The Women's Research and Resources Centre, 190 Upper Street, London N1. A comprehensive research index and library, plus a small pamphlet-publishing venture are the basis of the WRRC. It provides a focus for study groups and organizes its own seminars, workshops and summer school.

The Writers' and Readers' Publishing Co-operative, 9-19 Rupert Street, London W1. Has an excellent list of politics, fiction, poetry, children's books and the cartoon-strip 'Beginners' series. They have recently formed a bookclub.

Women and Literature Newsletter, J. Batsleer/R. O'Rourke, CCCS, University of Birmingham, PO Box 363, Birmingham B15 2TT. Recently launched, it aims to make and strengthen contacts between women across the country working on aspects of women and literature; to keep research lists and information exchanges up to date; and eventually to become a forum for discussion.

Notes and references

Preface

1 There is as yet no detailed or accredited history of the Centre's inauguration and development. The best source is probably the series of Annual Reports issued each year which, in addition to charting important developments, also give a detailed account of seminar groups, research topics, etc.
2 Richard Hoggart, *The Uses of Literacy* (Penguin Books 1958).
3 The Centre was made independent and given a base, in the Faculty of Arts, to develop its own line of work following a Faculty of Arts Working Paper in 1972.
4 The most important single area of growth is in the Communications Studies and Cultural Studies degree courses in polytechnics, under the aegis of the CNAA. But Cultural Studies approaches are now to be found in many university courses and curricula, and in English, Media and Social Studies courses in further education and in schools. The term itself has gained wide currency.
5 Nine issues of *WPCS* were published independently before the journal was absorbed into the CCCS/Hutchinson series. Stencilled Papers are still published by and available from the Centre: the list includes over sixty titles.
6 To date the following titles have been published by Hutchinson: *Resistance Through Rituals, On Ideology, Women Take Issue, Working Class Culture*.
7 Paul Willis's work on the transition of working-class boys from school to work is reported in *Learning to Labour* (Saxon House 1977). The SSRC and Birmingham University are currently supporting a follow-up project on young manual workers. An SSRC project on 'Women, work and the family' is also being undertaken by Christine Griffin.
8 *Working Class Culture* is a volume of historical essays on this theme, edited by R. Johnson, J. Clarke and C. Critcher. The work of the Education Group will shortly appear in *Unpopular Education: Education and social democracy since 1944*. The History Group are currently preparing a special number on problems of 'history and theory'. A number of studies on aspects of the state in the 1880s–1920s period are to be drawn together in a volume on 'Citizenship and the interventionist state'.
9 For a guide to the new kinds of work which have made this break possible, see the selected bibliography to the English Studies section, below, pages 269-75.
10 The growing importance of historical work is evidenced not only in the work of the Cultural History Group, but also in an increasingly historical dimension to all our projects and a general privileging of concrete studies over purely 'theoretical' ones. We believe this return to 'concrete work' is vitally necessary and can be accomplsihed without falling back into a simple empiricism.

Chapter 1 Cultural Studies and the Centre: some problematics and problems

1 Different theoretical emphases are already reflected in the first issue of the journal. See, for example, the exchange between Alan Shuttleworth ('People and culture') and Stuart Hall ('A reply'), in *WPCS* 1.

2 There is still no 'journal of the field' as such. Its absence may have helped to keep the field 'open', but it may also have constituted a barrier to its coherent development. For a long time those interested in Cultural Studies had to track it down through a labyrinth of internal references.

3 At first the Centre was part of the English Department, and it remains in a Faculty of Arts. This may have somewhat inhibited the extension of the field to include sociological, historical and anthropological approaches. There was, for a long time, a lag between the image of the Centre and the kind of work it was actually doing. In part, the journal was designed to help close that gap.

4 For example, the Portsmouth CNAA BA degree is based on history and literature; the North-East London Polytechnic on an innovative kind of sociology course. Communications Studies has also provided a fruitful disciplinary base, though itself a 'hybrid' in disciplinary terms.

5 The size of the Centre staff has never adequately matched the actual numbers of research students supervised, the complexity of the field or the range of topics covered. It was not designated a 'growth' area and could not attract the scale of outside funding commensurate with its project. In less propitious economic times innovations of this kind in higher education will be even harder to get off the drawing-board.

6 In the early days most Centre students came from a literary background. But by the early 1970s we were admitting students with a 'humanities' or 'social science' disciplinary formation in about equal numbers. This is still the general pattern.

7 In practice, this distinction was not always easy to sustain, especially to those not directly familiar with our thinking. They assumed – wrongly, in our view – that a *descriptive* definition of the field was adequate.

8 Through the journal's life we printed few 'outside contributors', and all of those had close connections with the Centre and had given versions of their articles as seminars on some Centre occasion.

9 This grant was generously renewed shortly before Sir Allen Lane's death. Its great value was that it was not 'earmarked': we could therefore use it to launch new ventures. It was not large, but - in terms of the Centre's development - it was invaluable. Without it the Centre would have remained a loose grouping of graduate students working on broadly similar themes.

10 Stencilled Papers have been widely used, especially as practical course materials in a range of courses in universities, colleges and schools.

11 His thesis was subsequently published as *Images of Women* (Chatto and Windus 1975).

12 Richard Hoggart, *The Uses of Literacy* (Penguin 1958); Raymond Williams, *Culture and Society* and *The Long Revolution* (Penguin 1961 and 1965 respectively); E. P. Thompson, *The Making of the English Working Class* (Penguin 1968). Thompson's seminal critique of Williams first appeared in *New Left Review*, nos. 9 and 10, and has been a formative text for the Centre.

13 'Time, work discipline and industrial capitalism', *Past and Present*, no. 97 (December 1967).

14 See an early Centre Occasional Paper by Richard Hoggart, 'Contemporary cultural studies'. But *The Uses of Literacy* is the *locus classicus* of this method in practice.

15 See, *inter alia*, F. R. Leavis and Denys Thompson, *Culture and Environment* (Chatto and Windus 1933); the Leavis essays collected in *The Common Pursuit* (Chatto and Windus 1952); *Education and the University* (Chatto and Windus 1943), and, of course, the pages of *Scrutiny, passim*. Q. D. Leavis's *Fiction and the Reading Public* is also a seminal text in this respect (Chatto and Windus 1932).

16 The ever-regressing 'organic society' is definitively dismantled by Williams in *The Country and the City* (Chatto and Windus 1973).

17 Leavis's concern with language has parallels in Ezra Pound's early work: similar themes appear in other work which, in certain ways, differs radically – for example, that of Karl Kraus and Walter Benjamin. In the wake of structural linguistics 'language' has become the paradigm for culture in a quite different sense: see below, the section on 'The Structuralisms'.

18 Included in Leavis, *Education and The University*.

19 See the Introduction to *Culture and Society*, where the interaction between these key terms is discussed. See also *Keywords* (Fontana 1976).

20 Part I of *The Long Revolution* is the most important section from this viewpoint.

21 Williams discussed the weaknesses of English Marxism in the 1930s in the 'Leavis' chapter in *Culture and Society*.

22 Thompson comments on the political context of Williams's work of this period in his *New Left Review* critique. It is more fully illuminated in *Politics and Letters* (New Left Books 1979).

23 For a recent critique of the concept of 'community', see Dan Finn and Eve Brook, 'Critique of community studies', Stencilled Paper no. 44, CCCS, Birmingham.

24 The synthesizing texts here were Talcott Parsons, *The Structure of Social Action* (Glencoe, Ill.: The Free Press 1949), and *The Social System* (Glencoe, Ill.: The Free Press 1951). The most influential middle-range sociological theorists were Merton (see *Social Theory and Social Structure*, Glencoe, Ill.: The Free Press 1963) and Lazarsfeld, *passim*.

25 Shils, a collaborator of Talcott Parsons, has written extensively on this theme: see, *inter alia*, his essay in Jacobs (ed.), *Culture for the Millions* (New York: Van Nostrand 1961).

26 One of the few exceptions is an essay on ideology in Merton, *Social Theory and Social Structure*. The opening was never followed through. This absence is discussed by Stuart Hall in 'The sociology of knowledge: hinterland of science', in *On Ideology* (CCCS/Hutchinson 1978).

27 Perry Anderson, 'Components of a national culture', a brilliant and insightful essay, in R. Blackburn and A. Cockburn (eds.), *Student Power* (Penguin 1969).

28 Hoggart's Inaugural Lecture is reprinted in *Speaking to Each Other* (Chatto and Windus 1970).

29 The project was generously supported by the Rowntree Memorial Trust.

30 A. C. H. Smith, T. Blackwell and E. Immirzi, with an Introduction by Stuart Hall: *Paper Voices* (Chatto and Windus 1975).

31 Weber's *The Protestant Ethic and the Spirit of Capitalism* (Allen and Unwin 1930), a seminal example, had the added advantage of being explicitly counter-posed to Marxist explanations of the same phenomenon.

32 These arguments are extensively explored in Weber's *Methodology of the Social Sciences* (Glencoe, Ill.: The Free Press 1949).

33 Many of these texts are unavailable in English and have not been well covered in the secondary sources. But see Raymond Aron's *German Sociology* and Anthony Giddins (ed.), *Positivism and Sociology* (Heinemann 1974). For a recent discussion, see Ted Benton, *Philosophical Foundations of The Three Sociologies* (Routledge and Kegan Paul 1977); Paul Hirst, *Social Evolution and Sociological Categories* (Allen and Unwin 1976); and S. Hall, 'The Sociology of knowledge', in *On Ideology* (CCCS/Hutchinson 1978).

34 On 'interpretation', see M. Truzzi, *Verstehen* (Addison Wesley 1974). A useful recent study on Dilthey is H. Rickman, *William Dilthey* (Paul Elek 1979).

35 The phrase 'the two sociologies' was first used by Alan Dawe in a critical review of the sociological traditions. An important text in the Weber/Durkheim counter-position was the reinterpretation of Durkheim's *Suicide*, using Weberian categories, in Douglas's *The Social Meaning of Suicide* (Princeton University Press 1967).

36 Schutz's collected works were reprinted in this period by Martinus Nijhoff, The Hague. See also Berger's *Invitation to Sociology* (Penguin 1963), and P. L. Berger and T. Luckman, *The Social Construction of Reality* (Penguin 1971); for the links between this reworking and the early Marx, see Berger and Pullberg, 'The concept of reification', *New Left Review*, vol. 35 (1966).

37 The key text here was Garfinkel's *Studies in Ethnomethodology* (Englewood Cliffs, NJ.: Prentice Hall 1967). Garfinkel's and Schutz's concern with the social foundations of 'everyday knowledge' was seminal in the application of the term 'ideology' to common-sense categories. The extension of ethnomethodology to the analysis of conversation strategies was important, especially in the work of Sachs. The preoccupation with how sociologists came to know what they knew took self-reflexivity to its logical extreme, however, and proved to be a cul-de-sac.

38 For an overview of the 'Chicago School', see R. E. L. Faris, *Chicago Sociology* (University of Chicago Press 1967).

39 Howard Becker's *Outsiders* (Glencoe, Ill.: The Free Press 1963), was the breakthrough text here.

40 See Paul Willis, *Profane Culture* (Routledge and Kegan Paul 1978), and *Learning to Labour* (Saxon House 1977). The debate with subcultural theory and its methodology is evidenced in S. Hall and T. Jefferson (eds.), *Resistance through Rituals* (CCCS/Hutchinson 1976). The male-centredness of the tradition is discussed by Angela McRobbie and Jenny Garber in *Resistance through Rituals*. For recent work on the position of women, see *Women Take Issue* (CCCS/Hutchinson 1978) and forthcoming Centre work.

41 The status of experiential evidence with respect to structural analysis is lengthily discussed in Willis, *Learning to Labour*. See also Willis, 'Notes on method', pages 88–95 below.

42 See for example, R. Johnson, 'Histories of culture/theories of ideology', in Barrett, Corrigan, Kuhn and Wolfe (eds.), *Ideology and Cultural Production* (Croom Helm 1979), and 'Thompson, Genovese and socialist/humanist history', in *History Workshop*, no. 6 (Autumn 1978).

43 One thinks here of the work in 'ethnosemantics' and 'ethnolinguistics' comprehensively reviewed by Dell Hymes, for example in Hymes (ed.), *Language in Culture and Society* (Harper and Row 1966), and *Directions in Ethno-Linguistics* (Holt, Rinehart 1972); Mary Douglas's *Rules and Meanings* (Penguin 1973), *Purity and Danger* (Penguin 1970) and *Natural Symbols* (Barry and Rockliff 1970).

44 These historical traditions will be more fully discussed in *History and Theory* currently being prepared for publication in the CCCS/Hutchinson series. The 'culturalistic' problematic in which they are situated is critically reviewed by R. Johnson, 'Three problematics', in J. Clarke, C. Critcher and R. Johnson (eds.), *Working Class Culture* (CCCS/Hutchinson 1979).

45 This is made explicit in Berger and Luckman, *The Social Construction of Reality*. See the discussion in Hall, 'The sociology of knowledge'.

46 These connections are skilfully reviewed in Lichtheim's *Lukács* (Fontana 1970) – despite its polemical character – and in the essay by Gareth Stedman-Jones, 'The Marxism of the early Lukács', *New Left Review*, no. 70.

47 Perry Anderson, *Considerations of Western Marxism* (New Left Books 1976); also, *Western Marxism – A Reader* (New Left Books 1977).

48 The Merlin Press enterprise of reprinting Lukács's work began at this time with the translation of *The Historical Novel* (1962). See also Goldmann's *Hidden God* (Routledge and Kegan Paul 1964) and his influential essay on 'The sociology of literature', in *International Social Science Journal*, vol. 19, no. 4 (1967). Heinemann's translations of Adorno and Habermas also date from this period. Sartre's *Critique of Dialectical Reason* was still untranslated, though its arguments were familiar through their use in *New Left Review* and in Cooper and Laing's work: see *Reason and Revolution* (Tavistock 1964). But the methodological chapter, written earlier but incorporated in *The Critique*, was already a familiar and important text, *The Problem of Method* (Methuen 1963).

49 The concept of 'epistemological rupture', appropriated from Bachelard and Canguilhelm, was introduced in Althusser, *For Marx* (Allen Lane 1969) and substantially developed, in a more absolutist direction, in Althusser and Balibar, *Reading Capital* (New Left Books 1970), alongside the theory of 'symptomatic reading'. Both have had to be radically modified in application to be of value. Althusser himself modifies the position in *Essays in Self-Criticism* (New Left Books 1976). See the general critique of this privileging of the 'theoretical' level in E. P. Thompson's blistering anti-Althusser polemic, *The Poverty of Theory* (Merlin Press 1979). The Centre has found it useful to read texts for their underlying 'problematics' but has never succumbed to the method of reducing texts to their epistemes and has actively criticized the stigmatization of texts on the sole ground that their problematics can be declared 'historicist', 'empiricist', 'Lukacsean', etc., etc.

50 Althusser, *For Marx*.

51 The first appearance of the Nicolaus translation of Marx's *Grundrisse* (Penguin

1973), with Nicolaus's seminal introduction, was an important event: above all for the highly significant *1857 Introduction*, Marx's most extensive methodological text, which not only provided a methodological bench-mark but also allowed us to criticize the highly theoreticist epistemology which Althusser and Balibar had culled from it: see S. Hall, 'Notes on a reading of Marx's *1857 Introduction*', in *WPCS* 6.

52 It enabled concrete links to be forged, for the first time, between the Centre and groupings of sociologists, in which important convergences were developed: the Centre's link with the National Deviancy Conference, and thus with thinking in 'the new criminology', is a pertinent example. Similar convergences took place in Media Studies, as mainstream communications research abandoned its earlier functionalist stance.

53 Raymond Williams initiated this crucial work on the 'selective tradition' in *The Long Revolution* and *The Country and The City* and developed it, in relation to 'hegemony', in *Marxism and Literature* (Oxford University Press 1977).

54 There is an important resumé of the argument concerning the relation between 'texts' and 'practices' in Williams's *Marxism and Literature*.

55 The Marxist structuralists examined 'dominance' but not 'struggle and resistance'. The concept of 'hegemony', elaborated through Gramsci's work, was therefore the crucial site of the elaboration of this perspective. One way of reading this – in terms of incorporative, emergent and residual elements – was offered in Williams's 'Base and superstructure' essay (*New Left Review* no. 82, 1973), later reprinted in *Marxism and Literature*. A somewhat different approach is to be found in the overview article 'Sub-cultures, cultures and class', by Hall, Clarke, Critcher, Jefferson and Roberts, in *Resistance Through Rituals*. Important work in social history pointed in the same direction: for example, the collection by A. P. Donajgrodski, *Social Control In Nineteenth Century Britain* (Croom Helm 1977), including R. Johnson, 'Educating the experts: education and the state 1833-7'. Some of this historical work, like parallel trends in the sociology of deviance, did, however, compensate for the 'functionalism' of dominant cultures by a too-easy inversion into a 'social-control' perspective. For a critique, see G. Stedman-Jones in *History Workshop*, no. 5, and Jock Young in Fine *et al.* (eds.), *Capitalism and the Rule of Law* (Hutchinson 1979).

56 Benjamin's work was one of the earliest influences to stress the 'productionist' rather than the expressive view of cultural practice. The terms 'signification' and 'signifying practice', developed in early semiotics, reinforced the notion that meaning was not given but produced. This depended on a fracturing of the naturalized relation between the sign and the thing it referenced, elaborated in structural linguistics. In Media Studies, for example, the analysis which brought out the strategies by which dominant definitions were 'preferred' depended on Vološinov's concept of the 'multi-accentuality' of the sign: See Vološinov, *Marxism and The Philosophy of Language* (New York: Seminar Press 1973). Meaning was thus the product of a 'struggle in language, over meaning'. See, *inter alia*, S. Hall, 'Encoding and decoding in television discourse', (extracted below, pages 128–38); Hall, Connell and Curti, 'The unity of current affairs TV', in *WPCS* 9; the exchange between Ros Coward

and Connell, Curti, Chambers, Jefferson and Hall on this point in *Screen*, vol. 18, nos. 1 and 4 (1977-8).

57 We deliberately use the Althusserean formulation of 'instances' here in a general sense: the notion of clearly distinct and separable instances, established not only at an analytical level but also as a feature of concrete historical societies, is not thereby endorsed. However, the need for *some* analytical distinction, at a clearly specified level of abstraction, would be defended - the notion of 'relative autonomy' seems to require it - against some recent arguments (see Thompson, *The Poverty of Theory* and Williams, *Marxism and Literature*) that any such distinction is a false abstraction because it distinguishes analytically things which always appear connected in any concrete historical example and in 'experience'.

58 The very term 'materialist' is, of course, itself problematic. In some cases it has become little more than a shorthand cover term for 'economism'. It has also frequently been recruited to support the opposite positions which could in no sense be defined as 'materialist'. Nevertheless, in the face of the immensely powerful pull towards idealism in Cultural Studies, the project of a materialist theory of culture does establish certain rudimentary theoretical limit positions - for example, the determinate character of 'ideas'.

59 For a brief survey of the problems, see S. Hall, 'Rethinking the base/superstructure metaphor', in J. Bloomfield (ed.), *Class, Hegemony and Party* (Lawrence and Wishart 1977).

60 From his review of *The Long Revolution, New Left Review*, nos. 9 and 10.

61 See R. Williams, 'From Leavis to Goldmann', *New Left Review*, no. 67 (May/June 1971).

62 J.-P. Sartre, *The Problem of Method*.

63 This argument has recently been restated with great cogency in E. P. Thompson's *The Poverty of Theory*.

64 This was one of the seminal arguments of Marx's *1857 Introduction*; see Hall, 'Notes on a reading of the *1857 Introduction*'. But it was the generalized use of the models of language systems elaborated in structural linguistics which, more than anything else at this stage, made available the concept of 'systems of difference'. This break with a certain conception of 'totality' is one of the distinguishing 'structuralist' marks. For a highly formal elaboration of this break in a mode of theorization, see Part I of M. Foucault's *Archaeology of Knowledge* (Tavistock 1972).

65 The term 'over-determination' is a borrowing from Freud, by Althusser, in his seminal essay, 'Contradiction and over-determination', in *For Marx*.

66 This concept of the autonomy of different practices is the position to which a number of important theoretical tendencies subscribe: for example, Foucault in 'Orders of discourse' and *The History of Sexuality*, vol. 1 (Allen Lane 1979); Hirst, Hindess, Cutler and Hussain, in *Marx's Capital and Capitalism Today*, vols. 1 and 2 (Routledge and Kegan Paul 1977, 1978); also those tendencies represented by the journals *Screen, M/F* and *Ideology and Consciousness*. For an exchange on this and related questions, see that between the editors and Stuart Hall in *Ideology and Consciousness*, no. 3 (1979). For critiques of 'relative autonomy' from one of these perspectives, see Hindess, 'The concept of class', in Bloomfield, *Class, Hegemony and Party*, and 'Classes and politics

in Marxist theory', in Littlejohn, Smart, Wakeford and Yuval-Davis (eds.), *Power and the State* (Croom Helm 1978); and Hirst, in *On Law and Ideology* (Macmillan 1979).

67 This theoretical confrontation is explored in several places in *On Ideology*, especially in Hall, Lumley and McLennan, 'Politics and ideology in Gramsci'.

68 This surprising convergence – by no means the only one – can be deduced from a careful comparison between Althusser's 'Contradiction and over-determination' and Thompson's anti-Althusserean polemic in *The Poverty of Theory*.

69 In, for example, *Totemism, The Savage Mind* and the volumes on *Mythologies*. The roots of structuralism in structural linguistics are well exemplified in the chapters on language in *Structural Anthropology* (Basic Books 1963).

70 In, for example, *The Elements of Semiology* (Cape 1967); *Système de la Mode* (Paris: Editions du Seuil 1967); *Mythologies* (Cape 1972); see also the important but little-known essay, 'Sociology and socio-logic', in *Social Science Information* (CCCS translation 1970).

71 One of the clearest and most exemplary discussions of this change of focus in structuralism is to be found in Roger Poole's introductory essay to the Penguin edition of *Totemism* (1969).

72 Durkheim's *The Rules of Sociological Method* (1938) was, nevertheless, appropriated as a founding text of sociological positivism.

73 See Althusser, 'Marxism and Humanism', in *For Marx*: 'it is within this ideological unconsciousness that men succeed in altering the "lived" relation between them and their conditions of existence and acquiring that new form of specific unconsciousness called "consciousness" ' (p. 233).

74 In his inaugural lecture, *The Scope of Anthropology* (Cape 1967).

75 The rapid displacement of Lukács, Goldmann and the 'Frankfurt School' by the French structuralists is one of the most intriguing episodes in recent English intellectual history. Althusser's critique of 'Hegelianism' and his rehabilitation of the Marx of *Capital* as opposed to the Marx of 'alienation' and the *1844 Manuscripts* were two of the most important factors. One effect is to have established a major displacement between English Marxist theory and the Marxisms of American, German and Scandinavian Left intellectuals. As has so often been the case, the ghosts of Hegel and Kant continued to play an alternating shadow role in these ruptures. See Gareth Stedman-Jones's 'The Marxism of the early Lukács'.

76 *The Savage Mind* (Weidenfeld and Nicolson 1966), is the *locus classicus* of this cognitive universalism.

77 This emphasis on the 'reciprocity of exchange' in the definition of the social, as expounded by Durkheim and his 'School' – see M. Mauss, *The Gift* (Routledge and Kegan Paul 1970) – continues to mark much subsequent work – for example, that of some feminist anthropologists and the Lacanians.

78 Though most fully developed in the 'Ideology and Ideological State Apparatuses' essay in *Lenin and Philosophy and Other Essays* (New Left Books 1971), the seminal formulations first occur in the 'Marxism and humanism' essay in *For Marx*.

79 For an extensive discussion of the relations between the terms 'culture' and 'ideology' and their problematics, see Richard Johnson, 'Histories of culture/theories of ideology' in *Ideology and Cultural Production*, and 'Three

problematics' in Johnson, Clarke, Critcher (eds.), *Working Class Culture.*

80 The identification of these sites as 'ideological *state* apparatuses' was always a contentious and problematic point: but the focus on the sites and practices of ideologies, and their practico-social effects have a direct derivation from Gramsci, whose formulations, though less thoroughly elaborated, are in this particular preferable: for a discussion of this point, see Hall, Lumley and McLennan, 'Politics and ideology in Gramsci' in *On Ideology*.

81 Althusser was studiously ambiguous as to how strong were the parallels he intended to draw between his and Lacan's discussion of 'the Subject'. Much post-Althusserean theory in this area has progressed by way of the argument that Althusser abolished the integral Cartesian subject but left the question of 'subjectification' empty. It has been extensively filled by more substantial borrowings from Lacan. See, for example, the work of Heath, McCabe and Brewster in *Screen*, and Ros Coward and John Ellis, *Language and Materialism* (Routledge and Kegan Paul 1977). For a critical exchange on this point, see the Hall/Editorial Collective exchange in *Ideology and Consciousness,* no. 3. The concept of interpellation has been fruitfully developed, without its Lacanian overtones, by Laclau in *Politics and Ideology in Marxist Theory* (New Left Book 1977).

82 See, *inter alia*, Hall, 'Notes On a Reading of Marx's *1857 Introduction*'; Johnson, McLellan and Schwarz, *Economy, Culture and Concept*, CCCS Stencilled Paper no. 50; the relevant essays in *On Ideology*; Johnson's 'Histories of culture/ theories of ideology', and 'Thompson, Genovese and socialist-humanist history'; Johnson, in *Working Class Culture*.

83 See *Essays in Self-Criticism*.

84 The argument is best developed in Poulantzas's *Political Power and Social Classes* (New Left Books, Sheed and Ward 1973).

85 In *Lenin and Philosophy and Other Essays*.

86 The substitution of 'reproduction' seemed, for a time, a usefully non-reductionist way of posing the relationship between different practices and their 'conditions of existence', with a warrant in Marx's *Capital*. This was also Althusser's source, though he restricted it to the reproduction of the ideological conditions of labour power. The 'conditions of existence' formula, though still extensively employed (see Hirst and Hindess, cited in n. 66) seems increasingly an empty one, covering for a theory of autonomy.

87 The listing is, of course, based on a direct quotation from Gramsci.

88 Post-Althusserian theories of ideology, using Lacan's psychoanalysis and posing the question of ideology exclusively at the level of the 'positioning of the subject', tend to repeat this error from a different direction: here, too, all ideology is *dominant* ideology. Oppositional ideologies cannot be theorized from this position (see 'Texts, readers, subjects' below, pages 163–73).

89 A favourite phrase of Althusser's. But it was he who insisted that a term is not theoretically effective in the problematic of a text simply because it is inserted into its surface argument.

90 For example, in the essay on Althusser by McLennan, Molina and Peters in *On Ideology*.

91 From *Selections from the Prison Notebooks* (Lawrence and Wishart 1971), p. 177.

92 Though by no means universally used, the concept of 'hegemony' has been one of the Centre's organizing ideas.

93 *Prison Notebooks*, pp. 181–2.

94 This is an aspect which distinguishes the Centre's use of 'hegemony' from those which restrict it to questions of 'cultural power' and ideology. For an example of the opposing stress, which tends to assimilate Gramsci to the 'Frankfurt School', see Boggs, *Gramsci's Marxism* (Pluto Press 1976); also the discussion by Raymond Williams in *Marxism and Literature*.

95 In our usage the historical/conjunctural emphasis in Gramsci is essential, a sign not of his thought being left in its 'practical state' but of its proper theorization (though by no means fully developed) at the appropriate level of abstraction: definite historical societies at definite moments.

96 There seems to be a difference between 'early' and 'later' Foucault: see *Madness and Civilization* (Tavistock 1971) and *Birth of the Clinic* (Tavistock 1973), contrasted with *Discipline and Punish* (New York: Pantheon 1977) and *The History of Sexuality*, vol. 1 (New York: Pantheon 1978); *The Archaeology of Knowledge* (Tavistock 1972) and the essays collected in *Language, Counter-memory, Practice* (Blackwell 1977) mark the break. The latter deploy a new conception of the relationship of 'knowledge' to 'power', which remains, however, very general and unspecified. For critiques, see Poulantzas in *State, Power, Socialism* (New Left Books 1979), and Dews, 'Nouvelle philosophie and Foucault', in *Economy and Society*, vol. 8, no. 2 (May 1979).

97 The concept 'discourse', however, remains highly ambiguous. In current usage it is almost synonymous with 'practice' – but it silently absorbs the earlier meaning (the extended 'articulation of language over units larger than the sentence') without making the distinctions/convergences clear. Thus it blurs the key issue – if all 'practices' are mediated by language, what aspect of a practice is not language? – and favours a slide between these different meanings without confronting them. Foucault's unelaborated 'extra-discursive' is open to the same question: what is it? This issue is not resolved in recent contributions, which, however, assume its secured theoretical status: for example, C. MacCabe, 'On discourse', *Economy and Society*, vol. 8, no. 3 (August 1979).

98 Many writers, unable to resolve first-principle epistemological questions, seemed to be released, by Foucault's example, into the analysis of particular discursive formations. But Foucault's agnosticism about the connections between discursive formations remains troublesome and ambiguous. The relation to class formations frequently works its way back into his texts by another door, sometimes reappearing in an untransformed, even 'vulgar' form. For example: 'With the new forms of capital accumulation, new relations of production and the new legal status of property, all the popular practices that belonged either in a silent, everyday, tolerated form, or in a violent form, to the illegality of rights were reduced by force to an illegality of property . . . . Or, to put it another way, the economy of illegalities was restructured with the development of capitalist society . . . .' (*Discipline and Punish*, pp. 86–7). This has a disconcertingly familiar ring, not disguised by the phrase 'Or to put it another way', especially since what distinguishes his work, theoretically, among his followers is precisely his refusal to put it *that* way . . . .

99 The thesis of the 'no necessary reduction' of all contradictions to class contra-

dictions has been most elegantly stated by Laclau in *Politics and Ideology in Marxist Theory*, though not directly with reference to patriachal relations. See, *passim, Women Take Issue*.

100 See, especially, the Introduction to *Women Take Issue*.

101 The key text in this break was P. Macherey's *A Theory of Literary Production* (Routledge and Kegan Paul 1978). Also important were the two as yet untranslated books by R. Balibar and D. Laporte, *Les Français Fictifs* and *Le Francais National*, and Terry Eagleton's *Criticism and Ideology* (New Left Books 1976). See the recent discussion in Williams's *Marxism and Literature* and T. Bennett's *Marxism and Formalism* (Metheun 1979).

102 Hall, Clarke, Critcher, Jefferson and Roberts, *Policing the Crisis: 'Mugging', the State and Law and Order* (Macmillan 1978).

103 In the highly charged sectarian atmosphere which has sometimes disfigured these debates critical distinctions were frequently lost: for example, on one side the distinction between the 'empirical' moment in an analysis and 'Empiricism': on the other side that between the 'theoretical' and 'Theoreticism'. These have turned out to be mirror-images of one another. But it has not always proved easy to get beyond them.

104 From 'Problems of Marxism', in *Prison Notebooks*, pp. 438–9. These final pages, which reveal the distinct influence of Gramsci's work and example, very much reflect the author's position and should not perhaps be taken – except in general terms – as representing the Centre.

105 This is a difficult truth to learn but a hard and inescapable material fact: a point where the built-in 'idealism' of even radical intellectual work encounters the conditions of a real practice. Young researchers, rightly impatient for a change, have not always found it easy to appreciate the gap which divides the formulation of new goals from the transformation of a real practice. The result is sometimes that pessimism/optimism oscillation about which Gramsci was so eloquent and which led him to insist on 'pessimism of the intellect, optimism of the will'.

106 This is not the place or time to enter in detail into a discussion of how these factors have hampered us or of the crises and ruptures they precipitate from time to time. But their real effectivity should not be minimized in any full account. They have been and are divisive – and there are no short-cut resolutions to them. Others who set out on a similar path should in no way underestimate their cost.

107 The slogan is most frequently invoked by one side to stop the other from doing something – 'thinking' or 'doing'. It reflects the fatal empiricism/theoreticism split and, behind that, the social division of labour. The error arises from assuming that, some time long ago – in the 'age of innocence', perhaps – theory and practice were inextricably united, and it is the 'bad faith' of one side or the other which wilfully divides them. The fact is that in the present social division of labour they are remorselessly divided and separated, so that their 'unity' can only be produced *as a result*: it is the result of an effective articulation, about which there can be no prior guarantees. But here, as elsewhere, teleological thinking has made its mark – not least of all on the Left. The result is a widespread inability to develop a proper understanding of the role of intellectuals and the place of intellectual work. Either

Theory is everything – giving intellectuals a vanguard role which they do not deserve – or Practice is everything – which results in intellectuals denying their function in an effort to pass themselves off as 'something else' (workers, agitators, urban guerrillas). One of the deep problems for the Centre has been finding and sustaining a proper, disciplined understanding of the place, possibilities, limits and conditions of the 'intellectual function' in our society (the importance of the 'intellectual function', as Gramsci has defined it, is *not* the same thing as the importance of intellectuals as a social category!).

108 From *Prison Notebooks*, p. 334.

Chapter 2 Barrington Moore, Perry Anderson and English social development

1 Preface to the first German edition of *Condition of the Working Class in England*, in Marx and Engels, *On Britain* (FLPH ed. 1962). Cited below as *OB*.

2 Engels to Marx, 19 November 1844, *OB*, p. 533.

3 Marx, 'The crisis in Britain and the British Constitution' (1855), *OB*, p. 426.

4 There are different selections of the relevant items in *OB and Surveys from Exile* (Penguin Marx 1973).

5 Engels, 'On certain peculiarities of the economic and political development of England', *OB*, p. 529.

6 The most important items in the debate are: Anderson, 'Origins of the present crisis', *New Left Review*, no. 23; Nairn, 'The English Working Class', *New Left Review*, no. 23; Nairn, 'The nature of the Labour Party', *New Left Review*, nos. 27 and 28; E. P. Thompson, 'Peculiarities of the English', *Socialist Register*, 1965; James Hinton, 'The Labour Aristocracy', *New Left Review*, no. 32; Anderson, 'Socialism and pseudo-empiricism', *New Left Review*, no. 35; N. Poulantzas, 'Marxist political theory in G.B.', *New Left Review*, no. 43. Also relevant are Perry Anderson, *Lineages of the Absolutist State* (New Left Books 1975) and N. Poulantzas, *Political Power and Social Classes* (New Left Books 1973), esp. ch. 4.

7 Barrington Moore Jnr, *Social Origins of Dictatorship and Democracy* (Penguin 1967), p. 160.

8 For his choice see *ibid.*, pp. viii-x.

9 *ibid.*, p. xiv.

10 One wonders, in passing, how far this *is* a Marxist orthodoxy; evidently modern social classes have shaped capitalism, but Marx was well aware of the role of old or transitional classes, witness the key role of French peasantry in *The Eighteenth Brumaire*.

11 Barrington Moore, *Social Origins*, p. 505.

12 How far Moore himself is a Marxist is an interesting if idle speculation which is not taken further here. The curious might read the assessments of Genovese (a Marxist) and Rothman (an anti-Marxist), Moore's own reply to Rothman or the very interesting recent 'review of reviews' by Wiener. The references are: Eugene D. Genovese, *In Red on Black* (Vintage Books 1972) pp. 345–53; Stanley Rothman, 'Barrington Moore and the dialectics of revolution', *American Political Science Review*, no. 64 (1970); Jonathan M. Wiener, 'The Barrington Moore thesis and its critics', *Theory and Society*, no. 2 (1975). I am grateful to Keith McClelland for the first two of these references and to

Roger Grimshaw for the last.

13 Barrington Moore, *Social Origins*, p. 417.

14 *ibid.*, p. 418.

15 *ibid.*, p. 113.

16 Moore only hints at subsequent instabilities. His whole treatment (especially of peasantry) is consonant with *Class Struggles in France* and *The Eighteenth Brumaire*.

17 Cf. Barrington Moore, *Social Origins*, pp. 3–14, and Anderson, *Lineages*, pp. 113ff.

18 *Social Origins*, esp. pp. 8 and 20. Much of the criticism that follows is based on M. Dobb, *Studies in the Development of Capitalism* (Routledge 1946), ch. 1, which contains a critique of the post-Weberian concepts of capitalism.

19 For class before the industrial revolution, see Edward Thompson's recent essay, 'Patrician society, plebeian culture', *Journal of Social History*, no. 7 (Summer 1974), pp. 382–405.

20 Thompson, 'Peculiarities of the English', p. 330.

21 Poulantzas, *Political Power and Social Classes*, ch. 4.

22 'A Review of Guizot's Book', *OB*, p. 349.

23 Barrington Moore, *Social Origins*, p. 3.

24 *ibid.*, pp. 31–32 and 442–5.

25 *ibid.*, pp. 3 and 488–9.

26 'Lord John Russell', *OB*, esp. p. 465. I am grateful to Stuart Hall for indicating that Marx's satirical mode has deeper levels.

27 Especially in 'The elections in England – Whigs and Tories'; 'The Chartists'; 'Corruption at elections'; 'The crisis in England and the British Constitution' – all in *OB*.

28 Thompson, 'Peculiarities of the English', esp. p. 328.

29 Barrington Moore, *Social Origins*, p. 33.

30 Edward Thompson's masterpiece is mentioned only once in Moore's footnotes and is listed in the bibliography.

31 The Poor Law was intended to be a model both for an 'expert', bureaucratic style of administration and for a new social policy. I am grateful to Paul Richards for this view of the critical significance of the Poor Law struggle.

32 Barrington Moore, *Social Origins*, p. 486.

33 What follows is based on Anderson, 'Origins of the Present Crisis' unless another source is cited.

34 Nairn, 'Nature of the Labour Party', *New Left Review*, no. 35, pp. 21–2.

35 For Raymond Williams, 'corporate' means hegemonic – see 'Base and superstructure', *New Left Review*, no. 82. On the other hand, his interpretation is nearer the spirit of the original than is Anderson's.

36 'Origins', p. 34.

37 *ibid.*, p. 36.

38 *ibid.*, p. 36.

39 Anderson, 'Components of the national culture', in Alexander Cockburn and Robin Blackburn (eds.), *Student Power* (Penguin 1969), esp. pp. 225–6.

40 'Nature of the Labour Party', *New Left Review*, no. 28, p. 36.

41 'Peculiarities of the English', pp. 321–2.

42 'Origins', pp. 41ff.

43 Anderson, 'Socialism and pseudo-empiricism', pp. 30–1.
44 'Origins', pp. 12 and 13.
45 I am grateful to Peter Cain and John Mason for discussions pointing to the conclusion.
46 This criticism is convincingly made by Edward Thompson, who notes the importance of political economy and the whole liberal tradition.
47 Hinton, 'Labour Aristocracy', *New Left Review*, no. 32, pp. 72–5.
48 Readers of Gramsci will realize that it is difficult to give precise references to 'points of theory' in the *Prison Notebooks*. The interpretation that follows is based on the texts as printed in Quintin Hoare and Geoffrey Nowell Smith (eds.), *Selections from the Prison Notebooks of Antonio Gramsci* (Lawrence and Wishart 1971). It also owes much to collective Centre discussions.
49 Marx, *1844 Manuscripts*, ed. D. J. Struik (1973), p. 126.
50 I have drawn heavily here on Edward Thompson's work on the eighteenth-century system.
51 Cf. Anderson, 'Components', pp. 228–9.
52 For example, 'Then will the mask be torn off which has hitherto hidden the real political features of Great Britain', *OB*, p. 426.
53 If anything, English aristocracy (or the large landowners) became more exclusive in the period up to the 1880s, largely because of the state of the market in land which made 'buying in' extremely difficult before the 1870s. See F. M. L. Thompson, *English Landed Society in the Nineteenth Century* and 'The land market in the nineteenth century', *Oxford Economic Papers*, no. 9 (1957).
54 What follows is based on John Vincent, *The Formation of the Liberal Party* (Penguin 1967). I differ from Vincent in his view of artisan Liberal allegiances as somehow natural; this ignores the previous defeat of Chartism.
55 For the changing social basis of the Conservative Party, see James Cornford, 'The transformation of Conservatism in the late nineteenth century', *Victorian Studies*, no. 7 (1963).
56 New Left Books 1977.
57 *ibid.*, pp. 29–30, n. 21.
58 *ibid.*, p. 14.
59 *ibid.*, p. 31.

Chapter 3 Introduction to ethnography at the Centre

1 See p. 23.
2 A. Schutz, in M. Natanson (ed.), *Collected Papers I: The Problem of Social Reality* (The Hague: Nijhoff 1962); A. Schutz in A. Broderson (ed.), *Collected Papers II: Studies in Social Theory* (The Hague: Nijhoff 1964); A. V. Cicourel, *Method and Measurement in Sociology* (Glencoe, Ill.: The Free Press 1964); A. V. Cicourel, *Cognitive Sociology* (Penguin 1973).
3 H. Blumer, *Symbolic Interactionism* (Englewood Cliffs, N.J.: Prentice-Hall 1969); J. Young, *The Drug Takers: the Social Meaning of Drug Use* (Paladin 1972); S. Cohen, *Folk Devils and Moral Panics* (Paladin 1973).
4 P. Willis, *Learning to Labour: How Working Class Kids get Working Class Jobs* (Saxon House 1977).
5 A. McRobbie, 'Working-class girls and the culture of femininity' (unpublished

M.A. thesis, University of Birmingham, 1977); A. McRobbie, 'Working-class girls and the culture of femininity', in Women's Studies Group, *Women Take Issue* (CCCS/Hutchinson 1978); A. McRobbie, *Jackie: an Ideology of Adolescent Femininity*, CCCS Stencilled Paper no. 53 (1978).

6 D. Hobson, 'Housewives: isolation as oppression', in *Women Take Issue*; D. Hobson, 'A study of working-class women at home: femininity, domesticity and maternity' (unpublished M.A. thesis, University of Birmingham, 1978); also current Ph.D topic.

7 R. H. Grimshaw, 'The social meaning of scouting: ethnographic and contextual analysis relating to a Midlands industrial city' (unpublished Ph.D thesis, University of Birmingham 1978).

8 S. Hall and T. Jefferson, *Resistance Through Rituals* (Hutchinson 1976).

Chapter 5 Notes on method

1 See the ritual acceptance in most mainstream methodology texts of the role of 'quantitative methods' – even if their use is to be limited to 'pilot' or 'descriptive' studies. See, for instance, Selltiz *et al.* (eds.), *Research Methods in Social Relations* (Metheun 1966), ch. 3; J. Madge, *The Tools of Social Science* (Longman 1965), ch. 3.

2 For a useful discussion on 'objectivity' in positivism, see A. W. Gouldner, *The Coming Crisis of Western Sociology* (Heinemann 1970), pp. 102–4.

3 *WPCS*, nos. 7 and 8, reprinted as *Resistance Through Rituals* (Hutchinson 1976).

4 See, for instance, C. R. Shaw, *The Jack-Roller* (University of Chicago Press 1966); W. I. Thomas and F. Ananiecki, *The Polish Peasant in Europe and America* (University of Chicago Press 1927); F.M. Thrasher, *The Gold Coast and the Slum: A Study of 1,313 Gangs in Chicago* (University of Chicago Press 1928); N. Anderson, *The Hobo* (University of Chicago Press 1923).

5 W. F. Whyte, *Street Corner Society* (London: University of Chicago Press 1969).

6 See, for instance, H. S. Becker, *Outsiders: Studies in the Sociology of Deviance* (Glencoe, Ill.: The Free Press 1966); H. S. Becker *et al.*, *Boys in White* (University of Chicago Press 1961); H. S. Becker *et al.*, *Making the Grade* (New York: John Wiley 1965); N. Polsky, *Hustlers, Beats and Others* (Penguin 1971).

7 See D. Downes, *The Delinquent Solution* (Routledge and Kegan Paul 1966).

8 See S. Cohen (ed.), *Images of Deviancy* (Penguin 1971); S. Cohen, *Folk Devils and Moral Panics* (Paladin 1973); P. Rock and M. McIntosh (ed.), *Criminology and the Sociology of Deviance in Britain* (Tavistock 1974); L. Taylor (ed.), *Politics and Deviance* (Penguin 1973).

9 See, for instance, M. A. Plant, *Drug-takers in an English Town* (Tavistock 1974); J. Patrick, *A Glasgow Gang Observed* (Eyre Metheun 1973); H. J. Parker, *View from the Boys* (David and Charles 1974).

10 G. J. McCall, J. L. Simmons (eds.), *Issues in Participant Observation* (Addison-Wesley 1969); W. J. Filstead (ed.), *Qualitative Methodology* (Markham 1979).

11 My emphasis. B. G. Glaser and A. L. Strauss, 'Discovery of substantive theory: a basic strategy underlying qualitative research', in Filstead, *Qualitative Methodology*, p. 304 note.

12 See the literature on 'working hypotheses', and especially B. Geer, 'First days

in the field', in G. J. McCall and J. L. Simmons (eds.), *Issues in Participant Observation: A Text and Reader* (Addison-Wesley 1969).

13 See H. Blumer, 'What is wrong with social theory', in Filstead, *Qualitative Methodology*.

14 See McCall and Simmons, *Issues in Participant Observation*, chs. 2 and 3.

15 'Contamination' is often referred to; see, for instance, G. L. McCall, 'Data quality control in participant observation', in McCall and Simmons, *Issues in Participant Observation*.

16 Even when connections are admitted, the concern is specifically to rescue that which is 'scientific' for the sociological method. See McCall and Simmons, *Issues in Participant Observation*, p. 1.

17 See, for instance, the section on 'The quality of data' in McCall and Simmons, *Issues in Participant Observation*.

Chapter 6 Green Farm Scout camp

1 Such an invitation to a group of boys was given in the course of dealing with an emergency at this particular camp. After an incident with another boy one of the young Scouts escaped from the site and made his way home, thus dramatically breaking the exterior spatial rules of the camp. His absence motivated a large-scale search of the surrounding area. But happily the event turned out safely.

2 'Avuncularity' is here defined as a relation in which men and boys are orientated to a common task, outside the immediate context of the family.

Chapter 7 Housewives and the mass media

1 This extract is part of a longer study which looks at the culture of young working-class housewives at home with young children. The research was conducted by tape-recorded interviews and observation in their homes, and it covered many aspects of their personal experience both before they were married and in their present situation. For a fuller discussion, see D. Hobson, 'Housewives: isolation as oppression', in Women's Studies Group, *Women Take Issue* (CCCS/Hutchinson 1978); D. Hobson, 'A study of working class women at home: femininity, domesticity and maternity' (unpublished M.A. thesis, University of Birmingham, 1978).

2 In my present Ph.D. research I am looking at the production processes of various popular television and radio programmes, which involves interviewing and observing the programme makers in the encoding moment, and I will then move to the audience of those programmes to try to understand their decoding of the televisual texts.

3 The essential finding of the research from which this extract is taken was that it was the isolation of their lives which the women found most oppressive, coupled with their inability to escape from the home either to paid work or leisure activities (see Hobson, 'A study of working-class women at home').

4 For a fuller discussion of the absence of leisure activities, see *ibid*.

5 I. Connell, L. Curti and S. Hall, 'The "unity" of current affairs television', in *Culture and Domination, WPCS*, no. 9 (CCCS, University of Birmingham, 1976).

6 There has been some early work on the audience responses to radio serials.

Hertzog looked at the structure of audiences and their responses to programmes of a similar kind – daytime radio serials. She was predominantly concerned with the psychological responses of the audience to features within the text and relied on the 'uses and gratification' theory. Also, Arnheim looked at the content of daytime radio serials in an attempt to identify features to which the audience responded. Both these works are important starting-points for future research into the possible identification which women may make to radio and television programmes, since many of the features of the programmes analysed in Arnheim are common to the present television series watched by the women in my study. My own work in this study starts at a point where the audience selects from the given range of available programmes. I have not been concerned, in this article, so much with how they decode those programmes as with the structures which have mediated in their choice of programmes. See H. Hertzog, 'What do we really know about daytime serial listeners?', in P. F. Lazersfeld and F. N. Stanton (eds.), *Radio Research 1942–43* (New York: Duell, Sloan and Pearce 1944); R. Arnheim, 'The world of the daytime serial', in Lazersfeld and Stanton, *Radio Research 1942–43*.

Chapter 8 Introduction to Media Studies at the Centre

1 For an early counterposing of the two traditions, see L. Bramson, *The Political Context of Sociology* (Princeton University Press 1961).
2 R. Hoggart, *The Uses of Literacy* (Penguin 1958). 'Schools of English' is reprinted in *Speaking to Each Other* (Chatto and Windus 1970).
3 A. C. H. Smith, E. Immirzi and T. Blackwell, *Paper Voices* (Chatto and Windus 1975).
4 A. Shuttleworth, S. Hall, M. Camargo Heck and A. Lloyd, *Television Violence: Crime Drama and the Analysis of Content* (CCCS 1974).
5 Trevor Millum, *Images of Women* (Chatto and Windus 1975).
6 The manuscript of *Cure for Marriage* was drafted by Stuart Hall on the basis of a collection of seminar papers produced by the group (CCCS unpublished mimeo).
7 J. Halloran, P. Elliott and G. Murdock, *Demonstrations and Communication* (Penguin 1970).
8 For an early analysis of the crisis in broadcasting, see Stuart Hall, 'The external/internal dialectic in broadcasting', *Fourth Broadcasting Symposium* (University of Manchester, Extra-Mural Dept. 1972).
9 Roland Barthes, *Elements of Semiology* (Cape 1977), and *Mythologies* (Cape 1972).
10 See the 'Media' issue, *WPCS* 3 (CCCS 1972), including S. Hall, 'Determination of news photos', and Camargo Heck, 'Ideological dimensions of media messages'. See also articles on related themes in that volume by Rachel Powell, Bryn Jones, Ros Brunt.
11 Stuart Hall, 'Deviance, Politics and the Media', in P. Rock and M. McIntosh (eds.), *Deviance And Social Control* (BSA and Tavistock 1974); S. Cohen and J. Young (eds.), *The Manufacture of News* (Constable 1973); S. Hall, 'The structured communication of events', in *Getting The Message Across* (Paris: Unesco 1975); and 'Broadcasting and the state: the independence/impartiality couplet', unpublished paper to the International Association for Mass

Communications Research (University of Leicester 1976).

12 P. Hartman and C. Husband, *Racism And The Mass Media* (Davis Poynter 1973); P. Golding, *The Mass Media* (Longman 1974); P. Schlessinger, *Putting Reality Together* (Constable 1978), M. Tracey, *The Production of Political Television* (Routledge and Kegan Paul 1978). S. Chibnall, *Law and Order News* (Tavistock 1977). The Glasgow Media Group, *Bad News* (Routledge and Kegan Paul 1976). P. Golding and P. Elliott, *Making the News* (Longman 1979).

13 S. Hall, I. Connell, L. Curti, 'The Unity of current affairs Television', in *WPCS* 9; C. Brunsdon and D. Morley, *Everyday Television: 'Nationwide'* (BFI Monograph 1978).

14 Dave Morley, *Reconceptualizing The Audience*, CCCS Stencilled Paper, no. 9.

15 Stuart Hall, 'Encoding/decoding in television discourse', CCCS Stencilled Paper, no. 7.

Chapter 9 The ideological dimensions of media messages

1 *'Ideology and the State'* (New Left Books 1971), p. 153.

2 N. Poulantzas, *Political Power and Social Classes* (Sheed and Ward, New Left Books 1971), p. 207.

3 L. Althusser, 'Marxism and humanism', in *For Marx* (Allen Lane 1969).

4 E. Veron, 'The semanticization of political violence', in E. Veron *et al.* (eds.), *Lenguaje y Communicacion Social* (Buenos Aires: Nueva Vision 1969) (my translation).

5 *ibid.*

6 E. Veron, 'Ideology and the social sciences', in *Semiotica*, vol. 3, no. 1 (1971).

7 U. Eco, *La Struttura Assente* (Milan: Bompiani 1968). My translation.

8 *La Struttura Assente* (my translation).

9 Veron, 'Ideology and the social sciences'.

10 R. Barthes, *Elements of Semiology* (Cape 1967).

11 R. Barthes, *Mythologies* (Cape 1972).

12 The 'media' issue, *WPCS* 3 (1972).

13 *Screen*.

14 R. Barthes, *Writing Degree Zero* (Cape 1970).

15 R. Barthes, *S/Z* (Paris: Seuil 1970).

16 J. Baudrillard, *Le Système des objects* (Paris: Gonthier 1968); *La Societé de Consommation* (Paris: Gallimard 1970); *Pour une Critique de L'Economie Politique du Signe* (Paris: Gallimard 1972), p. 190 (my translation).

17 *Pour une Critique de l'Economie Politique du Signe* (my translation).

Chapter 10 Encoding/decoding

1 For an explication and commentary on the methodological implications of Marx's argument, see S. Hall, 'A reading of Marx's 1857 *Introduction to the Grundrisse*', in *WPCS* 6 (1974).

2 J.D. Halloran, 'Understanding television', Paper for the Council of Europe Colloquy on 'Understanding Television' (University of Leicester 1973).

3 G. Gerbner *et al.*, *Violence in TV Drama: A Study of Trends and Symbolic Functions* (The Annenberg School, University of Pennsylvania 1970).

4 Charles Peirce, *Speculative Grammar*, in *Collected Papers* (Cambridge, Mass.: Harvard University Press 1931–58).

5 Umberto Eco, 'Articulations of the cinematic code', in *Cinemantics*, no. 1.
6 See the argument in S. Hall, 'Determinations of news photographs', in *WPCS* 3 (1972).
7 Vološinov, *Marxism And The Philosophy of Language* (The Seminar Press 1973).
8 For a similar clarification, see Marina Camargo Heck, 'Ideological dimensions of media messages', pages 122–7 above.
9 Roland Barthes, 'Rhetoric of the image', in *WPCS* 1 (1971).
10 Roland Barthes, *Elements of Semiology* (Cape 1967).
11 For an extended critique of 'preferred reading', see Alan O'Shea, 'Preferred reading' (unpublished paper, CCCS, University of Birmingham).
12 P. Terni, 'Memorandum', Council of Europe Colloquy on 'Understanding Television' (University of Leicester 1973).
13 The phrase is Habermas's, in 'Systematically distorted communications', in P. Dretzel (ed.), *Recent Sociology 2* (Collier-Macmillan 1970). It is used here, however, in a different way.
14 For a sociological formulation which is close, in some ways, to the positions outlined here but which does not parallel the argument about the theory of discourse, see Frank Parkin, *Class Inequality and Political Order* (Macgibbon and Kee 1971).
15 See Louis Althusser, 'Ideology and ideological state apparatuses', in *Lenin and Philosophy and Other Essays* (New Left Books 1971).
16 For an expansion of this argument, see Stuart Hall, 'The external/internal dialectic in broadcasting', *4th Symposium on Broadcasting* (University of Manchester 1972), and 'Broadcasting and the state: the independence/impartiality couplet', AMCR Symposium, University of Leicester 1976 (CCCS unpublished paper).

Chapter 11 Television news and the Social Contract

1 Stuart Hall, 'The determinations of news photographs', *WPCS* 3 (1972).
2 Trevor Pateman, *Television and the February 1974 General Election*, BFI Television Monograph no. 3 (British Film Institute 1974).
3 Pateman, *Television and the February 1974 General Election.*
4 It is not possible here to detail the establishment of this paradigm, but the 1960s represent a moment of consolidation and crystallization in this field of broadcasting.
5 J. Galtung and M. H. Ruge, 'The structure of foreign news', in J. Tunstall (ed.), *Media Sociology* (London 1970).

Chapter 12 Recent developments in theories of language and ideology: a critical note

1 *Screen*, vol. 16, no. 2 (Summer 1975).
2 See the Editorial Statement and the 'Presentation' of 'The imaginary signifier' in *Screen, ibid.*

Chapter 13 Texts, readers, subjects

1 Steve Neale, 'Propaganda', in *Screen*, vol. 18, no. 3 (Autumn 1977).
2 M. Pêcheux, *Analyse Automatique du Discours* (Paris: Dunod 1969) and *Les Vérités de la Palice* (Paris: Maspero 1975). Cf. Roger Woods, 'Discourse

analysis: the work of Marcel Pêcheux', in *Ideology and Consciousness*, no. 2 (Autumn 1977).

3 L. Althusser, 'Ideology and Ideological State Apparatuses', in *Lenin and Philosophy and Other Essays* (New Left Books 1971).

4 Ernesto Laclau, *Politics and Ideology in Marxist Theory* (New Left Books 1977).

5 Frank Parkin, *Class Inequality and Political Order* (Macgibbon and Kee 1971).

6 See, for example, Colin McCabe, 'Realism and the cinema', in *Screen*, vol. 15, no. 2 (Summer 1974), and 'Realism and pleasure', in *Screen*, vol. 17, no. 3 (Autumn 1976).

7 For critiques or variants of the dominant *Screen* position on 'realism' see, *inter alia*, Christine Gledhill, 'Whose choice?', in *Screen Education*, vol. 24 (Autumn 1977); Tony Stevens, 'Reading the realist film', in *Screen Education*, vol. 26 (Spring 1978); and Dick Hebdige and Geoff Hurd, 'Reading and realism', in *Screen Education*, vol. 28 (Autumn 1978).

8 V. N. Vološinov, *Marxism and the Philosophy of Language* (New York: The Seminar Press 1973).

9 *ibid.*, p. 23.

10 Neale, 'Propaganda'.

11 *ibid.*, p. 34.

12 *ibid.*, p. 18.

13 Paul Willemen, 'Subjectivity under siege', in *Screen*, vol. 19, no. 1 (Spring 1978), p. 48.

14 P. Hardy, C. Johnston and P. Willemen, in papers from the Edinburgh Television Event, *Edinburgh 1976* (British Film Institute 1976).

15 Christine Gledhill, 'Recent developments in film criticism', in *Quarterly Review of Film Studies*, vol. 3, no. 4 (Fall 1978).

16 Claire Johnston, 'The subject of feminist film: theory/practice', in *Edinburgh Television Papers* (1979).

17 Hardy, Johnston, Willemen, in *Edinburgh 1976*.

18 Willemen, 'Subjectivity under siege', pp. 63–4.

19 Geoffrey Nowell-Smith, 'Editorial', in *Screen*, vol. 18, no. 3 (Autumn 1977).

20 *ibid.*, p. 5.

21 Gledhill, 'Recent developments in film criticism', p. 19.

22 Neale, 'Propaganda', pp. 39–40.

23 Willemen, 'Subjectivity under siege', pp. 66–7.

24 Basil Bernstein, *Class, Codes and Control* (Paladin 1973); Pierre Bourdieu and J.C. Passerson, *Reproduction* (Sage 1977); C. Baudelot and R. Establet, *L'ecole Capitaliste en France* (Paris: Maspero 1971). For an elaboration of this connection, see Dave Morley, 'Reconceptualizing the media audience', CCCS Stencilled Paper no. 9.

25 See the way this charge is levelled in Ros Coward's 'Class, culture and the social formation', in *Screen*, vol. 18, no. 1 (Spring 1977). See also the reply, I. Chambers, J. Clarke, I. Connell, L. Curti, S. Hall and T. Jefferson in *Screen*, vol. 18, no. 4 (Winter 1977/8).

26 For a critique, see Rosen, *Language and Class* (Bristol: Falling Wall Press 1972). For some Berstein reformulations, see the 1973 'Postscript' to *Class, Codes and*

Control, vol. 1; and his 'Classification and framing of educational knowledge'.

27 Willemen, 'Subjectivity under siege'.
28 Neale, 'Propaganda'.
29 John Ellis, 'The institution of the cinema', *Edinburgh Magazine* (1977).
30 Nicos Poulantzas, *Political Power and Social Classes* (Sheed and Ward, New Left Books 1971).
31 Laclau, *Politics and Ideology in Marxist Theory*.
32 Parkin, *Class Inequality and Political Order*.
33 See S. Hall, 'Encoding/decoding', pp. 128–38 above; and Morley, 'Reconceptualizing the media audience'.
34 Louis Althusser, 'Ideology and Ideological State Apparatuses'.

Chapter 14 Introduction to Language Studies at the Centre

1 Richard Hoggart, *The Uses of Literacy* (Penguin 1958), p. 27.
2 Raymond Williams, *The Long Revolution* (Penguin 1965), p. 40.
3 Hoggart, *The Uses of Literacy*, p. 17.
4 Roland Barthes, 'The rhetoric of the image', in *WPCS* (1971).
5 Stuart Hall, 'The determination of news photographs', *WPCS* (1972), p. 82.
6 *ibid*., p. 69.
7 Roland Barthes, *Elements of Semiology* (Cape 1967), pp. 89–90.
8 Barthes, *Elements of Semiology*, p. 90.
9 Roland Barthes, *Mythologies* (Cape 1972), pp. 129–30.
10 Iain Chambers, 'Roland Barthes: structuralism/semiotics', in *WPCS* 6 (1974), p. 55.
11 *ibid*., p. 57.
12 John Ellis, 'Semiology, art and the Chambers fallacy', *WPCS* 9 (1976), p. 129.
13 Chambers, 'Roland Barthes', p. 59.
14 See *WPCS* 3 (1972), p. 60.
15 Hall, 'The determinations of news photographs', p. 76.
16 V. N. Vološinov, *Marxism and the Philosophy of Language* (New York: Seminar Press 1973).
17 Rosalind Coward and John Ellis, *Language and Materialism* (Routledge and Kegan Paul 1977).
18 Important here would be, for example, the journals *Screen, Ideology and Consciousness* and *m/f*.
19 Louis Althusser, *Reading Capital* (New Left Books 1970).
20 Louis Althusser, 'On ideology and ideological state apparatuses', in *Lenin and Philosophy and Other Essays* (New Left Books 1971).
21 Ernesto Laclau, *Politics and Ideology in Marxist Theory* (New Left Books 1977).
22 Louis Althusser, 'Freud and Lacan', in *Lenin and Philosophy*.
23 Juliet Mitchell, *Psychoanalysis and Feminism* (Allen Lane 1974).

Chapter 15 Ideology and subjectivity

1 Roland Barthes, *S/Z* (Cape 1974).
2 Mao-Tse-Tung, 'On the correct handling of contradictions among the people', in *Four Essays on Philosophy* (Peking 1968), p. 116.
3 M. A. Macciocchi, *De la Chine*, rev. ed. (Paris: Seuil 1974), trans. as *Daily Life in Revolutionary China* (New York: Monthly Review Press 1972).

4 Louis Althusser, *Lenin and Philosophy and Other Essays* (New Left Books 1971).
5 Louis Althusser, 'On Ideology and Ideological State Apparatuses', in *Lenin and Philosophy*.
6 Louis Althusser, 'Freud and Lacan', in *Lenin and Philosophy*.
7 J. Kristeva, *La Révolution du Langage Poétique* (Paris: Seuil 1974).
8 Mao, 'On the correct handling of contradictions', p. 5.
9 Juliet Mitchell, *Psychoanalysis and Feminism* (Penguin 1975), p. 17.
10 See the Introduction in Anika Lemaire, *Jacques Lacan* (Routledge and Kegan Paul 1978).
11 Kristeva, *La Révolution*, p. 181.
12 *ibid.*
13 Charles Woolfson, 'The semiotics of working-class speech', in *WPCS* 9 (1976).
14 J. Kristeva, 'The ruin of a poetics', *20th Century Studies*, nos. 7-8, pp. 102-19.
15 V. N. Vološinov, *Marxism and the Philosophy of Language* (New York: Seminar Press 1973), p. 39. It now (1979) is clear that Vološinov's reference is to the concept of 'inner speech' developed by Vygotsky, Eikenbaum and others to describe the way in which the child's early syncretic egocentric speech is internalized under the pressure of the demands of sociality. See articles by Ronald Levaco and Paul Willemen in *Screen*, vol. 15, no. 4 (Winter 1974/5), especially pp. 54-8. Thus the relative autonomy perceived here will tend to be oriented around a traditional opposition between the subjective and the objective.
16 Kristeva, 'The ruin of a poetics', p. 105.
17 Philippe Sollers, 'A propos de la dialectique', in *Psychoanalyse et Politique* (Paris: Seuil 1974), p. 28.

Chapter 16 Theories of language and subjectivity

1 F. de Saussure, *A Course in General Linguistics* (Fontana 1974); see also R. Jakobsen, *Selected Writings* (The Hague: Mouton 1962).
2 Saussure, *A Course in General Linguistics*, pp. 198-9.
3 *ibid.*, p. 69.
4 *ibid.*, p. 133.
5 *ibid.*, p. 120.
6 *ibid.*, p. 17.
7 *ibid.*, p. 72.
8 *ibid.*, p. 14.
9 *ibid.*, p. 9.
10 *ibid.*, p. 71.
11 *ibid.*, pp. 103-4.
12 Jacques Derrida, *Speech and Phenomena* (Evanston, Ill.: Northwestern University Press 1973).
13 Jacques Derrida, *Of Grammatology* (Baltimore, Md.: Johns Hopkins University Press, 1974).
14 *ibid.*, p. 23.
15 For a recent, accessible and succinct introduction to Derrida, see D. C. Wood, 'An introduction to Derrida', in *Radical Philosophy*, no. 21 (Spring 1979).

16 Derrida, *Of Grammatology*, p. 35.
17 *ibid.*, p. 73.
18 *ibid.*, p. 91.
19 Sigmund Freud, *Complete Psychological Works* (Standard Ed., Hogarth), vol. 4, p. 277.
20 J. Lacan, *Ecrits* (Tavistock 1977), p. 19.
21 See, for example, Rosalind Coward and John Ellis, *Language and Materialism* (Routledge and Kegan Paul 1977).
22 Juliet Mitchell, *Psychoanalysis and Feminism* (Allen Lane 1974).
23 Coward and Ellis, *Language and Materialism*.
24 Michel Foucault, *The Archaeology of Knowledge* (Tavistock 1972).
25 Michel Foucault, *Discipline and Punish* (New York: Pantheon 1977).
26 Michel Foucault, *The History of Sexuality* (New York: Pantheon 1978).
27 Foucault, *The Archaeology of Knowledge*, p. 13.
28 *ibid.*, p. 52.
29 *ibid.*, p. 95.
30 *ibid.*, p. 122.
31 *ibid.*, p. 94.
32 *ibid.*
33 Foucault, *The History of Sexuality*, p. 93.
34 *ibid.*, p. 95.
35 Foucault, *Discipline and Punish*, p. 17.
36 Foucault, *The History of Sexuality*, pp. 155–6.
37 Ernesto Laclau, *Politics and Ideology in Marxist Theory* (New Left Books 1977).
38 Foucault, *The History of Sexuality*, p. 96.
39 A. Gramsci, *The Prison Notebooks* (Lawrence and Wishart 1971).
40 Louis Althusser, 'On ideology and ideological state apparatuses', in *Lenin and Philosophy and Other Essays* (New Left Books 1971).
41 Foucault, *Discipline and Punish*, p. 202.
42 See, for example, Paul Willis, *Learning to Labour* (Saxon House 1977).
43 Roland Barthes, *S/Z* (Cape 1974); *The Pleasure of the Text* (Cape 1975).

Chapter 17 Sexuality for sale

1 Karl Marx, *Grundrisse* (Penguin 1973), p. 94.
2 Karl Marx, *Capital*, vol. 1 (Penguin 1976), p. 165.
3 Judith Williamson, *Decoding Advertisements* (Boyars 1978), p. 13.
4 Marx, *Grundrisse*, p. 89.
5 Judith Williamson takes the concept of 'exchange values' from Marx's use of it as an economic definition: the value of commodities in terms of the embodiment of one identical social substance – human labour – which allows them to be exchanged with each other, irrespective of their use value, their individual bodily forms (Marx, *Capital*, vol. 1, ch. 1). But Williamson shifts its use to an ideological level (cf. Mauss's and Lévi-Strauss's 'symbolic exchange'). Thus it is used analogously rather than identically but always retains its relation to the commodity form: 'The ad translates these "thing" statements/use values to us as human statements; they are given a humanly symbolic "exchange value" ' (*Decoding Advertisements*, p. 12).

6 For more on this work of beautification in women's and girls' magazines, see A. McRobbie, 'Working-class girls and the culture of femininity' (unpublished MA thesis, University of Birmingham, 1977); J. Winship, 'A woman's world: *Woman* – an ideology of femininity', in Women's Studies Group, *Women Take Issue* (CCCS/Hutchinson 1978), and 'Woman becomes an "individual": femininity and consumption in women's magazines 1954–69', in *Sociological Review* monograph (1979). For more on the work of domesticity, see A. Oakley, *The Sociology of Housework* (Martin Robertson 1974), and A. Oakley, *Housewife* (Allen Lane 1974).

7 Rosalind Coward, 'Sexual liberation and the family', in *M/F*, no. 1 (1978).

8 Sigmund Freud, 'Fetishism', in *On Sexuality* (Penguin 1977).

9 John Berger, *Ways of Seeing* (Penguin 1972); H. Butcher, R. Coward *et al.*, 'Images in the media', CCCS Stencilled Paper, no. 31 (1974).

10 For Freud's discussion, in psychoanalytic terms, of scopophilia and exhibitionism, see 'Instincts and their vicissitudes' (1915), in *Complete Psychological Works* (Standard Edition, Hogarth), vol. 14.

11 Williamson defines a 'referent system' as a 'hollowed-out system of meaning' (*Decoding Advertisements*, p. 168), which refers to a reality but is 'lifted from the materiality of our lives' (*ibid.*, p. 74).

12 Griselda Pollock, 'What's wrong with images of women?', *Screen Education*, no. 24 (Autumn 1977), p. 29.

13 Marx, *Capital*, vol. 1, p. 165.

14 *ibid.*, pp. 164–5.

15 Freud, 'Fetishism'.

Chapter 18 Literature/society: mapping the field

1 Peter Wollen, *Signs and Meaning in the Cinema* (Secker and Warburg 1972).

2 Frye's 'The social context of literary criticism' is reprinted in Tom and Elizabeth Burns (eds.), *The Sociology of Literature and Drama* (Penguin 1973); Leavis's 'Literature and society', and the related 'Sociology and literature' are both in *The Common Pursuit* (Chatto and Windus 1952).

3 Introduction to Frye, *The Sociology of Literature and Drama*.

4 Perry Anderson, 'Components of a national culture', in A. Cockburn and R. Blackburn (eds.), *Student Power* (Penguin 1969).

5 *Culture and Society* and *The Long Revolution*, but also *Modern Tragedy* and *The English Novel*.

6 Hoggart's work, which is often (correctly) also identified as originating here, moves in a different direction: it extends the methods of 'close reading' of texts in the direction of 'reading a culture', and especially popular and working-class culture, where the 'texts' are, characteristically, not *literary* in the traditional sense.

7 All the formulations quoted in this paragraph are from *The Long Revolution* (Chatto and Windus 1961).

8 The formulations in this paragraph are all from 'From Leavis to Goldmann', *New Left Review*, vol. 67 (May/June 1971): reprinted as the Introduction to Goldman's *Racine* (River Press 1972).

9 'In studying such transformations it is always necessary to distinguish between the material transformation of the economic conditions of production, which

can be determined with the precision of natural science, and the legal, political, religious, artistic or philosophic – in short, ideological – forms in which men become conscious of this conflict and fight it out' (Marx, the Preface to *A Contribution to the Critique of Political Economy*, in K. Marx and F. Engels, *Selected Works* (Lawrence and Wishart 1968).

10 The problem with the base/superstructure model has always been how far the base actually determines the form of the superstructure. Engels (and now Althusser) insists that to postulate any too direct a determination by the base would be to oversimplify but that in the end (the last instance) it is *the* determining element. However, how one can conceive the last instance (or, in Althusser's sense, whether one can ever consider the base in isolation from everything else in a social formation) remains a problem. Adrian Mellor's paper on Goldmann in *WPCS* 4 (1973) contains a discussion of this question. See also Engels's letter to J. Bloch, in Marx and Engels, *Selected Works* (Moscow 1951), p. 443, and Althusser, *For Marx* (Allen Lane 1969).

11 See Althusser's tantalizingly brief essay, 'The "Piccolo Teatro" ', in *For Marx* (Allen Lane 1969); two brief essays in the Appendix to *Lenin and Philosophy and Other Essays* (New Left Books 1971); also Pierre Macherey, *Pour une théorie de la Production Littéraire* (Paris: Maspero 1970).

12 Especially the essays in *For Marx*.

13 Althusser, 'On the materialist dialectic', in *For Marx*.

Chapter 19 Recent developments in English Studies at the Centre

1 Raymond Williams, 'Base and superstructure', in *New Left Review*, no. 82 (November/December 1973).

2 *Marxism and Literature* (Oxford University Press 1977).

3 *Marxism and Literary Criticism* (Metheun 1976); *Criticism and Ideology* (New Left Books 1976).

4 R. Johnson, 'Histories of culture: theories of ideology', in M. Barrett *et al.* (eds.), *Ideology and Cultural Reproduction* (Croom Helm 1979).

5 Williams, *Marxism and Literature*, p. 5.

6 Eagleton, *Criticism and Ideology*, p. 22.

7 Williams, *Marxism and Literature*, p. 82.

8 Eagleton, *Criticism and Ideology*, p. 43.

9 *ibid*.

10 *ibid*., p. 44.

11 *ibid*., p. 101.

12 *ibid*., p. 161.

13 Walter Benjamin, 'The author as producer', in *Understanding Brecht* (New Left Books 1973); 'The work of art in the age of mechanical reproduction', in *Illuminations* (Fontana 1973).

14 Pierre Macherey, *A Theory of Literary Production* (Routledge and Kegan Paul 1978).

15 Eagleton, *Criticism and Ideology*.

16 Renee Balibar, *Les Français Fictifs* (Paris: Hachette 1974).

17 J. Dubois, *L'Institution de la Littérature* (Paris: Nathan 1978).

18 Williams, *Marxism and Literature*.

19 Macherey, *A Theory of Literary Production*.

20 Karl Marx, *Grundrisse* (Penguin 1973).
21 Dubois, *L'Institution de la Littérature.*
22 M. Naumann (ed.), *Gesellschaft–Literatur–Lesen* (Berlin: Aufbau-Verlag 1973).
23 E. Laclau, *Politics and Ideology in Marxist Theory* (New Left Books 1977).
24 Laclau, *Politics and Ideology*.
25 J. Culler, *Structuralist Poetics* (Routledge and Kegan Paul 1975).
26 H. R. Jauss, 'Literary history as a challenge to literary theory', in *New Literary History*, vol. 2, no 1 (Autumn 1970).
27 W. Iser, *The Implied Reader* (Baltimore, Md.: Johns Hopkins University Press 1974).
28 Naumann, *Gesellschaft–Literatur–Lesen.*
29 *ibid.*, p. 489.
30 B. Brecht, *Schriften zur Literatur und Kunst* (Frankfurt: Wemer Hecht 1966).
31 T. Roszak (ed.), *The Dissenting Academy* (New York: Vintage Books 1968).
32 F. Jameson, *Marxism and Form* (Princeton University Press 1971).
33 Raymond Williams, 'From Leavis to Goldmann', in *New Left Review*, no. 67 (May/June 1971).
34 See 'Joe Spriggs', in T. Pateman (ed.), *Counter-Course* (Penguin 1972).
35 For symptomatic comments, see *Wedge*, no. 1 (Summer 1977); *Wedge*, no. 2 (Spring 1978); *Wedge*, no. 3 (Winter 1978); K. Worpole, 'Oppositional culture': yesterday and today', in *Camerawork*, no. 11 (1978); 'Politics of writing', in *Radical Education*, no. 12 (1979), 'Alternative publishing', in *New Society*, no. 3 (May 1979).
36 See Kate Millet, *Sexual Politics* (New York: Doubleday 1970); John Berger, *Ways of Seeing* (Penguin 1972).
37 J. Rée in *Radical Philosophy*, no. 20 (1978).
38 F. R. Leavis, *Education and the University* (Chatto and Windus 1943).
39 R. Balibar, *Les Français Fictifs* (Paris: Hachette 1974).
40 Worpole, 'Alternative publishing'.
41 A. Gramsci, *Selections from the Prison Notebooks* (Lawrence and Wishart 1971).
42 Raymond Williams, 'Making it active', *English Magazine*, no. 1 (Spring 1979).
43 See Cynthia Cockburn, *The Local State* (Pluto Press 1977), but also Max Jäggi, Roger Müller and Sil Schmid, *Red Bologna* (Writers' and Readers' Co-operative 1977).
44 Worpole, 'Alternative publishing'.
45 M. Lane, *Commerce against Culture* (Pluto Press, forthcoming).
46 Raymond Williams, *The Long Revolution* (Chatto and Windus 1961).
47 Caroline Heilbrun, *Towards Androgyny: Aspects of Male and Female in Literature* (Gollancz 1973).
48 Patricia Meyer Spacks, *The Female Imagination* (Allen and Unwin 1976).
49 Roger Bromley, 'Natural boundaries: the social function of popular fiction', *Red Letters*, no. 7 (1978).
50 CCCS English Studies Group, 'Thinking about the thirties' in F. Barker *et al.* (eds.), *The Sociology of Literature: 1936* (University of Essex Press, forthcoming).
51 Winifred Holtby, *South Riding* (Collins 1936).

52 Clemence Dane, *The Woman's Side* (Herbert Jenkins 1926).
53 Ellen Dorothy Abb, *What Fools We Women Be* (Cassell 1937).
54 Vera Douie, *The Lesser Half* (Women's Publicity Planning Association 1943).
55 Ethel M. Wood, *Mainly for Men* (Gollancz 1943);
56 Neville Chamberlain (Hansard 1935).
57 Abb, *What Fools We Women Be.*
58. Winifred Holtby in Vera Brittain, *Testament of Friendship* (Macmillan 1940).
59 Winifred Holtby, *A New Voter's Guide* (Kegan Paul 1929).
60 Vera Brittain, *Testament of Friendship.*
61 Holtby, *South Riding.*
62 *ibid.*
63 *ibid.*
64 *ibid.*
65 *ibid.*
66 *ibid.*
67 *ibid.*
68 *ibid.*
69 *ibid.*
70 Walter Benjamin, 'Reply to Adorno', in *Aesthetics and Politics* (New Left Books 1977).
71 Culler, *Structuralist Poetics*; Robert Scholes, *Structuralism in Literature* (Yale University Press 1974).
72 English Studies Group, 'Thinking the thirties'.
73 Ministry of Education, *Youth's Opportunity* (1946).
74 Barbara Cartland, *Lord Ravenscar's Revenge* (Corgi 1978).
75 Barbara Cartland, *Blue Heather* (Rich and Cowan 1953).
76 Cartland, *Lord Ravenscar's Revenge.*
77 Cartland, *Blue Heather.*
78 Barbara Cartland, *The Black Panther* (Rich and Cowan 1940).
79 Cartland, *Lord Ravenscar's Revenge.*
80 Cartland, *Blue Heather.*
81 Cartland, *Lord Ravenscar's Revenge.*
82 Cartland, *The Black Panther.*
83 Cartland, *Blue Heather.*
84 Cartland, *The Black Panther.*
85 Cartland, *Lord Ravenscar's Revenge.*
86 Cartland, *The Black Panther.*
87 Cartland, *Blue Heather.*
88 *ibid.*
89 Cartland, *Lord Ravenscar's Revenge.*
90 Cartland, *Blue Heather.*
91 *ibid.*
92 Gramsci, *Prison Notebooks*, p. 405.
93 Raymond Williams, *Marxism and Literature.*
94 Colin Mercer, 'Culture and ideology in Gramsci', in *Red Letters*, no. 8 (1978).
95 Roger Bromley, 'Natural boundaries: the social function of popular fiction', in *Red Letters*, no. 7 (1978); 'Culture and Hegemony in the 1930s', BSA Conference Paper (1978).

96 Gramsci, *Prison Notebooks*, p. 324.
97 *ibid.*, p. 35.
98 John Ruskin, *Of Queen's Gardens* (1864, 1871).
99 Worpole, 'Politics of writing'.
100 Gramsci, *Prison Notebooks.*

Index